DISCOVERING AMERICAN HISTORY IN ENGLAND

An Illustrated Traveler's Guide

CATHERINE LEITCH

g
GILES

D Giles Limited, London

First published in 2007 by GILES
An imprint of D Giles Limited
2nd Floor
162-164 Upper Richmond Road
London SW15 2SL, UK
www.gilesltd.com

ISBN: 978-1-904832-38-6

Edited by Eleanor Lines
Copy-edited and proofread by Sarah Kane
Picture research by Sophie Spencer-Wood
Designed by Linda Wade Book Packaging and Design
Cover design by Mercer Design, London
Produced by GILES, an imprint of D Giles Limited, London
Printed and bound in China

CONTENTS

A SHORT HISTORY OF BRITISH–AMERICAN CONNECTIONS

In the twenty-first century, the term "special relationship" is often used to describe the connection between Great Britain and the United States. Ironically, Great Britain is the only sovereign country to have fought Americans twice on their own soil, but today the two countries are the closest of allies.

We can appreciate how this special relationship developed by looking at the lives of the real people who actually forged the connections between the UK and the US, starting with the very first links over four hundred years ago. Visiting the real places where these people lived can make history come alive. The footprints of explorers, early settlers, and revolutionaries can be found in castles and stately homes, in small towns, in mighty cathedrals and village churches, in landscape gardens, and ancient colleges. By following the footsteps of individuals, the larger movements of history can come into view.

We can also see that the relationship went both ways across the Atlantic Ocean. Native Americans were brought to England as early as 1585, and for almost four hundred years people from America have traveled to England to make lasting contributions to political and cultural life in Britain.

How did it start? English exploration of North America was motivated by international competition with Spain and France, and by economic goals – to discover a quicker way to sail to India and the Far East, and to find gold and other precious materials. According to Norse legend, Leif Ericson sailed to the New World in the year 1000, but the Spanish claim to be the first Europeans to have set foot in the New World. In 1492 an Italian navigator, Christopher Columbus, sailing in an expedition sponsored by King Ferdinand and Queen Isabella of Spain, discovered the islands of the Caribbean. Five years later an English expedition, also led by an Italian navigator, John Cabot (Giovanni Caboto), explored the coast of New England. Cabot's expedition actually landed on the mainland of North America, something Christopher Columbus never did.

The Spanish began exploring and colonizing the continent much

more rapidly than the English, and also began harassing the English attempts at settlements. When Elizabeth became queen, she supported the exploration and exploitation of the New World. With economic and political goals, the queen granted charters for ships that would attack Spanish vessels and bring their treasure back to England. English captains were required to turn the captured goods over to the monarch, keeping a percentage for themselves. It was a profitable business for both monarch and pirate (or "privateer" as they were called.)

Early English expeditions focused on exploiting the natural resources of the New World. Queen Elizabeth and King James I granted charters that allowed groups to explore the land and establish settlements. Voyages of exploration and mapping preceded attempts to build permanent colonies. The first colonies failed, and it was not until 1607 that the first permanent English settlement in North America was established – at Jamestown, Virginia.

In the 1620s and '30s waves of English people immigrated to America. By looking at their individual stories one can see the great surge of religious dissent sweeping over England at that time. Many of these groups saw immigration to the New World as a way to set up their own communities and live according to their beliefs. As more English settlers arrived and established new communities, various groups cooperated, merged, fought, separated, and grew. Life in the colonies presented serious challenges, both physical and philosophical, especially in the theocracy of New England. Religious dissenters could be banished, a serious verdict in an unknown and untamed environment.

As the English colonies grew rapidly, they soon absorbed or took over Dutch and Swedish colonies in the areas of New York and New Jersey. In 1643 the Massachusetts Bay, Plymouth, Connecticut, and New Haven colonies formed the New England Confederation – the English colonists' first attempt at regional unity. It took more than a century for this unity to reach its conclusion in the establishment of an independent nation.

The monarch could use grants of vast areas of land in the New World as a way of paying royal debts or of gaining favor with English aristocrats. In 1632 King Charles I granted the Maryland Charter to Lord Baltimore

(George Calvert) for land north of the Potomac River. Millions of acres in Virginia and Carolina were used as rewards for loyalty to the monarch. In 1681 a huge area of land which became the State of Pennsylvania was granted by Charles II to William Penn, a member of the Society of Friends (Quakers), in payment of a debt owed to Penn's father. The last of the original thirteen colonies to be established was Georgia, created in 1732 when King George II granted land to General James Edward Oglethorpe to set up a colony as a refuge for the poor and former prisoners.

English culture and education formed the foundation of the new civilization. Many of the earliest immigrants to America had attended Oxford or Cambridge Universities and often they had networked while studying law at the Inns of Court in London. New institutions in America developed with English support. John Harvard, who grew up south of the River Thames in Southwark, was instrumental in the development of a college in Cambridge, Massachusetts. Elihu Yale, who was born in America but returned to his ancestral home in Wales, made a substantial donation to a college that would later bear his name. More recently, many well-known Americans have come to England to study. American politicians and a president, Supreme Court justices, Nobel Prize winners, and "Dr. Seuss" have all attended Oxford or Cambridge.

Commerce and communication between England and the colonies were constant in both directions. As the colonies grew and prospered, Americans such as Edward Winslow and George Downing returned to England to have a significant impact on their native country. Political thinkers in England influenced American political philosophy. As political tensions between the two countries developed in the mid-eighteenth century, Americans in England tried to act as mediators. When the battle lines of the American War for Independence were drawn, names of old English families were prominent in both camps. Once full-scale war broke out, men who had been born in England were instrumental on both sides, not only in battle but also during its aftermath. With all these Englishmen fighting on opposite sides, one might almost think of the American Revolution as the final phase of the English Civil War.

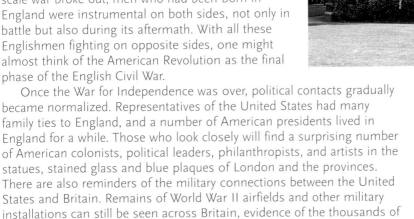

Once the War for Independence was over, political contacts gradually became normalized. Representatives of the United States had many family ties to England, and a number of American presidents lived in England for a while. Those who look closely will find a surprising number of American colonists, political leaders, philanthropists, and artists in the statues, stained glass and blue plaques of London and the provinces. There are also reminders of the military connections between the United States and Britain. Remains of World War II airfields and other military installations can still be seen across Britain, evidence of the thousands of young Americans who fought in both world wars. Military cemeteries serve as honored resting places for many of these young Americans who never returned home. Less formal reminders of wartime military ties can be seen in local memorials, military museums, and churches.

Over the years, Americans have been recognized and honored by successive British monarchs. Since World War II, more than sixty American citizens have been granted honorary knighthoods by the United Kingdom. The City of London has given its highest honor, the Honorary Freedom of the City, to three Americans. American philanthropists have also made great contributions to life in Britain. The original motivations for exploring the New World were economic – to find new sources of materials and easier routes for commerce. Over the centuries, these commercial and business links have worked both ways across the Atlantic.

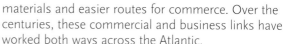

Evidence of American decorative arts, artistic and scientific creativity, and historical events can be seen in museums around England. Actors, poets, scientists, businessmen, showmen, and sportsmen from the United States have come to Britain to work and live. They have turned up in unexpected places – like Buffalo Bill at the Earl's Court exhibition center. An American was one of the most prolific contributors to the *Oxford English Dictionary*. London theaters have seen many performances by Americans, one London theater even having a memorial plaque to Judy Garland. And of course Sam Wanamaker was the driving force behind the creation of the new Globe Theatre.

In the late nineteenth and early twentieth centuries, the daughters of American families were frequently seen crossing the Atlantic in the direction of Europe. Between 1870 and 1914, 454 American heiresses married European nobles, 100 of them with British titles. A number of these women brought fortunes that contributed to the preservation of some of the most impressive stately homes in the country! One was the mother of the man who was voted "The Greatest Briton of All Time" – Winston Churchill. Another American became the first woman to take a seat in the House of Commons. And one American woman changed the course of British history by marrying a king who abdicated his throne for her.

British people show their interest in American history in unexpected ways. One of the most popular branches of the "living history" movement in Britain is the American Civil War! There are also re-enactment groups that focus on the period of the American Revolutionary War. For those who would like to experience a bit of (ersatz) America up close, there are two American theme parks in England, where the adventurous can pan for gold, or enjoy a cowboy show at "The Alamo."

Britain and America share more than four hundred years of common history. Exploring this history by visiting sites in England can be a learning experience, and can also be fun. Seeing connections can enhance a visit to England. Knowing where early immigrants came from, and why they left England, can help Americans understand their early history.

Appreciating the lasting contributions Americans have made in England can help us see that our special relationship continues, in both directions, across the Atlantic.

This history of the United States is biographically based and weaves together the stories of real people who contributed to the story of America. With only a few exceptions, individuals are included in this history only if there is something tangible left of their own story to see in England as one travels around the cities and countryside of this green and pleasant land. Sidebars on the pages of text tell of the places linked with the biographies. The Gazetteers provide contact information about each place mentioned, giving the British postcode wherever possible. This makes it very easy to pinpoint their location by using an internet map site such as www.multimap.com or www.streetmap.co.uk. Maps of London and regional areas are marked with places where something can be seen. In the text, when an individual name is highlighted in bold, it can be found in the index at the end of the book. Likewise, a place name in bold italics will be listed in the Gazetteers. Further information can be found at www.americanhistoryinengland.com

CHAPTER 1
EXPLORING THE NEW WORLD

LONDON The Columbus Screen at *Canary Wharf* was designed by Wendy Ramshaw.

LONDON A statue of Christopher Columbus stands at the corner of *Belgrave Square*.

MERSEYSIDE In the nineteenth century *Liverpool* became the gateway to the New World for thousands of British and European emigrants who sailed across the Atlantic to a new life in America. A statue in front of the Palm House in *Sefton Park* bears the inscription "**Christopher Columbus** – The discoverer of America was the maker of Liverpool."

The late fifteenth century saw the great sailing nations of Spain and Portugal expanding their empires – the race was on to discover a sea route from Europe to the East. China and India offered rich resources and huge markets but land travel was very difficult and time-consuming. Early English voyages of exploration took advantage of Italian expertise in ocean navigation and Europe turned westward in search of a sea route to the East. These expeditions led to the discovery of the American coast and the first connections between England and America.

The number of English expeditions crossing the Atlantic to explore the American coastline increased dramatically during the last part of the sixteenth century and beginning of the seventeenth. These voyages were very expensive undertakings that required the monarch's permission. Investors in London, Bristol, and other cities formed companies to raise the huge financial sums required to back an expedition, hoping to make fortunes by discovering a faster way to the Far East, or finding the legendary Cities of Gold. 🍃

Christopher Columbus

Christopher Columbus was a man with a plan. Growing up in Genoa, Italy, an important maritime center, he began working on a ship as a young man, and traveled to Portugal and Madeira. A group of Italian seamen lived in *Bristol* when Columbus visited the city in 1477, sailing on a Portuguese ship that was heading for Ireland and possibly as far as Iceland. He may have heard the rumors that sailors from Bristol had discovered the shores of a large land to the west, but had not reported it because they were sailing in regions that were "off limits" to them due to regional politics.

Years later, Columbus became convinced that, since the earth was round, it would be possible to reach the riches of the East by sailing west, and he thus approached potential financial backers in many parts of Europe. He sent his brother to England, hoping to interest the English monarch, but this effort was unsuccessful. Henry VII, newly on the throne, was focused on consolidating his power at home. It was under the patronage of King Ferdinand and Queen Isabella of Spain that Christopher Columbus sailed west across the Atlantic Ocean in 1492. After his expedition discovered the islands of the Caribbean, Columbus became celebrated as the man who "discovered America."

Richard Ameryck

Americans have long thought that the lands in the "New World" were named for Amerigo Vespucci, an Italian merchant and cartographer who sailed to South America. His reports and descriptions were incorporated in early maps of the area, and it is claimed that his name was used to identify the region. Recent historical research has come up with an alternative inspiration – Richard Ameryck, a wealthy merchant from **Bristol** who helped fund early Atlantic expeditions. Bristol was the second largest port in England and its ships may have been sailing to North America as early as 1470, secretly breaking a restriction on foreign fishing imposed by the King of Denmark. Ameryck's name (also written as Amerike) may have been used on early navigation maps of the area – years before **Columbus** sailed to the Caribbean.

John Cabot

John Cabot, known as the English navigator who discovered North America, was born in Italy, possibly in Gaeta near Naples. His name originally was Giovanni Caboto. "Caboto" in Italian meant "a coastal seaman." Cabot was a lifelong friend of **Christopher Columbus**. In 1493, when he learned of Columbus's journey to the West Indies, Cabot decided to attempt a similar voyage to try to discover the way to the riches of the Far East. When the Kings of Spain and Portugal were not interested in sponsoring Cabot's expedition, he traveled to England with the hope of approaching King Henry VII. The king had been unable to support Christopher Columbus's proposed voyage of exploration but, by 1496, he was more interested. He granted "letters patent" to John Cabot to "discover and claim a New World."

After organizing the expedition, Cabot left **Bristol** in May 1497 on the *Matthew*. He reached North America and probably sailed as far south as Massachusetts. When the *Matthew* returned to Bristol on 6 August 1497, Cabot was hailed as a hero and became a major celebrity. Encouraged by the king, Cabot set out on a second expedition, but never returned. His fate remains unknown, but he is celebrated as the adventurer from Bristol who discovered North America for the English.

BRISTOL In the *Church of St. Mary Redcliffe* there is a memorial to John and Joanna Brook. She was the daughter and heir of **Richard Ameryck**, after whom some Bristolians claim America is named.

Ameryck spent his later years at his Ashton Phillips Estate and his house still stands on Yanley Lane, Long Ashton, Somerset.

BRISTOL A replica of John Cabot's ship the *Matthew* is docked at the *Great Western Dockyard*.

The *Cabot Tower* was built in 1897 to celebrate the 400th anniversary of the original journey.

A whale bone in the American Chapel of the *Church of St. Mary Redcliffe* was reputedly brought back to Bristol by Cabot in 1497 and presented to the church as a symbol of the rich fishing grounds he had discovered. Today the whalebone rests near a model of Cabot's boat, presented to the church by the crew of the replica *Matthew* that sailed 500 years after the original.

The *Bristol City Museum & Art Gallery* has a painting that shows Cabot setting sail from Bristol.

YORKSHIRE The *Merchant Adventurers' Hall* in *York* is still used by the guild. A museum explains the guild system and the history of the Merchant Adventurers in York.

LONDON The *Museum in Docklands* has exhibits on the story of maritime trading in London including the formation of trading companies such as the **Muscovy Company** and the **East India Company**.

BRISTOL The Society of Merchant Venturers of the City of Bristol was established in 1552. Today a plaque marks the office building on the site, which is called the *Merchant Venturers' House*.

The *Merchant Venturers' Almshouses* were built in 1696 for sick and elderly sailors. The building still displays the coat of arms of the Merchant Venturers.

LONDON The illustration of the turkey in **William Strickland's** coat of arms is the earliest depiction of this fowl in England, according to the *College of Arms*.

YORKSHIRE At *St. Andrew's Church* in *Bridlington* the carving of a turkey on the back of the lectern is said to be in memory of William Strickland's lucky fowl.

Boynton Hall in *Bridlington* was purchased by William Strickland in 1549. Today it is a private home.

LONDON The *National Maritime Museum, Greenwich,* has an excellent collection of paintings, maps and other artefacts that show the history of British exploration in America.

Sebastian Cabot and the Muscovy Company

Sebastian Cabot claimed that, as a boy, he had accompanied his father on the expedition that reached Newfoundland. Lacking financial backing and political support in England, Sebastian sailed for the Spanish king from 1515 to the late 1540s. He discovered Brazil during this time. By 1551 Sebastian Cabot had returned to England. With the backing of King Edward VI, he founded an investment group known as "The Merchant Adventurers of England for the Discovery of Lands, Territories, Isles, Dominions, and Seignories Unknown." The group attracted some of England's most far-sighted and daring spirits, with investors, navigators, and adventurers including **Walter Raleigh** and **Humphrey Gilbert**. Eventually the group of over 200 investors raised more than £6,000 – a huge sum at that time. Sebastian Cabot was named Governor for Life by his sponsor, the Duke of Northumberland. The Merchant Adventurers backed many expeditions and voyages over hundreds of years. In 1555 Queen Mary Tudor granted the right to control all trade with Russia to a group of investors that later became the "Muscovy Company." This was the world's first joint-stock company. In 1587 the company sponsored an expedition to find a northwest passage to China. Led by John Davis, it explored the area between Greenland and Canada. **Henry Hudson**'s two expeditions, in 1607 and 1608, were backed by the Muscovy Company. His ships explored the coast of Greenland and areas north of the Artic Circle. The company lost its monopoly over trade to Russia in the late 1600s, but continued in existence until 1917. 🍃

William Strickland

William Strickland was a cabin boy with John Cabot on his first voyage to the New World, and is considered by some to be the first Englishman to have set foot on North American soil. Strickland is said to have introduced the turkey to England. He brought back some of the strange birds when he returned from several voyages to the New World. Selling them in Bristol, he saved his earnings until he was able to charter his own ship. He earned a fortune and a knighthood, and in his coat of arms, he proudly showed a turkey. 🍃

Sir Francis Drake and the *Golden Hinde*

In June of 1579, during his voyage round the world, Sir Francis Drake dropped anchor in a harbor he called Nova Albion, on the coast of what is now California. He stayed in this harbor for over five weeks repairing the *Golden Hinde*. Before leaving, he set up a monument with an engraved metal plate that has never been found. Drake returned to

England on 25 September 1580 – the first English captain to sail all the way around the globe. He was honored by Queen Elizabeth and grew to be very rich and famous. Drake became a privateer and conducted raids against the Spanish in the Caribbean. He also played a leading part in the English defeat of the Spanish Armada in 1588. 🌿

Sir Humphrey Gilbert

Humphrey Gilbert was a nephew of Queen Elizabeth I's governess. He was an early companion of the future queen. In 1578 Elizabeth granted Humphrey a charter to plant a colony in North America. He sailed from *Dartmouth* on 26 September 1578 with a large fleet, but bad weather forced them into port at Plymouth. In the end, this attempt to reach North America failed, and cost Gilbert his fortune, but it did have a long-lasting result – it got his half-brothers, Walter and Carew Raleigh, involved in exploration.

Humphrey Gilbert managed to organize another expedition in 1583. This reached Newfoundland, which he claimed for Queen Elizabeth I. On the return voyage to England bad weather struck and Gilbert's men urged him to get aboard the fleet's flagship. He refused, and stayed on his tiny ship the *Squirrel*. He was heard to say, "We are as near to heaven by sea as by land." Later that day the *Squirrel* disappeared and Humphrey Gilbert was lost. His half-brother **Walter Raleigh** continued the family tradition of exploration and adventure. 🌿

LONDON The *Golden Hinde* is docked at Horseshoe Wharf in *Southwark*.

PLACES CONNECTED WITH SIR FRANCIS DRAKE

LONDON Sir Francis Drake is commemorated at ***Westminster Abbey*** in the ***Navigators' Memorial***.

DEVON Drake lived near ***Sutton Harbour*** in ***Plymouth***, from where he left in 1577 on his voyage around the world. One of the statues in ***Hoe Park*** shows Sir Francis Drake looking out to sea.

Drake purchased ***Buckland Abbey*** from ***Richard Grenville*** in 1581 with the rewards he had been granted for his Spanish exploits on behalf of Queen Elizabeth I.

GLOUCESTERSHIRE Pieces of ebony furniture, possibly from the ***Golden Hinde***, can be seen in "Drake's Room" off the Kings Gallery at ***Berkeley Castle*** along with a large chest that belonged to Drake, who was a close friend of the Berkeley family.

Sir Walter Raleigh

Military service started early for Walter Raleigh. At fifteen, he was a volunteer in the Huguenot army in France. At twenty-

DEVON *Greenway* on the River Dart was built for Otho Gilbert. When he died in 1547, he left four children – John, Humphrey, Adrian, and Elizabeth. His widow married **Walter Raleigh** of Fardell. They had three children – Walter, Carew, and Margaret.

LONDON Walter Raleigh's statue stands in front of the *Greenwich Visitors' Centre*.

A painting in the collection at the *National Maritime Museum, Greenwich*, shows Raleigh claiming Virginia for England – although he never actually went to Virginia.

Arthur Barlowe was captain of one of the ships in the 1584 reconnaissance trip to North Carolina. He returned to England with two Native Americans – Manteo and Wanchese. They may have taught the rudiments of their language to some of the members of the 1586 expedition.

LONDON Virginia Dare's parents were married at *St. Clement Danes Church* on 24 June 1583. They moved to the parish of *St. Bride's, Fleet Street*, before they sailed to Roanoke. The reredos at St. Bride's is dedicated to the Pilgrim Fathers who sailed to American on the *Mayflower* in 1620.

four he sailed with his half-brother **Humphrey Gilbert** on an unsuccessful effort to reach North America. Walter was well known at court, and Queen Elizabeth gave him many honors. After putting down a rebellion in Ireland, he was made Captain of the Guard and was granted an estate in Ireland for his part in foiling the "Babington" conspiracy that had the goal of replacing Queen Elizabeth with Mary, Queen of Scots.

Walter Raleigh led several efforts at exploring and colonizing North America. In 1592 he fell out of favor with the queen when he secretly married one of her maids of honor, Elizabeth Throckmorton, without obtaining permission. The queen had him imprisoned in the *Tower of London*, but he was released after one of his ships brought back a huge treasure trove from a captured Spanish ship. He retired to the country and built *Sherborne Castle*.

Queen Elizabeth died in 1603. Her successor, James I, disliked Raleigh whose role in foiling the Babington plot had led to James's mother's execution. Raleigh had a long history of battling the Spanish, and James wanted to try to improve the English relationship with Spain. Accused of plotting to replace the new king with Arabella Stuart in the "Main Plot," Raleigh was tried, convicted, and sentenced to death by Lord Chief Justice **Sir John Popham**. Sent to the Tower of London, Raleigh was held prisoner there for thirteen years.

Desperate to be released, Raleigh promised King James that he would lead a new expedition that would bring back a fortune in gold for the king. James agreed on the express condition that Raleigh should not antagonize the Spanish. The expedition set off in 1616, but instead of Raleigh's triumphant resurrection, it led to a disastrous downfall. They didn't find El Dorado, and Raleigh's son was killed when the English attacked a Spanish settlement.

When Raleigh returned empty-handed, he was arrested. King James invoked the death sentence of 1603. On 29 October 1618 Raleigh was taken to Old Palace Yard (the large paved area between the *Palace of Westminster* and *Westminster Abbey*) to be beheaded in front of hundreds of people. He made a moving speech from the scaffold. It was reported that he felt the edge of the axe and said, "Tis a sharp remedy, but a sure cure for all my ills." 🍃

Virginia Dare and the Lost Colony of Roanoke

In 1584 **Walter Raleigh** organized an exploratory expedition to an area he had named "Virginia" in honor of Queen Elizabeth I, the Virgin Queen. The English landed on Roanoke Island, which is hidden from the open Atlantic by the barrier islands of the North Carolina coast. It was important to keep out of sight of Spanish ships sailing from their large bases in the

PLACES CONNECTED WITH WALTER RALEIGH

LONDON

Houses of Parliament – In the Tudor Room of the **House of Lords**, a fresco shows Walter Raleigh putting down his cloak for Queen Elizabeth I to walk across. In the Strangers' Gallery, there is a large mural with the inscription: "Queen Elizabeth the Fairie Queen with her knights and merchant venturers commissions Sir Walter Raleigh to sail for America to discover a new country."
Raleigh's name appears on the register of the **Middle Temple** in 1575, and on a painted shield on the paneling of the Temple Hall which reads
"Courtier, Soldier, Scholar, and Founder of Britain's Colonial Empire."
Crosby Hall, Chelsea Embankment – Raleigh had lodgings at Crosby Hall in 1601, in its original location in Bishopsgate. The hall was demolished in 1908 and the interiors used in 1926 at the new Chelsea site.
Raleigh was buried in the chancel of **St. Margaret's Church, Westminster**. The west window, above the entrance, commemorates the famous explorer. Funded with subscriptions from the USA, the window shows the US coat of arms and a verse by **James Russell Lowell**. There is another memorial to Walter Raleigh next to the east door.
College of Arms – Raleigh's coat of arms includes the cape he put down for Queen Elizabeth.
Tate Britain – *The Boyhood of Raleigh* by John Everett Millais shows an idealized scene.

OXFORD

Raleigh was an undergraduate at **Oxford University** in 1572.

DORSET

Raleigh built **Sherborne Castle** in 1594.

WARWICKSHIRE

Coughton Court in **Alcester** was Elizabeth Throckmorton's family home.

WILTSHIRE

Raleigh stayed at the **White Hart Hotel** in **Salisbury** for a few days in 1616 on his journey back to London after being arrested. He spent the time feigning madness and trying to write a letter of justification and apology to King James.

HAMPSHIRE

Raleigh's trial for treason was held at the Great Hall in **Winchester Castle** in December 1603. He was convicted of involvement in the Main Plot and was sentenced to death.

DEVON

Hayes Barton, a large farmhouse in **East Budleigh**, is celebrated as the birthplace of **Sir Walter Raleigh**. (In the City of Raleigh, North Carolina, a fashionable neighborhood is named "Hayes Barton.")
In 1561 Walter Raleigh's father was warden at the ancient **All Saints' Church** in **East Budleigh**. The Raleigh pew is on the north side of the nave.
A statue of Walter Raleigh was unveiled in **East Budleigh** in 2006.
Raleigh spent his childhood at **Compton Castle**, home to the Gilbert family for most of the last 600 years.

READ *Roanoke* by Lee Miller (New York: Arcade Publishing, 2001), which presents an intriguing theory as to what happened to the Roanoke Colony.

LONDON Roanoke expedition member John White made remarkable watercolors and drawings of the Indians and of the country's flora. These are preserved in the *British Museum*.

HAMPSHIRE The *Mary Rose*, docked in *Portsmouth*, is the only preserved sixteenth-century warship in the world. Visitors can get a good idea of what these ships were like by touring King Henry VIII's warship which sank in 1545 after a battle with the French.

CORNWALL *Stowe Barton Farm* in *Kilkhampton* is all that remains of the grand **Grenville** house, once called "the noblest house in the west of England." The house was demolished in 1739. *St. James's Church* in *Kilkhampton* has many Grenville memorials – reminders of its links with the wealthy family.

Caribbean and Mexico. Queen Elizabeth had authorized English captains to attack the Spanish ships and seize the treasure they were taking back to Spain. These "authorized" pirates were called privateers and were required to give the English monarch the captured ship and a share of the plunder. Walter Raleigh was not an official privateer but he did promote privateering, and his financial gains from this activity probably helped fund his expeditions.

Raleigh sent a second expedition to Roanoke with seven ships and 100 settlers. Queen Elizabeth wouldn't allow Raleigh, one of her favorite courtiers, to sail on the dangerous expeditions, so Raleigh's cousin **Richard Grenville** was commander of the fleet. They reached Roanoke Island in June 1585. When the fleet left, some colonists stayed behind. A year later, a fleet of thirteen large ships and several small boats under the command of **Sir Francis Drake** stopped at Roanoke Island, and evacuated the colony. On board were two products virtually unknown in Europe – the potato and tobacco, which may have been taken aboard when Drake stopped to reprovision his fleet in Cartagena, Columbia. The plants were introduced to Britain in 1585.

On 22 July 1587 Walter Raleigh's third expedition to North America reached Roanoke Island with 117 colonists in three ships. This time John White was governor of the group. Among the colonists were White's daughter Eleanor and her husband Ananias Dare. Their daughter, Virginia Dare, was born on 18 August 1587, the first English child to be born in America.

When the supply ships returned to England, John White went along to arrange more supplies and settlers for the colony. He was unable to return until 1590 because ships were not allowed to leave England while it was under threat of attack by the Spanish Armada. When White finally returned to Roanoke Island, he found it completely abandoned. The only clue as to what had happened was one word carved on a doorpost – "Croatoan" – the name of a nearby island. Nothing was ever found to explain what happened to the "Lost Colony" of Roanoke, and it remains one of America's great mysteries.

Virginia Dare disappeared along with all the other colonists. Her fate is still a mystery – did she die of illness or starvation, was she killed by Spanish raiders or did she perhaps grow up among the Indians of North Carolina?

Richard Grenville

Richard Grenville was born in 1542 into an important land-owning family who were related to several other families involved in the early exploration of America, especially the Raleighs and the Gilberts. His father Roger was a famous naval captain who died in the disastrous sinking of Henry

VIII's man-of-war *Mary Rose* off *Portsmouth* in 1545. Richard spent his childhood at *Buckland Abbey* and in 1559 was admitted to the *Inner Temple* in London to study law. The next year he went off to Hungary to fight the Turks. When he returned to England, he may have hoped to find glory and wealth by leading a major voyage of exploration to the New World, but he was disappointed when Queen Elizabeth appointed **Francis Drake** to that position. Grenville must have felt conflicting emotions when Drake returned in 1580 from his round-the-world voyage to become one of the most famous men in England. Drake also became very rich. He began purchasing property in Devon, and through an intermediary bought Richard Grenville's estate at Buckland Abbey.

Grenville's cousin **Walter Raleigh** organized his first expedition to the New World in 1584, and planned a second one for the next year. Because Queen Elizabeth refused to allow Raleigh to leave England on the expedition, Richard Grenville led the fleet of seven ships that sailed to Roanoke with 100 colonists.

Richard Grenville continued to be connected with the Roanoke Colony. In 1586 he returned with a small fleet looking for the military group left behind on Roanoke the year before. Grenville found the colony empty – the soldiers had been taken back to England by **Francis Drake**.

In 1591 Grenville sailed as second-in-command in an expedition sent to the Azores to capture a Spanish treasure fleet. His ship, the *Revenge*, was cut off from the rest of the English fleet. During the battle he was wounded and wanted to blow up his ship rather than be dishonored by being captured. His colleagues prevented this and Grenville was captured; he died on board a Spanish ship. 🍃

Bartholomew Gosnold

In 1602 Bartholomew Gosnold led an expedition to an area of North America that had not then been explored by the English, the area we now call New England. Gosnold's captain on his first expedition was Bartholomew Gilbert, a relative through Gosnold's father. Gosnold's wife, Mary Golding, was a granddaughter of Sir Andrew Judd, Lord Mayor of London, and a cousin of **Sir Thomas Symthe**, the powerful and wealthy investor who was central to financing early international exploration and trade. His cousin John was an usher to Queen Elizabeth and King James.

After seven weeks at sea, the 1602 expedition sighted land – a cape that later was named Cape Elizabeth, Maine. Heading south down the coast, they reached Plymouth, Massachusetts, on 14 May. Later they discovered a promontory which Gosnold named Cape Cod on account of

DEVON *Buckland Abbey* was a Cistercian monastery founded in 1278. In 1541, following the Dissolution of the Monasteries, it was purchased by Sir Richard Grenville. Francis Drake purchased Buckland Abbey in 1581.

When Grenville returned to England in 1585, he brought a Native American Indian – probably the first North American to visit England. The stranger was baptized in *St. Mary's Church, Bideford*, and was given the name of Rawleigh. He was entered in the parish register as "a natif of Wyngonditoia" (Virginia). Unfortunately, he died the next year, and is buried at St. Mary's.

Hoops Hotel, Bideford – the thirteenth-century inn is one of England's most famous. It was notorious as a meeting place for smugglers and seafarers such as **Sir Francis Drake, Sir Walter Raleigh**, and Sir Richard Grenville.

LONDON Bartholomew Gosnold studied law at the *Middle Temple* along with a friend from his years at the University of Cambridge – Henry Wriothesley, 3rd Earl of Southampton, who later became a patron of William Shakespeare.

SUFFOLK For 400 years *Otley Hall* was the home of the Gosnold family. It has been described as "one of England's loveliest houses."

LONDON Reports of Gosnold's adventures in the New World may have inspired scenes in Shakespeare's play *The Tempest*. The historical reconstruction of the *Globe Theatre* is a very evocative place to enjoy the Bard's plays!

There is a very interesting memorial to Gosnold's wife's grandfather Sir Andrew Judd at *St. Helen's Bishopsgate*.

SUFFOLK In June 2005 at the *Church of All Saints* in *Shelley*, near *Ipswich*, DNA material was taken from the remains of Elizabeth Tilney, Bartholomew Gosnold's sister. The body of his niece, Katherine Blackerby, was exhumed at the *Church of St. Peter and St. Mary* in *Stowmarket*. This will be checked against the remains found at Fort Jamestown.

BRISTOL At *St. Stephen's Church* a large framed oval memorial to **Martin Pring** is supported by a mermaid and merman.

the abundance of fish in that area. He named Martha's Vineyard after his daughter. On his return to England, Gosnold announced that he had found a more direct and quicker way to sail to the New World.

Soon Gosnold organized another expedition to the New World. Helped in recruiting colonists by his cousin **Edward-Maria Wingfield**, Gosnold was instrumental in getting **Captain John Smith** to join the expedition. This time the venturers did manage to build a lasting settlement, the first permanent English colony to be established in North America – Jamestown, named after the king who had given the company its charter.

Bartholomew Gosnold died of malaria at Jamestown on 22 August 1607. In 2003 archeologists excavating at the colonial Jamestown site found a grave inside the fort which they believe may be that of Gosnold. It is hoped that DNA tests will prove whether the body is indeed that of the explorer whom Captain John Smith described as "the prime mover behind the settlement" – one of the most important early explorers of America. 🍃

Martin Pring

Backed by the merchants of *Bristol*, Martin Pring sailed to the New World in 1603. He explored the area of Plymouth Bay, Massachusetts. Pring returned to Virginia in 1606 and mapped the coastline of Virginia. His maps may have been used by the Jamestown expedition, which sailed from London in December 1606. Martin Pring died in 1626 and is buried in Bristol. 🍃

George Weymouth

Although **Bartholomew Gosnold** found a quicker route to sail to America, many explorers were still hoping to do what **Christopher Columbus** had failed to do – find a way to get to China by sailing westward. On 2 May 1602, two ships backed by "the right Worshipfull Merchants of the Moscovie and Turkie Companies" sailed from London: the *Discovery* under Captain George Weymouth and the *Godspeed* under Captain John Drew.

The expedition reached Greenland on 28 June, headed toward North America, and then sailed northward, but were prevented from sailing into the Hudson Straits by ice and fog. On 19 July the crew mutinied and demanded to sail back to England. After Weymouth returned to Dartmouth on 5 August 1602, he claimed that there was good reason to think he had found the Northwest Passage. The two ships used in this expedition may have been the same *Discovery* and *Godspeed* used for the Jamestown expedition in 1606.

In 1605 Weymouth sailed to America in the *Arch-Angel* in

an expedition backed by **Henry Wriothesley** and **Sir Ferdinando Gorges**. Reaching Maine and sailing down along the coast of Massachusetts, they went ashore in the area of the Patuxet tribe, where they kidnapped five Indians. Manida, Sketwarroes, and Tisquantum (also known as Squanto) were presented to **Sir Ferdinando Gorges**, then governor of Plymouth. Nahanada and Assacumet were presented to **Sir John Popham** of *Hemyock Castle*. Nahanda was returned to his tribe in 1606 and Sketwarroes in 1607. Tisquantum came to play a very important role in the history of the early English presence in North America. 🍃

Squanto

Squanto was a member of the Patuxet tribe in Massachusetts. Kidnapped in 1605 by **George Weymouth**, Squanto lived in England for nine years. His was a life of incredible adventure. He became a living link between **Captain John Smith** who founded the Jamestown Colony in Virginia in 1607, and the Pilgrims who settled at the Plymouth Colony in 1620.

In 1614 **Sir Ferdinando Gorges** sent two ships to prepare for a colony in New England and to trade with the Indians. Squanto went along as an interpreter. Captain John Smith commanded one ship and Captain Thomas Hunt was in charge of the other. It was agreed that Squanto would help Smith for a short time, and then would be allowed to return home. When Smith was ready to return to England, he gave Squanto permission to travel back to his village. Unfortunately, Squanto met Captain Hunt who tricked him into going on board his ship. Squanto was imprisoned along with twenty-seven other young Indians who were all sold as slaves in Malaga, Spain. Eventually escaping, he returned to England. Squanto was taken back to New England in 1619 where he learned that all of his tribe had died from an epidemic, probably smallpox brought by the English colonists. He went to live among the Wampanoag tribe, near present-day Plymouth, Massachusetts. This is where he was when the Pilgrims reached Cape Cod in November 1620.

Imagine the Pilgrims' surprise on 11 March 1621 when an Indian walked into their Plymouth settlement and called out "Welcome Englishmen, Welcome Englishmen." The man spoke English! This was Samoset, who told them he would return with his friend who spoke better English. He returned with Squanto whom he introduced to the Pilgrims as "a native of this place who had been in England and could speak better English than himself." Squanto befriended the Pilgrims, taught them skills to survive in their new home, and acted as an interpreter with the Wampanoag tribe and its chief, Massasoit. Squanto probably was present at the first Thanksgiving celebration held by the Pilgrims. With the help

LONDON The northwest group of statues on the *Prince Albert Memorial* in Kensington portrays Native Americans.

SOMERSET The *American Museum in Britain, Bath*, has displays about Native American Indians, including Pocahontas.

LEICESTERSHIRE The *Church of St. Andrew* in *Stoke Dry* has a mural of St. Christopher painted in 1280–5. The mural shows two bowmen shooting St. Christopher. They are supposed to be modeled on American Indians, described in Norman ballads about Norman raids on the North American coast.

LONDON American Indians look proudly from the façade of *14 Prince's Gate, Knightsbridge*, which for many years served as the American ambassador's residence.

LONDON Richard Hakluyt was a pupil at *Westminster School*. Legend says that Richard Hakluyt's interest in mapping the New World was sparked when he visited the *Middle Temple*, where his cousin, also Richard, was a lawyer and consultant to maritime explorers.

OXFORD Richard Hakluyt studied at *Christ Church*. He received a BA in 1574 and an MA in 1577. He stayed on at Oxford as a lecturer in geography and cosmology.

LINCOLNSHIRE Hakluyt is shown in the Virginia windows at *St. Helena's Church* in *Willoughby*.

SUFFOLK In 1588 Hakluyt was appointed rector of *All Saints' Church* in the village of *Wetheringsett*.

LONDON In 1604 Hakluyt became chaplain of the hospital in the Savoy. The ancient *Savoy Chapel* is just off the Strand.

Richard Hakluyt was archdeacon at *Westminster Abbey* and is buried there.

DEVON The Lord Mayor and the people of *Plymouth* invite all Americans to join the city of Plymouth's Annual Thanksgiving Festival, celebrating its unique *Mayflower* and transatlantic heritage.

of Squanto's interpreting, Massasoit and Governor Carver made a peace treaty that lasted for at least fifty years.

Squanto chose to remain with the settlers. In the spring of 1621, the colonists planted their first crops in Patuxet's abandoned fields. Their corn crop proved very successful, thanks to Squanto, who taught them how to plant corn in hills, using fish as a fertilizer. Late in 1622 he became ill while guiding an expedition around Cape Cod. Squanto died in Chatham Harbor, Massachusetts, in November 1622. 🍃

Richard Hakluyt

Richard Hakluyt, born in 1552, became the best known English geographer of the sixteenth century. He had a great impact on the course of English exploration of America. Early English exploration was based on commercial goals, and while seamen needed accurate maps and geographical information, they were not always eager to share information with competitors. Hakluyt decided to compile as much accurate information as possible about the geography of the New World. When he accompanied Queen Elizabeth's ambassador to Paris in 1583 as his secretary and personal chaplain, Hakluyt gathered information about French, Spanish, and Portuguese navigators.

Richard was aware of the latest English expeditions and personally knew many of the people involved, including **Walter Raleigh**, **Bartholomew Gosnold**, **Gabriel Archer**, and **Edward-Maria Wingfield**. He used eye-witness accounts of expeditions in writing his most famous book. Hakluyt's view of the purpose of sailing to the New World was changing from finding trade routes to looking at the potential of the new land itself. He proposed to Queen Elizabeth that the unemployed and discontented of England could be sent to harvest the resources of America. He was a supporter of Walter Raleigh's effort to establish a colony, and was one of twelve directors of the company formed to back Raleigh's 1587 Roanoke expedition.

In 1588 Hakluyt returned from France and was appointed rector of **Wetheringsett, Suffolk** where he worked on two further editions of his *Principal Navigations* adding new stories he found in ships' logs, secret intelligence, and personal interviews. His books provide some wonderful stories of those early expeditions. In 1589 he became a director of the **Virginia Company** and in 1599 a consultant to the **East India Company**. As the 1606 expedition was being planned, Hakluyt was placed in charge of the religious care of James Town, the intended capital in the proposed colony of Virginia. He engaged the curate who actually traveled to Virginia and became known as the first minister in America – Robert Hunt. 🍃

The Virginia Company

The Virginia Company was created in 1606 with a charter granted by King James I. Two private stock companies were formed to establish colonies along the Atlantic coast of North America. The Company of Adventurers and Planters of the City of London was established for the "First Colony," and the Company of Adventurers and Planters of Bristol, Exeter, and Plymouth for the "Second Colony." These have become known as the London Company and the Plymouth Company. The charters specified that the London Company was to establish its colonies in the area we know as Virginia and the Carolinas. The Plymouth Company was granted territory in the area now called New England.

The London Company moved quickly after it received the letters patent. Much of the financial backing for the expedition was supplied by the Merchant Adventurers of London. On 19 December 1606 the colonists sailed toward Virginia in three small ships: the *Godspeed*, *Mary Constant*, and *Discovery*. The Jamestown settlement survived several years of extreme hardship to become the first permanent English colony in the New World.

The Plymouth Company backed an expedition sent out in 1607 with the support of Chief Justice **John Popham** and Sir **Ferdinando Gorges**, governor of the **Fort on the Hoe** at **Plymouth**. A colony was established in Maine, but the colonists were not able to sustain this settlement. It took a few years for the Plymouth Company to organize its next effort to establish a colony. Several expeditions were sent out to explore the coast. Native people were brought back to England where they lived for several years to learn English. In 1616 financial backers were sought for a new expedition. Finally, in August 1620, the *Mayflower* and *Speedwell* left **Southampton** on an expedition backed by the Plymouth Company. A group of English Pilgrims who had spent time in Holland were under contract as colonists. 🍂

The Popham Colony

George Popham and Ralegh Gilbert were the two main adventurers involved in the Plymouth Company's attempt to set up a colony in America. Their families were at the center of efforts to build colonies in the New World. George Popham's uncle was Chief Justice **John Popham**, who sentenced **Walter Raleigh** to death in 1603. Ralegh Gilbert's father, **Humphrey Gilbert**, was half-brother to Walter Raleigh.

On 18 August 1607 an expedition left Plymouth with 120 colonists and soldiers. In two ships, the *Gift of God* and the *Mary and John*, they explored the Maine coast, finally landing at the mouth of the Kennebec (then called the Sagadahoc)

SOMERSET *Hunstrete House, Hunstrete,* near Bristol, was one of the many properties owned by **John Popham** in the early 1600s. It is now a luxury country house hotel.

DEVON By the 1600s, *Hemyock Castle* in *Cullompton* and most of the village belonged to Sir John Popham.

BERKSHIRE *Littlecote House* near *Hungerford* became the property of John Popham in the 1590s. The house remained in the Popham family for 350 years. It is now a hotel.

SOMERSET At *St. John the Baptist Church, Wellington,* there is a magnificent tomb with effigies of Sir John Popham and his wife.

During the fifteenth and sixteenth centuries, many wealthy families set up charitable institutions around England. The Pophams funded an almshouse in *Wellington*. Built c. 1606, it served its original purpose until 1936 when the Mantle Street almshouses were converted into the *St. John Fisher Catholic Church*. Its high windows and gabled roofline give hints of its origin as an almshouse.

CAMBRIDGESHIRE Around 1600, John Popham lived at *Kimbolton Castle*. The Popham Gallery above the chapel is named for him, and his portrait hangs in the Queen's Room.

SOMERSET The ancient *Ashton Court* estate at *Long Ashton* has several associations with America, including **Richard Ameryck** and **Ferdinando Gorges.**

SOMERSET The beautiful Gorges tomb at *All Saints' Church* in *Wraxall* is a memorial to Sir Ferdinando's great-great grandparents Sir Edmund Gorges and his first wife Lady Anne Howard. She was the great aunt of two queens of England – Anne Boleyn and Catherine Howard.

River. Naming their settlement the Popham Colony after Sir John Popham, the colony's main patron, they built a fort and constructed the first ship built in Maine, a 50ft pinnacle called the *Virginia of Sagadahoc*. The colonists explored the area in the pinnacle, possibly going as far as Virginia.

George Popham became president of the Popham Colony but proved an ineffective leader. Before the end of December 1607, both the *Gift of God* and the *Mary and John* returned to England leaving only forty-five colonists behind. When the severe winter weather came early, the colony wasn't prepared. George Popham died in February and Ralegh Gilbert took over. Unfortunately, Gilbert wasn't an effective leader, either. He was a hothead and made unwise decisions.

Supply ships came in the spring and the colonists made an effort to continue. However, a third ship arrived in September with news that the colony's main patron, Sir John Popham, had died. Ralegh Gilbert's brother had also died, leaving his estate to Ralegh, who decided to return to England and claim his inheritance, which included **Compton Castle**. The colony was abandoned and everything that could be dismantled was loaded onto ships. Although it was a failure, the building of the Popham Colony later provided the English with support for their claims to Maine and New England. 🍃

Ferdinando Gorges

In 1596 Ferdinando Gorges was commissioned as governor of the castle and **Fort on the Hoe** in **Plymouth**, England. A friend of **Sir Walter Raleigh**, he became interested in plans for establishing colonies in the New World and supported the 1605 expedition led by **George Weymouth** to explore the coasts of Maine and Massachusetts in a quest for the resources of North America. When Weymouth returned to England in late July 1605 he presented five Indians to Sir Ferdinando, who took three of them: Manida, Sketwarroes, and Tisquantum. They were taken into his household where they lived for several years, learning English.

Sir Ferdinando Gorges was part of the formation of the Plymouth Company in 1606. The company was involved in several failed attempts at settlement. In 1614 Gorges sent two ships commanded by **Captain John Smith** to establish a plantation in New England and to trade with the Indians. **Squanto** went along as an interpreter. Smith produced many important maps on this voyage. The first use of the names "New England" and "Plimoth" appear on one of these. The Plymouth Company backed the expedition that sailed on the *Mayflower* in the autumn of 1620 with a mixture of Puritans and "strangers" who founded the "Plimoth Plantation."

Called the "father of colonization in America,"

OTHER LOCATIONS CONNECTED WITH SIR FERDINANDO GORGES

LONDON Edward Gorges (father of Sir Ferdinando) died in 1567. He was buried at
St. James's Church, Clerkenwell.

SOMERSET Birdcombe Court in **Wraxhall**, near **Bristol**, was the home of Gorges family for many years.
It is now a private home.

The Gorges Tomb at **All Saints' Church, Wraxall**, has figures of Ferdinando's great-great-grandparents,
Sir Edmund Gorges and his first wife Lady Anne
Anne Howard. She was the great-aunt of two queens of England – Anne
Boleyn and Catherine Howard – both wives of Henry VIII.

DEVON Gorges was governor of the **Fort on the Hoe** in **Plymouth** during the attack of the Spanish in
1595. The Royal Citadel is still in use by the military, but guided tours are given.

There is a monument to Sir Ferdinando Gorges at **St. Budeaux's Church, Plymouth**.

Ferdinando Gorges gambled his fortune on the dreams of great wealth from the New World and eventually lost his fortune by backing expeditions that did not succeed. Gorges lived out his last years at *Ashton Court* near Bristol, which belonged to his fourth wife. He died in May 1647 and was buried at *All Saints' Church, Long Ashton.*

Sir Robert Cecil

William Cecil served Queen Elizabeth as secretary of state and then Lord Treasurer until his death in 1598. His son Robert was trained to be a great statesman. Becoming a Member of Parliament in 1584, and secretary of state in 1596, Robert Cecil was in a prime position to influence the course of events. He was listed as an "adventurer" in the 1609 charter that King James granted to extend the territory of the Jamestown Colony. Cecil hired George Calvert to be his private secretary, a position that led to the Calvert family receiving a grant of land in the New World that became the State of Maryland.

Robert Cecil had a long, but not always happy, relationship with **Walter Raleigh**. Perhaps Cecil was jealous of Raleigh's popularity with Queen Elizabeth. Raleigh's privateering past involved frequent naval battles with Spanish ships, and Robert Cecil's efforts to improve English diplomatic relations with Spain led to his strong disapproval of Raleigh's escapades in the southern part of the New World. It has even been suggested that this political web

LONDON On 19 April 1607 **Henry Hudson** and ten crew members prayed at *St. Ethelburga's Church* before starting out on their expedition.

KENT In early May 1607 Henry Hudson sailed from *Gravesend* on his first expedition to North America.

LONDON The *Royal Exchange* was founded in 1570 by Sir Thomas Gresham, the greatest merchant of his time. Gresham was an investor in the **Muscovy Company**. The present Royal Exchange was built after the Great Fire of 1666. The weathervane on top is Gresham's emblem, a golden grasshopper.

LONDON A grasshopper can also be seen on Sir Thomas Gresham's tomb in *St. Helen's Bishopsgate, London*.

There has been speculation that Henry Hudson's wife and younger

may have contributed to the disappearance of Raleigh's **Roanoke Colony**. 🍃

Henry Hudson

Born c. 1570, by 1607 Henry Hudson was an experienced seaman and had a ship under his command, sponsored by the **Muscovy Company.** He was under orders from Sir Thomas Gresham and the group of wealthy merchants to try to find the Northwest Passage – the short route to China. Sailing from London on 23 April 1607, the small expedition spent three-and-a-half months exploring the coast of Greenland and areas north of the Artic Circle. They had reached the furthest point north attained by any English expedition, but had failed to find a passage through the ice. They returned to England in September, and in April 1608 Hudson sailed on his second voyage for the Muscovy Company, again trying to find a passage over the North Pole. This expedition also failed to find the fabled route, but Henry Hudson had established a great reputation as an explorer.

When the Muscovy Company decided against sponsoring another expedition, the Dutch East India Company offered financial backing for Hudson. On 6 April 1609 he sailed from Amsterdam on the *Half Moon*, looking for a northeast passage around the top of Norway. When the way was blocked by arctic ice-floes, Hudson sailed west towards Newfoundland and then south, exploring the eastern coast of America as far as the James River in Virginia. Turning back to the north, Hudson anchored off Sandy Hook, near the southern end of Manhattan Island. He claimed the land for the Dutch. Thinking that the wide river that headed north from this bay might lead to the passage he was seeking, Hudson sailed up the river as far as present-day Albany, New York, where rapids made the route impassable. Hudson sailed back across the Atlantic, landing at Dartmouth on 7 November 1609. He did not have a friendly reception – he was arrested for "voyaging to the detriment of his country."

Henry Hudson was placed under a form of house arrest with his family in the Royal Peculiar of St. Katherine's precinct next to the Tower of London. The backers of English settlements in North America saw his expedition for the Dutch East India Company as foreign competition, and felt that the information Hudson had given the Dutch might endanger their own plans. However, by this time Henry Hudson was one of the most experienced explorers of the New World, so his knowledge and abilities could not be wasted. A number of "Merchant Adventurers" banded together to fund a new expedition with Henry Hudson as the leader.

In April 1610 Henry Hudson left on his last expedition,

sailing aboard the *Discovery* with twenty crewmen and supplies for eight months. His son John was aboard. The *Discovery* sailed north through ice-floes into the vast cold waters of what is now called Hudson Bay. The weather was extremely harsh and the ship became ice-bound. The men barely managed to survive the arctic weather. When spring arrived and the ice started to break up, Hudson wanted to continue west, searching for the passage. The crew had suffered to the point where they could endure it no longer. They mutinied and, in June 1611, Henry Hudson, his son John and seven sick and lame crew members were placed in a small lifeboat and set adrift in the cold waters. The little ship disappeared from sight and the men aboard were never seen again. The men left on the *Discovery* somehow managed to sail the ship back to England. Of the twenty-two people aboard the ship when it began its journey, only eight returned. Four of these men were tried for the murder of Henry Hudson, but sympathy for what they had gone through led to their acquittal.

Henry Hudson's name and memory live on in the lands he explored – in the Hudson River, where he was the first European explorer to sail up the mighty river, and in Hudson Bay, where his expedition allowed the British to claim vast regions of Canada. 🍃

The East India Company

The East India Company was founded in December 1600 with a royal charter from Queen Elizabeth I, giving it a monopoly of trade with the East Indies. The charter conferred on the "Governor and Company of Merchants of London to the East Indies" the right to trade between the Cape of Good Hope and Cape Horn. The investors backed expeditions to explore trade routes to the East, such as the 1602 voyage of two small vessels, the *Discovery* under George Weymouth and the *Godspeed* under John Drew. Their orders were to find a northwest passage to China.

The East India Company established interests along the trade routes to India. Many of the investors became immensely wealthy, including **Elihu Yale**, who in 1718 made a donation worth £1,162 to the Collegiate School in Connecticut, later renamed Yale College in his honor. The company's influence with India grew. In the eighteenth century it took over the military rule of the country and governed India on behalf of the Crown.

The three ships that carried the tea that ended up in Boston Harbor in December 1773 were whale-oil ships chartered for use by the East India Company by Samuel Enderby & Co. of London, ship owners and whalers. The

children were kept at *St. Katherine's Dock* almost as hostages when he left on his last voyage.

The *East India Arms* pub in Leadenhall Street is a reminder of the vast company complex that was built in that part of London.

The *East India Club* was founded in 1849 for current and former employees of the East India Company.

From 1648 to 1726 *East India House* occupied the former mansion house of Sir William Craven on Leadenhall Street, the site where *Lloyd's of London* now has its modern office building.

St. Matthias's Church, Poplar High Street, was built in 1653 as an East India Company chapel. Many company employees lived in the area.

LONDON *Crosby Hall* in *Chelsea* was built in 1466–75 in Bishopsgate as a mansion for Sir John Crosby, a wealthy grocer. **Walter Raleigh** had lodgings there in 1601. In 1621–38 it was the headquarters of the **East India Company**. In 1908 the house was purchased by the Charter Bank of India and taken down. In 1926 the interiors were incorporated in the Tudor-style building of the Hostel of the British Federation of University Women in Chelsea. It is now a private home.

The *Museum in Docklands* focuses on the history of maritime trading in London including the formation of trading companies such as the Muscovy Company and the East India Company. The companies held lotteries to raise money – on display are some of the prizes offered.

Captain Cook at the
National Maritime Museum,
Greenwich, London

YORKSHIRE *Middlesbrough's* most famous son, **Captain Cook**, is commemorated with the "Bottle of Notes" sculpture which is made up of extracts from the journals of his voyages.

colonial unrest in America resulted in serious financial difficulties for the East India Company and led to restructuring in 1773 and 1784 that gave the British government more direct involvement in the company. After increasing problems in India, including uprisings by the company's Indian soldiers, the East India Company was dissolved in 1874. 🍃

Captain James Cook: Hawaii and Alaska

James Cook was born on 27 October 1728, one of nine children of a farm laborer. When he was fifteen, James was apprenticed to William Sanderson who had a general store in the village of **Staithes** in North Yorkshire. He worked there for a year and a half, but when he turned seventeen, he left Staithes and walked to **Whitby**, where he started work as an apprentice to a ship owner who specialized in coal transport.

In 1755 hostilities broke out in North America between the English and the French. James Cook enlisted as an able seaman on the *Eagle*. He was soon promoted and his rise in the navy seems almost meteoric. In 1759, during the Seven Years' War, General James Wolfe was in command of the largest British naval force ever to cross the Atlantic. The chief navigator of the fleet was James Cook.

In 1763 Cook was given the difficult task of charting the St. Lawrence River. For four years he surveyed the eastern coasts of Canada, producing charts so accurate that they were used until the early part of the twentieth century. His mathematical work was accepted at the top levels of science; he even contributed papers to the **Royal Society** on mathematical problems such as finding locations by the moon. These skills contributed to the British admiralty's selection of Cook to command an expedition of scientists and astronomers sent to the South Pacific to study an eclipse of the sun by Venus predicted to occur on 3 June 1769. Cook was given a crew of eighty men and the *Endeavour* for the expedition, which included eleven scientists. They left **Plymouth** in August 1768 on the first of his three great voyages. The expedition reached Tahiti in April 1769. After spending three months observing the transit of Venus, they continued on the voyage of exploration, charting the coast of New Zealand. These were the first Europeans to visit the coast of Australia. The *Endeavour* returned to England in July 1771 after almost three years at sea.

Just one year later, Cook left on his second expedition with two vessels, the *Resolution* and the *Adventure*. He had been promoted to commander and given charge of a new expedition to determine whether the south magnetic pole was on water or land, to claim land for England, to chart the

26

South Seas, and collect scientific data and samples. During this voyage Cook discovered Antarctica. He returned to England in July 1775, after another three year voyage.

In 1776 Cook was given a promotion to captain and a third mission – to find a northwest passage from the Atlantic to the Pacific Ocean. The expedition left Plymouth on 12 July 1776 aboard the *Resolution* and the *Discovery*. They sailed around Africa, stopped at Australia, New Zealand, and Tahiti and turned northwards passing the Hawaiian islands. The expedition sailed up the coast of Alaska into the Arctic Ocean until stopped by ice. Cook left his mark by naming many areas in Alaska. Then they sailed south.

After exploring the Hawaiian islands for eight weeks, the ships moored in Kealakekua Bay on the Kona coast of the Big Island of Hawaii. They were initially welcomed by the Hawaiians. There are even stories that Cook's appearance in some way led the native people to consider him to be a representative of the god Lono. The ships made their repairs and left the bay, but a mast on the *Resolution* was damaged and the expedition returned to the bay. This time they were met with hostility from the Hawaiians. A longboat from the *Resolution* was stolen and a guard killed. On 14 February 1779 Captain James Cook went ashore with sailors and marines to demand the return of the ship. A fight developed, stones were thrown, and Cook was stabbed and killed. The voyage continued under the command of Captain Clerke of the *Discovery*, returning to England in 1780.

Hawaii

Captain James Cook first glimpsed the islands of Hawaii on 18 January 1778 when he sighted the island of Oahu. He landed on the island of Kauai on 20 January. Twenty-five days later, during a conflict with the natives, Captain Cook was killed. The British expedition left Hawaii on 15 March 1778 and no other Europeans visited the islands until 1786, when two English commercial ships and two French naval vessels sailed into the waters of the Sandwich Islands (the name given to the islands by Cook).

In 1793–4 Captain Vancouver established a friendly UK–Hawaii relationship and gave a Red Ensign to the king. The Hawaiians seem to have liked this flag – they flew it for the next several years. During the War of 1812 between the US and Britain, an American asked King Kamehameha why he was flying the "enemy" flag. At that time the Hawaiians decided to combine the Union Jack and the Stars and Stripes into their distinctive flag. This flag remains in use today as the flag of the State of Hawaii.

In 1933 the Cook family cottage in *Middlesbrough* was sold. It was dismantled and re-erected in Fitzroy Gardens, Melbourne, Australia, as a museum. A memorial obelisk was erected on the original site.

State flag of Hawaii

SOMERSET The *American Museum in Britain*, near *Bath* has several Hawaiian quilts in its collection, which is the largest assemblage of American furnishings and decorative arts outside of the US.

YORKSHIRE LOCATIONS WITH
CAPTAIN COOK CONNECTIONS

James Cook was born on 27 October 1728, one of nine children of a farm laborer. He was baptized at **St. Cuthbert's Church** in **Marton**. The church registry records: "James ye son of James Cook day labourer baptied." A stained-glass window commemorates the achievements of James Cook.

The **Captain Cook Birthplace Museum** in **Marton** marks the site of Captain Cook's birthplace and provides insight into his youth, his early seafaring career at Whitby and his three great voyages of discovery to the South Seas and Americas.

As a boy James Cook worshipped at **All Saints' Church, Great Ayton**. Buried in the Cook family grave in the churchyard are Cook's mother, Grace Cook, and five of his brothers and sisters. In 1737 the Cook family moved to **Aireyholme Farm**, three miles outside of **Great Ayton**. James Cook's father went there to work as foreman for the lord of the manor of Great Ayton. Aieyholme is still a working farm.

The **Captain Cook Schoolroom Museum** in **Great Ayton** is housed in a building once used as a charity school where James Cook was educated.

The sculpture of James Cook on **High Green** in **Great Ayton** shows James at the age of sixteen, when he left Great Ayton to go to Staithes as an apprentice.

The handsome seventeenth-century house in **Whitby** where James Cook came to serve his apprenticeship is now the **Captain Cook Memorial Museum**. It belonged to Cook's master, the Quaker ship owner Captain John Walker. When the young Cook was not at sea, he lodged here in the attic with Walker's "other family" of apprentices. The house is now a museum celebrating Cook's Whitby years and his later achievements.

The **Whitby Museum** has a Captain Cook exhibit, with models of his ships *Resolution* and *Endeavour*.

A full statue of Captain Cook stands looking out to sea at **West Cliff** in **Whitby**. A carving of the *Resolution* is on the base of the statue.

The **Captain Cook and Staithes Heritage Centre** in **Staithes** features a complete recreation of Sanderson's shop where a young Captain Cook was once an apprentice.

The huge obelisk of the **Captain Cook Monument** on **Easby Moor** near Great Ayton is a landmark for many miles around.

In the graveyard of **St. Germain's Church, Marske**, overlooking the sea, a tombstone marks the grave of James Cook's father. He died in 1779, unaware that his famous son had died in Hawaii six weeks earlier.

LONDON LOCATIONS WITH CAPTAIN COOK CONNECTIONS

A full-length statue of Captain James Cook, perched dangerously on a ship's coiled rope, stands just inside the **Admiralty Arch** on **The Mall**.

The **Natural History Museum, Cromwell Road** has many drawings brought back from Captain Cook's voyages.

James Cook and Elizabeth Batts married in 1762 at **St. Margaret's Church** in **Barking**.

A plaque at **340 The Highway** in **Shadwell** marks the site at 126 Upper Shadwell where Cook lived from 1762 to 1763.

James Cook, the eldest son of Captain James Cook, was baptized at **St. Paul's Church** in **Shadwell** in 1763.

A plaque marks the site at **89 Mile End Road** where Cook lived from 1763 to 1788.

A statue of Captain Cook stands in the garden of the **National Maritime Museum, Greenwich**.

One of the treasures brought back from his third expedition was the journal kept almost daily by Cook. The journal is an invaluable source of information about the discoveries made on some of the most important voyages of discovery ever undertaken.

The Navigators' Memorial in **Westminster Abbey** honors Captain Cook, **Sir Francis Drake**, and Sir Francis Chichester.

The **National Portrait Gallery** has several portraits of Captain Cook, including one by John Webber which is on display.

The twenty-five-year-old Joseph Banks accompanied Captain Cook on the voyage of the Endeavour which spent three years from 1768 to 1771 exploring New Zealand and Australia. Banks became one of England's most famous botanists. He was president of the Royal Society for forty-two years and was instrumental in the development of Kew Gardens. A blue plaque commemorates his home at **32 Soho Square, London**.

OTHER LOCATIONS WITH CAPTAIN COOK CONNECTIONS

CAMBRIDGE There is a marble memorial to Captain Cook in Cambridge's Round Church, the **Church of St. Andrew the Great**. Cook's wife and two sons are buried there.

BUCKINGHAMSHIRE In the late eighteenth century, Admiral Sir Hugh Palliser was treasurer of the navy. He built a memorial to his friend Captain Cook in the grounds of **The Vache**, his estate in **Chalfont St. Giles**. It consists of a globe standing on an engraved plinth. The Vache is private property, but there is public access to the monument from Vache Lane.

DEVON A plaque at **58 Notte Street** in **Plymouth** marks Captain Cook's visit before the

Endeavour voyage. Cook sailed from Plymouth on all three of his historic expeditions.

COUNTY DURHAM A replica of the *Endeavour* is moored on the River Tees at **Stockton-on-Tees**.

OXFORD The collection of the **Pitt Rivers Museum** contains some 150 objects collected in the South Pacific by Johann Reinhold Forster and his son George during Captain James Cook's second voyage of discovery.

NEWPORT, RHODE ISLAND, USA

How did the remains of Captain Cook's ship the *Endeavour* end up at the bottom of the waters in Newport Harbor? The *Endeavour* was sold by the Royal Navy in 1775 and, renamed the *Lord Sandwich*, it was used during the American Revolution as a British troop transport ship and then as a prison ship. In August 1778 the *Lord Sandwich* and twelve other transport ships were scuttled in Newport Harbor to block the port against the possibility of aid from a threatening French fleet. The Australian National Maritime Museum is working with Rhode Island Marine Archaeology Project to identify the remains of the Endeavour which lie among hundreds of shipwrecks.

By an amazing coincidence, Cook's other ship the *Resolution* may also have ended its days in Newport. It is thought that the ship may have been sold and rechristened *La Liberté*. In 1793, working as a cargo carrier, she ran aground in the entrance to Newport Harbor. After being refloated and returned to dock, it was found that the old timbers had severely rotted and the ship was not worth repairing. After any usable wood was salvaged, the wreck was left to silt over. It precise location is uncertain, but research is being carried out to pinpoint the remains of one of the most important ships in maritime history.

CHAPTER 2
ENGLISH COLONIAL SETTLERS
IN AMERICA

During the first few decades of the seventeenth century, English settlers began to populate the eastern coast of North America. The hostility between Protestant England and Catholic Spain had a very significant influence on the course of English exploration and settlement of the New World. English privateers attacked Spanish treasure ships in the Caribbean and consequently the English had to hide their early southern settlements behind barrier islands for protection against vengeful Spanish raids.

The English–Spanish hostility was also played out in Europe, where opposition to Spanish Catholic rule of the Low Countries provided a training ground for many English soldiers and naval commanders. English regiments went to Holland to support the native Protestants there in their bid to throw off Spanish rule. Many of the early leaders of the first English colonies in America were men who had served together in the Low Countries. They were trained and experienced soldiers who had often won fame in battle. These were just the kind of men to send as commanders of expeditions into an unknown world. They knew each other well, and often their families were closely related by marriage or blood. After the decisive defeat of the Spanish Armada in 1588, the English no longer had to keep their ships and soldiers nearby to defend their island kingdom. They could turn their attention westward across the Atlantic, and they had the resources and energy to start what became a tide of immigration that transformed a continent.

In the late sixteenth century, the earliest English attempts to build settlements in the New World ended in failure, but once the first English settlements were established in America, many different groups of English people began to immigrate. These people came from many parts of England and were motivated by a variety of reasons – some came hoping for economic gain, others were inspired by religious ideals. They came in small groups and large and faced varying hardships.

EAST SUSSEX Robert Hunt was appointed chaplain to the Jamestown expedition by **Richard Hakluyt**. Hunt celebrated the first Holy Communion in the English colony. This event is commemorated in stained glass window in the *Church of All Saints, Old Heathfield*, where he had been rector.

KENT The twin towers of *Reculver Abbey* stand where a Saxon church was built in 699 on the ruins of an abandoned Roman fort. Robert Hunt served as vicar in the parish of Reculver from 1594 to 1602.

LONDON The First Settlers Memorial at *East India Dock* commemorates the three ships that sailed from Blackwall Docks in 1606.

The thirteen colonies that eventually joined together as the United States were begun by English men and women who would make lasting contributions to the social, political, religious, and economic life of the nation that developed over the next 400 years. 🌿

VIRGINIA
Jamestown – The First Permanent English Colony

The early English settlement of North America was driven by the hope of financial gain. After **Walter Raleigh** was convicted of treason and imprisoned in the Tower of London under a death sentence, the Virginia patent was available to new investors. A group of military men and merchants from London, Dorchester, Bristol, and other areas formed a corporation of stockholders known as the London Company and petitioned King James I for a charter to establish a settlement in North America. In granting a charter to the London Company on 10 April 1606, the king gave the investors three objectives: find gold, find a route to the South Seas, and find the **Lost Colony of Roanoke**.

Several experienced explorers were involved with the new venture. **Bartholomew Gosnold**, working with his cousin-through-marriage, **Edward-Maria Wingfield**, helped to find colonists for Jamestown. Gosnold was the nephew of **Sir Thomas Smythe**, the powerful and wealthy man who was centrally involved in international exploration and trade. The new company could base its plans on information gathered by the early voyages of Cabot, Weymouth, Grenville, and others, as well as on the writings of **Richard Hakluyt**. **Martin Pring** had explored the area of Plymouth Bay, Massachusetts, in 1603 and had mapped the Virginia coastline in early 1606.

On 19 December 1606 an expedition of three small vessels carrying 144 men sailed from a pier in *Blackwall* in East London (now *East India Dock*). There were seventy-one on the *Susan Constant* under Christopher Newport, fifty-two on the *Godspeed* under Bartholomew Gosnold, and twenty-one on the *Discovery* under John Ratcliffe. Robert Hunt went as chaplain, appointed by **Richard Hakluyt**, the geographer, who was rector of the expedition. The Atlantic crossing was very difficult. Forty-five died at sea. When the ships reached Virginia, they opened the "Sealed Box" of instructions sent with the expedition and learned that the governing council determined by the king included Wingfield, Ratcliffe, Gosnold, Newport, Kendall, Martin, and Smith. The group decided to exclude John Smith because he had been imprisoned during the voyage for allegedly trying to start a mutiny.

On 27 April 1607 they made landfall on American soil.

The first group to step ashore included **Edward-Maria Wingfield**, John Ratcliffe, **George Percy**, Gabriel Archer, and about two dozen men. The ships then sailed further upriver, and on 13 May 1607 the English colonists went ashore to establish their camp, which they named Jamestown. On 21 June, Rev. Hunt celebrated the first Communion service by an English clergyman in America.

The summer and autumn brought blistering heat, swarms of insects, unfit water, starvation, and Indian attacks. By the end of the autumn fifty more colonists had died, among them Bartholomew Gosnold. The adventurers were unsuited for the work and the colony needed a strong leader to help it survive. A leader did emerge – **John Smith**. He also dealt with the local Indians, which led to the most famous story to be passed down from the Jamestown Colony – that of Captain John Smith being saved from execution by the Indian princess **Pocahontas**. The precise facts of the event are shrouded in the mists of time, but it is true that Pocahontas became closely attached to the English colony.

Only thirty-eight English colonists were still alive when Captain Newport returned to Jamestown in January 1608 with food, supplies, and 120 more colonists. These new settlers also faced tremendous hardships. The winter of 1609 has been called the Starving Time. It is said that after the settlers ate all of their livestock, they were forced to eat their pets, mice, rats – and each other. Some colonists reportedly did turn to cannibalism, sneaking out at night to dig up the graves of both English and Indian dead.

In 1609 a fleet of nine ships sailed from England with supplies and 500 to 600 new colonists for Jamestown. One ship was lost and the *Sea Venture* was separated from the fleet in a hurricane. It crashed on the rocks off Bermuda. The 150 passengers on the *Sea Venture* all survived the wreck. Luckily, the group included carpenters and shipwrights. They salvaged tools and wood from the wreck of the *Sea Venture*, and within nine months built two small vessels, the *Deliverance* and the *Patience*. When this group of survivors arrived in Virginia on 24 May 1610, they found only sixty survivors alive at Jamestown – ninety per cent of the colony had died.

Thomas Gates decided to take the remaining settlers to Newfoundland where they could then sail for England. Jamestown almost repeated the story of failure of the Popham Colony. However, as the ships headed away from Jamestown, they met an English ship coming upstream and learned that supplies and colonists were on the way with the newly appointed governor of Virginia, **Lord De La Warr**. The survivors turned around and returned to Jamestown. The colony continued. 🍃

LONDON The three ships of the Jamestown expedition are shown in the stained-glass windows of *St. Sepulchre-without-Newgate*.

St. Sepulchre-without-Newgate was **Captain John Smith**'s home church. A brass plaque commemorates his burial at the church. The kneeler collection features designs based on people associated with the Jamestown expedition.

Sir Richard Saltonstall was a long-time supporter of Captain John Smith, who dedicated one of his books to Saltonstall. He is shown in the window at St. Sepulchre's Church. Saltonstall was sheriff of London in 1588 and Lord Mayor of London 1597–8. The Lord Mayor's official residence is at the Mansion House. Construction of today's *Mansion House* began in 1739.

SUFFOLK The cathedral treasury at *St. Edmundsbury Cathedral* in *Bury St. Edmunds* is dedicated to the original Jamestown settlers.

LONDON It is said that an account of the *Sea Venture*'s survivors' time on Bermuda, written by the expedition's historian William Strachey, was used by William Shakespeare when he wrote *The Tempest*. A great place to see the play is at Shakespeare's *Globe Theatre* in *Southwark*.

KENT Sir Thomas Smythe bought an estate at *Sutton-at-Hone* where he retired. He died there on 4 September 1625, at the age of sixty-seven, and was buried at *St. John the Baptist Church*.

WILTSHIRE *Corsham Court* was built in 1582 by Thomas "Customer" Smythe. The Elizabethan manor house is open for special tours.

KENT There is a beautiful monument to Thomas "Customer" Smythe in the south transept of *St. Mary the Virgin Church* in *Ashford*.

LONDON "Customer" married well – his wife Alice Judd was a daughter of the Lord Mayor of London, whose tomb can be seen in *St. Helen's Bishopsgate*. The daughter of Alice's sister Katherine married Bartholomew Gosnold.

The Early Years at Jamestown

After the first years of extreme hardship, struggle, and survival, the Jamestown Colony evolved from a tenuous outpost of adventurers into an established community of settlers. The early governors of the colony were motivated by the desire to maximize profits, and the site was basically run as a military work-camp. Disagreements developed among the investors in London as to the best policy for running the colony. The Court Party, led by **Thomas Smythe** and Robert Rich (later the 2nd Earl of Warwick) wanted to continue the policy of martial law. The Country, or Patriot Party, led by **Sir Edwin Sandys,** favored ending the servitude system and developing a more liberal form of government giving the settlers greater responsibility for running the colony. In April 1619 Sir Edwin Sandys became treasurer of the **Virginia Company**, and was able to give support to a more liberal policy.

1622 was a fateful year in Virginia. On Good Friday the Indians carried out a carefully planned uprising against English settlements along the James River, and 350–400 settlers were killed. Many of the survivors decided to return to England and large areas of Virginia were abandoned. By 1623 conditions were improving; more women had arrived and families were started. The settlers demanded a less military type of rule. They complained about what they saw as unfair and illegal acts by the governor. Because of an investigation and because the London Company was not making a profit for investors or the king, the Privy Council took over the running of the Virginia Company. In June 1624 the charter was revoked and the company declared bankrupt. Virginia became the first colony in America to be ruled directly by the Crown. 🍃

Sir Thomas Smythe

In the sixteenth century, the Port of London was pulsing with ships and goods from around the world. There was opportunity for well-connected and hardworking men to become fabulously wealthy and extremely powerful. Thomas Symthe was at the center of all this action. His father had been high sheriff of Essex. Sixteen when his father died and left him a farm with an income of £20 a year, Thomas sold the farm and went to London, where he became involved in many enterprises. In the 1550s he was named one of the royal commissioners charged with overseeing the business coming through the London quays. Later he was given the position of collector of customs duty on all foreign goods and merchandise brought into the ports of London, Sandwich, and Chichester for eleven years – a position that earned him the nickname "Customer."

"Customer" Smythe's son Thomas became an important player in the exploration and settlement of America. Like his father, he was overseer of virtually all the trade that passed through the Port of London, becoming immensely wealthy. In 1588 he loaned the huge sum of £31,000 to Queen Elizabeth. He raised additional funds for her to finance the fleet that defeated the Spanish Armada.

Thomas Smythe's position connected him with many people. In 1601 he was implicated in the plot by **Robert Devereux** to overthrow the ageing queen. Smythe was arrested, accused of complicity, and held in the **Tower of London**. Devereux was beheaded at Tower Hill on 25 February 1601. A number of the remaining prisoners were released after paying enormous fines – including Thomas Smythe. By sparing many of these conspirators' lives, Elizabeth may have contributed to a future plot. In 1605 seven Catholic conspirators who participated in the Essex Rebellion joined together in a plot to blow up Parliament and kill King James I – the Gunpowder Plot.

Queen Elizabeth died in March 1603 at **Richmond Palace**. The new king, James I, came to England from Scotland – the start of a fresh chapter began for many men. In May 1603 **Edwin Sandys** was knighted by King James at the **Charterhouse** in London. Thomas Smythe was knighted at the Tower of London. He regained his position of importance and became governor of several trading companies. He was a major investor in the colonization of Virginia. 🍃

Edward-Maria Wingfield

An experienced soldier, Wingfield fought for the Dutch against the Spanish "oppressors." Back in England, surrounded by talk of exploration, he soon became financially involved. Wingfield raised money for the "Fund for Support of our Colony in Virginia" by mortgaging his house, **Stonely Priory** in **Cambridgeshire**. He was the only person in the Jamestown expedition to be both an "adventurer" (risking his money) and "venturer" (risking his person). It was expected that he would be one of the leaders of the group.

At Jamestown, Edward-Maria Wingfield was elected president by the colony's council, and therefore could claim to be the first American president. Charges that Wingfield was overly harsh, hid food for himself, and was an atheist because he didn't carry a Bible at all times led the council to replace him with Gabriel Archer. Wingfield returned to England, cleared his name with the council, and recruited more colonists to go to Virginia. He was a guarantor of the Second Charter of Virginia in 1609 and a generous backer of the expansion of the Jamestown venture. 🍃

LONDON "Customer" Smythe's sister Elizabeth was related to George Washington. Elizabeth's son married Mary Washington, daughter of Lawrence Washington (born 1557), the brother of George Washington's fourth great-grandfather Robert Washington.

On 7 February 1601 a performance of William Shakespeare's play Richard II at the *Globe Theatre* in *Southwark* was attended by at least eleven conspirators who would take part in Devereux's Rebellion the next day.

In 1558 a royal commission set up fifteen principal quays or docks which regulated the type of merchandise to be loaded and stored. *Billingsgate Market* was for fish, corn, and salt. Johnson's Wharf and *Butler's Wharf* were for tar, iron, timber, hemp, cloth, skins, and eels.

The *Museum in Docklands* focuses on the history of maritime trading in London including the formation of trading companies such as the Muscovy Company. The exhibits also tell of the "Legal Quays" established by Queen Elizabeth I.

SUFFOLK *Orford Castle* was originally built in 1165–73. Sir Henry Wingfield, Knight of Rhodes, was governor of the castle in the 1480s. He was the fourth great-grandfather of Edward-Maria Wingfield.

MORE LOCATIONS WITH WINGFIELD CONNECTIONS

LONDON Edward-Maria Wingfield attended **Furnival's Inn** before being accepted at Lincoln's Inn in April 1576.

BERKSHIRE Wingfield family crests are among the many historic coats of arms in **St. George's Chapel** and **St. George's Hall** at **Windsor Castle**.

SUFFOLK The village of **Wingfield**
The original manor at **Wingfield Castle** was castellated in 1384. It is now a private residence – the only inhabited castle in Suffolk – and retains its original appearance.

Wingfield College was built in 1362 and was a college for secular priests until 1534.
Today it is home to Wingfield Arts & Music.

The **Church of St. Andrew**, built as the collegiate church of Sir John de Wingfield's Foundation, has Sir John's impressive monument, along with those of his great-great-grandson,
John de la Pole, 2nd Duke of Suffolk and his wife Elizabeth Plantagenet, sister of King Edward IV and King Richard III.

CAMBRIDGESHIRE Kimbolton Castle was owned in the 1500s by Charles Wingfield, Edward-Maria's uncle. Kimbolton is chiefly known as the place where Queen Catherine of Aragon spent her last years. In the 1600s the castle was rented to John Popham.

SUFFOLK The **Church of St. Mary** in **Letheringham** (near **Otley**) reflects the Wingfield family's 300-year presence and contains several beautifully preserved Wingfield brasses including one of Sir John Wingfield of Suffolk from 1389.

LEICESTERSHIRE Built 1130–50, the ancient **Church of St. Peter** in **Tickencote** (near **Stamford**) has many Wingfield family connections including a Wingfield window and a Wingfield memorial. The original 1433 great house came into the family in 1592. In 1947 the main manor was dismantled. The present manor building was built in the stable block. The setting is spectacular.

LINCOLNSHIRE *Grimsthorpe Castle* has been the home of the de Eresby family since 1516. Peregrine Bertie, Lord Willoughby, was was an investor in the Virginia Company and may have encouraged John Smith to go on the expedition.

Captain John Smith

The most memorable leader to emerge from the group of colonists at Jamestown, John Smith was at first not considered good material for leadership. Perhaps he antagonized the gentlemen leaders of the colony with his humble family background, combined with a natural confidence built on years of military experience. But he was charismatic and assertive, and his leadership helped hold together the colony when it was faced with disorganization and then terrible hardship.

The eldest son of a yeoman farmer, John Smith inherited land from his father, but he wanted a more adventurous life. In 1596 or 1597 he joined a group of English military volunteers serving in the Netherlands under Lord Willoughby, his father's landlord. For the next four years he fought for Dutch independence from the Spanish king Phillip II. After returning briefly to England, he joined the Austrian forces in their battles against the Turks. Smith claimed to have been captured by the Turks in Transylvania and sent to Constantinople as a present for the Pasha's wife, who fell in love with him. John Smith managed to escape and returned to England in 1604.

Probably through his military connections Smith became part of the Jamestown expedition that sailed from London in December 1606. Some claimed that during the voyage Smith tried to lead a mutiny, and for much of the trip he was kept in chains. In December 1607, while on a scouting trip to see what surrounded the new settlement, he was captured and brought before the Algonquin chief Powhatan. In his diary Smith wrote that the chief's young daughter (**Pocahontas**) saved his life by throwing herself between him and his would-be executioners. Smith was released and the Indians communicated that he and Powhatan were to be friends and Smith would be free to return to the English settlement.

On 10 September 1608 John Smith became the leader of the Jamestown settlement. After being injured in an accident in 1609 he was forced to return to England. He had a hard time finding another expedition to become involved with, but

LONDON Captain John Smith's statue stands to the side of *St Mary-le-Bow, Cheapside*, the church of the Cordwainers Guild to which he belonged.

MORE ABOUT CAPTAIN JOHN SMITH

LONDON John Smith died in June 1631 and was buried in the parish of **St. Sepulchre-without-Newgate**. A brass plaque above the probable site of his burial records his exploits as a soldier in Hungary. A stained-glass window at **St. Sepulchre**'s, given by his American biographer, Bradford Smith, shows John Smith between two of his most important supporters – Robert Bertie and Sir Samuel Saltonstall.

LINCOLNSHIRE St. Helena's Church in Willoughby

The American flag and the flag of the State of Virginia frame a plaque to the memory of John Smith. This was erected by the Jamestown/Yorktown Foundation of Virginia in 1960. A framed copy of the baptism register notes the birth of John Smith. The John Smith Window commemorates many significant events, beginning with Smith's baptism on 9 January 1579/80 in this very font. Also depicted are the Prince of Transylvania, who made Smith captain of 250 soldiers and awarded him the coat of arms, **Princess Pocahontas** of Virginia who saved Smith's life in 1607, and Frances Howard, Duchess of Richmond and Lennox, whose first husband was a patron of John Smith. The Virginia windows were a gift to the church from Philip L. Barbour of Kentucky, a biographer of John Smith. One panel shows Rev. Robert Hunt celebrating the first recorded Holy Communion service on the American continent.

Richard Hakluyt is shown presenting a copy of his *Discourse of Western Planting* to Queen Elizabeth I in October 1584.

KENT Pocahontas is thought to have been buried beneath the chancel of *St. George's Church* in *Gravesend*. The statue of her in front of the church is a copy of one that stands in Jamestown, Virginia. Her name is given as Rebecca Wrolfe in the parish register which states that "The Princess was 1616 Mar 2 buried in ye Chauncell." The Colonial Dames of America presented two memorial windows in 1914. One window represents the figure of Ruth, and the other Rebecca, her baptismal name.

NORFOLK Pocahontas is shown on the town sign of *Heacham*, John Rolfe's home town. The Rolfe family coat of arms is displayed in the *Church of St. Mary the Virgin, Heacham*, and there is a memorial to Pocahontas . Heacham Hall burned down in 1899.

he sailed to America again in 1614 on a mapping expedition, during which he named the region north of Virginia "New England." This was his last voyage to the New World. 🍃

Pocahontas

A very real person who played an important role in the history of Jamestown, Pocahontas was born around 1595, a daughter of Powhatan, the powerful Algonquin chief. Her formal name was Matoaka, but she was known as "Pocahontas" which meant "playful little girl." In early 1607 when three English ships sailed up the Powatan River, they were allowed to land, but Powhatan discouraged the would-be settlers from staying. Nevertheless, they soon started to build a settlement. In December, **John Smith** was exploring and seeking trade when Powhatan's men captured him and killed his two companions. Legend has it that Captain Smith was spared the same fate through the intervention of Powhatan's daughter Pocahontas. Pocahontas's life was linked with the English from that day until her death.

In a strange incident in March 1613, Pocahontas was kidnapped by **Samuel Argall**, who planned to exchange her for English prisoners being held by her father's tribe, and guns which the Indians had taken from the colony. However, her father did not rush to rescue Pocahontas. After being held for more than a year, she was offered the chance to return to her tribe, but she chose to stay with the English settlers. Soon John Rolfe asked the acting governor, Thomas Dale, for permission to marry Pocahontas. Rolfe had been one of the survivors of the *Sea Venture* wreck on Bermuda. His wife gave birth to a baby on the island, but the baby died on the island and the mother died soon after reaching Jamestown.

Pocahontas's father consented to her marriage, but did not attend the ceremony. Before her wedding Pocahontas was given a Christian baptism and the Christian name Rebecca. She and John Rolfe were married in April 1614. The Reverend Richard Bucke from **Wymondham** officiated at the wedding.

Pocahontas gave birth to a son, Thomas, in 1615. In early 1616, she sailed for England with her husband and son. A dozen Indians accompanied her. Feted by English society, Pocahontas was seen at the **Globe Theatre** and Blackfriars, escorted by people such as Lady De la Warr. Attending a royal masque at the **Banqueting House** of **Whitehall Palace** on 5 January 1617, Pocahontas was presented to Queen Anne. In March 1617, Rolfe and Pocahontas prepared to return to Virginia. Pocahontas's health was deteriorating. She was brought ashore at Gravesend, where she died on 21 March 1617. Pocahontas was buried at **St. George's Church** in **Gravesend**. She was about twenty-two years old.

MORE PLACES LINKED WITH POCAHONTAS

LONDON One of the young Indians who came to England with Pocahontas stayed on after she decided to sail back to Virginia in 1617. He was baptized at the church of **St. Martin-in-the-Fields, Trafalgar Square**, on 10 September 1619 as Georgius Thorp in honor of George Thorpe, the founder of a college at Henricus, Virginia. Unfortunately, Georgius died in October 1619 and was buried at St. Martin's.

LONDON George Percy was the son of the Earl of Northumberland, whose London home was **Syon Park** in **Brentford**. Pocahontas knew George in Jamestown. When she traveled to England, he helped find a house in Brentford for her to live in. The house, called Boston Manor, stood where the Brentford Post Office sorting office is now. The present Boston Manor was built soon after Pocahontas died.

OXFORD On display at the **Ashmolean Museum** is a leather garment called "Powhatan's Cloak," brought back from Virginia by **John Tradescant the Younger**. It is claimed that it belonged to Pocahontas's father.

SOMERSET The American Museum in Britain in **Claverton** near **Bath** includes a large collection of Native American artifacts. One exhibit focuses on the life of Pocahontas.

NORFOLK Wymondham Abbey has a memorial to the Reverend Richard Bucke who performed the wedding ceremony of Princess Pocahontas and John Rolfe.

John Rolfe left his son Thomas in England with relatives and returned to Virginia. Father and son never saw each other again. John later remarried in Virginia. It is believed he died in the Indian Massacre of 1622. 🍂

George Percy

George Percy, a younger son of the 8th Earl of Northumberland, sailed to Jamestown with **John Smith** in 1607. He wrote one of the few surviving accounts of the first days of the colony. When Smith was injured and returned to England in 1609, Percy served as the next president of the colony's council. He stayed at Jamestown for five years and then returned to England. When **Pocahontas** traveled to England with her husband John Rolfe, Percy found a house in Brentford for them to live in. George Percy continued to be involved with the **Virginia Company** investments. 🍂

Thomas West, Lord De La Warr

Like many of the other early leaders of the Jamestown Colony, Thomas West served in Holland fighting against the Spanish. West was part of an important family – his mother Anne Knollys, was a cousin of Queen Elizabeth I and served her as Chief Lady of the Bedchamber.

Thomas West became the 3rd Baron De la Warr when his

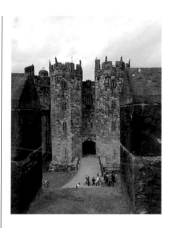

NORTHUMBERLAND *Alnwick Castle* is the Percy family seat.

LONDON *Syon Park, Brentford*, is the Duke of Northumberland's house on the River Thames.

YORKSHIRE The Northumberland Chapel in *Beverley Minster* has beautiful Percy family tombs.

KENT The famous gardens at *Sissinghurst Castle* were created by Vita Sackville-West. In the library the sign on a nineteenth-century portrait of Lady De la Warr mentions the connection with the early governor of Virginia, and the State of Delaware. An earlier Lady De la Warr escorted **Pocahontas** in London.

LONDON Thomas West was married at *St. Dunstan-in-the-West* in 1596 to Cecily, daughter of Sir Thomas Shirley of Sussex.

KENT *Knole* in *Sevenoaks* has been the home of the Sackville family since 1603. The West and Sackville families united in 1864 when George John West married Elizabeth Sackville, sister of the 4th earl.

SURREY *Richmond Palace* was home to kings and queens of England from 1125 to 1688. **Thomas Dale** was knighted by King James I at the palace on 6 June 1606. The old palace gatehouse and parts of the wardrobe are all that remain of the Tudor palace.

GLOUCESTERSHIRE *St. Leonard's Church* in *Tortworth* has two monuments to two Thomas Throckmortons. One was the father of Elizabeth Throckmorton who married Thomas Dale.

father died in 1602. He married Cecily Shirley, daughter of Sir Thomas Shirley of Wiston, West Sussex. West was one of the largest investors in the London Company. When the 1609 charter was put into effect, allowing the London Company to appoint an absolute governor for the colony, Thomas West was named the first governor of Virginia (rather than of the Jamestown Colony).

West sailed to Virginia in 1610 with three ships carrying 150 new colonists. After three-and-a-half months, they arrived just as the Jamestown colonists were sailing downriver to abandon the settlement. Lord de la Warr managed to persuade the colonists to return to the colony, and the settlement survived. In 1613 he was granted 8,000 acres of land in Virginia, which he called the "West and Shirley Hundred" after himself and his wife. The name "Shirley" lives on in the Shirley Plantation in Charles City, Virginia's oldest plantation. Thomas West returned to England in 1611, but in 1618 he sailed back to Virginia after hearing of the oppressive rule that **Samuel Argall** had imposed on the colony. West died on 17 June 1618, before the ship reached Virginia.

Thomas West also had close ties to the Massachusetts Bay Colony. His elder sister Elizabeth (whose godmother was Queen Elizabeth) married Henry Pelham the Elder of **Michelham Priory**, and his younger sister Penelope married Henry's son by his first wife. Their son became the first treasurer of **Harvard College**. 🍃

Thomas Dale

A professional soldier who enlisted in the army in 1588, Thomas Dale served in Holland with the same group as **Thomas West**. In early 1611 Dale was sent to Virginia with supplies and settlers. Dale served as "high marshall" of Virginia under Sir Thomas Gates.

The colony in Virginia was starting to evolve from a military camp into a more self-supporting community. Some of the early servants came to Jamestown under terms of indenture and these were expiring – the servants became free laborers or tenant farmers. Thomas Dale introduced changes in the land laws so that a man who cultivated the soil was given a chance to become the owner. More colonists were arriving, and, with grants of lands called "hundreds," new settlements grew up along the James River – the West and Shirley Hundred, the Flowerdew Hundred, the Berkeley Hundred.

In May 1616 Thomas Dale sailed for England on board the *Treasurer* along with John Rolfe, **Pocahontas**, and ten other Powhatan Indians. He died from an illness in the East Indies on 9 August 1619. 🍃

George Yeardley

George Yeardley also gained military experience fighting against the Spanish in Holland. Yeardley was the captain of the *Sea Venture*, the ship wrecked on Bermuda. He was appointed deputy governor in 1616, but the chairman of the London Company, **Thomas Smythe**, did not approve. Smythe and his friends in the Court Party managed to elect their man **Samuel Argall** to be governor, and he was sent to Virginia in 1617. Unfortunately, Argall proved to be "arrogant, self-willed, and greedy of gain," and was removed from office after the death of **Lord De La Warr**. The "mild and popular" Yeardley was re-elected governor and remained in office until his death in November 1627. 🍃

Temperance Flowerdew

The daughter of Anthony Flowerdew of **Hethersett, Norfolk**, Temperance was born around 1590. She sailed to Jamestown aboard the *Falcon*, one of the fleet of ships sent in 1609 to replenish the fledgling settlement. Temperance spent her first winter in Virginia suffering through the "Starving Time." She returned to England, perhaps on the ship captained by George Yeardley. In 1613 Temperance Flowerdew and **George Yeardley** were married in London. They returned to Virginia and Yeardley received a grant of a thousand acres of land in Virginia. He named it the Flowerdew Plantation. Their son Argall (named for the colonial governor) married into the Custis family, and was an ancestor of **George Washington**. After Yeardley's death, Temperance married **Governor Thomas West**, but she died a year later. 🍃

Samuel Argall

Born in **East Sutton, Kent**, in November 1580, Samuel Argall's grandfather, Thomas Argall, had been secretary to Thomas Cromwell, King Henry VIII's chief minister who played an important role in legalities surrounding the annulments of Henry's marriages to Anne of Cleaves and Katherine Howard.

A mariner and adventurer who served as vice admiral of the fleet during the British victory over the Spanish at Cadiz in 1596, Samuel Argall became involved with the effort to explore and settle lands in America. He was employed by the **Virginia Company** and commanded one of the ships that sailed to Jamestown in the 1609 supply fleet. In 1610 he was named admiral of Virginia. It was Samuel Argall who organized the kidnapping of **Pocahontas** in March 1613.

In 1616 Samuel Argall was named deputy governor of the Jamestown Colony, with the backing of **Thomas Smythe** who believed a harsh system of martial law was best for the

LONDON George Yeardley was born in London and baptized at *St. Saviour's Church* (later *Southwark Cathedral*) on 28 July 1588.

NORFOLK Temperance Flowerdew's father Anthony was from *Hethersett*.

KENT Samuel Argall's mother is buried at *All Saints' Church, Maidstone*, beside her second husband Lawrence Washington, a collateral forebear of George Washington. His memorial features a crest with the Stars and Stripes of the Washington family.

There is a memorial to Samuel Argall's father Richard in the *Church of St. Peter and St. Paul* in *East Sutton*. Richard's widow Mary Scott married Lawrence Washington.

Samuel Argall was knighted by King James I at *Rochester Castle* in 1622.

colony. He ruled the colony in 1616–19 and was accused of being unduly harsh on the colonists. Argall was generally hated in Jamestown. In 1619 a general reorganization of the Virginia Company led to a great change in the way the colony was governed. **Sir Edwin Sandys** was elected treasurer of the company. His more enlightened view of the future of the colony led to the appointment of **George Yeardley** as governor and captain general. Yeardley informed the colonists that they would enjoy the same rule of common law as in England. He established the first legislature in the colony. The Virginia House of Burgesses met for the first time on 30 July 1619 in the choir of the Jamestown church.

Samuel Argall was recalled to London and again faced charges about the harshness of his actions. He was eventually exonerated and in 1620 was given command of a ship and fought in an expedition against Algiers. In 1625 Argall commanded a fleet of twenty-six ships in an unsuccessful attack against Cadiz. He died the following year. Argall is remembered as a harsh, autocratic ruler of the Jamestown Colony. 🍃

WORCESTERSHIRE *Ombersley Court* became the **Sandys** family seat around 1559. The present house was built for the Sandys family in 1722–6 and the family still live here.

When *St. Andrew's Church, Ombersley*, was rebuilt in 1825–9, only the thirteenth-century chancel was retained. This is now the Sandys mausoleum and has several family tombs.

The name of the *Crown and Sandys Arms Hotel* in *Ombersley* recalls the loyalty of Samuel Sandys, sheriff of Worcestershire, who was a son of Archbishop Edwin Sandys. Samuel raised a regiment for the king during the Civil War. Unfortunately Samuel Sandys was captured by Parliamentary forces during the Battle of Worcester in 1651.

St. John's Church in *Wickhamford* has two extraordinary monuments. One commemorates Samuel Sandys and his wife Mercy Culpeper. The second is to his son Edwin Sandys, who died three weeks after the father. Samuel Sandys was the elder brother of Sir Edwin Sandys, treasurer of the London Company.

Sir Edwin Sandys

Sir Edwin Sandys was instrumental in the establishment of both the Jamestown and Plymouth colonies. Sir Edwin's father, also Edwin, was vice-chancellor of Cambridge University in 1553 when King Edward VI died. The possibility that Mary Tudor would become queen – and thus a Catholic would sit on the throne – stirred much opposition among the Protestant leaders in England. Edwin Sandys supported the faction that tried to place Lady Jane Grey on the throne. When Mary Tudor became queen, she showed her displeasure – Lady Jane Grey and her young husband were executed. Edwin Sandys was arrested and thrown into the **Tower of London**. He was lucky, though, and was able to obtain a release. He left England with a group of other exiles and traveled in Switzerland and Germany.

'Bloody' Mary died in 1558 and Henry VIII's Protestant daughter Elizabeth became queen. Edwin Sandys returned to England and was made Bishop of Worcester in December 1559. In 1570 he was appointed Bishop of London and in 1576 he became Archbishop of York. His son, also named Edwin, was born in 1561 in Worcester. The younger Edwin Sandys went to Scotland, and accompanied James VI of Scotland as he traveled down to London to become enthroned as King James I of England.

On 10 April 1606 King James granted a charter to the **Virginia Company**, permitting English investors to create colonies in America. Edwin Sandys was appointed to His

Majesty's Council for Virginia in March 1607. In April 1619 he became treasurer of the company, much to the king's disapproval. Sir Edwin was suspected of "harbouring designs to establish a republican or puritan state in America," ideas a king would not be likely to encourage. Sandys was soon implementing his ideas. He set up a committee to organize the regulations for the colony, to select a form of government, to appoint magistrates and officers, and to define their duties.

Sandys had a long-term vision of the future for the colonists sent to America. He saw beyond the immediate goal of profit on investment to a permanent colony that would provide relief from British overpopulation and expand the market for English goods. He also saw the necessity of encouraging women to travel to Jamestown. Having families would bind the colonists to the New World. Between 1619 and 1621, he sent forty-two ships and 3,750 men and women to Virginia. He urged the colonists to diversify their crops and become more self-reliant. Unfortunately, they did not follow his advice. For many years the colony was run as a one-crop business venture – tobacco.

Sandys's administration of the colony had a long-lasting impact. The so-called Great Charter of 1619 marked the beginning of self-rule in America. The meeting of the Assembly of Burgesses in Jamestown on 30 July 1619 is celebrated as the first representative government to meet in America. Sandys was criticized for his part and in 1621 he was imprisoned, suspected of plotting to create a Puritan state with republican government in America. As treasurer of the Virginia Company, Sandys also supported the efforts of the Leyden group of Pilgrims to gain a charter to immigrate to the New World. He was a long-time friend of the Pilgrim leader **William Brewster**. In fact, his father, the elder Edwin Sandys, Archbishop of York, had fired William Brewster from his job as postmaster and removed him from **Scrooby Manor**.

Sir Edwin Sandys died in 1629. He never traveled to America, but his vision and work helped to transform the Jamestown Colony. He also supported the Pilgrims in starting the Plymouth Colony. 🌿

Henry Wriothesley

Henry Wriothesley's grandfather, Thomas Wriothesley, was a lawyer who worked for Thomas Cromwell. He was involved in the suppression and torture of those who opposed the establishment of the new Protestant Church after Henry VIII broke with the Catholic Church. Interestingly, Thomas's son Henry was raised as a Catholic. When members of leading Catholic families conspired with foreign forces, principally

OXFORD Edwin Sandys received a BA in 1579 and an MA in 1583 from *Corpus Christi College*.

LONDON The younger Edwin Sandys studied law at the *Middle Temple*. He was elected to Parliament in 1586.

On 11 May 1603 Sandys was knighted by King James I at *Charterhouse*.

KENT *St. Augustine's Church* in *Northbourne* has an ornate funerary monument to Sir Edwin Sandys and his wife. On the 350th anniversary of the foundation of Virginia a memorial tablet was placed near the tomb by the American and British Commonwealth Association of the United States in "grateful memory of Sir Edwin Sandys."

WEST SUSSEX Henry Wriothesley was born at *Cowdray Castle* in *Easebourne* near *Midhurst* on 6 October 1573. In 1793 the castle was destroyed by fire and is now a romantic ruin.

HAMPSHIRE The Dissolution of the Monasteries created lots of work for lawyers and meant that properties all over the country were suddenly up for sale. In 1538 Thomas Wriothesley purchased *Beaulieu Palace* at *Beaulieu* near *Brockenhurst*.

CAMBRIDGE At *St. John's College* and then later at the *Middle Temple, London*, Henry was a friend of **Bartholomew Gosnold**. Wealthy, handsome, and well educated, Henry became a patron of the arts, and a friend and supporter of dramatists, especially William Shakespeare. Many people speculate that Henry Wriothesley was the person to whom Shakespeare dedicated his sonnets.

LONDON Robert Devereux was the last person to be executed on Tower Green. He was held in a tower on the northwest corner of the *Tower of London* for two weeks before his execution on 25 February 1601. This was named the Devereux Tower in his memory.

the Spanish, to bring a Catholic monarch to England, the Catholic Henry Wriothesley, 2nd Earl of Southampton, was on the edge of some of these plots. As a result, he was held in the **Tower of London** for four years. His son Henry was only eight years old when his father died in 1581 and he became the 3rd Earl of Southampton. The young Henry was placed in the care of William Cecil, Lord Burghley, and was brought up as a Protestant.

Lord Burghley was an inveterate manipulator. He began negotiations with Henry's mother to discuss marriage with Burghley's granddaughter. Henry was not persuaded. He paid a £5,000 fine rather than marry Lady Elizabeth de Vere. When he did marry in 1598, it was in secret to Elizabeth Vernon, a lady-in-waiting to Queen Elizabeth. As when **Walter Raleigh** married Elizabeth Throckmorton without permission in 1592, the queen was furious.

Henry's next problem almost led to his execution. In 1599 he served with **Robert Devereux**, 2nd Earl of Essex in putting down the Irish Rebellion. When Devereux led an attempted overthrow of the queen on 8 February 1601, Henry Wriothesley was arrested with others. He was sentenced to death, but this was changed to life imprisonment. When James I took the throne, he showed mercy to many prisoners. Wriothesley was released and restored to favor at court. He became involved with some of the major groups of investors in the exploration of the New World. As a member of the **Virginia Company**, he backed some important expeditions, including **George Weymouth**'s voyages in 1605 and 1614. In June 1620 Wriothesley replaced **Edwin Sandys** as treasurer of the Virginia Company.

Unfortunately, court politics became more dangerous. George Villiers was a favorite of the king and a rising star. In February 1623 Villiers was created Duke of Buckingham. Henry Wriothesley fell out with Villiers and left court. In 1624 he volunteered, with his son James, to lead a troop of English volunteers to fight for the Netherlands against Spain. Shortly after arriving in the Netherlands, both he and his son died of fever. 🍃

THE WRIOTHESLEYS AND THE MONTAGUS

LONDON The 4th Earl of Southampton died in 1667 with no son to inherit his title. His estates were divided between his three daughters, with **Beaulieu Palace** in **Hampshire** going to the youngest, Elizabeth, who married the Earl of Northumberland. After Northumberland died, Elizabeth married Ralph Montagu, who became the 1st Duke of Montagu. In 1675–80 Ralph built a home in London, Montagu House in Bloomsbury. In 1753 Montagu House was purchased by the government to hold the national collection of antiquities. Over the years the property was enlarged, demolished, and rebuilt – as the **British Museum, Great Russell Street**.

NORTHAMPTONSHIRE Boughton House near **Kettering** was home to Ralph Montagu who married Elizabeth Wriothesley, daughter of the 4th Earl of Southampton and widow of the Earl of Northumberland.

BEDFORDSHIRE Woburn Abbey is the seat of the dukes of Bedford. Rachel Wriothesley married William Russell, son of the 1st Duke of Bedford.

BUCKINGHAMSHIRE Chenies Manor House came into the Russell family in 1526. It is one of the loveliest medieval manor houses in England. Many family members are buried in the Bedford Chapel of **St. Michael's Church, Chenies**.

Francis Wyatt

Francis Wyatt was born at **Boxley Manor, Kent**, in 1575. His great-grandfather served on diplomatic missions to Spain for King Henry VIII and his grandfather Thomas Wyatt the Younger had been executed at the **Tower of London** in 1554 after attempting a rebellion when Queen Mary planned to marry King Philip of Spain. Wyatt's property and estates were confiscated, and the family reduced to poverty. When King Henry VIII's Protestant daughter Elizabeth became queen, she showed some tolerance towards those who had opposed Mary. Part of the Wyatt property was returned to the family in 1571, but not however ownership of **Allington Castle**.

After marrying Lady Margaret Sandys, niece of **Sir Edwin Sandys**, Francis became closely involved with the Virginia Colony. In January 1621 he was elected governor and captain general of Virginia. He arrived in Virginia in October 1621 bringing instructions that reflected Edwin Sandys's more progressive view of government for the colony. In 1626 he was replaced by George Yeardley. In 1639 Francis Wyatt returned to Virginia as the royal governor. 🍃

VIRGINIA AFTER JAMESTOWN

After a decade of struggling against a harsh environment and hostile natives, the English settlement at Jamestown had become a stable colony. Its investors felt confident of some financial success. The vast land and resources began to attract more interest from English investors. A variety of groups applied for permission to start colonies along both sides of the James River. Patents were issued for grants of land that were called "hundreds." Among these large tracts of land were the Flowerdew Hundred, Smith's Hundred, West Hundred, Shirley Hundred, and Berkeley Hundred. 🍃

KENT In 1539 Thomas Cromwell gave *Aylesford Priory* to **Thomas Wyatt** who owned nearby Allington Castle. It is now a Carmelite retreat center.

The Wyatts owned *Allington Castle* until it was confiscated following "Wyatt's Rebellion" in 1554. *Boxley*, near *Maidstone*, was the Wyatt family seat. When Francis Wyatt's father died in 1641, he was called back to England, where he inherited Boxley Hall.

In 1621 Francis's younger brother Haute traveled to Jamestown. He served as rector in the colony for four years, returning to England to become the rector of the *Church of St. Mary and All Saints, Boxley*. The church has a Wyatt monument and a memorial to George Sandys (1577–1643), brother of Sir Edwin Sandys.

OXFORD The collection at the *Ashmolean Museum of Art and Archaeology* was based on the rarities and oddities gathered by John Tradescant the Elder. His son, John the Younger, traveled to the Jamestown Colony several times and brought back plants from the New World.

GLOUCESTERSHIRE *Berkeley Castle* is the hereditary seat of the **Berkeley** family. The castle was completed by Maurice de Berkeley in 1153.

OXFORD William Berkeley attended *Merton College* and then studied law at the *Middle Temple, London.*

LONDON *Berkeley Square, Bruton Place,* and *Stratton Street* all lie in the area of the original Berkeley estate.

John Berkeley built Berkeley House on the London property given to him by King Charles II. His descendants sold it in 1696 to the 1st Duke of Devonshire, who built the grand *Devonshire House* on *Piccadilly,* across from what is now the Ritz Hotel.

LONDON William Berkeley was buried in 1677 at the *Church of St. Mary the Virgin* in *Twickenham.* Buried in the same church in 1678 was John, Lord Berkeley, who received the royal grant for New Jersey from King Charles II in 1664 along with **George Carteret.**

The Berkeley Family

In 1618, just eleven years after the Jamestown settlers arrived, a group of Gloucestershire merchants and gentlemen formed the Berkeley Company. The group negotiated a grant of 8,000 acres on the James River for a private colony to be called the Berkeley Hundred. In September 1619, thirty-eight settlers sailed from **Bristol** aboard the *Margaret.* When they arrived in Virginia on 4 December 1619, they went ashore and offered thanks for their safe arrival. They decreed that the day would be honored annually. Today a plaque at Berkeley Plantation commemorates this as the first American Thanksgiving celebration.

The Berkeley family was involved with the development of Virginia almost from the beginning of the English presence there. Sir Maurice Berkeley and his wife both held stock in the **Virginia Company.** Their eldest son, William Berkeley, purchased the governorship of Virginia from **Sir Francis Wyatt** and was named governor in 1641. Berkeley came from an old, aristocratic family and had conservative ideas about the colony. He hoped to replicate the aristocratic hierarchy of old England. The pattern of a few aristocratic families owning large estates and becoming leaders in both social and political life became strongly entrenched in the Virginia Colony, in contrast to the New England colonies where the Church was the most important factor in the government and social life.

During the English Civil War, William Berkeley's brother John fought loyally for King Charles I, and accompanied Queen Henrietta Maria into exile in France. In 1649, while in exile, Charles II gave a grant of six million acres of land in Virginia to seven men who had been loyal to him – Sir John Berkeley, John Lord Culpeper, his brother Thomas Culpeper, Sir William Morton, Sir Dudley Wyatt, Ralph Lord Hopton, and Henry Lord Jermyn. 🍃

The Culpepers and Fairfaxes

In 1673 King Charles II further confused the situation in Virginia by giving more than five million acres, including some land included in the earlier grant, in a thirty-one-year grant to Thomas Culpeper and the Earl of Arlington.

Governor William Berkeley tried to make Virginia a haven for exiled royalists, but a Puritan group from England forced him to leave office during the Commonwealth period. Because William maintained good relationships with the Virginia Puritans, he managed to keep his private estate. In the 1670s Berkeley's leadership was challenged by a colonial, Nathaniel Bacon, a cousin of Berkeley's wife **Frances Culpeper Berkeley.** The ensuing uprising resulted in an attack on

Jamestown. The colony was burned to the ground. King Charles II recalled Berkeley and in 1675 the king gave Thomas Culpeper, 2nd Baron Culpeper, the right of succession to the governorship of Virginia. William Berkeley left Virginia in May 1677 to return to England, but died before he was able have a hearing and clear his name.

Thomas Culpeper did not travel to Virginia until 1680. When he died in 1689, his estate went to his only legal child, Catherine, who married Thomas, 5th Lord Fairfax. Their son, Thomas Fairfax, inherited the proprietorship of five million acres of the Northern Neck of Virginia through his mother. Thomas sent his cousin William Fairfax to Virginia to manage the estate. Sir William's daughter Anne married Lawrence Washington, elder son of a Virginia family. His younger brother George became important in the history of America.

In 1745 the Privy Council confirmed Thomas Fairfax's claim to the grant. In 1747 he moved to Virginia, becoming the only British peer to live permanently in colonial America. **George Washington** was an energetic young surveyor hired by Thomas Fairfax to map his lands west of the Blue Ridge Mountains. A friendship developed between the loyal English peer and the young, hard-working widow's son. Washington's military experience fighting with the British Army in the French and Indian Wars, and his growing dissatisfaction with British rule of the American colonies, began a path that was to lead Washington to become the first president of the United States. 🍃

Frances Culpeper Berkeley

One woman linked many of these strands of early Virginia history – the Berkeleys, the Culpepers, and the Fairfaxes. Frances Culpeper was born in Kent, the youngest child of Sir Thomas Culpeper, one of the original proprietors of Charles II's 1649 Northern Neck grant. He lost most of his English property during the English Civil War, and in 1650 the family immigrated to Virginia. At eighteen, Frances married Samuel Stephens, governor of the Albemarle settlement in North Carolina. Samuel Stephens died in 1669, and six months later Frances married Sir William Berkeley, the colonial governor of Virginia, who was in his early sixties.

The Bacon Rebellion brought Frances's cousin Nathaniel Bacon into direct conflict with her husband. Bacon had been studying law at **Gray's Inn, London**, for ten years when he had a passionate affair with Miss Elizabeth Duke. Her father opposed the match and said he would disown his daughter. Bacon married her, and then decided there would be more opportunity for him in the colonies. His father helped him buy two plantations in Henrico County.

WEST SUSSEX Culpeper family brass memorials lie beneath a carpet in the chancel at *St. Peter's Church, Ardingly*. These are some of the finest medieval brass memorials to be found anywhere in England.

WEST SUSSEX *Wakehurst Place* near *Ardingly* came into the Culpeper family with the marriage of Richard Culpeper (1435–1516) and Margaret Wakehurst. Richard's brother Nicholas Culpeper (1437–1510) married Margaret's sister Elizabeth. The marriages seem to have taken place after the sisters were abducted and taken to London by the brothers. However, both marriages were long and happy. In 1963 Wakehurst Place was bequeathed to the nation and is now managed by the *Royal Botanic Gardens, Kew*.

KENT John Culpeper of Feckenham lies buried in the chancel of the church at *Hollingbourne*. He invested in the **Virginia Company** under the charter of 1609, and in 1610 made one of the largest individual subscriptions to the "supply" that saved the Jamestown Colony.

KENT Frances Culpeper was baptized at the Culpeper Chapel in *All Saints' Church, Hollingbourne,* on 27 May 1634. A memorial in the church reads: "To the lasting memory of John, Lord Culpeper, Baron of Thoresway, Master of the Rolles and Privy Counsellor to two Kings, Charles the First and Charles the Second."

Nathaniel Bacon was intelligent, self-confident, and charismatic. He seemed to have difficulty in accepting a situation he didn't like – and he didn't like the way the colonial government administered the Virginia Colony. He felt the taxes were oppressive and the government was not representative of the large group of small landowners. He thought the government did not provide enough defense against hostile Indians. When Nathaniel led an uprising against the governor, Frances supported her husband. She even traveled to England to try to raise support for armed resistance to the rebellion. The rebels attacked and destroyed the Berkeley mansion in Virginia, "Greenspring," considered the finest country home in colonial America. Frances was furious. She backed her husband in his harsh treatment of the rebels. After Nathaniel died of a fever in October 1676, the remaining rebels were defeated.

Sir William Berkeley returned to England in 1677 to defend his policies, but died before he was able to clear his name. Thomas Culpeper, who replaced William Berkeley as governor of Virginia, was another of Frances's cousins. When she was about forty-four years old, Frances Culpeper Stephens Berkeley married Colonel Philip Ludwell, a Virginia landowner. She never gave up her title, and continued to be called Lady Frances Berkeley. When she died in the 1690s, Lady Frances was buried at Jamestown. It is said that, after Pocahontas, she was the most important woman in Virginia in the seventeenth century. 🍃

MORE LOCATIONS ASSOCIATED WITH THE BERKELEY, CULPEPER, AND FAIRFAX FAMILIES

KENT The heirs of Sir Richard Smythe sold **Leeds Castle** to Sir Thomas Culpeper of Hollingbourne. Sir Thomas in turn sold it to his brother Sir John, whose son, Thomas Culpeper, 2nd Baron of Thoresway, replaced William Berkeley as governor of Virginia. His daughter Catherine Culpeper inherited Leeds Castle. She married Thomas, 5th Lord Fairfax, and her son, Thomas Fairfax, 6th Lord Fairfax, was born at Leeds Castle in 1692. When Thomas died, he left five million acres in Virginia to his brother Robert who lived at Leeds Castle. This property in Virginia was confiscated at the end of the American Revolutionary War.

The Lady Chapel of **St. Mary's Church** in **Goudhurst** has many monuments associated with the Culpeper family. The earliest brass on the floor commemorates John, son of John Bedgebury, who died in 1424. His widow Agnes married Walter Culpeper and their son John Culpeper is a direct ancestor of Thomas Culpeper, 2nd Baron, of Virginia.

KENT cont. Bedgebury Manor in **Goudhurst** is one of the oldest manors in England, having a deed of gift dated 815. The estate came into the Culpeper family when Walter Culpeper married Agnes Roper in 1425.

Most of the present structure of **St. Peter's Old Church** at **Pembury** was built in 1337 by John Culpeper of Bayhall. On the western buttress of the chancel the arms of the Culpeper family are carved into the stone. An old Culpeper tombstone is set into the floor of the chancel.

YORKSHIRE Fairfax House in **York** was built in the 1740s, and acquired in 1759 by Viscount Fairfax as a gift for his daughter Anne.

LONDON In 1908 Albert Kirby Fairfax, a member of the Virginia branch of the family, claimed the title of Baron Fairfax and was confirmed by the Committee of Privileges of the House of Lords as the 12th Baron Fairfax of Cameron. Thus an American took his rightful seat in the **House of Lords**.

An interesting Culpeper connection is with Henry VIII's fifth wife, Catherine Howard, and one of her lovers, Thomas Culpeper. Catherine's mother was Joyce Culpeper, so Catherine and Thomas were distant cousins. After being convicted of adultery, Thomas Culpeper was beheaded at Tyburn on 10 December 1541 and Catherine was executed at the **Tower of London** on 10 February 1542.

NOTE Today Berkeley Plantation in Virginia is an American historical site. Two US presidents were descendants of the second owner of Berkeley – William Henry Harrison (ninth president) and Benjamin Harrison (twenty-third president). Website: www.berkeleyplantation.com

MASSACHUSETTS
Pilgrims, Puritans, and Separatists

For centuries, religion and politics were closely intertwined in England. After King Henry VIII threw off the control of the pope and established the Church of England, the tensions between the Catholic Church and the Protestant movement grew stronger. Catholic countries like Spain threatened England at home with possible invasion by the Spanish Armada, while Protestant countries like Holland welcomed England's help in fighting for their independence from Spain. An individual's religious beliefs weren't just a personal matter – they were important to a government that wanted to preserve itself. Being different could seem a threat, and the state took steps to protect itself.

In England the Church was basically an arm of the government. The Church of England had an elaborate structure – the hierarchy started with the king as head of the Church, went down through the archbishops of Canterbury and York, to the bishops, and finally to the thousands of vicars throughout the country. The government exercised an important role in naming the high officials of the established

SUFFOLK The Walpole Congregationalists were one of hundreds of sects that flourished in the seventeenth century, including the Grindletonians, Muggletonians, Ranters, Claxtonians, Salmonists, Brownists, Levellers, Diggers, Sea Green Men, and the Family of Love. When the Pilgrims emigrated by the thousands, the *Old Chapel* in *Walpole* was set up in 1649 by Nonconformists who stayed in England. It is one of the oldest Nonconformist meeting houses in the country. The dignified interior gives an atmospheric example of the simple environment preferred by the early Dissenters and Separatists.

CAMBRIDGE *Emmanuel College* was founded in 1584 by Sir Walter Mildmay, Queen Elizabeth's Chancellor of the Exchequer. The goal of this new college was to train preaching ministers for the Church, and it quickly became known as a "nursery for Puritans." Several leaders of the Walpole Congregationalists were students there. Of the first hundred college-educated men to immigrate to America, thirty had studied at Emmanuel College.

LONDON There is an impressive monument to Walter Mildmay at *St. Bartholomew the Great, Smithfield.*

ESSEX *"Guy Harlings,"* the home of the Mildmay family in *Chelmsford,* is located across New Street from the Cathedral Close.

ESSEX In *Chelmsford Cathedral* the tomb of Sir Thomas Mildmay and his lady, Alice, shows their eight sons and seven daughters.

Great Graces in *Little Baddow* was the home of Henry Mildmay, Sir Walter's nephew. Sir Henry was a powerful Puritan supporter who was a Member of Parliament and sheriff of Essex. His wife's brother sailed to Massachusetts with John Winthrop.

church and controlled many aspects of daily religious life. The monarch could sponsor a new prayer book or a new version of the Bible, and decree that it must be used in all churches. Appointment as a vicar brought expectations that the appointee would support the government or lose his job, income, and home.

In the late 1500s and early 1600s Protestant religious ideas infiltrated from Europe into England, and hundreds of religious sects developed. People who did not adhere to the official doctrine and practices of the Church of England were called "Nonconformists." This included "Puritans" who wanted to simplify and purify the rituals of the existing Church and "Separatists" who wanted to leave the Church of England to set up their own church. One group of Separatists who escaped to Holland looking for religious freedom became known as the "Pilgrims."

These groups were a challenge to the government's control of religion; some of them espoused overtly political goals. Many refused to attend church, or to donate money to the Church. They were seen by the government as a direct challenge to its authority. Failure to kneel before a church altar could bring harsh punishment, and selling or distributing non-approved religious tracts could and did result in a death sentence. It was a dangerous time. The Church and government tried to control the growing religious dissatisfaction with rules and regulations, backed with judicial power. Nonconformist vicars and congregations were turned out of their churches. Dissenters who preached in public were arrested. Religious groups that tried to leave England without permission were jailed. But the new ideas continued to spread.

England was a country with an old and revered educational system. Many families sent their sons to be educated at Cambridge or Oxford. But sometimes education led these sons to think independently and develop strong personal beliefs that differed from the state-imposed thought system. In the late 1500s, **Cambridge University** became a hotbed of Nonconformist religious beliefs. Students from towns and villages in Lincolnshire, Nottinghamshire, East Anglia, and Cambridgeshire became some of the leading fathers of Puritan and Separatist congregations. Some of them led the establishment of colonies in the New World.

The early English immigrants to America came from many backgrounds and areas of the country. Some were the sons of wealthy families with fathers who were lawyers, vicars, and even courtiers with royal connections. A few even had titled fathers. After the initial wave of investors and adventurers looking for profit in Virginia, the next group of immigrants were by and large from less privileged backgrounds – farming families, tailors, shopkeepers, and carpenters. They were less motivated by the goal of making a fortune, and more by the hope of starting a new life. Driven by religious zeal, they hoped to establish communities where they could follow their new beliefs. This diversity in backgrounds led to some dissension in the early colonial period, especially in Massachusetts, where conflicts developed over theology, leadership, and personal freedom.

Walpole Old Chapel, Suffolk

The Pilgrims who sailed on the *Mayflower* in 1620 were on the whole not wealthy. They had spent many years trying to escape the control of the religious authorities in England. Many spent the years in Holland doing manual labor and unskilled jobs. When the Pilgrims sailed to the New World, they missed their intended landing point near the Hudson River, landing instead in Massachusetts. They believed that they had landed outside the jurisdiction of any organized government, so they pledged themselves in a formal written agreement to abide by "just and equal laws" decided by leaders of their own choosing. This was the "Mayflower Compact" – the first written document outlining self-government in America. The Pilgrims were Separatists who emphasized individual righteousness before God, and the freedom of religion from political control.

The Puritans who started coming to Massachusetts with the Massachusetts Company in 1630 were an entirely different group. Many of them were well educated and had been in positions of some influence or authority. While some were trying to evade the heavy hand of **Archbishop William Laud**, many saw their goal as that of establishing a "shining city on a hill" – a "purified" perfect version of the existing religious community. There was no need, and no desirability, for the individual to decide what was best – the governors based their decisions on what the Bible said. They were sure they knew what was best for the community, and had the power to enforce their opinions.

These clashing goals and philosophies led to conflicts in the new communities. **Anne Hutchinson, John Wheelwright, Roger Williams**, and others, were banished by the Puritans for their religious individualism. The questions of individual rights, separation of Church and State, government control of ideas, the rights and duties of the individual to participate in democratic government, the desirability of diversity in local communities – these issues were present in the early days of English colonies in America and are still hotly debated in the United States today.

LINCOLNSHIRE *Tolethorpe Hall* in *Little Casterton* near *Stamford* was the birthplace of **Robert Browne**, who could possibly claim to be the "Father of the Pilgrim Fathers." His father was cousin to Lord Burghley, treasurer to Queen Elizabeth I.

"Trouble-Church" Browne wasn't the only Puritan preacher with a name that reflected his religious connections. In 1653 Cromwell summoned a Fleet Street preacher named "Praisegod Barebones" to sit in the House of Commons.

Two of "Trouble-Church" Browne's descendants stood their ground against the British troops at the **Battle of Lexington and Concord** in 1775.

LONDON The *Clink Prison Museum* was where Nonconformists were imprisoned for religious disobedience.

Robert "Trouble-Church" Browne

An early Nonconformist leader, Robert Browne attended **Cambridge University**, and then started a Separatist congregation in Norwich in 1580. It is said that Queen Elizabeth herself gave him the name "Trouble-Church." (Robert's father was a cousin of Lord Burghley, treasurer to Queen Elizabeth I.) Constantly in trouble with the law, he was arrested and jailed for a short time. In 1582 Browne published several tracts explaining his religious beliefs, including the assertion that Christians had the right to share in the selection of their preachers and teachers. This was a direct challenge to the authority of the church hierarchy and the government; they reacted quickly. In 1583 a proclamation was issued against buying, selling or owning the writings of Robert Browne and his friend Robert Harrison, who was also a Separatist dissenter. Two members of the Norwich congregation were arrested, tried, and hanged for selling Browne's work.

In August 1582 Browne moved a small congregation of religious dissenters to Holland, setting a precedent followed several decades later by the group that came to be known in America as the "Pilgrim Fathers." Robert Browne eventually returned to Tolethorpe. In 1591 he submitted to the Church of England and was appointed rector at Adchurch, Northamptonshire. For the next thirty years he managed to avoid significant problems, but in 1626 he preached again without permission, promoting his Nonconformist beliefs. The Church of England excommunicated him in 1630. In 1632 Browne was sentenced to prison after he assaulted the parish constable. He was taken to Northampton jail on a cart cushioned with a feather bed. He died in jail in 1633.

In 1592 London's Separatist Ancient Church of Southwark was formed. The next year fifty-six members of the congregation were arrested and thrown into London's notorious prisons – the **Clink**, Fleet, and Newgate. Some of these Separatists were also hanged. Members of the Ancient Church of Southwark followed Browne's example and moved to Holland looking for religious freedom. Robert Browne's ideas influenced other young men who attended Cambridge, including **William Brewster**, **John Smyth**, and **Richard Clyfton**. 🌿

William Laud

Educated at **St. John's College, Oxford**, William Laud served as a chaplain to King James I. Laud became Bishop of London in 1628 and in 1633 was appointed Archbishop of Canterbury by King Charles I, on whom he had a huge influence, persuading the king that he was right in his stand against Parliament in the growing disputes that led to the

English Civil War. Laud was virulently anti-Puritan and determined to stamp out Nonconformists. From 1629 to 1640 he was one of the most powerful men in England. Puritans were hunted down, persecuted, and executed on his orders. But once the king lost power, Laud faced a reversal of fortune himself. He was arrested in 1641 on articles of impeachment brought by **Sir Henry Vane**. Held in the **Tower of London** for three years, Laud ably defended himself in his trial for treason. Finally, he was condemned by special decree and executed on Tower Hill on 10 January 1645. 🍃

LINCOLNSHIRE *Gainsborough Old Hall* is one of the most complete surviving medieval houses. The Hall has a "Mayflower Pilgrims" exhibition.

A large Separatist congregation developed at *Gainsborough* and included some of the Mayflower Pilgrims, such as William Brewster.

In *Gainsborough* a former Congregationalist chapel has been renamed the *John Robinson Memorial Church*.

John Smyth

John Smyth led a congregation of Separatists who worshipped secretly at **Gainsborough Old Hall** after being outlawed by King James I in 1604. The Hickman family came under pressure from the Bishop of Lincoln to stop allowing the Separatists to worship in the Hall. Finally the Separatists decided they had to leave England to find a place where they could follow their religious beliefs. In 1607 John Smyth and a group of forty to sixty followers sold their properties and moved to Holland, where they joined the First Church at Amsterdam, also known as the Ancient Brethren. In Holland, Smyth embraced a number of strange opinions and his church broke up. 🍃

John Robinson

After beginning his religious career in **Norwich**, John Robinson's Nonconformist beliefs brought him into conflict with the local bishop, and he decided he could not continue as a member of the Church of England. He returned home to **Sturton-le-Steeple** and became the first pastor to the group that became the "Pilgrim Fathers." John Robinson moved with the Pilgrims to Leyden and intended to follow the first group to America, but he died in Holland in 1625. His wife Bridget's sister Catherine was married to John Carver. The Carvers sailed on the *Mayflower* and John Carver became the first governor of the Plymouth Plantation. 🍃

NOTTINGHAMSHIRE John Robinson was born in 1576 at *Crossways* in *Sturton-le-Steeple*. His family home still stands at Cross Street just north of the *Church of St. Peter and St. Paul*.

NORFOLK After his marriage to Bridget White of Sturton-le-Steeple, John Robinson moved to *St. Andrew's Church*, the only church in *Norwich* to have a thatched roof.

Richard Clyfton

At Cambridge Richard Clyfton's religious beliefs had been influenced by the ideas of **Robert Browne**. Clyfton served as rector of **All Saints' Church, Babworth**, from 1586 to 1605. His preaching attracted many followers and he was eventually accused in Chancery Court of being a "nonconformist and non-subscriber." His "offences" may have been not wearing the cap and surplice during ceremonies, not using the sign of the cross in baptism and not bowing at the name of Jesus. He was deprived of his

NOTTINGHAMSHIRE An Elizabethan silver chalice used by Richard Clyfton can still be seen at *All Saints' Church* in *Babworth*.

church in 1605 and led his congregation from Babworth to **Gainsborough** to worship with John Smyth's group. Next they moved to **St. Wilfred's Church** in **Scrooby** and then changed congregations again to join the Separatists who worshipped at **William Brewster**'s manor house. Richard Clyfton sailed to Holland with the Pilgrims in 1608, where he died in Amsterdam in 1616 at the age of sixty-three. 🍃

William Brewster

NOTTINGHAMSHIRE William Brewster was born in *Scrooby* in 1566/7. When he was appointed Master of the Postes, the position came with a residence, the *Scrooby Manor House*, which had formerly been a wing of the medieval palace of the Bishop of York. Today Scrooby Manor House is private property, and can be visited by prior arrangement only.

Leaving **Cambridge University** before he graduated, William Brewster seemed destined for a career in government service but his mentor fell from favour and Brewster returned to his home in Scrooby. He found employment as "Master of the Postes" with the Archbishop of York, **Edwin Sandys**, who provided a manor house for his residence. The job of postmaster was a prestigious one, which involved keeping horses and supplies for the Royal Mail carriers, and providing an inn for the riders. In 1602 Brewster was attending Richard Clyfton's church in Babworth when he met the twelve-year-old **William Bradford**, who was to become his life-long friend. In 1606 Brewster set up a Separatist church at **Scrooby Manor**. This did not sit well with his employer and landlord, Archbishop Sandys, who began to harass Brewster. On 30 September 1607 he lost his job as postmaster. Nonconformists were finding it harder to worship and live as they wished to in England, and by 1607 Brewster's congregation was ready to try to leave England. William Brewster served as elder of the Pilgrim Separatist congregation after their arrival in Leyden. He immigrated to America on the *Mayflower* and became a much-loved religious leader of the Plymouth Colony. William Brewster died in 1644. 🍃

The *Pilgrim Fathers' Inn* in *Scrooby*, built in 1771, is a nice place to have lunch when visiting the area.

William Bradford

SOUTH YORKSHIRE The *Manor House* near the church in *Austerfield* is known as "Bradford's House" and is said to have been **William Bradford**'s childhood home.

In 1602, when he was twelve years old, William Bradford joined **Richard Clyfton**'s church in **Babworth**. Later Bradford went with Clyfton to worship at **Gainsborough Old Hall**, and in 1609 he immigrated to Holland to join other Separatists there. Bradford and his wife sailed to Massachusetts on the *Mayflower*. Tragically on 7 December 1620 she fell overboard and drowned while the ship was anchored in the Provincetown Harbor. William Bradford became the second governor of the Plymouth Plantation and was elected to that office thirty times. Bradford was an effective leader who maintained friendly relations with the Native Americans. He encouraged the colonists to support themselves with fishing, trade, and agriculture. He recorded the Pilgrim Fathers' odyssey in his book, *History of Plimouth Plantation*. 🍃

A commemorative plaque in the courtyard of *St. Helena's Church, Austerfield*, notes William Bradford's baptism in 1589. Inside, a beautiful stained-glass window tells the Pilgrims' story. The north aisle of the church was restored by the Society of Mayflower Descendants.

The story of William Bradford and the Pilgrim Fathers is presented at *Austerfield Field Centre* in projects schoolchildren do about local history.

Edward Winslow

Recruited by **William Brewster** to work with a printer in Leyden, Edward Winslow moved to Holland and helped produce anonymous Puritan tracts that were smuggled to England. King James's government ruled these pamphlets to be treasonable, and the printers went into hiding. In 1620 Edward Winslow sailed on the *Mayflower* with his wife, child, and two servants.

Edward's diplomatic skills were put to work when the new Plymouth Colony began having dealings with the local Indians. In 1621 he negotiated a treaty with the Indian chief, Massasoit, and was helped in dealing with Massasoit by **Squanto**, the Indian who had been taken to live in Plymouth, England, in 1605 by **Captain Weymouth**. This treaty lasted until it was broken by the Indian leader King Philip in 1675.

Edward Winslow's effectiveness in representing the Plymouth Colony came to the attention of Oliver Cromwell, the future Lord Protector of England, who recruited Winslow to work on various committees and commissions for the English government, including raising money and equipment, for the naval wars against the Dutch and Spanish. The English government sent Edward Winslow as a commissioner on an expedition to attack Spanish possessions in the West Indies, under General Venables and Admiral William Penn. On 8 May 1655, near Jamaica, Winslow died of a fever and was buried at sea off Hispaniola in the Caribbean. 🍃

THE PILGRIMS LEAVE ENGLAND

In September 1607 the Scrooby congregation traveled to **Boston, Lincolnshire**. A ship was hired to take them to Holland, where earlier Separatist groups such as the Ancient Brethren of Southwark had gone. They were supposed to be met secretly at the mouth of the River Witham, but the Pilgrims were betrayed by the captain of the ship. The local authorities captured many of the group and held them in the **Guildhall** at **Boston** before their trial. All except seven returned penniless to Scrooby. **William Bradford** was the youngest of those imprisoned in Boston. He was released after a month while **Richard Clyfton**, **John Robinson**, and **William Brewster** were held for the next assizes (trials).

In the spring of 1608, a group of these Separatists, including thirty women and children, walked forty miles from Scrooby to the Humber Estuary where they were met by a Dutch ship. As they were boarding, an armed group approached, coming to capture the illegal emigrants. The boat sailed away with those who were on board, leaving many of the women and children on shore. The local authorities did not know what to do with the homeless, miserable women

WORCESTERSHIRE On the north wall of the nave of *St. Peter's Church* in *Droitwich* there is a memorial to Edward Winslow, christened here on 20 October 1595. The Winslow vestry was dedicated in 1973 to the memory of Edward Winslow, a Pilgrim Father.

Edward Winslow attended King's College (now *The King's School*), *Worcester*, from 1606 to 1611.

LONDON Edward Winslow's parents were married at *St. Bride's Church, Fleet Street*. Edward was married there on 4 November 1594. The reredos at St. Bride's is dedicated to the Pilgrim Fathers.

LINCOLNSHIRE Visitors to the *Guildhall* in *Boston* can see the courtroom where the Pilgrim Fathers were tried in 1607, and the cells where they were imprisoned.

In the eighteenth century *Fydell House* belonged to a family of wine merchants and mayors of *Boston*. By 1938 the house was in a state of disrepair, but donations from Americans were used to save and repair it. The American Room was dedicated for the use of American visitors.

A stone monument on the banks of the *River Witham* near *Boston* marks the spot where the Separatist Pilgrims were arrested attempting to escape to Holland in 1607.

YORKSHIRE The Pilgrims finally escaped from English religious intolerance in 1608 from a small inlet at Killingholme. The 20ft-high *Pilgrims' Monument* in *Immingham* near *Grimsby, Humberside,* commemorates their flight to Holland.

NOTTINGHAMSHIRE *Worksop Library* has a permanent exhibition dedicated to the **Pilgrim Fathers.** Bassetlaw District Council provides an internet history of the Pilgrims' story. www.bassetlaw.gov.uk/pilgrim-fathers

KENT The *Canterbury Environmental Centre* now occupies the *Church of St. Alphege* where Robert Cushman was married in 1606.

James Chilton, a tailor born in *Canterbury* in 1583, was, according to legend, the first of the Pilgrims to step ashore at Plymouth Rock in Massachusetts.

LONDON **Thomas Weston** belonged to the Ironmongers' Company, one of the great livery companies of the City of London. *Ironmongers' Hall* is located at *Shaftesbury Place* near the Museum of London.

and children. By August 1608 they were allowed to leave England, and the families were reunited in Holland.

The group of Pilgrims first moved to Amsterdam, where a small congregation of Brownists still lived. However, disagreements developed, and they moved on. They settled in Leyden, supporting themselves with poorly paid, semi-skilled work in the woolen, leather, and metal trades. In Holland the Pilgrims were living in a strongly Catholic country, surrounded by a culture in which they did not feel their children could grow up as they wanted. Finding life difficult and their religious community under great strain, they made the momentous decision to risk everything and sail to the New World. 🍃

PREPARING TO ESTABLISH A COLONY

Before the Pilgrims could sail for America, they had to find a legal way to establish a community there. John Carver and **Robert Cushman** went to London to seek a patent from the **Virginia Company** for a colony on the James River. The company was interested but King James refused to allow the Pilgrims to practice their religion as they wished. Cushman and Carver approached wealthy Puritans in London, including **Sir Edwin Sandys** (the son of the Archbishop of York), an MP and governor/treasurer of the Virginia Company, who was a family friend of **William Brewster**. It was through the assistance of Sir Edwin Sandys that the Pilgrims were able to obtain a patent to settle in North America. 🍃

Robert Cushman

Robert Cushman was a grocer in **Canterbury**. At a trial before the church wardens of St. Andrew's (now demolished) in November 1603, Cushman was excommunicated, but was later given absolution. He joined the Scrooby congregation of Separatists and moved to Holland with them. His son Thomas, born in St. Andrew's parish, Canterbury, married Mary Allerton in Plymouth. She lived until 1699 and was the last of the Pilgrims to die. Robert Cushman returned to England to act as an agent for the Pilgrims. He died at Canterbury in February 1625. 🍃

Thomas Weston

London merchant Thomas Weston had business dealings with the Pilgrims in Holland. A somewhat unscrupulous entrepreneur, he became involved in the financial negotiations for the proposed expedition and efforts to find investors. About seventy London "Merchant Adventurers" invested in a plan to help finance the Pilgrims' travel, and in return the Pilgrims would send furs, other natural resources, and goods that they produced back to England. Finally, King James agreed to allow the Pilgrim group to immigrate as a result of their agreement to behave quietly and be faithful subjects of the king.

Carver and Cushman presented the agreement to the group in Leyden. After much debate, a set of ten articles of agreement was drawn up, but not all of the Pilgrims would sign the contract. The Pilgrims did not have a large financial nest egg and the group was forced to sell £60 worth of their supplies to pay for the voyage. Fewer than half of the group actually decided to leave Holland. 🌿

SAILING FOR AMERICA

The Pilgrims' agents next looked for ships that could be hired or purchased. They couldn't afford new or large ships, and in the end they settled on the *Speedwell* and the *Mayflower*. **John Carver** remained in Holland to purchase the *Speedwell*, which the Pilgrims planned to keep in America for fishing and coastal trade. **Robert Cushman** negotiated the hire of the *Mayflower* to take the Pilgrims from Holland to America. The contract was signed in what is now a restaurant in Canterbury's Palace Street. The port books indicate that the *Mayflower* was a trading ship which had already seen decades of service in both the wine and fishing trades. 🌿

Christopher Jones

Part-owner and captain of the *Mayflower*, Christopher Jones was born in **Harwich, Essex**. In 1611 he settled in Rotherhithe on the south side of the Thames in London, a popular place for sea captains to live. His children were baptized at **St. Mary's Church, Rotherhithe**. Jones was an ideal captain for the trip since he had previously sailed across the Atlantic, taking cattle to the Viginia settlement.

Sixty-six Pilgrim settlers left the port of Delfshaven, Holland on 22 July 1620 on the *Speedwell*, which headed to Southampton to join the *Mayflower* that had sailed from London. The two boats sailed from **Southampton** on 5 August. After a few days at sea, the *Speedwell* was found to have leaks. The ships turned into **Dartmouth** for repairs. Almost two weeks later they set out once more. Again, the *Speedwell* started to leak. This time they put into **Plymouth**, where it was decided to abandon the *Speedwell*. About twenty would-be colonists were left in Plymouth, since the *Mayflower* could not hold all of them. On 6 September 1620, the *Mayflower* alone sailed westward from Plymouth with 101 passengers. 🌿

ESSEX Many early voyages of exploration sailed from *Harwich*, and the captains who almost certainly would have attended services at *St. Nicholas's Church* included Hugh Willoughby, **Sir Francis Drake**, and Martin Frobisher. **Captain Christopher Jones** was married twice at St. Nicholas's.

The *House of Christopher Jones*, his birthplace, still stands in *Harwich*.

LONDON The *Mayflower* sailed from a dock close to the present-day *Mayflower Pub* in *Rotherhithe*. (Then it was called "The Shippe.") Today memorabilia connected with the *Mayflower* and *Pilgrims* decorate the rooms and add to the historic feeling of the ancient pub. In the summer it is nice to sit outside on the wooden deck and listen to the water slapping the timbers.

One passenger left behind when the *Speedwell* failed to sail for America was Phillipe De Lannoy (or de la Noye), a direct ancestor of **President Franklin Roosevelt**. Phillipe arrived in Massachusetts the following year aboard the *Fortune*.

BUCKINGHAMSHIRE The buildings at *Old Jordans Quaker Meeting House* in *Jordans* include the "Mayflower Barn," which was reputedly made of timbers from the dismantled *Mayflower*.

SHROPSHIRE *Shipton Parish Church* has a memorial plaque to the four More children on the *Mayflower*, placed in the church by the Massachusetts Society of Mayflower Descendants.

LONDON A hundred girls and boys from the *Bridewell Hospital* orphanage were sent to Virginia in 1619. The project was so successful that the governor requested a hundred more. All the children received grants of land on coming of age. Two carved wooden statues of a boy and girl at *St. Bride's, Fleet Street* represent children from the parish school at the time when orphans were sent to the New World.

SURREY On *West Street* in Dorking, a blue plaque marks *Mullins House*, where William Mullins and his family lived.

TYNE AND WEAR The Hilton (Hylton) family have been recorded in Country Durham since before the Normans arrived in England. St. Katherine's Chapel was built in about 1157. The *Hylton Castle* that still stands in *Sunderland* was actually the gatehouse of a much larger castle.

The *Mayflower* Passengers

The 101 passengers aboard the *Mayflower* when it sailed from Plymouth included thirty-five Puritan "Saints" and sixty-six "Strangers." The story of one particular group of children was very poignant. It was a practice at that time for abandoned or orphaned children to be sent on ships to help with the work on board. On the *Mayflower* were four children from the More family of **Shipton, Shropshire**. Their father had disowned them when he found out that he was not their natural father. They were placed in an orphanage and then chosen to sail on the *Mayflower*. Elinor, Jasper, Richard, and Mary More were taken under the care of families going on the ship. Jasper and Mary died in 1620, possibly during the voyage, and Elinor died the next year. Richard lived to be eighty years old.

The most famous of the "Stranger" passengers was to be John Alden, a relative of Captain Jones. Priscilla Mullins was also on the ship. Her father William Mullins was a fairly well-to-do shoe and boot dealer in Dorking, Surrey, who purchased shares in the Pilgrims' joint-stock company, becoming one of the Merchant Adventurers. His wife Alice, daughter Priscilla, and son Joseph all sailed on the *Mayflower*. Only Priscilla survived the first winter. **Henry Wadsworth Longfellow** wrote about the marriage of John and Priscilla in his poem *The Courtship of Myles Standish*. It became a classic tale of the Pilgrim era, even though its story about a love triangle had little basis in fact.

Several American presidents were descendants of *Mayflower* passengers. John Alden and Priscilla Mullins had ten children. Among their descendants were **Presidents John Adams** and **John Quincy Adams**, poet **Henry Wadsworth Longfellow** and Vice-President Dan Quayle. Presidents Ulysses S. Grant and **Franklin D. Roosevelt** and astronaut **Alan Shepherd** were descendants of Richard Warren. Franklin Roosevelt was also related to Isaac Allerton, as was President Zachary Taylor. John Howland was an ancestor of **President George Bush** and First Lady Edith (Carow) Roosevelt (wife of **Theodore Roosevelt**). Richard Nixon and Gerald Ford were descendants of John Howland's brother Henry. **Winston Churchill** was descended from John Howland's brother Arthur. 🌿

MASSACHUSETTS AFTER THE *Mayflower*

The situation at the Plymouth Colony was very tenuous on 20 November 1621 when a second ship, the *Fortune*, finally arrived from England. One of these new Pilgrim arrivals was **Robert Cushman**, the grocer from Canterbury who had negotiated the hire of the *Mayflower*. Of the 101 passengers who had traveled on the *Mayflower* only fifty-one were still alive when the *Fortune* arrived. 🌿

William Hilton

William Hilton of **Biddick, County Durham**, was also aboard the *Fortune*. The Hiltons were an ancient family in that part of England, dating back to at least the year 900. During the early seventeenth century some of the family developed Nonconformist religious leanings.

From 1615 to 1619 Lady Mary Hilton employed **John Davenport** as a preacher in the chapel at **Hylton Castle** in **Sunderland**. Davenport sailed to America in 1637 on the *Hector* and became a founding father of New Haven, Connecticut.

In July 1623 the ship *Anne*, accompanied by the *Little James*, arrived in Plymouth bringing new settlers and many of the remaining wives and children who had been left behind in Holland. The Plymouth Colony was beginning to grow. 🍃

TYNE AND WEAR One of the oldest churches in England, *St. Peter's Church* in *Monkwearmouth* was built in AD 674. Originally part of a monastery, its most famous scholar was the Venerable Bede, a monk who lived from 672 to 735 and wrote the first history of the Anglo-Saxon people. In the chancel there is a carved altar tomb with a monument to a member of the Hilton family.

MORE PLACES ASSOCIATED WITH THE *MAYFLOWER*

ESSEX Four people from **Billericay** sailed on the *Mayflower*: Christopher Martin (a victualler of ships who lived in the High Street), his wife, Mary, Soloman Prower, and John Langerman. **Chantry House** on the High Street is said to have been Martin's family home. Local legend says that the *Mayflower* immigrants from Billericay ate their last meal at the Chantry House before going to meet the ship. In 1655 a town in New England took the name of Billericay to commemorate the origins of some of the first settlers.

The church register at **St. Mary Magdalene's Church** in **Great Burstead** records the marriage of Christopher Martin. Church records also show that at Easter 1612, Martin refused to kneel for Holy Communion, which was taken as proof that he had Protestant leanings. He purchased four shares in the Virginia Company from **George Percy**, perhaps hoping to immigrate to Jamestown. Martin spent time with the Pilgrims in Leyden and was elected to be a governor of the *Speedwell*, but the other passengers did not approve of him. They reported he was rude and profane. Martin managed to transfer onto the *Mayflower* with some other *Speedwell* passengers. The church has a beautiful *Mayflower* window and plaque to commemorate Christopher Martin.

NORFOLK Two brothers from **Redenhall** sailed on the *Mayflower*. Edward Fuller was baptized on 4 September 1575 at **St. Mary's Church**, Redenhall, and Samuel Fuller was baptized on 20 January 1580. Their eight brothers followed them to the New World.

NOTTINGHAMSHIRE In **All Saints' Church, Babworth**, a replica of the *Mayflower* is a reminder of ties with the Pilgrim Fathers. **Richard Clyfton** was rector of the church from 1586 to 1605. The Elizabethan silver chalice used by Clyfton can still be seen at All Saints'. The track along which Brewster and Bradford used to travel to Babworth from the Great North Road is still called the Pilgrims' Way.

A picture of the *Mayflower* hangs in the church nave at the

Church of St. Peter and St. Paul, Sturton-le-Steeple. William and Susanna White, with their son, Resolved, from Sturton-le-Steeple sailed on the *Mayflower*. Their second child was the first "Englishman" born in the New World. They named him Peregrine, a reference to the traveling they had done to reach America.

BEDFORDSHIRE John and Joan Tilley were married in the parish of **Henlow** on 20 September 1596. Their daughter Elizabeth was baptized in the **Church of St. Mary the Virgin** in 1607. They sailed on the *Mayflower*. Elizabeth married John Howland, also a Pilgrim. A plaque was placed in the church in 1989 by the Pilgrim Howland Society.

HAMPSHIRE The **Mayflower Memorial** is located near the place where the *Mayflower* and the *Speedwell* left Southampton in 1620. The Pilgrims left the city through the **West Gate** to board their ships. A tower stands to commemorate the event and a plaque on West Gate records the Pilgrims' sailing.

DEVON In **Bayard's Cove, Dartmouth**, overlooking the mouth of the River Dart, a memorial in the stone of the cobbled Quay records the docking of the *Mayflower* and *Speedwell* and the sailing of the Pilgrim Fathers to the New World.

The **Island House** on the **Barbican, Plymouth**, is believed to be where the Pilgrims spent their last night in England. The Council for the Governing of New England was set up here in 1635.

The **Mayflower Memorial** on the **Barbican**, from which the *Mayflower* finally set sail for the New World. There are several plaques at the site. A memorial archway at the **Mayflower Steps** stands above the water at the Barbican.

LONDON In the **House of Lords Corridor** in the **Palace of Westminster**, a large mural shows "The Embarkation of the Pilgrims for New England."

The place name of "Plimoth," where the new colony was established, was first used on the map **Captain John Smith** made in 1614.

NOTE Plimoth Plantation in Plymouth, Massachusetts, is a recreation of the colony established by the Pilgrims. Today visitors can go aboard a replica of the *Mayflower* at Plymouth Rock, Massachusetts.

The Weston Colony

Not everyone connected with the early settlement of America was idealistic or religious. **Thomas Weston** was involved in the early financial arrangements for the Pilgrims' expedition, but he turned out to be a very shady character. A year after the *Mayflower* sailed to America, he was accused of selling an English cannon to a Turkish pirate. In July 1622 all his assets were seized by the king's officers, but Weston had fled to America months earlier.

After receiving a charter to set up a colony, Weston sent

a small ship with six or seven settlers and a crew to find an area for their group. They reached Plymouth in May 1622 and took advantage of the food the settlers there gave them, even though there was little to spare.

Pressed to establish his own colony, Weston and his men moved to a site known as Wessagusset. Most of the men in his group were totally unprepared to work. Before many months they were starving and freezing. They began stealing food from the Indians, who decided to attack the small colony. Word of this plan reached the Plymouth Colony, and Miles Standish was sent to try to sort out the situation. He found the English men starving, naked, and in desperate shape. A confrontation with the Indians left two dead.

On advice from Standish, the Wessagusset Colony was abandoned in the spring of 1623 by most of the settlers, some going to Plymouth, some going to the fishing stations in Maine, some returning to England. Those remaining were killed by the Indians. In 1623 Robert Gorges issued a warrant for Weston's arrest and the seizure of his ship. Weston argued that he could not be held responsible for the conduct of the settlers in his absence. Governor Bradford of the Plymouth Colony supported Weston, perhaps remembering the work he had done to get financial support for the original Pilgrim expedition. Weston's ship was returned to him and he was allowed to leave. He sailed off, heading south. Weston lived out the remainder of his years on his 1,250-acre estate in present-day Maryland, dying in 1647. 🍃

The Dorchester Company

Dissatisfaction with the Church of England was widespread throughout England in the early 1600s, but not all the early English settlers in Massachusetts were Separatists who wanted to start a new religion in the New World. The Dorchester Company of Adventurers had a largely economic motivation – they hoped to exploit the abundance of seafood that fishing vessels found in the North Atlantic. The **Reverend John White** was a major supporter of the Dorchester Company from its beginnings in 1623. He thought a colony in Massachusetts represented an economic opportunity for his community, and also a chance to set up a reformed Anglican church.

In 1623 the Dorchester Company sent a small ship, the *Fellowship*, with thirteen men aboard, who started a colony on Cape Ann, just north of the Plymouth Colony. Roger Conant traveled to Massachusetts with the Pilgrims, but he become disillusioned with their strict religious code. In 1625 Conant decided to leave Plymouth and was invited to join the Dorchester Colony, which had grown to over 100 men. Conant

DORSET *St. Peter's Church* in *Dorchester* has a monument to Rev. John White in the porch, which has the inscription: "In this porch lies the body of the Rev. John White ... he greatly set forth the emigration to the Massachusetts Bay Colony, where his name lives in unending remembrance." In the church there is a model of the ship *Mary and John* which took the **Dorchester Company** colonists to America.

John White lived behind St. Peter's Church at the *Old Rectory* on *Colliton Street* in *Dorchester*. A plaque says John White was "The Organiser of the Dorset Emigrants who Sailed on the 'Mary and John' 1630 and were some of the Original Founders of Massachusetts USA."

In the Superdrug store in *Dorchester* a medieval doorway that was originally in the rectory has a plaque that state that in 1624 "White was instrumental in forming a colony known as Dorchester in Massachusetts USA."

DEVON Roger Conant was baptized on 9 April 1592 in *All Saints' Church* in *East Budleigh.* The Conant family is remembered here with their coat of arms.

LONDON In November 1618 Roger Conant married Sarah Horton, also of East Budleigh, at the Church of St. Anne's, Blackfriars (which was destroyed in the Great Fire and not rebuilt). He and his wife went to the Plymouth Colony in 1623, probably on the ship *Ann.*

LINCOLNSHIRE The Puritan leaders held a conference at the Earl of Lincoln's manor house in *Sempringham* in 1629. St. Gilbert's Priory and Castle no longer stand, but the *Church of St. Andrew* remains.

A stained-glass window at *Lincoln Cathedral* commemorates the lead ship of the Winthrop Fleet, the *Arbella.*

A plaque in *St. Botolph's Church* in *Boston* is a memorial to the five men from Boston who became governors of Massachusetts: Richard Bellingham, Thomas Dudley, Francis Bernard, John Leverett, and Simon Bradstreet.

was appointed governor of the colony, which was struggling to survive. In 1626 this settlement split. Conant led the small group of Dorchester colonists south to settle in an area known as Naumkeag. The name of the settlement was subsequently changed to "Salem," the Hebrew word for "peaceful."

Back in England, the Reverend John White was still a major supporter of the Dorchester Colony, handling the arrangements for financing, transportation, and supplies, and encouraging new families to join the colony in Massachusetts. On 20 March 1630 a second group with 140 colonists from Somerset, Dorset, and Devonshire, sailed from Plymouth aboard the *Mary and John.* They put ashore at Nantasket on 30 May and found pasture for their cattle at Mattapan, later renamed Dorchester, in honor of John White, of Dorchester, England.

Two weeks after the group of settlers from the Dorchester Company had landed in Massachusetts, the **Winthrop Fleet** reached the same shore. The Dorchester group tried to co-exist with the Puritan settlers, but by 1637 the Dorchester colonists decided to leave Massachusetts because they felt they could no longer live with the religious and governmental policies of the strict Puritans. Sixty men, women, and children of the Dorchester congregation headed south to the Connecticut Valley. They settled on land that the Plymouth people had purchased from the Indians, and changed the name of the settlement to "Dorchester." In 1637 the name was changed for the final time, to "Windsor." 🍂

The Winthrop Fleet

King Charles I granted a charter for a new colony to the Massachusetts Bay Company on 4 March 1629. Although set up to be a commercial company with the aim of making a profit from trade, the promoters were also intent on establishing a colony where a Puritan church would be free from all outside interference. On 25 July 162, **John Cotton, Thomas Hooker**, and **Roger Williams** met at **St. Gilbert's Priory** at **Sempringham, Lincolnshire**, near Boston, at the manor house of Theophilus Clinton, 4th Earl of Lincoln, noted Puritan supporter. Williams urged that the colony separate completely from the Church of England. This policy was not adopted. At the same time another group was meeting in London at the home of Thomas Goffe, deputy governor of the company. At this meeting it was decided to move the whole governing body of Puritans to Massachusetts and settle a full colony rather than just setting up a trading station. This decision led to the immigration of tens of thousands of Puritans to New England and the rapid growth of the English presence in North America.

The religious goals of the colony attracted much support from Puritan groups, and many licenses to migrate were applied for. The Puritans used their control of the plans to make sure that the new settlers supported their religious ideals. On 7 April 1630 the first four ships of the Winthrop Fleet left London for the New World. These ships were followed by many others over the next few months. The flagship was a ship named the *Eagle* which was renamed the *Arbella* in honor of Lady Arbella Clinton Johnson, the sister of the 4th Earl of Lincoln. She and her husband, the Reverend Isaac Johnson, sailed with the fleet.

Among the nearly one thousand Puritans who sailed to New England with the Winthrop Fleet were:

Edmund Quincy, whose descendants **John Adams** and **John Quincy Adams** were the second and sixth presidents of the USA.

Richard Bellingham, Francis Bernard, John Leverett, and Simon Bradstreet, all of whom became governors of Massachusetts.

LINCOLNSHIRE *Alford* was Anne Hutchinson's birthplace. *Alford Manor House* hosts an exhibition on early American settlers from Lincolnshire.

Roger Williams, who clashed with Winthrop and was banished from Massachusetts.

Anne Hutchinson, later banished from the Massachusetts Bay Colony.

Descendants of **Robert "Trouble-Church" Browne** of Lincolnshire. Their descendants were in the front line at the first battle for American independence – Solomon Brown of Lexington, Massachusetts, fired the first shot that drew British blood on the Lexington Green. His first cousin, John Brown of Lexington, was one of the six "Minute Men" killed by the British on the morning of 19 April 1775.

John Winthrop

John Winthrop was born into a wealthy Suffolk family. Connected through marriage to the founder of **Emmanuel College, Cambridge**, John's father was for many years the auditor of Trinity and St. John's colleges. John had a strict Puritan upbringing at Groton Manor, and entered **Trinity College, Cambridge**, in 1602, at the age of fourteen. He became a justice of the peace and held court at Groton Hall. After studying law at the **Middle Temple, London**, he worked with Parliament, preparing bills for legislative committees. In March 1629 King Charles I decided to govern without

SUFFOLK John Winthrop's grandfather, Adam Winthrop, made the family fortune in the beautiful village of *Lavenham* selling broadcloth.

LONDON Adam Winthrop was a member of the *Clothworkers' Company*, and master in 1551.

SUFFOLK A stained-glass window in *St. Bartholomew's Church* in *Groton* was given to the church in memory of John Winthrop by American descendants. In 1975 the American branch of the Winthrop family contributed toward the restoration of the tower and west end of the church.

ESSEX John Winthrop and Mary Forth were married at the *Church of St. Mary and All Saints* in *Great Stambridge* on 16 April 1605. A window donated by American descendants hangs above the font in which two of Winthrop's children were baptized.

DERBYSHIRE The house in *Derby* where John Cotton lived as a boy, and the church where he was baptized, no longer exist, but the Derby Grammar School buildings are still there. The Tudor building he knew is now called "St. Peter's Hall."

LINCOLNSHIRE At *St. Botolph's Church* in *Boston* visitors can see John Cotton's pulpit and a modern stained-glass window that commemorates Cotton's farewell address to the group of Puritans who emigrated in 1630. The church's Cotton Memorial Chapel was restored in 1857 by citizens of Boston, Massachusetts.

Parliament, and Puritan leaders were carried off to the Tower. In June, Winthrop's commission as an attorney of the Court of Ward and Liveries in London was withdrawn when the king cancelled his crown appointment. · .

John's background and legal training served him well – the shareholders of the company elected John Winthrop to be governor of the Massachusetts Company before the expedition left England. Because the company charter allowed the colony to be governed from Massachusetts, John joined the Puritans in New England. He served as governor of the Massachusetts colony for twelve terms. John Winthrop has been described as the "Father of New England." He died in Boston, Massachusetts, on 26 March 1649 and is buried in Kings Chapel, Boston, Massachusetts. 🌿

The Massachusetts Bay Colony

John Cotton was admitted to *Trinity College, Cambridge*, when he was thirteen. After graduating he was elected a fellow of Trinity College, and then he became head lecturer and dean at *Emmanuel College*. Although Emmanuel was known as a "nursery for Puritans," Cotton had not yet become a Puritan himself. However, he was an outstanding preacher who impressed people with his directness and simplicity.

In 1612 Cotton became vicar of the influential church of *St. Botolph's* in *Boston, Lincolnshire*, where he remained for twenty years. He became more strongly Puritan in his beliefs and, in 1615, began to question some of the ceremonies of the established church. His reputation spread throughout that region of England, and people from the surrounding areas traveled to hear him preach. **Anne Hutchinson** and her family, including her brother-in-law **John Wheelwright**, were greatly influenced by John Cotton. In 1630, when Cotton preached to members of the Massachusetts Company who were preparing to sail from Southampton, he claimed it was God's will that the Puritans should inhabit all the world.

Charles I became king in 1625, and in 1628 **William Laud** was named Bishop of London. The bishop had great influence on the king, increasing the official opposition to the Nonconformists. John Cotton's influence and Puritan leanings attracted Laud's attention. In 1632 legal action was begun against him. Knowing this, Cotton left Boston and hid in London for several months. Cotton eluded the authorities who were on watch for him at the ports. For a time he hid with Henry Whitefield at *Ockley Rectory*, near *Guildford, Surrey*. In July 1633 Cotton sailed for Massachusetts aboard the *Griffin*. Within a few weeks of his arrival, he was appointed teacher for the First Church in Boston, a position he held until his death in 1652.

John Cotton and John Winthrop were the leading members of the Massachusetts Bay Colony. Along with the council they attempted to establish a community ruled by religion – a theocracy where the clergy could and should dictate the laws for the good of the group. His authoritarian stand became clear in his opposition to **Anne Hutchinson**, who had been a faithful follower in Lincolnshire. He came to believe that her philosophy of individual freedom was a threat to the community, and he joined in the vote to banish her from the colony in November 1637. Despite his stand on the power of the clergy to rule the colony, John Cotton was a beloved member of the Massachusetts community and had a great influence on religious and civil matters in the colony. 🌿

John Eliot

The man who came to be known as the "Pastor to the Indians" graduated from *Jesus College, Cambridge*, in 1622. During the next several years he worked in *Little Baddow* as an assistant at the school run for the children of Nonconformists by **Thomas Hooker**. John Eliot's religious beliefs made it impossible for him to obtain a preaching or teaching position within the Church of England. Hooker fled to Holland in 1630 and Eliot left England with the **Braintree Company** on the *Lyon*, reaching Boston in November 1631.

The Puritans in the Massachusetts Bay Colony had two goals – to found a community where they could worship as they wanted, and to bring the message of the Bible to the native peoples. John Eliot took this second aim and made it his life's work. He visited the Indians to learn their language. Within a few years he could preach to them in their own words. In 1649 the English Parliament created the Society for the Propagation of the Gospel in New England, and Eliot began his translation of the Bible into the Algonquin language. It took ten years. In 1661 1,500 copies of the New Testament in Algonquin were published – the first Bible printed in the New World.

In 1675 hostility between colonists and Indians led to what was called King Philip's War (named for the epithet used by one of the Indian leaders). Many of the local Indians were taken to an island in Boston Harbor. Most of them died during the harsh winter. Nearly all of the first edition of the Algonquin Bible was destroyed. Eliot's dreams of peaceful co-existence between the English settlers and the Native Americans were shattered. His death in 1690 effectively ended the attempt to evangelize the Algonquians in their native tongue, but his goal of education for all children continues to be important in America today. 🌿

John Cotton's daughter married Increase Mather. They were the parents of Cotton Mather, one of the last great Puritan preachers of Massachusetts. Cotton Mather was a judge at the Salem witch trials in 1692, at first insisting on the importance of spectral evidence. Later, after the hangings, he came to question some of the actions. He was also influential in the founding of **Yale College**.

HERTFORDSHIRE Parish records at the *Church of St. John the Baptist* in *Widford* show the marriage of John Eliot's parents in 1598 and the birth of their son in 1604. A window at the church is dedicated the memory of John Eliot.

CAMBRIDGE On 20 March 1619 John Eliot entered *Jesus College* as a pensioner. ("Pensioners" were those who paid their own bills at the university.) He graduated in 1622.

ESSEX A plaque placed in *All Saints' Church* in *Nazeing* by the National Society of the Descendants of John and Elizabeth Curtiss is dedicated "In Memory of all the members of this church who emigrated to America." Eliot's sister Sarah was married to John Curtiss's nephew.

CAMBRIDGESHIRE John Eliot was ordained at *Ely Cathedral* according to a memorial plaque at Roxbury Latin School in Roxbury, Massachusetts, founded by Eliot in 1645. It is America's longest continuously operating school.

ESSEX A plaque at *Cuckoos Farmhouse* in *Little Baddow* commemorates the school run by Thomas Hooker and John Eliot between 1626 and 1631.

ESSEX *Barrington Hall, Hatfield Broad Oak*, was the home of Sir Francis Barrington and his wife Lady Joan Cromwell Barrington, an aunt of Oliver Cromwell. For a time **Ezekiel Rogers** was the Barrington family chaplain. **Roger Williams** was chaplain to the family of her daughter Elizabeth Barrington Marsham.

SUFFOLK *St. Mary's Church* at *Haverhill* has a memorial to John Ward, father of three Puritan preachers.

YORKSHIRE A stained-glass window commemorating Ezekiel Rogers was donated to *St. Peter's Church* in *Little Weighton* in 1994 by friends from New England.

Rawley Manor Hotel in *Little Weighton* was once the rectory to St. Peter's Church, and home to Ezekiel Rogers.

COUNTY DURHAM *Raby Castle* has been the Vane family home since 1626.

The Ward Family and Ezekiel Rogers

In 1620 **Haverhill** in Suffolk was known as a Puritan town. John Ward, the famous Puritan preacher at **St. Mary's Church**, had sons who became influential Puritan preachers themselves. The eldest, Samuel Ward, called a "hot-head" by some, encouraged immigration to Massachusetts. His brother Nathaniel Ward graduated from **Emmanuel College** in 1603. His Puritan leanings brought him to the attention of **Archbishop Laud**, who tried and convicted Nathaniel of Nonconformism. He was stripped of his church position, and sailed for Massachusetts in 1634. His legal training came in very useful. He compiled the "Body of Liberties," which was adopted by the General Court in December 1641. This was the first code of laws established in New England. Nathaniel Ward returned to England in 1647 and was able to resume his work as a preacher.

The Wards had a step-brother who also became an important Puritan leader in the Massachusetts colony. After John Ward died, his widow Susan remarried. Her second husband, Richard Rogers, was the father of Ezekiel Rogers who served as chaplain to Sir Francis Barrington. With Sir Francis's support, Rogers was appointed assistant pastor at **St. Peter's Church** in **Little Weighton** in 1619, a post he held for seventeen years. When Church authorities sent out a decree that pastors should encourage their congregations to play ball and sports on the Sabbath, Ezekiel Rogers refused to allow his parishioners to participate. After Archbishop Laud suspended him, Rogers spent three years preaching in private homes. In 1638 Rogers sailed to Massachusetts where he became an important addition to the theocracy of Puritan Massachusetts. He was a member of a council of clergy appointed to discuss and decide questions of church law, which was the law of the colony. Rogers didn't believe in freedom of individual belief – he saw the minister as "leader" and "ruler," and did not believe that individual private members should be allowed to make speeches in church assemblies.

Henry Vane

Few people know that a governor of Massachusetts was executed on **Tower Hill** in London. Henry Vane could be considered one of America's earliest heroes. His father, Sir Henry Vane the Elder, was an advisor to King Charles I and served as the Comptroller of the Royal Household and later as secretary of state. The younger Henry entered the diplomatic service and traveled in Europe. When he returned to London in 1632, he had developed Puritan beliefs and could not support the absolutist government of Charles I.

The intolerance of the Church of England made Vane's

religious beliefs dangerous in England. In 1635 he sailed to Massachusetts and joined the Puritan colony in Boston, hoping to enjoy greater religious freedom. His abilities, education, and family background meant he was soon given significant responsibilities. In 1636 he was elected governor of the colony of Massachusetts. Henry Vane tried to bring religious tolerance into the colony's strict Puritan government. He had a hatred of religious bigotry, and did not approve when **Anne Hutchinson** was accused and tried because she refused to submit to the doctrines of the colony's leaders. As a result, **John Winthrop** and the General Court of Massachusetts opposed Vane's re-election in 1637.

In August 1637 Vane returned to England. Elected to Parliament in 1640, he became joint treasurer of the navy. In the years before the English Civil War Vane became an opponent of the Royalist Party and even refused to keep the fees of office paid to him by the government. He opposed the concept of a state church. Vane was not a strong anti-monarchist; as late as 1648 he voted for a continuance of the monarchy. But, he did play a central role in the downfall of **Archbishop Laud**. In 1641 he backed the articles of impeachment against Laud. Laud was executed in 1643.

Henry Vane refused to take an oath approving the king's execution, only swearing to be faithful to the new government. He served as a member of Cromwell's government, but his ideas of reforming elections and representation in Parliament brought him into direct disagreement with Oliver Cromwell. After Oliver Cromwell's death and Richard Cromwell's abdication, Vane regained his position as a leader in government.

King Charles II returned to England on 29 May 1660 and was crowned on 23 April 1661. He set about exacting revenge on members of the Commonwealth government. Henry Vane became a target, and in 1661 he was brought to trial on a capital charge. He was found guilty, mostly on the evidence that he had gone to work on the day of King Charles I's execution and therefore must have approved of it.

The political and religious ideals that Henry Vane voiced in Parliament and in Massachusetts are a vital part of the life of the United States today – individual religious freedom and the separation of Church and State. Vane made an important contribution towards the acceptance of these ideals in America with the work he did on the granting of a charter for the Colony of Rhode Island by Charles II in 1663. The charter guaranteed religious freedom and self-government. **Roger Williams**, a friend of the idealistic Puritan, said the people of the colony should honor the name of Henry Vane for ever. 🌿

KENT *Fairlawne* in *Plaxtol* was the family home of Sir **Henry Vane** the Younger. It is now a private house.

LONDON Henry Vane the Younger was educated at *Westminster School*, and graduated from *Magdalen College, Oxford.*

A blue plaque marks *Vane House, Rosslyn Hill, Hampstead*, where Henry Vane lived.

King Charles I was executed at the *Banqueting House* on 30 January 1649.

On 14 June 1662 Henry Vane was taken to *Tower Hill* for his execution. When he attempted to give a speech from the scaffold, trumpets and drums were played to drown out his voice, so he handed a paper to his friends for publication after his death. It read: "It is a bad cause that cannot bear the words of a dying man."

KENT Sir Henry Vane the Younger is buried at *St. Giles's Church, Shipbourne*.

READ The poet John Milton was a friend and neighbor of Henry Vane in Kent. He addressed Sonnet 17 to Sir Henry Vane in celebration of Vane's courageous positions on religious toleration and the separation of Church and State.

LINCOLNSHIRE Anne Hutchinson was from a Puritan family in Lincolnshire. Her father, Francis Marbury, was imprisoned for preaching against the established church. In the 1590s he was headmaster at the grammar school in *Alford*. When Anne was fourteen, her father was appointed to *St. Martin's Church* in *London*. In 1634 Anne sailed to Massachusetts with her husband and children. In 1636 her husband's younger sister Mary and her husband, **Rev. John Wheelwright**, a Lincolnshire preacher, also joined the Puritans in Massachusetts.

Anne Hutchinson

Anne Hutchinson had strongly held beliefs about how religion should be practiced. After immigrating to the Massachusetts Bay Colony, she began holding meetings and giving lectures, becoming the first woman preacher in America. Her philosophy of individual freedom of worship brought her into conflict with the Puritan leaders of the colony. She was tried and convicted of heresy and sedition. **John Eliot** disagreed with Anne's religious beliefs and was a member of the group that interrogated her.

Banished from the colony in November 1637, Hutchinson moved to Rhode Island along with her family. In 1642 her husband died and Anne moved to Connecticut. The following year she and most of her children were killed in an Indian attack. Her brother-in-law **John Wheelwright** was also banished from Massachusetts because of his opposition to the colony's leadership, and with others he moved north to New Hampshire.

In October 1770 Anne Hutchinson's great-great-grandson Thomas Hutchinson was appointed governor of Massachusetts. He corresponded with George Grenville, the Whig prime minister who was responsible for unpopular measures in America – the Sugar Act and the Stamp Act. Letters written by Hutchinson to Grenville were made public in Britain, and were the catalyst for the Privy Council hearing to which **Benjamin Franklin** was summoned in January 1773. Franklin faced a humiliating trial which forced him to decide whether he was a British citizen who lived in America or an American who was independent of Britain. 🌿

ESSEX In the *Braintree Town Hall* Council Chamber mural shows many scenes from the history of Braintree, including the "Sailing of the Braintree Company in the Lyon, 1632."

The Braintree "Company of Twenty-Four" was a system of local government that oversaw town business through a municipal council. This became a model for Puritan government in New England.

The *Braintree District Museum* has an exhibition about the Braintree Company and a good model of the *Lyon*.

The Braintree Company

On 22 June 1632 a group of emigrants left England aboard the *Lyon*, a ship which had made the journey to Massachusetts a year earlier. This time 123 passengers from **Braintree, Essex**, including fifty children, made the ten-week voyage. The colonists of the Braintree Company had been encouraged by the charismatic Nonconformist preacher **Thomas Hooker** to move to America in order to find religious freedom.

More colonists from Braintree sailed from Essex to the new colony over the next months. By 1640, a large group of Essex Puritans had moved to the Wollaston/Merrymount Colony in Massachusetts and renamed it Braintree. In 1636 many members of the Braintree Company went to Connecticut with Thomas Hooker where they established a model of democratic government that influenced the subsequent government of the United States.

At least four presidents of America were direct

descendants of Essex people who immigrated with the Braintree Company. **John Adams** was the great-grandson of Henry Adams, who sailed on the *Lyon*. Three presidents have been descendants of the Hooker family: Calvin Coolidge, **Franklin D. Roosevelt**, and William Howard Taft. 🍃

John Bridge

John Bridge, originally of Rayne Road, Braintree, England, started the school that was to develop into **Harvard University**. A statue in Harvard Square, Cambridge, Massachusetts, has the inscription:

"JOHN BRIDGE 1578–1665 left Braintree, Essex County, England 1631 as a member of Rev. Mr. Hooker's Company. Settled here 1632, and stayed when that company moved to Connecticut."

NEW HAMPSHIRE
John Wheelwright

Many of the early Puritan immigrants to New England were related by blood and marriage, and also connected to the Puritans who led the English Commonwealth. John Wheelwright's second wife was Maria Hutchinson of **Alford**, a sister of **Anne Hutchinson**'s husband, William Hutchinson. Wheelwright's Puritanism brought him into disfavor with **Archbishop Laud**. After he was suspended from his employment for Nonconformism, he immigrated to America, sailing for Boston, Massachusetts, aboard the *Griffin* in 1634 at the same time that Anne and her husband were sailing to America.

John Wheelwright agreed with many of his sister-in-law's opinions on religion, even though they went against some of the policies of the governing Puritans in Massachusetts. When he preached a sermon against a fast that had been decreed by the General Court in 1637, he was accused of sedition and contempt. Found guilty, Wheelwright was banished from the colony. Wheelwright and a group of his followers left Massachusetts in 1638. They headed north and established a settlement which they named Exeter. When the Boston Puritans claimed this was still within their jurisdiction, Wheelwright's group obtained a grant of land from **Sir Ferdinando Gorges** and moved further north to Maine.

The following year, after Wheelwright admitted that he had been partially in the wrong, his banishment was lifted and he returned to Massachusetts. About 1657 Wheelwright traveled back to England, where he met with a friend from his days at Cambridge – Oliver Cromwell. John Wheelwright returned to Massachusetts where he served as a preacher in Salisbury, New Hampshire. He died on 15 November 1679, aged eighty-seven. 🍃

ESSEX The *Deanery Church of St. Mary the Virgin* in *Bocking* has a magnificent window donated by "James J. Goodwin Esq and the Rev. Francis Goodwin, DD, American citizens, to the Parish of their Ancestors." Local tradition says that Mr. William Goodwin of Lyons Hall, Bocking, was the leader of the Braintree Company and that Thomas Hooker stayed with the Goodwin family at Lyons Hall.

LINCOLNSHIRE John Wheelwright was born around 1592. He entered the ministry of the Church of England, serving as vicar of *Holy Trinity Church* in *Bilsby* near *Alford*, from 1623 to 1633.

CAMBRIDGE In 1614 John Wheelwright graduated from *Sydney Sussex College*, where he knew Oliver Cromwell.

LEICESTERSHIRE *St. Peter's Church* at *Tilton-on-the-Hill* was the Hooker family church. Thomas's father and mother are probably buried in the churchyard. Their deaths are noted in the church records.

Thomas Hooker was born in *Marefield* on 7 July 1586. The Hooker family home was either Marefield Farm or Marefield Manor Farm, sixteenth-century farmhouses in the tiny village (both are now private homes).

CAMBRIDGE Thomas Hooker entered *Queens' College* in 1604 as a sizar (self-paying student). When he received a Dixie Scholarship, he moved to *Emmanuel College*.

ESSEX On a wall near *Chelmsford Cathedral* a plaque states, "Thomas Hooker, 1586–1647, Founder of the State of Connecticut, Father of American Democracy." The cathedral's south porch was enriched in 1953 by "Essex friends of the American people."

SURREY In 1620 Hooker took on the position of curate at *St. George's Church* in *Esher*, where he lived in the household of Francis Drake, a cousin of the famous explorer of the same name. Drake lived at *Wayneflete Tower*, a thirteenth-century manor house that was enlarged into a palace by Bishop Wayneflete. Only the gatehouse remains today.

CONNECTICUT
Thomas Hooker
"Father of American Democracy"

The Puritans who sailed to America with the **Braintree Company** had been encouraged to move to the colony by the charismatic Puritan preacher, Thomas Hooker, who had studied at **Emmanuel College, Cambridge**, Sir Walter Mildmay's "nursery for Puritans." In late 1625 or early 1626 Thomas Hooker moved to **Chelmsford** as lecturer at the **Cathedral Church of St. Mary the Virgin**. Being appointed lecturer was still possible for Puritans for whom the position of vicar was increasingly closed. He made no attempt to hide his Puritan leanings and was a very charismatic preacher. His preaching electrified many people around the countryside, winning converts by the thousands. Thomas Hooker became more outspoken in his Puritanism, and was soon on the list of clergy being hunted down by **Bishop William Laud**.

Forced to leave Chelmsford because of his religious views, Hooker moved to **Little Baddow** where he started a school for the children of Nonconformist families. For a while his assistant was **John Eliot**, who later became known as "Pastor to the Indians." In and around the secluded village, Puritans were quietly holding meetings, secretly discussing their religious ideas, opposition to the king, and plans for the future. When King Charles I attempted to force landowners to make loans to the monarch, Sir Francis Barrington of **Hatfield Broad Oak, Essex**, refused to pay. Although he was seventy-six years old, he was imprisoned in **Marshalsea Prison** in **London** along with his son-in-law Sir William Masham. Sir Francis died as a result of his imprisonment. His wife, Lady Joan Barrington, was an aunt of Oliver Cromwell.

In 1630 Thomas Hooker was ordered to appear before the Court of High Commission in London for Nonconformist preaching. He fled to Holland, and lived for three years before immigrating to America with his wife and children aboard the *Griffin*. His friend **John Cotton** also sailed on the *Griffin*. They headed for a New World which they would help to shape in fundamental ways. Hooker and Cotton were two of the most famous English preachers to make the journey to New England.

Thomas Hooker became a minister in Newtown, Massachusetts (later renamed "Cambridge"). In 1636 he moved with his congregation to Connecticut, largely because he opposed the strict control the Puritans exercised over the Massachusetts colony. Hooker felt that each congregation should be able to select their own leaders and set guidelines for their communities. The Puritans insisted on following what they said were the Old Testament guidelines, enforcing a strict theocracy where church leaders opposed any religious differences.

Thomas Hooker delivered a sermon before the Connecticut General Court that inspired the Fundamental Orders of Connecticut, the first written constitution in America focusing on the civic rights and responsibilities of members of the community, rather than on religious duties. The Fundamental Orders are seen as a precursor of the Federal Constitution of the United States. Because of this, Thomas Hooker has been called the "Father of American Democracy."

New Haven and the Early English Settlers

Reverend John Davenport and Theophilius Eaton arrived in Boston, Massachusetts, on 26 June 1637 with a group of Puritans on board the *Hector*. After studying at **Merton** and **Magdalen Colleges, Oxford**, Davenport had been employed by Lady Mary Hilton as a preacher at the chapel at **Hylton Castle, County Durham**, from 1615 to 1619. He moved to London where he was elected lecturer and curate of the church of **St. Lawrence, Old Jewry**. Davenport preached before the Virginia Company of London and became a member of the company in 1622. After he was appointed vicar at St. Stephen's, Coleman Street, London, influential members of the congregation switched church funds in order to support Davenport. This congregational independence was fiercely opposed by Bishop Laud. Davenport eventually fled to Holland before immigrating to Massachusetts.

Theophilius Eaton

A successful merchant who spent several years in Denmark as an agent of King Charles I, Theophilius Eaton returned to London as a strict Puritan. Eaton decided to immigrate to America to escape persecution and sailed to the New World with his wife, Anne Lloyd Yale, the widow of Thomas Yale and grandmother of **Elihu Yale**. Also with the group was John Brockett, surveyor, from **Brocket Hall** in **Hertfordshire**.

The Puritans urged the new arrivals to stay in Boston, but Davenport, Eaton, and others hoped to set up a new community and create a Christian utopia. The group sailed south, looking for an advantageous location for trading. On 24 April 1638 the ships sailed into the harbor that they first called Quinipiac and later renamed New Haven. The local Indian tribe, the Quinnipiacks, agreed to sell the land to the Puritans in exchange for thirteen English coats and a pledge of protection against the raiding Pequots and Mohawks. Eaton

ESSEX At *Cuckoos Farmhouse* in *Little Baddow* a plaque notes that Thomas Hooker and John Eliot had a school here between 1626 and 1631.

Hooker and Eliot worshipped at the *Church of St. Mary the Virgin* in *Little Baddow*. Near the altar is the ornate tomb of Sir Henry Mildmay.

Great Graces in *Little Baddow* was the home of Sir Henry Mildmay, a powerful Puritan supporter who was an MP and sheriff of Essex. His great uncle was Sir Walter Mildmay, founder of *Emmanuel College, Cambridge*. Sir Henry's brother-in-law sailed to Massachusetts aboard the *Arbella* with John Winthrop.

Three US presidents were descended from the Hooker family – Calvin Coolidge, Franklin D. Roosevelt, and William Howard Taft.

LONDON John Davenport was lecturer and curate at *St. Lawrence, Old Jewry*.

HERTFORDSHIRE The original *Brocket Hall* in *Welwyn* was built in 1239 and rebuilt in 1440.

LONDON The trial of King Charles I was held in *Westminster Hall*, which is the oldest surviving part of the *Houses of Parliament*. A copy of King Charles I's signed death warrant is on view.

CAMBRIDGESHIRE *Hinchingbrooke House, Huntingdon,* was the Whalley family home. **Edward Whalley's** mother was Frances Cromwell, a sister of Oliver Cromwell's father.

SURREY Edward Whalley was the warder of Charles II while he was held at *Hampton Court Palace.* After Charles escaped temporarily, he sent Whalley a thank-you letter.

LONDON Another man who died as a result of Charles II's retribution was Isaac Pennington, the step-grandfather of **William Penn's** first wife Gulielma Springett. Pennington did not sign the king's death warrant, but he was a commissioner of the High Court of Justice. After the Restoration he was convicted of treason. Held in the *Tower of London,* he died in 1661.

was chosen as the first governor of the colony and continued in office until his death in 1658. The town plan of New Haven was laid out by John Brockett, based on a grid of nine squares. In accordance with old English custom, the central square, now the Green, was designated a public common.

The new colony's opposition to rule from England was tested in 1661 when the king's officers came to New Haven searching for two fugitives. Charles II had been restored to the throne of England and he embarked on a program of retribution against those who ordered his father's death. Many regicides had to flee England. **Edward Whalley** and William Goffe were two of the judges who had sentenced Charles I to death. Whalley was the son of Oliver Cromwell's aunt and Goffe was Whalley's son-in-law. These two regicides fled to America and spent time in New Haven where they were hidden in a cave by townsfolk. (Today Judges' Cave, on top of West Rock in New Haven is reached by the Regicides Trail.) The two men left New Haven and secretly traveled to Milford, Connecticut, where they lived in hiding for three years. When the king's officers followed them here, they moved on to Hadley, Massachusetts, where they lived for the rest of their lives in a secret room in the home of Rev. John Russell. 🍃

The Reverend Henry Whitfield

The Reverend Henry Whitfield had been a friend to many of the Puritan leaders who were taking their congregations to Massachusetts. **John Cotton, John Davenport,** and **Thomas Hooker** had at times taken refuge in Whitfield's rectory in **Ockley** while hiding from **Bishop Laud**. Finally, in 1638, after refusing to read *The Book of Sports* to his congregation, Whitfield himself led thirty-nine persons from **St. Margaret's Church** in **Ockley**, near **Guildford**, to become the original settlers of Guilford, Connecticut. Their names are engraved on the memorial window at St. Margaret's. In 1650 Henry Whitfield returned to England to work in a position in the newly empowered Puritan church under Oliver Cromwell. He died in 1657 and is buried in **Winchester Cathedral**. 🍃

Elihu Yale

David Yale was a young man who found the strict Puritan theocracies of New Haven and Massachusetts hard to tolerate. David had sailed to the New World aboard the *Hector* with his stepfather **Theophilius Eaton**, his mother Anne Lloyd Yale Eaton, and his three siblings. In 1638 they were part of the group that founded New Haven, Connecticut, but in 1641 David moved from New Haven to Boston. His son Elihu was born in Boston on 15 April 1649. In 1652 David took his wife and children back to the Yale family home in Wales and then to London, where he became a prosperous merchant. His son Elihu entered the service of the **East India Company** and went to India with the company in 1671, staying there for twenty-seven years. He was one of the governors of Madras who got into trouble because of their private trading – but only after they had amassed fortunes! Generous with the wealth he accumulated, Elihu Yale considered donating his money to a college at Oxford, but instead, in 1718 he donated a gift worth £1,162 and a book collection to the Collegiate School of Connecticut in Saybrook, Connecticut. The school subsequently moved to New Haven and was eventually renamed **Yale College** in his honor. 🌱

RHODE ISLAND
Roger Williams

Growing up in the Holborn district of London, near the great Smithfield plain, where fairs were held and religious dissenters were burned at the stake, Roger Williams was educated at **Charterhouse**, where the governors included the Archbishop of Canterbury and the Lord Chancellor. Capable students who graduated from the school received a modest allowance enabling them to further their education at **Pembroke College, Cambridge University**. Roger graduated in 1627. He soon became close friends with **John Cotton** and **Thomas Hooker**, two dedicated Puritans. In 1629 Williams met with Cotton and Hooker at **St. Gilbert's Priory, Sempringham, Lincolnshire**, to discuss their plans to set up a colony in America. Williams urged that the colony should separate completely from the Church of England. His suggestion was not accepted.

In 1629 Williams accepted the post of chaplain to Sir William Masham at Otes in Essex. He fell in love with Sir Williams's daughter and proposed marriage, but her parents made it clear he would not be accepted, probably because of their different social levels. Within a few months, Roger had married Mary Barnard, a member of Lady Masham's household, and in 1630 they boarded the ship *Lyon* sailing for New England.

Roger Williams was very assertive in expressing his religious beliefs, and tensions soon developed. He believed the Puritan leaders should express repentance for having been members of the Church of England. He also felt that they were wrong to punish individuals who expressed personal beliefs that didn't follow the official dogma. His denunciation of the law requiring every man to make a contribution to the Church was a serious challenge to the financial support of the Church. He maintained that the land

WALES The Yale Chapel at *St. Tysilio's Church, Bryn Eglwys, Clwyd* is built over the entrance to the family vault.

Elihu Yale died in 1721. The epitaph on his tomb in *St. Giles's Churchyard, Wrexham*, tells the story of his life:
"Born in America, in Europe bred,
In Africa travell'd, and in Asia wed,
Where long he liv'd and thriv'd,
in London dead.
Much good, some ill, he did;
so hope all's even,
And that his soul thro mercy's gone to Heaven.
You that survive and read this tale,
take care
For this most certain exit to prepare:
Where blest in peace,
the actions of the just
Smell sweet, & blossom in
the silent dust."

SUFFOLK Dudley North purchased *Glemham Hall* in *Little Glemham* in March 1708. His wife, Catherine, was the daughter of Elihu Yale. Glemham Hall received many treasures through the generosity of Elihu Yale.

LONDON Roger Williams was born in London about 1603. He was christened at *St. Sepulchre-without-Newgate*.

LONDON In 1611 Thomas Sutton purchased the buildings of the Charterhouse monastery to establish a charitable hospital for eight elderly gentlemen, and a school for forty boys. A plaque commemorates Roger Williams who attended *Charterhouse School*.

ESSEX Roger Williams and Mary Barnard were married at *All Saints' Church* in High Laver on 15 December 1629.

Roger Williams's employer, Sir William Masham, was the son-in-law of **Sir Francis Barrington** of *Barrington Hall, Hatfield Broad Oak*. Lady Barrington was an aunt of Oliver Cromwell.

LINCOLNSHIRE The castle and priory no longer stand in *Sempringham* where the Puritans held an important conference in 1629, but the *Parish Church of St. Andrew* remains.

ESSEX The original *Copford Hall* has disappeared, but the present Hall is the residence of the descendants of **John Haynes**. The house can be seen from the park that surrounds the church.

St. Michael and All Angels, Copford, was the parish church of the Haynes family. It was described by Pevsner as "the most remarkable Norman parish church in the county."

NOTE See Chapter 1 for details of Henry Hudson's voyages of discovery.

belonged to the Indians and that the king had no right to give it away. To Puritan leaders, these were very dangerous opinions. In 1635 Williams was summoned to appear before a court in Boston on a charge of heresy. After the trial, he was ordered to leave the colony.

Roger Williams left Massachusetts in the spring of 1636 and moved further south with a group of followers to start a new colony they called Providence on land granted to them by the Narragansett Indian chiefs. In 1663 the "Royal Charter for the Colony of Rhode Island" was granted by King Charles II. It guaranteed religious freedom in the colony which was established as self-governing, with Benedict Arnold (grandfather of the Revolutionary War general) as governor and Roger Williams as one of his assistants. Roger Williams died in early 1683. 🍃

John Haynes
A life-long friend of **Thomas Hooker**, John Haynes came from *Copford* in **Essex**. He moved to Massachusetts and then Connecticut with him. Haynes was appointed a freeman of Newtown, then an assistant, and then third state governor. He banished **Roger Williams** from the colony. Haynes was the first governor of Connecticut, and was then governor every alternate year for the rest of his life. 🍃

NEW YORK
Henry Hudson
Henry Hudson was the first English explorer to sail up the mighty river that now bears his name, but in 1609 he was sailing for the Dutch East India Company and he claimed the land along the river for Holland. English colonies along the Atlantic coast began encroaching on the Dutch and, by 1664, the English were so powerful that just sailing their warships into the waters near Manhattan was enough to lead the Dutch director general, Peter Stuyvesant, to surrender without firing a shot. The Dutch colony known as New Amsterdam was renamed New York, after the lord high admiral, James, Duke of York, who later became King James II. 🍃

Queen Anne and the Indians
King James's daughter, Queen Mary II, supported Protestant emigration from France, after King Louis XIV revoked the Edict of Nantes in 1685, forcing the Huguenots to leave his country. During Anne's reign thousands of people from the Palatine area of western Germany fled to the Protestant countries of Holland, Sweden, and England. In London the number of refugees making their way across the Channel kept growing and the British government tried to deal with

the situation by turning back new arrivals when it could. Large encampments formed at **Blackheath**, Greenwich, Camberwell, Kensington, Tower Ditch, and other areas. About 15,000 people were in these camps. Local conditions grew unhealthy and unsafe. Families were often reduced to begging and working at the worst possible jobs. Local people attacked the refugees, claiming that the foreigners would take their jobs, spread disease or resort to crime.

When a group of these refugees petitioned Queen Anne for permission to sail to the English colonies in America, it seemed a useful way to deal with several problems. It would provide much-needed labor in New York, act as a possible buffer between the French colonies in Canada and the growing English presence in New York, and offer a way to deal with the growing number of refugees. In 1708 Queen Anne sponsored the first group of Palatine immigrants and in October fifty-six colonists sailed aboard the *Globe*. During the next two years several fleets of ships with thousands of refugees sailed for America, sponsored by the British government.

In 1710 Peter Schuyler, the mayor of Albany, New York, brought five chiefs of the Iroquois Confederacy to England. Schuyler thought the visit would impress the Indians with the power and grandeur of Britain, and might encourage the British to give more support to the colonial forces opposing the French in upper New York. Four of the Indian chiefs were presented to Queen Anne at **St. James's Palace**. These Indian chiefs visited the encampment at Blackheath where thousands of Palatine refugees were living. It is said that they were so moved by the conditions of these refugees that they offered to share land in America with them. 🍃

MARYLAND
George Calvert, Lord Baltimore

Educated at **Trinity College, Oxford**, George Calvert became private secretary to Robert Cecil. After Cecil died, Calvert became a clerk to the Privy Council. A favorite of King James I, he was appointed a principal secretary of state in 1619 and was given a manor in Ireland. The king created him Baron Baltimore in the Irish peerage.

In 1620 Calvert purchased a plantation in Newfoundland and went there in 1627 to explore the area. Returning the following year with about forty colonists, it was soon apparent that the cold weather would make a permanent settlement difficult. Calvert traveled south to Virginia, but he was met with hostility because of his Catholic faith. He wrote to Charles I requesting a grant of land in the warmer southern region, and in 1632 the king gave Calvert a new grant in the area now known as Maryland and Delaware. When George

LONDON The group of figures at the base of the statue of Queen Anne in front of *St. Paul's Cathedral* includes an American Indian.

At *Westminster Abbey* there is a memorial to Mr. Henry Warren, a Londoner born in Greenwich, who bought land on Manhattan Island and named the plot Greenwich Village.

YORKSHIRE George Calvert 1st Lord Baltimore was born in 1580 at *Kiplin*. The present *Kiplin Hall* was built in 1620 to designs by Inigo Jones.

LONDON George Calvert was buried at *St. Dunstan-in-the-West, Fleet Street,* in 1632.

Calvert died, his son Cecil Calvert took up the grant and named the area Maryland, in honor of King Charles's queen Henrietta Maria. Lord Baltimore set guidelines for religious tolerance in the colony. Maryland became one of the most tolerant of the American colonies. 🍃

THE CALVERT FAMILY

SURREY The **Woodcote Park** estate in **Epsom** was inherited by Charles 3rd Lord Baltimore, in 1692. Frederick Calvert, 6th Lord Baltimore, was forced to leave Constantinople after being accused of having a private harem. When he died in 1771 he named his thirteen-year-old illegitimate son Henry Harford as his heir. Henry lost all his property holdings in America during the Revolutionary War, but he did make a claim of £400,000 to Parliament for compensation after the war was over. Over the next thirty years he received over £100,000 in compensation, which was the second largest amount awarded by Parliament. Henry Harford inherited a fortune from his father, even without the Maryland property, and he lived a lavish lifestyle. The title of Lord Baltimore, however, ended when his father died.

In 1913 Woodcote Park was purchased by the Royal Automobile Club for use as a golf club. A beautiful drawing room from this mansion was purchased by 1927 and installed in the Museum of Fine Arts at Boston, Massachusetts. The original Woodcote mansion burned down in 1934 and was replaced with a new building that reproduces some of the features of the original house.

LONDON In 1995 several groups from Maryland sponsored the creation of a memorial to Cecil Calvert, 2nd Lord Baltimore who had lain in an unmarked grave in **St. Giles-in-the-Fields** for over 250 years. On 7 May 1996 *Pride II*'s captain and crew brought a 250lb memorial in a procession through the streets of London to the church. The memorial itself was carved by a Baltimore stonemason and surrounded with white marble from the steps of Baltimore rowhouses.

The Maryland State flag is the only one of the US state flags to be based on ancient English heraldry. The coat of arms adopted by **George Calvert**, the 1st Lord Baltimore, included a shield that combined the yellow and black colors of his paternal family and the red and white colors of his maternal family, the Crosslands.

KENT *Knole* in *Sevenoaks* is the seat of the Sackville-West family. In 1813 Elizabeth Sackville, sister of the 4th Duke of Dorset, married George John West, 5th Earl De la Warr, and combined the Sackville and West family names.

DELAWARE

The State of Delaware was named after **Thomas West, Lord De La Warr**, governor of Virginia. In 1610 **Captain Samuel Argall**, from the Jamestown Colony, was seeking shelter from a storm and sailed into a large bay north of Virginia. He named the bay after the first governor of Virginia governor, and later the river and then the state took the name (*see page 33 above*). 🍃

PENNSYLVANIA
William Penn

William Penn was not just a wealthy young man who got involved with a religious sect that was unacceptable to his father. William grew up during a stormy time of religious and political revolution in England and was involved in some of the most important religious, political, and legal developments of his time.

Much of young William's childhood was spent in Wanstead, Essex, while his father was away with the navy. William Penn entered **Christ Church, Oxford**, but was expelled because he refused to conform to Anglican beliefs. At Oxford, William met members of the Society of Friends (the Quakers), who were pacifists. He became active in their political battles for freedom of religion, freedom of assembly, and the right of trial by jury. When his beliefs led William into conflict with the authorities, his father tried to keep him away from trouble by sending him to France, hoping he would abandon his religious beliefs. While traveling in Europe, William met **Algernon Sidney** who became a close personal friend. Sidney influenced the liberal scheme of government and law that Penn later developed for the Pennsylvania Colony.

In 1667 William was part of a Quaker congregation that was arrested and jailed on a charge of riot. In 1668 he was in trouble again for writing *The Sandy Foundation Shaken* which was seen as an attack on the Church of England. He was given a life sentence for "crimes against the Crown and Christianity," which resulted in his imprisonment in the **Tower of London**. William was released after serving only a few months of the sentence, probably through his father's intervention. However, in 1671, the younger Penn, now a devout Quaker, was sent to **Newgate Prison** for six months after being convicted of holding an "unlawful, seditious and riotous assembly." Penn's crime had been to lead a service of prayer in the street when he arrived at the Quaker meeting house and found it locked by soldiers. His trial had an important impact on the course of British legal history. When the jury in his trial voted to acquit Penn, the judge kept them locked up without food, water or heat, until they voted to convict. On appeal, Chief Justice Vaughan upheld the right of juries to reach a verdict without pressure or interference. William Penn's trial set the legal precedent that a jury could not be forced to bring in a pre-determined verdict.

Admiral Penn loaned a large amount of money to the king and, on his death, this debt was owed to his son. William proposed to the king's council that he be granted land on the Atlantic seacoast in lieu of the monies owed. King Charles II probably thought he had found a way to get rid of this young Quaker nuisance, so out of "regard to the memorie and meritts of his late father," gave the younger Penn a huge tract of land in North America. William thought

LONDON William Penn was born at Tower Hill and was baptized on 24 October 1644 at the church of *All Hallows by the Tower*.

William Penn plaque,
All Hallows by the Tower

LONDON The original *Newgate Prison* was built around 1188 by King Henry II. It became infamous as a filthy, chaotic place of detention where people were held before their trials. It was also where the condemned were held before being executed. The prison was finally closed and demolished in 1902, and the new *Central Criminal Court* was built on the site.

Pepys Garden is on the site where Admiral Penn and Samuel Pepys lived on *Seething Lane* in the 1660s. The great English diarist of the seventeenth century, Pepys worked in the Naval Office with Admiral Penn and mentions the young William in his diaries.

BUCKINGHAMSHIRE William Penn is buried next to both of his wives in the Quaker burial ground at *Jordans*.

LONDON *Czar Street* in *Deptford* is near the location of John Evelyn's house Sayes Court. The name commemorates the time when Peter the Great spent several months as Evelyn's house guest. A group of statues on at *Greenwich Quay, Deptford* also commemorates the tsar's visit.

of naming the colony "New Wales" or "Sylvania." The king intervened and named it, in honor of the admiral, "Pennsilvania," or Penn's Woods. Governor William Penn did not actually live in his colony for very long. He traveled to North America in 1682 and stayed for two years. He returned to his colony in 1699 for another two years.

One unusual relationship William Penn had was with Peter the Great, tsar of Russia. As a young man Peter the Great traveled to Europe and stayed in London for four months in 1697–8, living near Greenwich in the house of John Evelyn. During this time he visited the Friends Meeting House in Deptford, where he discussed religion with the Quaker William Penn on several occasions. One can only wonder how different the world would be today if William Penn had convinced the great Russian tsar to become a Quaker! 🍃

George Fox

A devoutly religious young man, George Fox began work as an apprentice shoemaker and shepherd, but was soon wandering the countryside preaching outdoors. He could stand for hours shouting his message criticizing social

PLACES WITH WILLIAM PENN CONNECTIONS

SOMERSET The Penn family was originally from the west of England. William Penn's grandfather, Giles Penn (1570/80–1641) was a prosperous merchant. With his brother William he carried on trade in far-flung areas. He died in Fez, Morocco. In 1636 he was involved in a raid on the Barbary pirates to rescue English captives, a dramatic raid that greatly boosted his naval career. The captain of this raid was **George Carteret** of Jersey. Thirty years later Carteret and John, Lord Berkeley were the proprietors of the colony of New Jersey. Interestingly, Giles's grandson, William Penn, was a member of the group that bought this land from Carteret's widow. And there was another coincidence associated with that naval raid. The vice admiral of the fleet was John Pennington; his cousin Isaac Pennington had a step-granddaughter, Gulielma Springett, who became William Penn's first wife. Isaac Pennington died in the Tower of London in 1661, as a result of his participation in the trail of King Charles I.

BRISTOL Giles Penn was married at the church of **St. Mary Redcliffe** in 1600. Admiral Penn was baptized at the church on 23 April 1621 and was buried at St. Mary's in 1670. Admiral William Penn's memorial at St. Mary Redcliffe contains his armor.

William Penn often visited Bristol, the home of his second wife, Hannah Callowhill. There is a statue of William Penn in **Millennium Square**.

ESSEX As a boy William Penn attended Bishop Harsnett's School in **Chigwell** (now **Chigwell School**.)

OXFORD William Penn studied at **Christ Church**. His portrait now hangs in the College Hall.

HERTFORDSHIRE A memorial plaque notes that William Penn and his first wife, Gulielma Marie Springett, lived at **Basing House, Watersmeet, High Street, Rickmansworth**, for five years. The stone above the tablet is from Pennsbury, Pennsylvania, the ancient home of William Penn on the Delaware River. The **Three Rivers Museum** at Basing House has exhibits about William Penn.

The Pennsylvanian pub on the **High Street** in **Rickmansworth** illustrates the town's connection with the famous Quaker leader.

SOMERSET A plaque on the front of the **Crown Hotel** in **Wells** gives a glimpse into the dangerous times that faced William Penn in 1685. This plaque was presented by Michael Fentum and unveiled by Thatcher Longstreth in June 1979.

LONDON In 1665 William Penn entered **Lincoln's Inn** to study law.

In March 1686 William Penn rented rooms in **Holland House** in **Kensington** to be near the court at **Kensington Palace**. Every day hundreds of petitioners would stand outside the house petitioning Penn, hoping he could help them by intervening with King James II to ease religious repression against Quakers.

BUCKINGHAMSHIRE The seventeenth-century farmhouse of **Old Jordans** at **Jordans** near Beaconsfield was home to an early Friends meeting house. William Penn attended Quaker meetings here. He died on 30 July 1718, at the age of seventy-three, and was buried in the Quaker cemetery. On the site is the "Mayflower Barn," reportedly built from timbers of the dismantled *Mayflower*. Legend says it was sold and taken apart when its sailing days were over, and used to build this barn.

The **Crown Inn** in **Penn** is a wonderful creeper-clad seventeenth-century inn that was originally built by the Penn family, relatives of William Penn.

In 1760 the Stoke Manor estate was purchased by Thomas Penn, the son of William Penn, when he moved to England after the Penn family left Pennsylvania, where they were very unpopular for levying taxes that were considered unfair. Thomas tore down part of the dilapidated structure and remodeled it between 1792 and 1808, paying for it with the compensation he received from the new Commonwealth for the loss of his family's lands in Pennsylvania following the American Revolution. The Penn family owned Stoke Park until 1848.
Part of the historic parkland of the estate, designed by Capability Brown and Humphrey Repton, is now the home of **Stoke Park Golf Club**.

DORSET John Penn, grandson of William Penn, was governor of the **Island of Portland** for some time in the late 1700s. In 1800 he built **Pennsylvania Castle** on the Island of Portland on land given to him by **King George III**. The castle was a hotel in the 1980s but was sold and converted into a private home.

WARWICKSHIRE George Fox was born in July 1624 at Drayton-in-the-Clay, now called *Fenny Drayton*, and baptized at *St. Michael and All Angels,* which had a Puritan congregation.

LANCASHIRE As a result of the vision George Fox had on *Pendle Hill* the Friends ("Quaker") movement was formed. NOTE: Pendle Hill is also now the name of a Quaker educational and conference center established in 1930 in Wallingford, near Swarthmore, about eleven miles outside of Philadelphia, Pennsylvania.

CUMBRIA *Swarthmoor Hall* in *Ulverston* was the home of Judge Fell and his wife Margaret.

LONDON George Fox died in London in 1691 and is buried at the Dissenters' burial ground, *Bunhill Fields, City Road.*

CUMBRIA The Quaker Tapestry at the *Friends Meeting House* in *Stramongate, Kendal,* is a celebration of 350 years of Quaker insights and experiences embroidered in seventy-seven panels of specially woven wool cloth. Many of the panels include people, places, and events connected with American history.

injustices and religious practices. He was jailed many times for disturbing the peace, encouraging people not to attend Anglican church services and encouraging them to refuse to pay tithes to the Church. In 1650 Fox told Judge Bennett that the judge should "quake before the word of the Lord." This led to his followers being called "Quakers," a term which they considered derogatory. They came to be called "The Society of Friends."

During the Civil War, Fox was jailed for refusing to take arms. In 1652 he had a vision on Pendel Hill that inspired him to preach a gospel of brotherly love. When he wasn't in prison, he traveled the countryside preaching his religious vision and building a large group of followers. In 1652 Fox first visited **Swarthmoor Hall**, which became an important meeting place for the Friends.

By 1660 Fox had made more than 20,000 converts and had missionaries in Ireland, Scotland, Wales, and the American colonies. He sailed for Barbados in 1671 and visited the colonies of Maryland, New Jersey, and New England, to preach his message. One of his most ardent supporters was **William Penn**, who heard Fox preach at Oxford and in Ireland. When King Charles II gave William Penn a grant of a huge track of land in the colonies, Penn extended an invitation to Europe's religiously persecuted people to come to Pennsylvania, which he called the "Holy Experiment." Many members of the Society of Friends came from England, Scotland, Ireland, and Wales. They had a lasting impact on the new colony, teaching tolerance and the respect for individual conscience and beliefs. 🍃

CAROLINA

King Charles I was defeated in the English Civil War and executed on 30 January 1649. In 1660 his son returned from exile and was crowned as Charles II. He was generous to those who had been loyal to the royal cause.

Although there had been a grant of the Province of Carolina to Sir Robert Heath in 1629, no real effort had been made to settle the colony, and after the restoration of the monarchy, King Charles II declared the initial patent void. He made several new grants of land in America to those who had shown loyalty to the monarchy during the Civil War and the Commonwealth period. In 1663 and 1665 the king granted the proprietorship of Carolina to eight royal supporters:

1. **Edward Hyde, 1st Earl of Clarendon** (Lord High Chancellor)
2. **George Monck, Duke of Albemarle** (Master of the King's Horse and captain general of all his forces)
3. **William Lord Craven** (an old friend of the king's father)
4. **John Lord Berkeley**

5. **Anthony Ashley Cooper** (Lord Chancellor and later made 1st Earl of Shaftesbury)
6. **Sir George Carteret** (Vice-Chamberlain of the Household)
7. **Sir William Berkeley** (who, as governor of Virginia, encouraged the colony to remain loyal to Charles II during the Commonwealth period)
8. **Sir John Colleton** (who supported the royal cause in Barbados).

These busy English politicians were focused on affairs at home rather than on their colony in America. Of the original board of proprietors, several died within a few years – John Colleton in 1666, Albemarle in 1669, and Clarendon in 1674. John Berkeley took no interest in the colony after the first five years. For a few years, **Ashley Cooper**, Lord Shaftesbury, took a personal interest in developing the colony, but as his concerns in England demanded his attention, his involvement in the colony lessened. 🍃

Anthony Ashley Cooper

As a young man who had inherited baronetcies when his father died early, Anthony Ashley Cooper was raised by relatives and educated by Puritan tutors. At the beginning of his political career he was elected to the Short Parliament. But Ashley Cooper was a man whose affiliations shifted from one side to the other during the English Civil War and afterwards. Initially he supported the king, not too surprising for a man whose father-in-law was the king's Lord Keeper in Coventry. However, his royalist affiliation was weakened by personal doubts about the abilities of Charles I. Cooper eventually switched sides to support the Parliamentarians in 1644, and was later a member of the Council of State for Oliver Cromwell. Ashley Cooper supported the restoration of the monarchy under King Charles II; elevated as Lord Ashley, he became a member of the "Cabal," a secret behind-the-scenes group of advisors to the king. The group was named for the lords who were part of it: Clifford, Arlington, Buckingham, Ashley, and Lauderdale.

Of all the proprietors of Carolina, only Ashley Cooper showed much interest in the early development of the colony. His name is remembered in two rivers in South Carolina – the Ashley and the Cooper. He was also very busy with affairs in England. In 1672 he became Lord Chancellor and was elevated to Earl of Shaftesbury. Because Charles II had no legitimate heir, his illegitimate son, the Duke of Monmouth, made an attempt to be recognized as the heir to the throne, in place of the king's Catholic brother, James, Duke of York. Shaftesbury supported the Duke of Monmouth

LONDON The names of the "lord proprietors" of Carolina are still prominent in Mayfair and along the Strand in London: *Albemarle Street, Clarges Street, Clarendon Street, Craven Street,* and *Shaftesbury Avenue. Berkeley Square, Bruton Place,* and *Stratton Street* are related to the Berkeley family.

LONDON *Shaftesbury Avenue* begins at Piccadilly Circus and heads east through the theater district of London. The statue of Eros at Piccadilly Circus can be seen as a pun on Anthony Ashley Cooper's title of Lord Shaftesbury – the shaft of love has been released from Eros' bow and is buried near Shaftesbury Avenue.

OXFORD Ashley Anthony Cooper attended *Exeter College* but left after being involved in a student riot.

NOTE Another Anthony Ashley Cooper, the 10th Earl of Shaftesbury, was in the news recently. The playboy earl disappeared in Europe in 2004. After his mutilated body was discovered in the French Alps, the brother of the earl's third wife was arrested and accused of his murder. The earl's eldest son, also named Anthony, became the 11th earl, but only a few months later the twenty-seven-year-old aristocrat died suddenly of a heart attack. His younger brother, Nicholas Ashley Cooper, who was working as a DJ and music promoter in New York, became the 12th Earl of Shaftesbury in May 2005.

The *Duke of Albemarle* pub,
6 *Stafford Street, London*

LONDON In Mayfair, *Clarges Street* was named for George Monck's wife Anne Clarges.

LONDON In the 1730s the successors to the Earl of Craven bought a small estate in the area north of Kensington Gardens in order to move the pest house he had built in Soho after the Great Plague of 1665. *Craven Street* and *Craven Hill* are reminders of Lord Craven, a royal proprietor of Carolina.

and was charged with high treason. These charges were later withdrawn, but in 1682 Shaftesbury fled to Holland, and died the next year. 🍃

George Monck

Beginning his military career supporting King Charles I, George Monck fought on the Royalist side at the beginning of the English Civil War. He was captured at the Battle of Nantwich in 1644. For a time he was held prisoner in the **Tower of London**. When he was unable to pay for any living comforts in the Tower, King Charles sent him a well-appreciated gift of 100 pounds with which he managed to improve his situation. Cromwell's Parliament offered Monck the opportunity to resume his military career by going to help quash the Irish rebellion.

After Oliver Cromwell's death in 1658 Monck at, first, supported his son Richard, but at the same time he was communicating with supporters of Charles II. He played an important role in the return of Charles II by working to bring about the dissolution of Parliament and the calling of a more Royalist-oriented Parliament. His strategy of working with both sides was rewarded when he was named a Knight of the Garter, Master of the Horse, and commander in chief by the king who then gave him the titles of Baron Monck, Earl of Torrington and Duke of Albemarle. In 1663 he was one of the "lord proprietors" granted rights in the Province of Carolina. He remained a naval commander; his last battle was in 1667 when he helped in the defense of Chatham when the Dutch fleet sailed up the Thames. Monck died on 3 January 1670, "like a Roman General with all his officers around him." 🍃

William, 1st Earl of Craven

One of the richest men in England, William, 1st Earl of Craven was a loyal supporter of the monarchy. In 1663 he was named as one of the proprietors of the Colony of Carolina. Lord Craven was particularly devoted to Elizabeth, daughter of King James I. In 1612 she married Frederick, Elector Palatine, who was offered the crown of Bohemia after the Diet of Bohemia deposed the Roman Catholic king. Craven was wounded several times fighting in support of Frederick, who was defeated in 1620. After Frederick died in 1632, Elizabeth continued to live in Holland until 1660 when her nephew was invited to return to England as King Charles II. Craven was still devoted to Elizabeth. There is speculation that he built his mansion at **Hamstead Marshall** in the style of Heidelberg Castle as a home for the "Winter Queen." Unfortunately, she died before the mansion was completed.

Ashdown Park in *Berkshire* was built in the early 1660s, reportedly when the earl was fleeing the plague in London. The house was constructed in the style of the palatial homes of Holland where Elizabeth lived for many years. 🍂

Edward Hyde, 1st Earl of Clarendon

Edward Hyde was an MP before the English Civil War, but he was a moderate critic of King Charles I. He gradually changed his position and by 1641 was an informal advisor to the king. He was made guardian to Charles, Prince of Wales, and fled with him to Jersey in 1646. In the latter years of the exile, Hyde became a close advisor to Charles II, who named him Lord Chancellor in 1658. When the monarchy was restored, Charles raised Edward Hyde to the peerage as Lord Hyde of Hindon, and then created him Earl of Clarendon. In 1660 his daughter Anne Hyde married Charles's younger brother, James, Duke of York. They had two daughters, Anne and Mary, who became successive queens of England after James was forced from the throne in 1689. In 1663 Hyde was named one of the lord proprietors of the Carolina Colony. Unfortunately his political success came to an end in 1667 after the Dutch victories in the Second Anglo-Dutch War. Blamed for financial failures brought on by the war, he fled to exile in France and died in Rouen on 9 December 1674. 🍂

George Carteret

From a ruling family on the Isle of Jersey, George Carteret was a loyal supporter of King James I and his sons. He was rewarded with large land grants in Carolina and the present New Jersey. In 1729 the descendants of the other original proprietors agreed to sell their claims back to the Crown, but George Carteret's grandson John Carteret refused. As a result he gave up the right to participate in government. His share of the colony was defined as a sixty-mile-wide strip in North Carolina, adjoining the Virginia boundary; this became known as the Granville District.

Several of the proprietors of Carolina received other grants of land in America. The Berkeley family and George Carteret were early proprietors of areas that became the American states of New Jersey and New York. 🍂

NEW JERSEY

The **Berkeley family** was closely tied to the fortunes of the monarch before and after the English Civil War. They had a powerful position in the English court, having been lords of the manor of Bruton in Somerset for at least 200 years. Before the Civil War Sir John Berkeley was a loyal supporter of the monarch and entertained King Charles I in his home.

BERKSHIRE *Ashdown Park* near *Lambourn* remained in the Craven family until 1956 when it was given to the National Trust.

The Craven mansion at *Hamstead Marshall* was destroyed by fire in 1718 and partially rebuilt. The original mansion was demolished in 1813 and the Craven family sold the property in 1984.

LONDON Excavations at *Brown's Hotel* on *Albemarle Street* have found part of the foundations of Clarendon House, built in 1666 and demolished in the 1680s. The Clarendon Room is named for this connection.

Hyde died in France; later his body was returned to England and was buried in *Westminster Abbey*, where a tomb was built in honor of the grandfather of two queens.

SOMERSET *St. Mary's Church* in *Bruton* has a memorial to Sir Maurice Berkeley, ancestor of George, William, and John Berkeley. The church also has a Bruton Chapel, built in 1749 by Sir Charles Berkeley.

GLOUCESTERSHIRE *Berkeley Castle*, the hereditary seat of the **Berkeley family**, was built by Lord Maurice de Berkeley in 1153. For nearly 1,000 years, twenty-five generations of Berkeleys have commanded this ancient site.

LONDON **William Berkeley**, colonial governor of Virginia, was buried in 1677 at the *Church of St. Mary the Virgin* in *Twickenham*. John, Lord Berkeley, who, along with George Carteret, received the royal grant for New Jersey from King Charles II, was buried at the same church in 1678.

In 1696 John Berkeley's descendants sold Berkeley House to the 1st Duke of Devonshire who built a huge city mansion – *Devonshire House*. The site is just across from today's Ritz Hotel.

BEDFORDSHIRE In 1667 **George Carteret** purchased *Haynes Park Manor* in *Haynes Church End*.

He fought for the king and led a successful military campaign in the southwest of England. In 1643 he was named commander in chief of the Royalist forces in Devonshire and governor of the city of Exeter. King Charles I sent his pregnant queen to stay in Exeter under Berkeley's protection. Unfortunately the Royalist forces were defeated at Exeter, and the city surrendered to Sir Thomas Fairfax. Lord Berkeley was part of the escort that accompanied Queen Henrietta Maria, and several of the royal children to France. He was also part of an unsuccessful attempt to free King Charles I from his captivity at Hampton Court.

During the Commonwealth period, John Berkeley stayed on the Continent as a professional soldier. He fought against the Spanish in Flanders, but when the Duke of York became an ally of the Spanish John switched and fought for them. In 1660, when Prince Charles was invited to return to England and the monarchy was restored, John Berkeley returned also, and was granted high office. Berkeley served as Lord Lieutenant of Ireland from 1670 to 1672.

The Berkeley family received many honors from King Charles II. The oldest brother, George, who inherited the title Baron Berkeley, was elevated to earl. John Berkeley was given land in Piccadilly, London, on which a great family house was built. The second brother, William, was named governor of Virginia by Charles I in 1641, succeeding Francis Wyatt.

Charles II gave his brother James, Duke of York (later King James II), a grant of land in America. Later James divided his grant, keeping the northern part for himself. This area later became New York. In June 1664 James signed documents that granted land west and south of a line on the Delaware River to two proprietors, John, Lord Berkeley and **George Carteret**. The grant was partly given to compensate for debts James owed. The area was named New Caesaria (New Jersey) after Carteret's home – the Isle of Jersey. In 1674 Lord Berkeley sold his share to John Fenwick, a Puritan.

George Carteret was born around 1610 into one of the ruling families of the island of Jersey. During the English Civil War, Jersey was initially divided between Royalists and Parliamentarians. After the death of George's uncle, Philippe de Carteret, lieutenant governor of Jersey, during a siege of the Parliamentarians at Elizabeth Castle, George led the retaking of the island for the Royalists. To raise funds, George turned to capturing "enemy shipping" – including ships owned by the Parliamentarians. His piracy was legitimized when King James I made Carteret vice admiral of the Channel Islands. The king's son Charles arrived in Jersey with 300 retainers in 1646 and stayed at Elizabeth Castle for ten weeks. After the execution of King James I, Jersey was the first place to proclaim Charles II as the new king.

George Carteret continued to be close to Charles, and when the king entered London on the day before his coronation in 1660, Carteret was with him. His loyalty was rewarded by the king in 1663 when he was named as one of the proprietors of the Carolina Colony. In 1664 Carteret received part of the large grant of land in the northern colony that became New Jersey. After his death in 1680, Carteret's land in East Jersey was auctioned off to a group of twelve men, one of whom was **William Penn**. 🍂

GEORGIA
James Oglethorpe

James Oglethorpe was born in London on 21 December 1698. He studied at Oxford for a short time, and entered the army around 1714. In 1722 he was elected to Parliament for Hazlemere, a constituency he continued to represent for thirty-two years. Soon he focused his attention on the terrible conditions people faced in debtors' prisons. Oglethorpe proposed the creation of a colony that would offer these people a way to have a new start in life. A new southern colony was also seen as a potential buffer between the Carolina colonies and the Spanish colonies in Florida.

In 1732 King George II granted Oglethorpe and a group of twenty other people the land between the Savannah and Altamaha Rivers. The colony was named Georgia in honor of the king. In January 1733 James Oglethorpe and thirty-five families (about 150 people) arrived in Charleston, South Carolina. They explored the Savannah River and settled on a site known as the Yamacraw Bluff, laying the foundations for the city of Savannah. In April 1734 Oglethorpe returned to England, bringing with him ten members of the Yamacraw tribe, including the chief Tomochichi, his wife Scanauki and his nephew Toonahowi. They stayed at Oglethorpe's family home **Westbrook** in **Godalming** for about four months, and visited Whitehall and **Eton College**, where Tomochichi gave a speech. On 1 August 1734 the Indians were presented to King George II and Queen Caroline at **Kensington Palace**.

New settlers were arriving in Georgia, including 150 Scottish Highlanders sent to protect the colonists. Joining the Georgia settlement were also a group of German Protestants who had fled religious persecution in Europe and were living in England. Oglethorpe appealed to the government for more money to support the new colony, but the amount they granted was quite inadequate, so he was forced to mortgage his home, Westbrook, to raise funds. The money was eventually repaid, but the mortgage of the house contributed significantly towards the survival of the colony.

BERKSHIRE George Carteret had a country residence at *Cranbourne Lodge* in *Windsor Great Park*.

WILTSHIRE John Carteret's daughter, Sophia, married **William Petty, 2nd Earl of Shelburne**, who became 1st Marquess of Lansdowne, the prime minister who negotiated the Treaty of Paris at the end of the American Revolution. She is buried at *Bowood* in *Calne*.

SURREY In 1688 Sir Theophilius Oglethorpe purchased *Westbrook Manor* in *Godalming*. Theophilius and his wife Eleanor were close to King Charles's brother James, who later became King James II. Theophilius accompanied James when he went into exile in France, and then returned to Westbrook in supposed retirement. Theophilius was secretly part of a campaign to support James as "the king across the water." An arrest warrant was issued. When he was captured, he was given a lenient punishment and returned to Godalming. He swore allegiance to King William III. A few months later his ninth child was born, a son who was named **James Edward Oglethorpe**.

LONDON On 23 December 1696 James Oglethorpe was christened at *St. Martin-in-the-Fields* by the Archbishop of Canterbury.

BERKSHIRE James Oglethorpe attended *Eton College* and in 1731 he received an an MA from *Corpus Christi College, Oxford*.

LONDON On 15 September 1744, in the King Henry VII Chapel in *Westminster Abbey*, Oglethorpe married Lady Elizabeth Wright, the only daughter of Sir Nathan Wright, and heiress of *Cranham Hall* in the village of *Cranham, Essex.*

LONDON There is a memorial to Sir James Wright, the last royal governor of Georgia at *St. Margaret's, Westminster.*

John Wesley outside St. Paul's Cathedral, London

James Oglethorpe lived in Georgia for nine years. When he returned to England in July 1743, he faced legal charges brought against him by unhappy colonists. At his trial his name was cleared, and he was able to repay the mortgage on his home, Westbrook. He also married an English heiress, Elizabeth Wright, and they spent their honeymoon at Westbrook, attended by a Chickasaw Indian chief who had come to England with Oglethorpe. 🍃

John and Charles Wesley

John and Charles Wesley, the founders of Methodism, went to Georgia in order to spread their Christian message to both the colonists and the Indians. They sailed from Gravesend aboard the *Simmonds* in October 1735 with their father's good friend, **James Oglethorpe**. Charles Wesley served as Oglethorpe's secretary for Indian affairs for a while. The two brothers found life in the southern colony very difficult. Accusations of scandal disillusioned Charles, who returned to England in December 1736. John stayed on for another year, but also became discouraged and returned to England. Their theological beliefs and practices developed into the Methodist church which became an important Protestant denomination in the United States. 🍃

PLACES ASSOCIATED WITH
JAMES OGLETHORPE

SURREY Westbrook Chapel in the **Church of St. Peter and Paul** in **Godalming** is named for the Oglethorpe family home. Several family members are buried here. A plaque and flag from the State of Georgia were presented on the 250th anniversary of the founding of Georgia, and a chandelier was presented by the people of Georgia in 1992 on the 300th anniversary of James Oglethorpe's birth.

The Yamacraw who came to England with Oglethorpe in 1734, including Chief Tomochichi, his wife Scanauki, and his nephew Toonahowi, stayed at Oglethorpe's family home **Westbrook** in **Godalming**, for about four months, and visited Whitehall and Eton.

The **Godalming Museum** has a number of exhibits about the life and career of James Oglethorpe.

ESSEX For the last forty years of his life, James Oglethorpe lived at **Cranham Hall** in **Cranham**, the family home of his wife Elizabeth Wright. Oglethorpe was buried in a vault under the chancel floor at **All Saints' Church, Cranham**. In 1993 there was a special ceremony in the church when representatives of Oglethorpe University in Atlanta, Georgia read a proclamation and placed flowers on the tomb.

LOCATIONS WITH
JOHN WESLEY CONNECTIONS

LONDON

John Wesley's statue is in front of **Wesley's Chapel**. The "Cathedral of World Methodism" was built in 1778. Designed by the famous architect, George Dance the Younger, the original pillars supporting the gallery were ships' masts from the naval dockyard at Deptford, a gift from King George III. They were replaced in 1891 by the present pillars of French jasper, a gift from various Methodist churches overseas.

At **Nettleton Court, Aldersgate Street** (near the entrance to the Museum of London) is John Wesley's Conversion Place Memorial ('The Aldersgate Flame') – a modern bronze sculpture with a facsimile of Wesley's journal for 24 May 1738.

A small pulpit at **St. Giles-in-the-Fields** has the inscription, "From this pulpit, formerly in West Street Chapel in this parish, John and Charles Wesley preached regularly during the years 1743–1791."

St. Giles Cripplegate is an ancient church from which Samuel Annesley (grandfather of John and Charles Wesley) was expelled for Nonconformism in 1662.

There is a blue plaque on the building at **24 West Street** near **Cambridge Circus** where John Wesley had his first Methodist chapel.

Charles Wesley died on 29 March 1788 and was buried, as he had requested, in the churchyard of **St. Marylebone Parish Church**. In the memorial garden next to the church there is an obelisk in memory of Charles, his wife Sarah, and their two sons.
Charles lived and died in nearby Great Chesterfield Street (now **Wheatley Street**) where the site is marked by a plaque on the King's Head public house.

John and Charles Wesley were members of the **Fetter Lane Moravian Church**. However, they eventually split with it because of disagreements over theological issues, and went on to found the Methodist church. The Fetter Lane Moravian Church is now located in Chelsea.

YORKSHIRE

John Wesley was born at the **Old Rectory** in **Epworth** in 1703. The house was rebuilt in 1709 after a fire. Americans financed much of the restoration. Samuel Wesley, father of John and Charles Wesley, was rector of **St. Andrew's Church** in **Epworth** from 1695 to 1735. After John Wesley was ordained, he served as curate here for a while, but later his religious beliefs came into conflict with the established church, and he was denied access to the church, and he famously stood on his father's tomb and preached.

The **Wesley Memorial Church** in **Epworth** was built in 1888–9 as a memorial to the Wesley brothers. It provides services and programmes for the local community and information for visitors.

Epworth's market cross was another early pulpit used by John Wesley.

John Wesley visited **Sheffield** frequently. He first preached in Sheffield in June 1742 and his final visit was in July 1788 at the age of eighty-five.

John Wesley preached many times in **Paradise Square**, a lovely Georgian square. A plaque commemorates the most memorable occasion, 15 July 1779, when he recorded in his journal: "I preached in Paradise Square, Sheffield, to the largest congregation I ever saw on a weekday."

A stained-glass window in the chapter house of **Sheffield Cathedral** depicts John Wesley preaching in Paradise Square. In the cathedral you can also see the desk which he used while preaching.

OXFORD
John Wesley became a fellow at **Lincoln College** in 1726. He began to meet with a group of like-minded individuals, forming what became known as a "Holy Club." In 1732 the term "Methodists" was first used to describe these men meeting in Oxford – it reflected the method and order of their lives.

BRISTOL
John Wesley built the very first Methodist chapel, **The New Room**, in Bristol in 1739. It was here that John Wesley chose Francis Asbury to be the first Methodist missionary to go to the New World. Charles Wesley chose to settle in Bristol and it was here that he wrote many of his hymns, such as "Love Divine All Loves Excelling" and "Hark the Herald Angels Sing."

COUNTY DURHAM
The **Methodist Chapel** in **Newbiggin-in-Teesdale** is believed to be the oldest Methodist chapel in the world in continuous use, from 1759. There is a display of local history and Methodism, including a pulpit that John Wesley used. The **Wesley Manse** is nearby.

CHAPTER 3
AMERICAN INDEPENDENCE

For a period of 160 years, the English colonies in America
remained part of the expanding British Empire. Over the years
the various colonies were administered in a variety of ways –
as royal colonies, private proprietorships, and self-governing
colonies. There was even a penal colony. The colonies
coalesced into thirteen geographical entities spread across a
vast land. They did not look to each other for support or
decisions about government or economy – they were all
subjects of the British monarch and were under the control of
Parliament. However, this was to change in the 1770s.

European politics contributed to the American move
towards independence. The Seven Years' War (1756–63) in
Europe was based on the rivalry between Britain and France to
control overseas colonies. This competition led to a series of
"French and Indian Wars" in North America. The hostilities
ended in 1763 with the Treaty of Paris. The French ceded
Canada and all its territory east of the Mississippi River to
Britain, and Spain agreed to surrender Florida to Britain. From
these territorial gains, it seemed that Britain had won the war,
but there were many unanticipated consequences.

The British economy was seriously strained by the long
struggle. British leaders felt that special colonial taxes were
enitrely justified by the high cost of years of fighting and the
continued need to keep a large military presence in North
America. Colonial merchants felt they were being financially
disadvantaged by taxation and trade regulations. They also felt
they were given no voice in the government that was
controlling their lives and economy. The British government's
responses to the concerns and complaints from their
American colonies seemed only to create more problems.

Despite efforts on both sides of the Atlantic to mediate
the tensions, war broke out. Military action united the
thirteen disparate colonies. Six years of bloody fighting
between cousins ended with the Battle of Yorktown in 1781.
The formal end of the war, the Treaty of Paris of 1783, created
a new nation – the United States of America. 🍃

Algernon Sidney

Algernon Sidney was one of several English political thinkers who greatly influenced the political philosophy of the leaders of the American Revolution. He had a particular influence on the writers of the American Declaration of Independence through his important work *Discourses Concerning Government*. **Thomas Jefferson** said this was one of the most important foundations of his own political thinking.

KENT Completed in 1341, *Penshurst Place* was the family home of **Algernon Sidney**, who was born in 1622.

LONDON Algernon Sidney's mother was Dorothy Percy, daughter of the 9th Earl of Northumberland, whose London home was *Syon Park* in *Brentford*. Algernon's portrait hangs in the corridor just past the print room.

During the English Civil War, Sidney joined the fight for parliamentary government, taking up arms against King Charles I. When Charles II returned to England in 1660 to restore the monarchy, he chose voluntary exile in Europe. During this exile Sidney wrote his famous book. He also befriended the young **William Penn**, whose father had sent him to Europe to distance him from his involvement with religious Nonconformists in England. He was influential in the development of Penn's liberal ideas of government and laws for the Pennsylvania Colony.

After traveling in Europe for nearly twenty years, Sidney returned to England and tried to work towards an independent Parliament under the restored monarchy. In 1681, after King Charles dismissed Parliament in a move to ensure the succession of his Catholic brother, Sidney joined a plot to restore representative government. A group of young aristocrats planned to assassinate King Charles II and his brother James at Rye House in Hertfordshire as they traveled from the horse races at Newmarket back to London. This became known as the Rye House Plot. The royal brothers did not travel as planned and the assassination was never attempted, but the plotters were exposed. Algernon Sidney was convicted on flimsy evidence that amounted to guilt by association and was executed on *Tower Hill* on 7 December 1683.

St. James's Palace, London

LONDON George William Frederick, the son of Frederick, Prince of Wales, was born on 4 June 1738 at *31 St. James's Square*. His grandfather, King George II, had thrown the Prince of Wales out of the family residence at nearby *St. James's Palace*, calling his son Frederick "the greatest ass and greatest liar ... the greatest beast in the world." Frederick rented Norfolk House from the Duke of Norfolk in time for his son to be born.
The music room from Norfolk House has been installed in the *Victoria and Albert Museum*.

King George III

King George III is probably the British monarch who most influenced American history. He became king in 1760 and his long reign lasted sixty years. George III is often called the king who "lost America," but it is probably unfair to place all the blame on him. The British Parliament had grown in power over the previous century. After the Commonwealth period, the restoration of the monarchy in 1660 brought back a king (Charles II), but one with much less control over government policy. In the "Glorious Revolution" of 1689, King James II was forced to leave the throne. William and Mary were invited to come from Holland as joint monarchs. This led to a further decrease in the power of the royal ruler. When Queen Anne died in 1714 without an heir, her distant cousin was invited to come from Hanover to become the English king as George I.

George III was the first Hanoverian king to be born in England and the first to learn English as his native language. During the reigns of George I and George II, Parliament and ministers became accustomed to exercising a significant amount of power in a government headed by kings who did not know the country well and spoke little English. During the first twenty-five years of his reign, George III faced criticism from the Whig Party, which led the government and wanted to prevent the king from increasing his power. George III was more directly interested in government policy than previous Hanoverian kings, and the Whigs didn't like it. The political gamesmanship between the Tories and the Whigs, the king's supporters and those who sympathized with the colonials, played an important part in decisions made over the years leading up to and during the American War for Independence (or American Revolutionary War). 🍃

Charles Townshend

Charles Townshend was Chancellor of the Exchequer in the 1760s. When his political opponents voted for a reduction in the land tax, the unexpected result was significantly lower tax income for the British government. Townshend looked across the Atlantic and came up with a plan to tax goods such as lead, glass, paper, and tea which Britain exported to the colonies. His opponents predicted that it would cost the government dearly. Some even said the taxes would lead to the loss of the colonies! In America the colonists saw the taxes as harsh and even illegal.

The main effect of the Townshend Duties was to unify opposition in several of the colonies, resulting in an effective boycott of British products. Almost no revenue was generated for the British government, and the Sons of Liberty (*see page 92*) gained significant support throughout New England. When the Massachusetts colonial legislature circulated a petition condemning the Townshend Acts and calling for unified colonial resistance, the British government dissolved the Massachusetts General Court. The situation in the colonies was becoming very tense. 🍃

OPPOSITION TO BRITISH POLICY
Lord North and the American Revolution

When George III's father died, his young son came under the influence of his widow's friend, John Stuart, the Earl of Bute. In May 1762 George appointed Bute to be his prime minister, even though he was unpopular, a poor speaker, and

LONDON A statue of King George III in Roman costume stands in the forecourt at *Somerset House* and a statue of George III on horseback stands at the junction of *Cockspur Street* and *Pall Mall East*.

SURREY King George III suffered from debilitating periods of illness when he seemed to be mentally unbalanced. In November 1788 he was kept at a royal cottage at *Kew Gardens* during his illness.

BERKSHIRE King George III died at *Windsor Castle* on 29 January 1820. There is a large statue of the king on the Long Walk at *Windsor Great Park*.

NOTE For a moving portrayal of the unhappy illness of George III, see the film *The Madness of King George*.

NORFOLK In 1619–21 Sir Roger Townshend built an up-to-date *Raynham Hall* at *West Raynham*.

There are a number of Townshend family memorials at *St. Mary the Virgin Church, West Raynham*. The Townshend Society of America contributed towards the restoration of the church and the bells, which were recast at the *Whitechapel Foundry* in *London*.

DORSET The original High Cliff House was built around 1770 by John Stuart, the 3rd Earl of Bute. The present romantic French chateau-style *Highcliffe Castle* was built 1830–4 by his grandson Lord Stuart de Rothesay. **Gordon Selfridge** rented Highcliffe Castle in the 1930s.

OXFORDSHIRE *Wroxton Abbey* became a private home after Henry VIII dissolved the monasteries in 1536. It belonged to the North family from 1668 to 1932. In 1963 Wroxton Abbey was sold to Farleigh Dickinson College of Madison, New Jersey.

All Saints' Church in *Wroxton* has several impressive monuments including an exquisite memorial to **Lord North**, prime minister during the American Revolution.

LONDON The *National Portrait Gallery* has several portraits of **Isaac Barré** and **John Wilkes**. This portrait of Isaac Barré is by Gilbert Stuart (oil on canvas, 1785).

NOTE Wilkes Barre, Pennsylvania, was named in honor of the two Members of Parliament who spoke out in opposition to the government's harsh policies towards the American colonies.

pompous. His ministry lasted less than a year. After a series of short-lived prime ministers, in 1770 George appointed a man who proved to be effective, Frederick North.

As prime minister, North initially took a conciliatory approach to the American colonies; he repealed four out of five of the Townshend Duties, keeping only the one on tea. The British tried reinforcing their troops in Massachusetts, but the increased troop presence led to further tensions. The situation in America reached a combustible level. On 5 March 1770, the day the Townsend Duties were repealed in London, fighting between the British and colonists broke out in Boston. British troops fired on a group of Boston citizens, and "The Boston Massacre" left five or six colonials dead. This seemingly small action gave American "patriots" a rallying point. It seemed that every effort by the British government to deal with the situation in America just led to further strengthening of the colonial opposition.

In 1772 the British decided that judges in the Massachusetts court would be paid by custom-house receipts rather than by the colony, which effectively meant that law in the colony was controlled directly from London. As a result, various colonies set up "committees of correspondence," which were a first step towards the unification of all the American colonies. These committees were first started in Massachusetts and Virginia, inspired by young colonial men like **Arthur Lee** who had studied or lived in London and knew of the Bill of Rights Society and Constitutional Society that had developed with the support of **John Wilkes**. In England, colonial agents like **Benjamin Franklin** were working tirelessly to try to avoid war. There were members of the British government and members of Parliament who also had doubts about the effectiveness of the harsh tax policy. Some members of Parliament became known for their opposition to the government's policies. 🌿

Isaac Barré

Born in Dublin in 1726 and educated at Trinity College, Isaac Barré joined the British Army and was sent to Canada during the French and Indian Wars. He returned to England and was elected to Parliament where his opposition to the government was soon clear. When the Stamp Act was introduced in the ***House of Commons*** in February 1765, Barré was the single most vocal opponent, going so far as to predict rebellion in the colonies over the proposed policy. In a speech that became famous, Barré called the British colonists in America the "Sons of Liberty," a label the revolutionists proudly adopted when they organized to oppose the Stamp Act. 🌿

John Wilkes

Born in London in 1727, John Wilkes was the son of a successful distiller in Clerkenwell. He led a very dissolute life, perhaps funded by his wife's money. He was a member of the notorious and secretive Hell-fire Club, but was expelled after which he turned against a fellow member, the Earl of Bute, who had been appointed prime minister in May 1762. Wilkes started a weekly publication, *The North Briton*, which criticized Bute and the government. Serious problems developed in April 1763 after he attacked the king's speech at the Opening of Parliament in Issue 45 of *The North Briton*. His main criticism was of the king's praise of the Treaty of Paris which ended the Seven Years' War. Wilkes was accused of misuse of parliamentary privilege by making public speeches made in Parliament. He was expelled from the House of Commons and imprisoned. Wilkes was released and reinstated in Parliament after the Chief Justice ruled that as a Member of Parliament Wilkes was protected from arrest and the charge of libel.

Parliament then voted that a member's privilege from arrest did not extend to the publishing of seditious libel. Wilkes was charged again and this time he fled to Paris. He was found guilty, *in absentia*, of obscene libel and seditious libel. Wilkes returned to England in 1768, having run out of money. On 10 May 1768 a crowd of around 15,000 gathered outside the **King's Bench Prison** in **Southwark** chanting "Wilkes and Liberty," "No Liberty, No King," and "Damn the King! Damn the Government! Damn the Justices." The troops guarding the prison may have been inflamed by the mood of the crowd, or perhaps were afraid that the crowd would try to free Wilkes. They opened fire, killing seven people. The incident became known as the "Massacre of St. George's Fields" and led to significant disturbances all over London.

On 8 June 1768 Wilkes was sentenced to twenty-two months' imprisonment, and was expelled from the House of Commons. The general public showed strong support of Wilkes. In February, March, and April 1769, he was repeatedly re-elected as MP for Middlesex. On all three occasions the elections were overturned by Parliament. On 20 February 1769 a group met at the London Tavern to discuss ways to help the imprisoned champion of the people's rights. The Bill of Rights Society was formed, with the initial objective being to "maintain and defend the liberty of the subject (i.e. Wilkes) and to support the laws and constitution of the country."

John Wilkes's experience in prison did not temper his willingness to take a stand for his beliefs. After his release in 1770, he joined the campaign for the freedom of the press.

LONDON John Wilkes's statue stands on *New Fetter Lane* near *Fleet Street*.

BUCKINGHAMSHIRE *West Wycombe Park* was the home of Francis Dashwood, founder of the Hell-Fire Club. A portrait of **Benjamin Franklin** hangs in a room here.

Medmenham Abbey on the River Thames was leased to Sir Francis Dashwood. He and his wealthy friends held secret rituals as part of the infamous Hell-Fire Club and called themselves the "Monks of Medmenham."

The *Hell-Fire Caves* were excavated in the 1750s by Sir Francis Dashwood. The tunnels and caverns were reputedly the site of bizarre rituals and debauched antics when the Hell-Fire Club held secret meetings in the caves. Among the figures of members of the club is **Benjamin Franklin**.

LONDON The Hell-Fire Club first met in May 1746 at the *George and Vulture* tavern.

LONDON John Wilkes died on 26 December 1797 and was buried at the *Grosvenor Chapel, South Audley Street.*

WEST SUSSEX The 1st Duke of Richmond was the son of Charles II and his French mistress Louise de Keroualle. In 1697 he purchased *Goodwood House* as a hunting estate. The first horse race was held on the Goodwood course in 1801. Now during late July the "Glorious Goodwood" races are held on what has been called "the most beautiful racecourse in the world."

LONDON John Singleton Copley's famous painting *The Death of the Earl of Chatham* in the *National Portrait Gallery* portrays the dramatic death of the 3rd Duke of Richmond after a speech calling for a withdrawal of British troops from America.

LONDON *Crosby Hall*, built in 1466–75 on Bishopsgate as a mansion for Sir John Crosby, a wealthy grocer, was the head office for the **East India Company**. from 1621–38. The interiors were stored until 1926, when it was rebuilt in Chelsea.

The government was trying to prevent the publication of reports of parliamentary debates, but Wilkes decided to publish the debates *verbatim*. The government reacted by ordering the arrest of Wilkes's printers. Eventually, it became accepted that the press had the right to report, comment on, and criticize parliamentary debates. John Wilkes is considered to be one of the important campaigners who helped establish the freedom of the press in Britain. 🍃

Charles Lennox, 3rd Duke of Richmond

Charles Lennox was a radical Whig Member of Parliament who opposed **Lord North**'s American policy and supported parliamentary reform. In December 1775 he declared that the resistance of the colonists was "neither treason nor rebellion, but it is perfectly justifiable in every possible political and moral sense." Forced to admit that he had supported the radical views on which **John Wilkes** and John Horne Tooke had been brought to trial for high treason, Lennox resigned from the cabinet and left government. He retired to his home at ***Goodwood*** where he focused his efforts on building a race course. 🍃

The Boston Tea Party

The Boston Tea Party was one of the most important symbolic events leading up to widespread armed conflict in America. A group of American colonists boarded English ships in Boston Harbor and destroyed the cargo. What led to this inflammatory act of commercial vandalism?

The economic downturn suffered in England as a result of the Seven Years' War meant that some English companies were unable to sell their stocks of goods. This was certainly true for the **East India Company**, which had large stores of tea it was unable to sell in England. Parliament's attempt to resolve this problem was to have long-lasting consequences. The Tea Act, passed in 1773, allowed the East India Company to ship its tea directly to the American colonies without paying the regular export duty. Perhaps Parliament thought the colonials would be pleased to be able to buy cheaper tea from the East India Company. They apparently did not anticipate the reaction of the colonial tea merchants whose businesses were threatened with bankruptcy by the special privileges granted to English companies.

Throughout the colonies, protests were organized and Americans were encouraged to boycott cheap tea, much as they had boycotted the taxed commodities under the Townsend Acts six years earlier. The protests escalated and plans were made to prevent the East India Company from unloading its cargoes in colonial ports. In Boston the royal governor and shipping agents refused to give in to the colonial opposition and in December 1773 three whaling ships loaded with tea from the East India Company docked in Boston Harbor. The *Dartmouth*, the *Eleanor*, and the *Beaver* quickly attracted the attention of protesting Americans. A large group of spectators gathered on the dock. On the evening of 16 December, about 150 men dressed as Indians passed through crowds of spectators and went aboard the ships. Seizing around 340 tea chests, they broke them open and threw the tea into the sea. News of the Boston "Tea Party" spread throughout the colonies, and similar acts of resistance were staged in other seaports.

Lord North tightened his policy of control of the colonies, and decided to make Boston an example of how opposition would be met with serious consequences for the Americans. In 1774 Parliament passed the so-called Coercive Acts closing the Port of Boston, drastically reducing the powers of self-government in the Massachusetts colony, ordering the quartering of British troops in the colonists' barns and houses, and allowing royal officers accused of crimes in Massachusetts to be tried in other colonies or in England.

American colonial agents and representatives in England realized the potentially devastating consequences of the Coercive Acts and tried to warn the lawmakers. Their advice and petitions were ignored. **General Thomas Gage** was sent to Boston to enforce the harsh new policy, and the momentum towards open war increased. Within a year the **Battle of Lexington and Concord** marked the first organized military conflicts of the American War for Independence.

The Thatched House Tavern Petition

In the eighteenth and early nineteenth centuries "The Thatched House" was a tavern on the western side of **St. James's Street, London**, near St. James's Palace. In its large public rooms, politicians met to debate the latest issues, fencing duels were conducted, speeches and addresses were made. The Thatched House Tavern was a rendezvous of wits, politicians, and men of fashion by the time of the American Revolution. Naturally, colonial Americans frequented this fashionable meeting place where they could rub shoulders with the most important and interesting men in London. On 26 March 1774, one of the most important meetings of American colonials in Britain took place when twenty-nine of them met at the tavern – a meeting that focused their minds on the relationship between the British government and the people back in America.

These men included lawyers, merchants, inventors, diplomats, and even a couple of spies. They signed a

LONDON The tea that was sent to Boston was loaded onto the ships at *Sugar Quay* on the *River Thames*.

The *East India Club* was founded in 1849 for current and former employees of the **East India Company**.

The *Hamilton House Hotel, Greenwich,* was the home of the Enderby family, ship owners and whalers, who chartered two of the ships that took the tea to Boston. The whaling house of Enderby & Sons is mentioned by **Herman Melville** in the greatest whaling novel of all time, *Moby Dick*.

LONDON The *East India Arms* on *Fenchurch Street* is a small reminder of a huge trading empire that moved out from the docks of London to operate around the world. The East India Company was created in 1600 when Queen Elizabeth I granted a charter to a group of over 200 London merchants, giving them a monopoly of trade with the East Indies. Within a few years the City of London was home to the company's offices, timber yards, foundries, rope works, gunpowder mills, and warehouses.

LONDON The *Thatched House Tavern* was located on the site of 69 St. James's Street, where in 1843–5 the original Conservative Club was built. The Carlton Club stands on the site today. The tavern was demolished in 1814.

LONDON The "Petition of Stephen Sayer and others, Natives of America, praying that the Boston Port Bill may not pass into a Law" was presented at the *Houses of Parliament* on 28 March 1774.

NOTE The South Carolinian signers of the Thatched House Tavern petition and the Declaration of Independence were related in a complex web of family ties. Many are remembered in Charleston, South Carolina, and their homes and burial places are part of an historical walking tour.

LONDON Many men connected with American history have been held prisoner at the *Tower of London*. These include **Henry Laurens**, **William Penn**, **Walter Raleigh** (reconstruction of his cell, above), **Thomas Smythe**, **Henry Vane**, **Robert Devereux** (Lord Essex), **Thomas Wyatt**, **John Lord Berkeley**, and **William Disney**.

NOTE Interestingly, **Stephen Sayre's** family home in Bordentown, New Jersey, was purchased in 1816 by Joseph Bonaparte, Napoleon's elder brother.

petition urging Parliament not to pass an act closing the Port of Boston in retaliation for the **Boston Tea Party**. The petition was presented to the House of Lords, the House of Commons, and **King George III**. However, the closing of the port was carried out. This became the first of the "Intolerable Acts" or "Coercive Acts" that greatly angered the colonists and led to a growing unity of their opposition to British rule.

Among the twenty-nine signatories of that petition at the Thatched House Tavern were:

- **Stephen Sayre** – graduate of the College of New Jersey (which became **Princeton University**), and a merchant in London. He belonged to the Bill of Rights Society and in 1773 was elected a sheriff of London. In 1775 Sayre was arrested and thrown into the **Tower of London**, accused of high treason, allegedly having planned to kidnap the king. Sayre was eventually released.
- **William Lee** – having come from Virginia to conduct business, he became an alderman of the City of London and was elected sheriff of London in 1773. Lee was considered a diplomat and "born troublemaker."
- **Arthur Lee** – William's brother, known as "America's first spy," was a secret agent for the Continental Congress.
- **Benjamin Franklin** – a prominent and respected scientist and public servant
- **John Williams** – inspector general of the Boston customs, and married to Benjamin Franklin's niece
- **Hugh Williamson** – a doctor who witnessed the Boston Tea Party and brought the news to London
- **John Boylston** – wealthy merchant from Boston
- **Edward Bancroft** – writer and inventor; a double-agent who was the most successful spy for the British during the American Revolution
- **Thomas Barker** – merchant and lawyer from North Carolina
- **Ralph Izard** – future US senator from South Carolina; a graduate of Christ's College, Cambridge.
- **Thomas Pinckney** – from South Carolina. Educated at *Westminster School* and *Oxford University*. His brother and cousin signed of the US Constitution. He later served as American minister to England (1792–4).
- **Henry Laurens** – from South Carolina; future president of the Continental Congress. In 1780 he was arrested by the British while trying to arrange a purchase of arms from Holland. He was held in the *Tower of London* until released in exchange for General Cornwallis.

Benjamin Franklin

Arguably the most important American ever to live in London, Benjamin Franklin was born in Boston, Massachusetts, on 17 January 1706, Franklin came to London briefly as a young man, hoping to establish himself as a printer, but after a year or so he returned to Philadelphia. By 1757 he was an internationally acclaimed scientist. Franklin was sent to London to negotiate with the heirs of **William Penn** who were ruling the colony in a heavy-handed way. He lived in London for the next sixteen years.

Franklin worked tirelessly to improve understanding between Britain and its American colonies. When Parliament passed the Stamp Act in 1765, he argued that it was the colonists who had in fact aided the British throughout the French and Indian Wars. In 1774, when news of the **Boston Tea Party** reached London, the government proposed to retaliate. Franklin joined other colonial Americans in London to present a petition of protest. Franklin was not making friends in Parliament.

Parliament used a controversy about letters to remove Franklin as postmaster general of the colonies. At this time the royal governor of Massachusetts was Thomas Hutchinson, the great-great-grandson of **Anne Hutchinson**, the feminist Puritan preacher who had been banished from the Massachusetts colony. Hutchinson was corresponding with George Grenville, the Whig politician who was responsible for some of the most hated British policies in America – the Sugar Act and the Stamp Act. After Grenville died, letters written to him by Hutchinson were passed to Benjamin Franklin. In the letters Hutchinson wrote about the weakness of the royal government in Massachusetts, and the need for a strong military force to support it; he condemned the conduct of Samuel Adams and the other popular leaders as seditious, and described the hostile mood of the people of Boston. He wrote that he had reluctantly come to the conclusion that Massachusetts should be governed with "an abridgment of what are called English liberties." Benjamin Franklin had been a loyal British citizen and perhaps he thought that making these letters public would help the British government understand why the colonies were worried and upset.

Franklin was charged with stealing the Hutchinson letters and making them public. A trial was held, attended by the Privy Council and a large audience that included the Archbishop of Canterbury, the philosopher Edmund Burke and Franklin's friend, the scientist **Joseph Priestley**. British high society attended, seeming to enjoy the sight of the humiliation of the upstart American. The sixty-eight-year-

OXFORDSHIRE Benjamin Franklin's father was a wool-dyer in Banbury. In 1683 he decided to immigrate to America with his wife and three children.

NORTHAMPTONSHIRE The village of *Ecton* was home to the Franklin family for centuries. Benjamin Franklin great-grandfather, grandfather Thomas, and father were born in the village. Franklin himself visited in 1758 to search for his family. Today parts of the Franklins' smithy can be seen in the back yard of the *Three Horseshoes Inn*. The family home where Thomas lived has an inscription over the door.

Thomas Franklin (d. 1702) and his wife Eleanor (d. 1711) are buried in the churchyard at *St. Mary Magdalene Church, Ecton*. There is a tablet that describes their relation to Benjamin Franklin. A bronze tablet, unveiled by the American consul-general in 1910, commemorates Benjamin Franklin's connection with the village.

LONDON As a young man, Franklin worked in a printing shop that operated in a chapel at the *Church of St. Bartholomew the Great, Smithfield*.

WEST SUSSEX The *Franklin Tavern* in Brighton has a nice portrait of the president on the pub sign. The landlady doesn't know of any link with Franklin, but they do decorate for the 4th of July and have an "American Motown" evening.

SHROPSHIRE Colonel Richard Lee was born in Shropshire in 1617/18. The **Lee** family lived at *Coton Hall* near *Alveley, Shropshire*, from the 1300s until 1821 when the home was sold by Harry Lancelot Lee. At nearby *Acton Burnell, St. Mary's Church* has the tombs of Sir Richard Lee (d. 1591) and Sir Humphrey Lee (d. 1632).

YORKSHIRE In eighteenth-century America, wealthy families in Virginia often sent their sons to England to be educated. Richard Henry Lee, a great-grandson of "The Colonel," was educated at Wakefield Academy. He returned to Virginia when he was nineteen.

BERKSHIRE Arthur attended *Eton College* and then studied medicine at Edinburgh University, from which he graduated in 1765.

LONDON In June 1769 Arthur Lee and Stephen Sayre were elected to membership in the *Framework Knitters Company* in a show of support for John Wilkes.

old Franklin remained silent throughout the trial, refusing to present a defense. He later said that this experience forced him to realize that he was an American in Britain and not an Englishman living in America. Nine months later, having wound up his business and personal affairs in England, Benjamin Franklin sailed for home. The day he stepped off the boat he became a member of the Continental Congress. He played an important part in the American struggle for independence, and was given the honor of being appointed the first American ambassador to France. Benjamin Franklin died in Philadelphia at the age of eighty-four, on 17 April 1790. 20,000 people attended his funeral. 🌿

The Lee Family of Virginia

William and Arthur Lee, brothers who signed the Thatched House Tavern petition, were members of the Lee family of Virginia, descendants of Colonel Richard Lee, who traveled to America with **Sir Francis Wyatt**, when Wyatt returned to Virginia to become the royal governor of the colony. In 1641 Richard Lee married Anne Constable, the niece of Sir Francis. Theirs grew to be one of the most important families in early American history.

Colonel Richard Lee's great-grandson Arthur Lee studied at **Eton College** and the University of Edinburgh, where he received a medical degree in 1764. Arthur Lee went back to Virginia for a while and then returned to London. He studied law at **Lincoln's Inn** and the **Middle Temple**, and practiced in London from 1770 to 1776. Arthur's political tracts explaining and supporting the American cause were distributed throughout America and Europe. He was made an alderman of the City of London. In July 1773 he was appointed sheriff of London. William was active in business and became involved in the local politics of London, which often focused on issues that were parallel to the concerns in the colonies – the power of Parliament, taxation, commercial freedom.

Arthur Lee contributed a specific link between England and America that was to have very significant consequences. He was a member of the Society for the Bill of Rights in London, which was formed to provide support for the radical politician **John Wilkes**. Lee wrote a letter to Samuel Adams in which he outlined his plans to develop corresponding societies that would serve to facilitate communication with provincial allies. Samuel Adams and others in Massachusetts developed this idea into the committees of correspondence that proved to be vital in the growth of revolutionary unity in the colonies. In Virginia, elder brother Richard Henry Lee was instrumental in starting the committees of correspondence there.

MORE ABOUT BENJAMIN FRANKLIN

LONDON Franklin's trial before the Privy Council was held in the Cock Pit located where the **Old Treasury Building** stands today at **70 Whitehall, Westminster**.

36 Craven Street is the only existing house in the world where Franklin actually lived. It opened as the **Benjamin Franklin House Museum** on 17 January 2006 – his 300th birthday.

In 1956, on the 250th anniversary of Benjamin Franklin's birth, the **Royal Society of Arts** established the Benjamin Franklin Medal, which is conferred on individuals, groups, or organizations that have made important efforts to promote Anglo-American understanding. Recipients have included the Americans John Hay Whitney, **Paul Mellon**, J. William Fulbright, Kingman Brewster, **Sam Wanamaker**, Ambassador Philip Lader, and Colin Powell.

Franklin was a member of the **Royal Society**. The society has a portrait of Franklin by Joseph Wright of Derby.

The **National Portrait Gallery** has six portraits of Benjamin Franklin. **Madame Tussauds** has a waxwork figure of Franklin.

Peter Collinson (1694–1768) specialized in trading with the American colonies and sent Benjamin Franklin the instruments for his electrical experiments in Philadelphia. Ridgeway House, where Collinson lived, is now part of **Mill Hill School.** It is marked by a plaque.

CUMBRIA Benjamin Franklin visited **Whitehaven** in 1772 to see William Brownrigg, the leading scientist in the area. Franklin went down one of the local coal mines to study the fossils.
He also visited Brownrigg at Ormathwaite, near **Keswick** on **Derwentwater**, in the English Lake District to demonstrate his oil-on-water experiment.

OXFORD Franklin, who only completed the second grade, was awarded an honorary doctorate by the **University of Oxford** in the 1760s, thereby becoming Dr. Franklin.

BUCKINGHAMSHIRE At Sir Francis Dashwood's home **West Wycombe Park** there is a portrait of Franklin on display. Benjamin Franklin was rumored to have been a member of Sir Francis Dashwood's secret club. He is among the waxwork figures on display in the **Hell-Fire Caves** near **West Wycombe**.

KENT Franklin attended service in **Tenterden** in 1774 when he and **Joseph Priestley** stayed in Woodchurch Road. In May 1976 a Franklin descendant unveiled a plaque at the **Unitarian Meeting** House to mark the Bicentenary of American Independence. The Meeting House has a painting of Franklin.

HAMPSHIRE Franklin stayed at the **Star Hotel** in **Southampton** on his voyage from France to America in 1785.

READ *The First American* by H.W. Brands. New York: Doubleday Books, 2000.
Murder in the Hell Fire Club by Donald Zochert. New York: Holt, Rinehart, and Winston, 1978.

LONDON On display at the *National Army Museum, Chelsea,* among the British uniforms of the eighteenth century, are a painting of the **Battle of Lexington and Concord**, as well as a model layout of the final battle of the American Revolutionary War. This scarlet coat with green facings (c. 1770) is an "officer's coatee" associated with the 49th Regiment of Foot.

LINCOLNSHIRE It isn't clear who fired first at the Battle of Lexington, but some claim that the first shot to draw English blood was fired by Solomon Brown of Lexington. His cousin, John Brown of Lexington, was one of the "Minute Men" killed by the British on Lexington Green. The Browne family, relatives of **Robert "Trouble-Church" Browne**, had come to Massachusetts from Tolethorpe Hall in *Little Casterton,* near *Stamford,* with the **Winthrop Fleet**.

LONDON General **Hugh Percy**'s portrait hangs in *Syon Park, Brentford,* the home of his family. General Percy became the 2nd Duke of Northumberland.

READ *Paul Revere's Ride* by David Hackett Fischer. New York: Oxford University Press, 1994.

In London, William and Arthur Lee were well placed to gather information about the king and Parliament that would be helpful to American colonial leaders. The Lee brothers passed information back to the colonies at the risk of being charged with treason. They were labeled "vagrant Americans" and "pestilent traitors" by Members of Parliament. The Continental Congress was aware of their abilities, and named Arthur as its secret agent in London – he thus became America's first "official" secret agent. They both worked closely with **Benjamin Franklin**. Arthur Lee, Benjamin Franklin and Silas Deane were appointed commissioners to the French court. By June of 1776 both brothers had left London and moved to Paris. 🌿

The Battle of Lexington and Concord

The first major military battle of the American Revolution was fought at Lexington and Concord, Massachusetts, on 19 April 1775. Two of the most outspoken rebel leaders, Samuel Adams and John Hancock, were known to be attending meetings in Concord and spending the night in Lexington. The colonials had seized a large amount of gunpowder from a British fort at Portsmouth in December and were storing it in Concord. They also had number of cannon and mortars, and were planning to move these out to other rebel communities.

British commander **General Thomas Gage** planned to send a secret expedition to seize the colonial militia's cannon and ammunition, and to arrest Adams and Hancock. A British force of about 700 men left Boston around midnight on 18 April and moved towards Concord, hoping to surprise the rebels. However, warning of their movements had been leaked to the rebels. Perhaps a stable lad heard an indiscrete remark, or a soldier let some information slip to the colonial family where he was quartered. There is even speculation that the information may have come from General Gage's American wife, **Margaret Kemble Gage**.

The colonists kept watch to make sure they knew what the British troops were doing. A warning system was planned. Lanterns would be hung in the tower of Old North Church in Boston to signal troop movements – "one if by land or two if by sea." On the evening of 18 April 1775, Thomas Davies, born in **Sudbury** in **Suffolk**, held two lanterns high in the Old North Church tower to signal the waiting Paul Revere that "The Redcoats are coming!" William Dawes (also originally from **Sudbury**) rode along with Paul Revere to broadcast the warning.

When the advance British troops arrived in Lexington they were met by about seventy armed men. The British commander gave an order to surround and disarm the colonials. After a skirmish in which eight local men were killed, the British moved toward Concord hoping to seize cannon that were reportedly hidden at a local farm. When they got to North Bridge in Concord they were met with a larger group of armed militia who offered organized resistance. When British Brigadier General **Hugh Percy** arrived in Concord with the relief column, the British troops had broken rank and were in a confused retreat. Percy managed to bring the troops under control and led a retreat back to Boston.

In the battle the American casualties numbered 96 men killed, wounded or missing. The British total was 273. The Battle of Lexington and Concord was a turning point in the move towards full revolution. The confrontation proved to the colonials that they could fight successfully against the might of the British Army. 🍃

English Support after the Battle of Lexington and Concord

American colonials weren't the only people in London spurred into action by news of events at Lexington and Concord. A document that outlined the attack and "atrocities" by British soldiers against local citizens was sent to London by the Provincial Congress and actually reached the British public before the official report sent by **General Gage**. A number of groups in London and throughout Britain opposed royal policies and military power. There was even a "Patriotic Society" that supported candidates for Parliament who would "try to restore America's right of taxation by representation of her own choice."

The Bill of Rights Society was formed in 1769 to help support **John Wilkes**, but by 1771 some members wanted to focus their work on parliamentary reform. The Bill of Rights Society was wound up, and the Constitutional Society created. John Horne (who later added the surname "Tooke") was a leading member of both groups. He led members of the Constitutional Society in signing a newspaper advertisement published on 5 June 1775 calling for contributions to aid the American colonists injured in the hostilities in Massachusetts. The appeal for "the relief of the widows, orphans, and aged parents of our beloved American fellow-subjects, who faithful to their character of Englishmen, preferred death to slavery, were, for that reason only inhumanly murdered by the King's Troops at or near Lexington and Concord" was held to be illegal. The publishers were found guilty, fined and imprisoned for a year. However, funds were collected and sent to the Massachusetts Council in care of **Benjamin Franklin**. 🍃

LONDON Support for the colonials in Massachusetts continued on many levels in England. In July 1775 at their annual "Festivity to Liberty" the Middlesex electors toasted "all those American heroes who like men nobly prefer death to slavery and chains." Opposition to royal power and government policies was even heard in some of the private gentlemen's clubs in St. James's, especially at *Brook's Club, 60 St. James's Street*. The Whig group that met at Brooks included Members of Parliament such as **John Wilkes** and Isaac Barré, well known for their support of the colonials.

LONDON In 1777 John Horne was convicted of sedition for his support of the American victims of the **Battle of Lexington and Concord**. He was sent to the *King's Bench Prison* in *Southwark* for a year. Horne continued to be prominent in the circles of radical political thought, and supported the goals of the French Revolution. In 1794 he was again arrested and charged with treason; this time he spent six months in the *Tower of London* before being acquitted of the charges. **Thomas Paine** visited Horne at *Chester House*, his home in *Wimbledon*.

READ *Disaffected Patriots: London Supporters of Revolutionary America 1769–1782* by John Sainsbury. Kingston, Ontario: McGill: Queen's University Press, 1987.

EAST SUSSEX *Firle Place* has been the home of the Gage family for more than 500 years. Portraits of **General Thomas Gage** and **Margaret Kemble Gage** by David Martin (pictured above and right) hang in the family dining room. **Benjamin West**'s portrait of Elizabeth Gideon, wife of the 2nd Viscount Gage, hangs in the drawing room.

An interesting American document hangs in the Pine Corridor at *Firle Place* – an address giving the Freedom of New York to General Gage in 1773.

On the reverse is a document of May 1775 of the Provisional Congress of Massachusetts rescinding honors given to General Gage and criticizing his role in commanding the military opposition to colonial militia. It was signed by Joseph Warren, president of the Provisional Congress, who was killed only weeks later at the Battle of Bunker Hill.

Thomas Gage

Thomas Gage was a major in the British Army when his unit, **44th Regiment**, was sent to America in 1755 to fight in the French and Indian Wars. In 1758 Colonel Gage married **Margaret Kemble**, of Morris Town, New Jersey, daughter of one of the influential men in the colonies. In 1759 Gage participated in the conquest of Canada and was appointed military governor of Montreal. In 1763 he was appointed commander in chief of British forces in North America.

In February 1773 Thomas Gage returned to England, but tensions were growing in America, especially in Boston after the infamous "Tea Party" of 16 December 1773. Parliament voted to close the Port of Boston and force the colonists to pay for the tea that had been destroyed. In 1774 Thomas Gage was appointed to succeed Thomas Hutchinson (the great-great-grandson of the banished **Anne Hutchinson**) as governor of Massachusetts and was sent to Boston with orders to bring the people to submission.

Thomas Gage may have personally questioned the imposition of harsh taxes on the American colonies, but he was determined to enforce the laws passed by Parliament. He threatened arrest for anyone who conspired against the rules, and decided to take control of weapons and military stores held by local militia. On the night of 18 April 1775 he sent a large force on a secret mission to Lexington and Concord to seize cannon and ammunition held by the colonists in those towns. The British defeat at this battle was a turning point in American armed opposition to the British.

On 17 June Gage sent a large force to dispatch colonists who were gathering on a hill in Boston. Technically the British won this "Battle of Bunker Hill." Out of their force of around 2,400 men, there were 1,054 casualties. The colonials suffered between 300 and 600 dead or wounded – but they lost their position when the British regulars overran the colonials' defensive line. The Battle of Bunker Hill became a rallying point of resistance against the British. It proved that the colonials could stand up to the might of the British Army. And it opened the eyes of the British to the determination of the Americans. 🌿

Margaret Kemble Gage

Margaret Kemble Gage's life shows the difficult choices that people had to make at the time of the American War for Independence. She was born in New Brunswick, New Jersey, in 1734. Her father, Peter Kemble, was one of the wealthiest and most prominent men in America. When his daughter married Colonel Gage in December 1758 it was surely a time of happy family rejoicing. Peter Kemble had known Thomas

Gage during his time as a student at **Westminster School** in London, and now Gage was rising in the British command. In 1763 he was named commander in chief of the British forces in North America. This was before outright hostilities between the British Army and colonial militias, and Gage was given the Freedom of the City of New York. However, the situation was growing more divisive.

While General Gage and Margaret spent several months in England in 1773, threats of violence were becoming more frequent in Massachusetts. Gage was named governor of Massachusetts and sent to deal with colonial resistance to British rule. Margaret Kemble Gage returned to America in 1774. She soon realized how divided the American colonials were becoming and the difficulty of her own position.

George Washington visited the Kemble home in New Jersey in May 1773 on his way to register his stepson at King's College in New York (later renamed Columbia University). A few days later, Washington dined with General Gage, with whom he had served during the French and Indian War. Within two years these former military colleagues would be leading opposite sides in a long and bloody war, and Margaret Kemble Gage would be torn between the two sides. In 1775 she told a friend that "she hoped her husband would never be the instrument of sacrificing the lives of her countrymen."

Margaret's life shows the terrible divisions of a civil war, where a country is not invaded by another nation, but instead fights to divide itself. Families are forced to choose sides, and the choices are not easy to make. She saw her own family divided by the demands of war — two brothers remained loyal to Britain and left America at the end of the war. Two other brothers sided with the revolutionaries and managed to keep the family estate intact.

When General Gage was sent to Massachusetts in 1774, both the British and the colonial "patriots" could see that armed conflict might not be far off. Soon after the British defeat at the **Battle of Lexington and Concord**, Margaret Kemble Gage was sent to England and never returned to her homeland. She sailed on the *Charming Nancy* along with 170 wounded British soldiers who were being sent to the **Royal Hospital Chelsea.**

General Gage returned to England in November 1775 and was relieved of his command of the army in North America. He remained in the army, and his subsequent career was uneventful. He was eventually promoted to the rank of full general. Unfortunately, but perhaps not surprisingly, his marriage to Margaret Kemble was not a happy one after they returned to England. He died in 1787 and Margaret survived

Margaret Kemble's family shows the divided loyalties of the American colonials – her father Peter supported the colonial side, but three of her brothers fought for the British. One brother was a British officer who served under Thomas Gage and had what seemed to be a promising military career. Once his brother-in-law was recalled to Britain, however, Stephen's career was plagued with disappointments. He stayed in the British Army until 1805 when he sold his British property and returned to live in the family home in New Brunswick. Another brother joined the opposition and swore an oath to the colonists. This may have saved the Kemble home from being destroyed by the rebels. Margaret Kemble Gage's portrait by David Martin hangs in the Gage family home at *Firle Place, East Sussex.*

LONDON A blue plaque marks the house at *41 Portland Place* where General Gage lived after he returned from America.

NORTHUMBERLAND *Alnwick Castle,* the second largest inhabited castle in England, has been home to the Percy family (earls and dukes of Northumberland) since 1309.

YORKSHIRE *Beverley Minster* has the Northumberland Chapel and several Percy tombs.

LONDON *Syon Park* is the London home of the Duke of Northumberland.

BERKSHIRE Hugh Percy attended *Eton College* from 1753 to 1758.

Hugh Percy's father, the 1st Duke of Northumberland, had an illegitimate son who left a fortune to the People of the United States to found "an Establishment for the increase and diffusion of Knowledge." (*See James Smithson in Chapter 8.*)

him by thirty-seven years until 1824, dying when she was ninety.

Hugh Percy

Hugh Percy was born into one of the wealthiest and most powerful families in Britain. His father, a Yorkshire baronet named Hugh Smithson, married Lady Elizabeth Seymour, daughter of the Duke of Somerset. Through his wife's family, he was made Earl of Northumberland. His last name was changed to Percy by a special Act of Parliament in 1750. In 1766 he was elevated to Duke of Northumberland. His son was born Hugh Smithson, but he became Hugh Percy when his father's name was changed. He began his military career in 1759 and fought in Europe during the Seven Years' War. In 1763, when he was twenty-one, he was elected to Parliament. His wife was the daughter of the Earl of Bute, a close friend of **King George III**. Percy later divorced Lady Anne Stuart.

The Duke of Northumberland and his son were part of the growing opposition to Tory policies in North America. Meanwhile, Hugh Percy's military career was progressing quickly. It was the practice at that time for well-to-do young men to purchase their ranks in the army. Percy purchased a captaincy and a few years later he purchased a commission as a lieutenant colonel. In 1764 he was made a colonel and aide-de-camp to the king. Hugh Percy went to Massachusetts as the commander of the 5th Foot Regiment in Boston which landed in Boston on 5 July 1774. Nine months later came the **Battle of Lexington and Concord** which proved to be a military disaster for the British.

Percy was the only British officer whose reputation gained anything from the Battle of Lexington and Concord because he was able to save many men by his success in leading an orderly retreat, but his military career was tarnished by his perceived sympathies with the American cause. General Gage was recalled to Britain in October 1775 and was replaced by the more hard-line General Howe. Percy finally requested leave to go back to Britain and left America in May 1777, never to return. Hugh Percy became the 2nd Duke of Northumberland in 1786, and died in 1817.

John Montresor and Nathan Hale

In planning his military actions, **General Gage** used maps of the city and harbor of Boston drawn by Captain John Montresor, an officer in the Royal Engineers Corps who drew many of the important maps used by the British in the French and Indian Wars, and during the American Revolution. Montresor was the vital witness to one of the most iconic scenes of patriotism of the American Revolution. On 22 September

1776 Nathan Hale, a twenty-one-year-old schoolteacher and Yale graduate, was sentenced by the British to be hanged as an American spy. Hale was on a secret mission for **General Washington**, carrying documents about British fortifications and defensives when he was captured. John Montresor stayed with Hale while preparations were made for the execution. Later that day Montresor, on a mission to discuss an exchange of prisoners, told Alexander Hamilton (then a captain of artillery) that Hale had impressed everyone with his calm dignity. Montresor also reported Hale's last words as: "I only regret that I have but one life to lose for my country." 🍃

The Declaration of Independence

Representatives from all thirteen of the British colonies in North America met in Philadelphia in the Second Continental Congress, which developed from the committees of correspondence. By the time the congress opened on 10 May 1775, armed conflict had begun. A month earlier British troops and American colonists fought each other in the **Battle of Lexington and Concord**. The Continental Congress stated that Britain had declared war on the colonies. In some matters, the congress seemed to move quickly – a Continental army was established, with **George Washington** as its commander. Silas Deane was sent to France as the ambassador of the United States.

Seeking to explain their motivations in a legalistic manner and to encourage more colonists to support them, on 7 June 1776 Richard Henry Lee placed a motion before the congress:

"Resolved: That these United Colonies are, and of right ought to be, free and independent States, that they are absolved from all allegiance to the British Crown, and that all political connection between them and the State of Great Britain is, and ought to be, totally dissolved."

Four days later a committee was created to draft a declaration for the "Lee Resolution"; it consisted of **John Adams** of Massachusetts, **Benjamin Franklin** of Pennsylvania, **Thomas Jefferson** of Virginia, Robert Livingston of New York, and Roger Sherman of Connecticut. Thomas Jefferson did most of the writing, and on 28 June a draft was read in the congress. From 1–4 July the congressmen debated and revised the document. On 2 July they voted to declare idependence from Britain, and on 4 July 1776 the Declaration of Independence was approved and adopted as the formal document stating the grievances and philosophy that had led the colonies to take this action. 🍃

EAST SUSSEX A map drawn by John Montresor hangs in the Pine Corridor at *Firle Place*. The map is a plan of the City of New York, and shows important buildings, farms, and fortifications on Manhattan Island, including the wall built to keep out hostile Indians – from which came the name of Wall Street.

NOTE: A play has been written about this episode in the American Revolution: *The Interrogation of Nathan Hale by Captain John Montresor of HRM Expeditionary Forces* by David Stanley Ford. Woodstock, IL: Dramatic Publishing, 1997.

LONDON Outside the *American Law Library* at the *Middle Temple* hangs a reproduction of the American Declaration of Independence with the names of five members of Middle Temple who were among its fifty-six signatories marked with red stars: Arthur Middleton, Edward Rutledge, Thomas Hayward, Thomas Lynch, and Thomas McKean.

KENT Silas Deane died on board ship sailing from Gravesend to Boston, 23 September 1789 and was interred in the cemetery at *St. Leonard's Church* in *Deal*.

ESSEX In 1623 John Russhe was baptized at *St. Andrew's Parish Church, Boreham*. In 1683 he immigrated to Byberry, Pennsylvania. His grandson Benjamin Rush was a signatory of the Declaration of Independence.

The "Washington Window" at *All Saints' Church* in *Maldon* was presented by the citizens of Malden, Massachusetts in 1928 and dedicated to the memory of Lawrence Washington, **George Washington**'s great-great grandfather. The window shows among other things the signing of the Declaration of Independence.

Whitechapel Foundry, London

ESSEX The spectacular south porch at *Chelmsford Cathedral* was enriched in 1953 by "Essex friends of the American people." The windows on the eastern side feature symbols of the United Kingdom. The western window has many American symbols including the arms of George Washington, an eagle holding an olive branch, the stars and stripes of the American national flag and the motto *E pluribus unum.*

GLOUCESTERSHIRE In *Gloucester Cathedral* an American flag and plaque note that John Stafford Smith (born 1750) was the organist at the cathedral and wrote the tune to the "Star-Spangled Banner" as a drinking tune for his men's club.

Places in England where
the "Stars and Stripes"
can be found:

LONDON *St. Paul's Cathedral –
the American Memorial*
CAMBRIDGE *Little St. Mary's Church*
COUNTY DURHAM *Durham
Cathedral*
KENT *All Saints' Church, Maidstone*
OXFORDSHIRE *Sulgrave Manor*
SOMERSET *Bath Abbey*
BRISTOL *Clifton College*
SUFFOLK *Church of St. Peter and
St. Paul, Lavenham*
TYNE AND WEAR *Washington Old Hall*
YORKSHIRE *Selby Abbey
and York Minster*

The Liberty Bell

The Liberty Bell was ordered on 1 November 1751 from the **Whitechapel Foundry** in **London** to hang in the Philadelphia State House – now Independence Hall. It was made to celebrate the fiftieth year of the Constitution of Pennsylvania. The bell weighed one ton and was inscribed:

"Proclaim Liberty throughout all the Land to the inhabitants Thereof."
(Lev. 25:10)

The bell was delivered to Philadelphia in September 1752. When it was first rung in 1753, the bell cracked and had to be recast by Pennsylvania workmen. From 1753 until the Revolution, it was used to announce meetings, protest taxation, celebrations, and tolled in mourning. The Liberty Bell rang on 8 July 1776 for the announcement of the **Declaration of Independence**. It was buried from September 1777 to June 1788 to prevent its capture by the British. The bell next rang on 16 April 1783, at the proclamation of peace and was rung thereafter on state occasions. It cracked again on 8 July 1835 when tolling the death of Chief Justice John Marshall. The bell was repaired to ring on 22 February 1846, **George Washington**'s birthday, but it immediately cracked again. It has rung only twice since, on 6 April 1917, when America declared war on Germany and on 6 June 1944, announcing Allied landings in Normandy.

The Whitechapel Foundry was commissioned to cast the Bicentennial Bell in 1976. It now resides in Philadelphia with its illustrious predecessor and bears the inscription:

"FOR THE PEOPLE OF THE
UNITED STATES OF AMERICA
FROM THE PEOPLE OF BRITAIN
4 JULY 1976
LET FREEDOM RING"

The "Stars and Stripes" and the "Star-Spangled Banner"

Just as the **Liberty Bell** was made in England, other symbols of the United States had their origins in the native country of many of her first citizens. The design of the American flag with its stars and stripes may have been influenced by the family crest of ancestors of **George Washington**, who had emigrated from **Sulgrave Manor** during the English Civil War in the 1650s. The tune of the American national anthem was written as a drinking song by a church organist from Gloucester. 🌿

SIGNATORIES OF
THE DECLARATION OF INDEPENDENCE

The Declaration of Independence was approved by delegates to the Second Continental Convention in Philadelphia on 4 July 1776. Many of the fifty-six men who signed the document were descendants of English, Irish, and Scottish emigrants who had crossed the Atlantic in the 170 years since the three ships left the Blackwall Dock in London to sail to Virginia and establish the Jamestown Colony. Those signatories who had close links with England include:

1 *John Adams* of Massachusetts

2 *Samuel Adams* of Massachusetts – he and John Adams were cousins. Their great-grandfather was Henry Adams who emigrated from *Braintree, Essex*.

3 *Carter Braxton* of Virginia – spent two years in England in his early twenties.

4 *Charles Carroll* of Carrollton of Maryland – was a very wealthy young man who was sent to France at age eight to be educated. In 1757 he moved to London, and commenced the study of law. He returned to America in 1764. The last surviving signatory, his granddaughter Marianne Caton Patterson was the second wife of Richard Wellesley, elder brother of the Duke of Wellington.

5 *Samuel Chase* of Maryland – his father was an English Episcopalian clergyman who immigrated to America. In 1783 Samuel Chase was sent to England by the Maryland legislature to attempt to recover money that the legislature had invested in the Bank of England before the war. He remained for nearly a year and succeeded in recovering $650,000.

6 *Samuel Huntington* of Massachusetts – in the early 1660s Simon Huntington, his wife Margaret and children left Norwich in Norfolk for New England. Simon died during the voyage, but Margaret survived and settled in Roxbury, Massachusetts. One of their descendants was Samuel Huntingdon (born 1731).

7 *Thomas Heyward* of South Carolina – studied law at the *Middle Temple* in London.

8 *Francis Hopkinson* of New Jersey – his father, Thomas Hopkinson, a lawyer born in London, immigrated to America in 1731. His mother was a niece of the Bishop of Worcester, England, and Francis studied in England with him for two years.

9 *George Clymer* of Pennsylvania – his father emigrated from Bristol.

10 *Benjamin Franklin* of Pennsylvania

11 *Elbridge Gerry* of Massachusetts – his father, Thomas Gerry, left Newton, England, in 1730.

12 *Button Gwinnet* of Georgia – born in 1732 at *Down Hatherley, Gloucestershire*, where his father Samuel was vicar of *St. Mary and Corpus Christi Church*.

12 **Thomas Jefferson** of Virginia – his mother was born in **Shadwell, London**, and baptized at **St. Paul's, Shadwell**.

13 **Richard Henry Lee** of Virginia – attended school in Wakefield, Yorkshire, before returning to Virginia.

14 **Thomas "Lightfoot" Lee** – a younger brother of Richard Henry Lee

15 **Francis Lewis** of New York – was born in Wales. In the care of his uncle, dean of St. Paul's Cathedral, he was educated at **Westminster School** and entered business in London.

16 **Thomas Lynch** of South Carolina – was educated at **Eton College**, **Cambridge University**, and the **Middle Temple, London**. He returned home in 1772, deciding he did not like the legal profession.

17 **Arthur Middleton** of South Carolina, graduated from **Westminster School**, **Trinity Hall, Cambridge** (1773), and studied law at the **Middle Temple**. His great-grandfather Edward Middleton immigrated to Barbados in 1678 and then to South Carolina. Arthur's wife was Mary Izard, whose cousin Ralph Izard signed the **Thatched House Tavern** petition. Arthur's father, Henry Middleton, was second president of the Continental Congress, and built Middleton Place in Charleston, South Carolina.

18 **Robert Morris** of Pennsylvania – was born in Liverpool, in 1734. When he was about thirteen years old he came to America with his father, who was engaged in the tobacco export business.

19 **Benjamin Rush** of Pennsylvania – his grandfather, John Russhe, was baptized in 1623 at **St. Andrew's Parish Church, Boreham, Essex**.
He immigrated to Byberry, Pennsylvania, in 1683.

20 **Richard Stockton** of New Jersey – his grandfather Richard Stockton left England before 1670.

22 **Roger Sherman** of Connecticut – at least eleven members of the Sherman family emigrated from Essex during the years 1633–40. Among their descendants were a co-founder of Rhode Island, a signatory of the Declaration on Independence, a framer of the Constitution, General W.T. Sherman of the US Civil War, a vice-president of the US from 1808 to 1812, and two famous admirals in the Second World War. The family is remembered in the **Church of St. Mary the Virgin** in **Dedham, Essex**.

23 **John Morton** of Pennsylvania – his stepfather was a well-educated surveyor from England.

24 **Thomas Nelson** of Virginia – was sent to **Eton College** at fourteen years of age, and from there to **Cambridge University**.

25 **William Paca** of Maryland – entered the **Inner Temple, London**, as a student on 14 January 1762, and was admitted to the Bar in 1764.

26 **Edward Rutledge** of South Carolina – studied law at **Oxford University** and the **Middle Temple** and was admitted to the Bar.

John Paul Jones

John Paul ran away from home in Scotland when he was twelve to find adventure on the sea. For a time he served as a mate on a slave ship, but he was disgusted by the slave trade and returned to England. He was accused of murder when he flogged a ship's crewman so severely that he died. The charges were dropped that time, but he was later again accused of using his authority too harshly. This time there were hostile witnesses, and John Paul decided it was time to make a new start. He fled the ship and started a new life in Virginia with a new surname – Jones.

In the early years of the American Revolution he offered his services to the new government and was given a commission. John Paul Jones became an energetic seagoing opponent of the British – attacking their ships at sea, and raiding along the British coastline. On 22 April 1778 Jones led the Continental marines from the USS *Ranger* in an audacious raid on the Cumbrian port town of **Whitehaven**. Whitehaven was a place Jones knew well – it was just across the Solway Firth from the village where he had been born.

John Paul Jones reported directly to **Benjamin Franklin**, who was in France trying to negotiate official support for the Americans' cause from the French government. Jones seems to have appreciated the attention Franklin paid him; when Jones was given a French ship to command, he rechristened it the *Bonhomme Richard* in honor of the character that had made Franklin famous in his *Poor Richard's Almanac*.

On 23 September 1779 John Paul Jones engaged the British Royal Navy flagship *Serapis* off **Flamborough Head, Yorkshire**, in what became the US Navy's first great sea battle. It made Jones a hero of the American Revolution. After two of the *Bonhomme Richard*'s cannon had exploded, the British captain offered Jones the chance to surrender, to which he famously replied, "I have not yet begun to fight." As the *Bonhomme Richard* sank, Jones and his crew won the battle and took command of the British ship. 🍃

Chief Joseph Brandt

Chief Joseph Brandt was a Mohawk Indian whose tribe was from an area in upper New York. Born in 1742, he was given the Indian name Thayendanega, meaning "he places two bets." During his youth he became a friend and protégé of Sir William Johnson, the British superintendent of the northern Indians in America. He and several other young Mohawk Indians were selected by Johnson to attend Moor's Charity School for Indians at Lebanon, Connecticut – the school which in future years was to become Dartmouth College.

Chief Joseph thought American independence from

SCOTLAND The *John Paul Jones Cottage Museum* is in *Kirkbean* where the naval hero was born in 1747.

Defending *Whitehaven*

CUMBRIA *Whitehaven* was the site of John Paul Jones's raid in April 1778. One of the cannon spiked by Jones and his men was recovered from the sea in 1964. Mounted on a replica trunnion and placed on the South Beach, it is a fitting memorial to Jones's daring raid on Whitehaven.

YORKSHIRE In the summer of 2001, the remains of a ship were discovered in *Filey Bay*, near *Scarborough*, by underwater divers. It has been claimed to be the wreck of John Paul Jones's ship the *Bonhomme Richard*.

NOTE John Paul Jones is buried in the chapel crypt at the US Naval Academy, Annapolis, Maryland.

LONDON Chief Joseph's portrait hangs in the print room at *Syon Park, Brentford*. Major John Norton's portrait (above) also hangs in the print room there. He was Teyoninhokarawen, an Indian leader during the War of 1812.

LONDON The present *Freemasons' Hall* was built in 1927–33, and is the central meeting point for the more than 8,000 Lodges around the UK.

WARWICKSHIRE Benedict Arnold's ancestor William Arnold emigrated from *Leamington* in 1587 and was one of the fifty-four proprietors in the first settlement of Rhode Island.

LONDON Benedict Arnold is buried in the crypt of *St. Mary's Church, Battersea*, beside his wife and daughter. The stained-glass window in the church has the British and American flags. The plaque that marks Arnold's burial place in the crypt has the inscription:

> "TWO NATIONS WHOM
> HE SERVED IN TURN
> IN THE YEARS
> OF THEIR ENMITY
> HAVE UNITED
> IN THIS MEMORIAL
> AS A TOKEN OF THEIR
> ENDURING FRIENDSHIP"

Britain would mean that the native peoples would lose their lands, so he urged tribes of the Six Nations Confederacy to support the British. Chief Joseph became the principal tribal war chief of the Six Nations, and in 1776 received a captain's commission in the British Army. Shortly after this the British authorities took him to England, hoping to impress him with the power and resources of the British king and government. Brandt wanted to protest the policy of the commander of British forces in Canada, who refused to let the Six Nation tribes fight with the British against the American revolutionaries. Brandt made a very positive impression on the leaders of British government and society. He was invited to stately homes; members of the British Cabinet fawned over him; and portraits of him were painted by many of the leading artists of the day, including Romney and Reynolds. He was also assured that the Indian forces would be used more effectively in the battle against the Americans. During this visit Chief Joseph was made a member of the Freemasons. His Masonic apron was presented to him by **King George III**.

Chief Joseph returned to America and saw action in the Battle of Long Island. During the next five years he was involved in many battles. When the Revolution ended, he retained his commission in the British Army and was granted 675,000 acres in Ontario where he established the Grand River Reservation. Chief Joseph returned to England in 1785 seeking compensation for Mohawk losses during the Revolutionary War. This was granted, along with funds for the first Episcopal Church in Upper Canada. During this visit he was presented to King George III. He is reported to have said, "I bow to no man for I am considered a prince among my own people. But I will gladly shake your hand." 🍃

Benedict Arnold

Benedict Arnold was born in Connecticut in 1741. Sent to school in Canterbury, England, he was forced to return home because of family financial difficulties. He left home at fifteen to join the Connecticut army which was marching north to counter the French invasion. Soon tiring of the discipline and hard work of the army, Arnold deserted and went home. By 1775 he was captain of the governor's guard in Connecticut. When news of the Battle of Lexington reached New Haven, he assembled the guard and offered to lead them to Boston, even though others suggested it might be wiser to wait for orders. When Arnold and his men threatened to break into the weapons store, the selectmen opened it, and the group marched to Cambridge. This impetuous bravado was typical of his career. He antagonized other officers with his hot temper, and sulked when he didn't get the praise he thought he deserved.

George Washington gave Arnold several command positions. He joined General Schuyler as the Americans prepared to fight against the British at Saratoga, New York. After a personal quarrel, Arnold threatened to leave the battlefield. He was removed from command, but stayed and continued to fight. He rushed onto the field of battle without orders, breaking through the enemy lines. His leadership spurred the Americans to fight on and the British Army was defeated. Although he had been a hero, he was bitter about the way Gates and Congress had treated him.

George Washington named Arnold commandant of Philadelphia when the city was recaptured from the British. In Philadelphia, the widower met and married Peggy Shippen, the daughter of the wealthy Loyalist judge Edward Shippen. Arnold was soon enjoying a much more lavish lifestyle than he could afford. Peggy introduced him to **Major John Andre**, chief of intelligence for British general Henry Clinton. By May 1779 Arnold was bargaining with the British. He offered the strategic fort of West Point, along with 20,000 American soldiers, in exchange for a British commission and £10,000. When Major Andre was captured, Arnold immediately defected to the British side. After the war, he moved to London, but couldn't find work he deemed appropriate. It seemed the British didn't trust him. He died in London in 1801, unknown and penniless. 🌿

John Andre

John Andre is honored by the British as a hero with a memorial in Westminster Abbey. Americans see him as the spy who turned **Benedict Arnold** into a traitor. Born in London in 1751 into a Huguenot family, he joined the British Army in 1770. Four years later he was assigned to the Royal Fusiliers in Canada. Andre's career in military intelligence may have started after he was captured in November 1775 following an American battle. He was taken to Lancaster, Pennsylvania, as a prisoner of war. On this journey he stayed in many American forts, and made secret drawings of these military installations. When he was released in a prisoner-exchange, he presented these drawings to the British general William Howe who rewarded him with a promotion to captain. In 1778 the British appointed Andre to be their chief of intelligence. His greatest coup as a spy-master was the successful recruitment of Benedict Arnold, who provided the British with invaluable information along with maps and other documents. Unfortunately, American soldiers captured John Andre with these incriminating documents. Arnold was

LONDON A blue plaque marks the house at *62 Gloucester Place* where Arnold lived.

LONDON General Burgoyne surrendered to the Americans at the Battle of Saratoga. A blue plaque marks the house at *10 Hertford Street, Mayfair,* where he lived. Burgoyne was baptized at *St. Margaret's, Westminster,* educated at *Westminster School,* and is buried under a simple stone in the north cloister at *Westminster Abbey.*

LONDON Major John Andre was buried in the nave of *Westminster Abbey.* A memorial was erected in his honor.

The figure of William Pitt the Elder in the *Westminster Abbey* waxworks was made in 1779 by Patience Lovell Wright, a New Jersey woman who had set up a studio in London. She is considered America's first great sculptor. Mrs. Wright's waxworks exhibition of prominent people was popular with Londoners. She made waxwork busts of many of the most important people of the day including of **King George III** and **Queen Charlotte**. A good friend of **Benjamin Franklin**, Mrs. Wright was also an intelligence agent acting for the American cause. She passed information on to Franklin and other American leaders.

LONDON Several impressive statues of Charles Cornwallis are found in the *Foreign and Commonwealth Office.*

There is a large monument to Cornwallis in the south transept of *St. Paul's Cathedral.*

SUFFOLK Now home to Culford School, *Culford Hall, Culford,* near *Bury St. Edmunds,* was the home of the Cornwallis family from 1659 to 1824. The church has a memorial to the family.

LONDON Henry Laurens was held prisoner in the *Tower of London.*

View of the Byward Tower, the *Tower of London*

court-martialed and found guilty of spying on 29 September 1780. He was hanged three days later, on 2 October 1780. In accordance with the laws of military tradition, his body was returned to the British. 🍃

Charles Cornwallis

Charles Cornwallis went to **Eton College**, and after purchasing a commission in the British Army, he studied at a military school in Italy. When his father died in 1762 he inherited the title of earl. Even though Cornwallis voted against some of the government's Acts that he felt were too punitive towards the colonies, he still was favored by **King George III**. On 1 January 1776 Cornwallis sailed to America and saw action in many battles during the Revolution. Cornwallis was given command of the British forces in the South. In October 1781 he commanded British troops at the Battle of Yorktown. With naval aid from the French, the Americans won the battle and Cornwallis surrendered. He was held until exchanged for **Henry Laurens**, an American who was imprisoned in the **Tower of London**. Following the war, Cornwallis turned to diplomacy. He served as governor general of India where his administration was seen as very positive and successful. In Ireland he was responsible for putting down the Rebellion of 1798 and enabling the union of Ireland and Britain. Cornwallis returned to India and served as governor general of Bengal. 🍃

Henry Laurens

Henry Laurens was born in 1724 in Charleston, South Carolina, and became a successful merchant and planter. He was a delegate to the Continental Congress and was president during much of the group's 1777–8 stay in Yorktown, Pennsylvania. Laurens was sent on a diplomatic mission to Holland in 1780, to negotiate support for the American colonies. His ship was stopped by a British man-of-war and Laurens was captured and imprisoned in the **Tower of London** as a traitor. He remained a prisoner until 1782 when he was exchanged for the British general, **Lord Cornwallis**, who had been captured during the last battle of the Revolutionary War. He apparently did not have strong feelings against the country that imprisoned him; he stayed in England after his release. There were rumors that he had a romantic relationship with Elizabeth Vernon, daughter of his jailor. It was also said that Elizabeth smuggled Laurens's patriotic writings out of the Tower in her underwear. He returned to South Carolina in 1786 and died in 1792. In his will he left a bequest to Elizabeth Vernon. 🍃

Thomas Paine

Thomas Paine received little formal education. He joined the British Excise Service in 1762, and was sent to **Alford, Lincolnshire**, as the excise officer in an area where there was known to be a lot of smuggling. Paine established his office at the **Windmill Inn**, and worked there for about a year, until he was suddenly fired, possibly by a corrupt supervisor. In 1768 he was reinstated as an excise officer in **Lewes, East Sussex**. He attended local meetings to discuss and argue about his fairly radical ideas, such as backing the American colonies in their demands for political rights. He also began writing and publishing political tracts.

Paine's early political essays seem to be based on his personal situation, such as his plea that the salaries of excise officers be raised, which he claimed would increase their efficiency and reduce corruption. His employers did not seem to appreciate his helpful suggestions – he was fired from his job. Meanwhile his marriage had broken up and he was having financial difficulties, so he may have been looking for a new start in life when he met **Benjamin Franklin** in London. In 1774 Paine immigrated to America, probably with the encouragement of Franklin, and became an influential and controversial writer on politics and religion.

In 1776 Paine published his famous political pamphlet *Common Sense*, which explained the American colonies' position on independence from Great Britain. The pamphlet became an enormous bestseller – almost everyone in America at the time seems to have read it! Because of his importance in the propaganda war in the colonies, Paine was honored by American revolutionary leaders. In 1784 New York State gave Paine a grant of 277 acres in New Rochelle. But this exalted position was not to last.

After the end of the war in America, Paine traveled to France, then back to England, where in 1791 he published *Rights of Man* in defense of the French Revolution. There was a lot of negative feeling in England about the French Revolution at this time. Paine's new book was censored so he fled to France, where he was imprisoned. During this time he worked on *Age of Reason*, in which he elaborated his views on religion, especially his harsh criticism of organized religion. Benjamin Franklin urged Paine not to publish the book, but Paine went ahead. As a consequence, he was labeled an atheist by church authorities. Paine returned to America in 1802, with the help of then-president **Thomas Jefferson**, but found that his political writings and service in the Revolution were now mostly forgotten, overshadowed by his unpopular religious philosophy. Paine died a social outcast in 1809. He was denied burial in a churchyard on

WILTSHIRE Henry Laurens was held at the *White Hart Hotel* in *Salisbury* after being captured by the British in 1780.

LINCOLNSHIRE A statue of Thomas Paine stands in front of the *Windmill Hotel* in *Alford* and a plaque on the hotel commemorates the time that Paine lived there.

LONDON Paine lived at *Angel Square* when he wrote *The Rights of Man*. A momument commemorates Paine's writings.

NORFOLK Paine was born at *Thetford* on 29 January 1737. His democratic and humanitarian ideals may have started to form during his years at Thetford, which was the site of an assize court, a goal, and the local gallows. The town was regarded as one of the rotten boroughs and Tom may have grown up listening to grumbling complaints about the local political situation.

The *Thomas Paine Hotel* in *Thetford* claims to be his birthplace. A magnificent black and white Tudor merchant's house is now the *Ancient House Museum*. It has displays about Thomas Paine, *Thetford*'s most famous son.

NORFOLK A gilded bronze statue of Thomas Paine was installed in 1964 in front of the *King's House* in *Thetford*. (Other statues of Paine stand in New Rochelle, New York; Bordentown and Morristown, New Jersey; Paris, France.)

READ *The Trouble with Tom: The Strange Afterlife and Times of Thomas Paine* by Paul Collins. New York: Bloomsbury, 2005.

EAST SUSSEX Paine lived at *Bull House, Lewes High Street*, from 1768 to 1774. It is now the headquarters of Sussex Archaeological Society. For several years, Tom Paine Project festivals have been held in Lewes from 4–14 July (American Independence to Bastille day) to mark the role played by Paine in both eighteenth-century uprisings.

The Headstrong Club met at the *White Hart Hotel* in *Lewes*. Paine joined the debates, often being awarded the prize for being the "most obstinate haranguer." A copy of the US constitution now hangs in the "American Room." The Headstrong Club was disbanded by the government in the 1790s in an effort to stop radical debate. Reborn in 1987, it meets regularly at the *Royal Oak* pub where a plaque reminds readers of Tom Paine's part in the original club.

Thomas Paine married Elizabeth Ollive at *St. Michael's Church* in *Lewes* on 26 March 1771.

LONDON Paine visited John Horne Tooke at his home at *Chester House* on *Wimbledon Common*.

The website of *Windsor Castle Pub* in *Kensington* says that Thomas Cobbett's son sold a skeleton to the landlord to settle a beer debt and that the bones of Thomas Paine are buried in the pub's cellar.

account of his being labeled an atheist. He was buried at his farm in New Rochelle.

Thomas Paine's story has a bizarre coda. Ten years after he died, another English political writer, **William Cobbett**, decided Thomas Paine should have a monument. He had Paine's bones exhumed and took them back to England. Unfortunately, the monument was never built. Cobbett reportedly kept Paine's bones in a trunk in his attic. When Cobbett died in 1835, his son tried unsuccessfully to auction them. What happened next is a matter of some confusion. In 1850 a Unitarian minister claimed to have Paine's skull and right hand. In the 1930s a woman in Brighton claimed to have his jawbone. There were rumors that the bones had been made into buttons. A Sydney businessman claimed he purchased Paine's skull while on vacation in England. He sold it to an Australian who said he was the descendant of an illegitimate child of Thomas Paine. The president of the Thomas Paine Historical Association says that DNA testing may be done to settle the claims.

William Cobbett

William Cobbett, "The Poor Man's Friend," was a colorful and free-speaking character who was entirely self-educated. The man who became a famous pamphleteer and social commentator started out life as a crow-scarer and plowboy. He left home when he was nineteen and went to London where he found work as a lawyer's clerk. In 1783 he joined the army and served in Canada from 1783 to 1791. When he returned to England, his political outspokenness was unappreciated and he was forced to leave, going to the United States where he lived from 1792 to 1800. In the new democracy his fiery political views were considered too radical. He attacked people with whom he disagreed – including **Joseph Priestley** and **Thomas Paine**. Cobbett moved back to England, and returned to publishing. His recording and publishing of parliamentary debates was later taken over by Hansard. For some time he published the *Porcupine Gazette* and then in 1802 started the *Political Register* as a weekly Tory report.

Cobbett traveled extensively around England on horseback, giving political speeches and printing accounts of his tours in the *Political Register*. His *Rural Rides* described social conditions in rural England and the oppression of agricultural workers, expressing views that were considered radical. When he opposed the use of flogging in the army, he was fined £1,000 and sentenced to two years in prison. When he was released from prison he escaped to America again, and lived in rural Long Island, New York, from 1817 to 1819.

Returning to England with the bones of Thomas Paine, William Cobbett pursued his interest in politics. He was elected to Parliament in 1832 and used his position to continue his campaign for the rights of laborers and the poor. One of the best political commentators of his day, his political views and outspokenness earned him the title of "The Poor Man's Friend." Among many other radical political ideas he supported was the demand for "wider suffrage and the ballot; for the selection of civil servants on the basis of merit rather than rank or family; and for the elimination of the public workhouse." 🍃

Banastre Tarleton

Banastre Tarleton purchased a commission as a cavalry officer in the British Army in 1775, and in May 1776 he arrived in North America with the British military re-enforcements under **General Charles Cornwallis**. He was involved in many skirmishes and battles in the conflict in New Jersey and Pennsylvania. By 1778 he had been promoted to lieutenant colonel and put in charge of the British Legion, a group of American Loyalists who were given British military training. In December 1779 Tarleton was transferred to the southern campaign and a company of British Dragoons was added to his command. Tarleton gained a reputation as a cruel and ruthless soldier when he led his cavalry in an attack on unprepared Americans at Waxhaw, North Carolina, in May 1780. Men without weapons were hacked to pieces by the British, and legend says that one of the prisoners taken was the thirteen-year-old Andrew Jackson. This future president of the United States received a serious sword wound as punishment when he refused to clean mud off a British officer's boots.

In October 1781 Banastre Tarleton was captured during the siege of Yorktown. He eventually returned to England and was considered to be a military hero. He was elected to Parliament from Liverpool for six sessions. Tarleton died in 1833. British military historians may consider him to be a dynamic cavalry leader, but in America his legacy remains one of brutal treatment of patriotic civilians. He has been called the most hated British officer to serve in America. (His character is said to be the model for the sadistic Loyalist officer in the movie The Patriot.) 🍃

Lord Shelburne and the Treaty of Paris

William Petty had conflicting thoughts about the American colonies. He disagreed with the British government policy in the 1760s of taxing the colonies, but in 1782 he did not readily agree with the demands to recognize America as an

SURREY William Cobbett was born in *Farnham* in 1763. The farmhouse where he was born became a pub named the "Jolly Farmer". In the 1970s it was renamed the *William Cobbett*.

SURREY William Cobbett's tomb stands just outside the door of *St. Andrew's Church* in *Farnham*. The *Museum of Farnham* has exhibits on Cobbett.

HAMPSHIRE A memorial to the "Poor Man's Friend" stands on the village green at *Botley*. Inside the Market Hall are two engravings of William Cobbett. Cobbett first lived at Botley House (demolished). Later he rented a house (then called "Botley Hill") with 106 acres of farmland. His farming schemes were not always successful – he planted wheat when prices were falling, and tried growing American trees which did not transplant successfully.

LONDON Joshua Reynolds's portrait of Banastre Tarleton at the *National Gallery, Trafalgar Square* (bequeathed by Mrs Henrietta Charlotte Tarleton, 1951), shows him in the green jacket of the Green Horse Guards, the cavalry group he commanded in America.

MERSEYSIDE A plaque marks the house on *Water Street, Liverpool,* where Tarleton lived from 1802 to 1833. He was a Member of Parliament for Liverpool.

HEREFORDSHIRE Tarleton married Susan Priscilla Bertie in 1798. They spent their last years at Leintwardine House. He died on 25 January 1833 and was buried at the *Church of St. Mary Magdalene* in *Leintwardine.* A large memorial to Banastre Tarleton can be found in the vestry of the church.

OXFORD William Petty attended *Christ Church,* but left without a degree to join the Foot Guards.

LONDON *Lansdowne House* near *Berkeley Square* was Lord Shelburne's London home.

WILTSHIRE Lord Shelburne's country estate was *Bowood House* near *Calne.* The estate built by the 1st Earl of Shelburne in 1754 was in a very dilapidated condition after World War II, and the main house was demolished in 1955. Joseph Priestley's laboratory at Bowood has been designated an International Historic Chemical Landmark.

READ *The Life and Adventures of William Cobbett* by Richard Ingrams. London: HarperCollins, 2005

independent nation. In his early twenties he was elected to the *House of Commons,* but he decided not to take the seat, serving as an aide-de-camp to King George II instead. When his father died, he became the 2nd Earl of Shelburne, but because the title was an Irish one he did not gain a seat in the House of Lords.

Under Prime Minister William Pitt, Shelburne was appointed secretary of state for the Southern Department, which included the American colonies. His personal conciliatory attitude towards the colonies led to responsibilities for American affairs being removed from his control, and he thus resigned from government. After traveling in Europe for a year, he returned to England and hired as his private librarian and tutor to his son **Joseph Priestley,** who was one of England's best-known scientists.

Following the Battle of Yorktown in October 1781, it became clear that the American colonies were "lost." Changes in the British government brought Whigs into office. In 1782 **Lord North** was replaced as prime minister by the Marquess of Rockingham. He died after only fourteen weeks in office, and the king asked the Earl of Shelburne to form the next government. This was a crucial time for the new American colonies. **Benjamin Franklin, John Adams,** and John Jay were in Paris to represent the United States in negotiations for the formal treaty that would end the American Revolution and recognize the creation of a new nation – the Treaty of Paris. Both were aware that Lord Shelburne might be replaced by a prime minister who would be much harder to deal with, so pressure was on to reach an agreement. The preliminary treaty was signed on 30 November 1782.

In March 1783 Lord Shelburne was forced from office. He never held office again, and spent most of his time at his estate at *Bowood.* But he had been at the right place at the right time to play a vital role in the negotiations that established the United States of America.

MEMORIALS RELATED
TO THE AMERICAN WAR FOR INDEPENDENCE

The Triumphal Arch built by Sir Thomas Gascoigne at **Parlington Hall** in **West Yorkshire** is
the only monument in Britain that celebrates the American victory in its War for Independence. The
design of the arch was inspired by the Arch of Titus in Rome.
The inscription along the top reads:
"Liberty in North America Triumphant MDCCLXXXIII"

There are several memorials in **Westminster Abbey** to American and British military men who
commanded troops during the French and Indian Wars, the American Revolutionary War,
and the War of 1812:

Major John Andre – British spy who was captured on a mission to meet the American traitor
Benedict Arnold to negotiate the surrender of West Point. Andre was tried and hanged. His body was
returned to the British.

General John Burgoyne – British general who surrendered to the Americans at Saratoga.
He was baptized at St. Margaret's, Westminster, and educated at Westminster School.
He is buried in the North Cloister under a simple stone.

George, 3rd Viscount Howe – killed in 1758 on an expedition to Ticonderoga in New York State.
His monument in the northwest tower chapel of the nave was erected by the
Province of Massachusetts.

Colonel Roger Townshend – British officer killed on an expedition to Ticonderoga,
New York State, 1759. His monument includes two figures of Native Americans.

St. Margaret's, Westminster
Sir Peter Parker – a Briton who died in a skirmish on the
American coast during the War of 1812

Barnardus La Grange – "an American loyalist" who died in 1797

St. Paul's Cathedral, London
Charles Marquis Cornwallis – British military leader during the American
Revolutionary War. There is a large memorial to him in the south transept.

George Washington – American military leader and first president of
the United States. There is a small bust of him in the crypt of St. Paul's Cathedral.

Grosvenor Square, London
The Diplomatic Gates – a gift of the National Committee for the Bicentennial
to commemorate the 200th anniversary of the signing of the Treaty of Paris which brought
a formal end to the Revolutionary War.

OTHER CONNECTIONS WITH THE AMERICAN REVOLUTIONARY WAR

Royal Green Jackets Museum
Winchester, Hampshire

23rd Foot — Royal Welsh Fusiliers
re-enactment group: www.geocities.com/the23rdfoot

The Continental Marines
www.marine76.8m.com/
Formed in 2000 to take part in the John Paul Jones Festival at Filey,
the Continental Marines re-enactment group has the advantage of portraying
the only American regiment to have actually landed in Britain during
the Revolutionary War!

CHAPTER 4
MILITARY CONNECTIONS

The Treaty of Paris of 1783 officially recognized the transformation of thirteen British colonies into one nation called the United States. The relationship between the new nation and the country from which much of its population came was a dynamic one. After more than two hundred years, the relationship is still one of some tension and uncertainty.

Linked by history, language, economic ties, and personal relationships, the United States and the United Kingdom have been military foes and military allies. The two countries fought each other on American soil just thirty years after the Treaty of Paris in the War of 1812. As their relationship matured, they became allies, and fought side by side in two world wars, defending their common political systems and cultural heritage. 🍃

The War of 1812
By ratifying the Treaty of Paris in 1783, Great Britain recognized the establishment of a new independent nation in America and agreed to end formal hostilities. However, signatures on a document did not guarantee a peaceful future, and American efforts to carry on maritime commerce with Europe often encountered British opposition. British involvement in the Napoleonic Wars meant they needed more ships and sailors for their naval battles against the French. The British navy often harassed ships from the new nation, and carried out a policy of impressing the Americans – capturing American ships and forcing the sailors to serve in the British navy.

After a British ship attacked an American ship, USS *Chesapeake* in 1807, **President Thomas Jefferson** declared an embargo on American shipping, barring US merchants from exporting goods. This hurt American merchants and led to a depression. The embargo was repealed in 1808 just before James Madison took office as the fourth US president. When British forces continued to seize American ships, a group of

LONDON In the dining hall of the *Royal Hospital Chelsea* a number of military banners and flags are on display, including four American flags captured by the British during the War of 1812.

At *St. Margaret's Church, Westminster,* a monument commemorates Sir Peter Parker who died in 1814 during a skirmish on the American coast.

Teyoninhokarawen, known as **Major John Norton**, was an important link between the Indians and the British military during the War of 1812. The son of a Scottish mother and a Cherokee Indian father who joined the British Army in the French and Indian Wars, John was born in Scotland. He returned to America and became a leader of the Cherokee nation. His portrait hangs in the print poom at *Syon Park* in *Brentford.*

LONDON General Edward Pakenham, commander of British forces during the Battle of New Orleans, was killed during the conflict. He is remembered at the *Pakenham Arms, London*, and with a statue in the south transept of *St. Paul's Cathedral*. He was the brother of Catherine Pakenham who married Arthur Wellesley, Duke of Wellington.

GLOUCESTERSHIRE A plaque and American flag at *Gloucester Cathedral* commemorate John Stafford Smith. A member of the Anachreonic Society, in 1780 he composed the music for a song to be sung at their meetings. Titled "To Anachreon in Heaven" it was inspired by a sixth-century Greek poet and was about the pleasures of wine and love. Francis Scott Key set his words for the "Star-Spangled Banner" to Smith's tune.

SUFFOLK According to local historian Barry Wall, woolen bunting made in *Sudbury* was used to make the giant American flag that flew above Fort McHenry in the War of 1812.

American politicians calling themselves the "War Hawks" backed a more aggressive policy. In June 1812 President Madison declared that the United States was at war with Britain.

The United States was still a nation in the process of creation. With a national army consisting of only about 7,000 regular soldiers, the Americans attempted an ill-prepared invasion of Canada. The American navy and privateers attacked British ships, capturing 500 British vessels during 1812 and 1813. The British fleet moved toward the American coast with orders to "destroy and lay waste." On the night of 24 August 1814, the British attacked Washington, D.C. The American arsenal, docks, and weapons stores were destroyed. The White House was burned. This was the scene of one of America's symbolic acts of heroism when First Lady Dolley Madison refused to leave the White House until **Gilbert Stuart**'s portrait of **George Washington** was safely removed. The government administration fled the city, and the British invaders moved to the northeast.

British vessels moved towards Baltimore, hampered by the American forces firing on them from Fort McHenry. The British bombarded the fort for twenty-five hours and attempted a landing with 1,000 men. When the British commander was killed, their troops withdrew and Baltimore was saved. The commander of Fort McHenry ordered a large, clean American flag to be raised. Francis Scott Key was aboard a British warship trying to negotiate the release of an American prisoner. When the sun rose, he saw the Stars and Stripes still flying over Fort McHenry. He then wrote the verses that finish:

> "Oh! say, does that star spangled banner yet wave
> O'er the land of the free and the home of the brave?"

The staggering costs of the Napoleonic Wars led the Duke of Wellington to urge negotiations to end the war with America. On 14 December 1814 the Treaty of Ghent was signed. America's greatest "victory" in the war came weeks after the peace treaty was signed in Europe. News of the treaty had not reached General Andrew Jackson who led his troops in a great battle and victory over the British at New Orleans. 700 British troops were killed and 1,400 wounded, while only thirteen Americans were killed and fifty-eight wounded. The victory insured that the British carried through with official ratification of the Treaty of Ghent.

So, the French contributed a second time to an American victory over the British. Without the need to fight a costly war in Europe, the British could have turned their full attention to defeating the new American nation. As it was, the Americans were able to claim that they won the war, and with the defeat of the British, were given a long period of peace to build and strengthen the new United States. 🍃

American Prisoners of War

During the War of 1812, American prisoners captured at sea were transported back to Britain. At first the prisoners were kept in old ships and congested buildings in **Plymouth** in **Devon**, but in the spring of 1813 they were marched overland to **Princetown** where they joined French prisoners who had also been captured. On 31 December 1814 there were more than 3,300 American prisoners at Dartmoor. Approximately 270 American prisoners died at the prison – some from the terrible conditions that prevailed there, and some at the hands of British troops who fired on them during riots. Their brutal mistreatment was investigated after the war by a commission that awarded compensation to the families of those who had died. An attempt is currently being made to erect a memorial to the Americans who died while in British captivity. 🍃

The 44th Regiment of Foot Soldiers

The 44th Regiment of Foot was one of the many units of the British Army to be involved in fighting the colonial rebels during the American Revolutionary War. The regiment was ordered to North America in 1755 to fight in the French and Indian Wars, and many of the unit were wounded or killed at the Battles of Monongahela and Ticonderoga. The 44th moved to Ireland in 1765, but was ordered back to Boston, Massachusetts, in 1775 as part of the strengthening of British forces after the Boston Massacre and the **Battle of Lexington and Concord.**

Thomas Gage was appointed major of the regiment in February 1747. Whey they returned to Boston in 1775 he had become General Gage and was in charge of the British forces in North America. (*See Chapter 3 for details about General Gage.*) During the next five years the 44th Regiment of Foot participated in many of the important military campaigns – the New York Campaign, Philadelphia Campaign, and the Battle of Monmouth Court House. In 1780 they were sent to Quebec and in 1786 returned to England. The 44th Regiment of Foot returned to fight on American soil again after President Madison declared war on Britain in June 1812. They were part of the battle force that sailed up the Chesapeake Bay to fight in Washington and Baltimore. 🍃

DEVON On its "Door of Unity" *Prysten House* in *Plymouth* has a memorial tablet presented by the Society of the Daughters of 1812 to commemorate a battle when the American brig Argus saw action against the British ship *Pelican*. The captain and a midshipman of the Argus were killed and are buried in Plymouth. A memorial service is held here annually on 30 May.

Once a hotel, then the prison officers' mess, the Dartmoor Prison Museum and High Moorland Visitor Centre in Princetown opened in 1993.

DEVON The *Church of St. Michael and All Angels* in *Princetown* is the only church in England to have been built by French and American prisoners of war.

The *44th Regiment of Foot* is a "living history" and re-enactment society that portrays the life of the British Army regiment from 1800 to the Battle of Waterloo in 1815. Each year the group participates in many events throughout Britain in locations such as *Hatfield House*, Highclere Castle, and Waltham Abbey. Visitors are welcome to come and see this historic unit "in action."
www.44thregiment.itgo.com
The 41st Regiment of Foot Re-enactment Society focuses on a British regiment that was based in Canada during the War of 1812. The 41st Regiment took part in the capture of Fort Detroit and Fort Niagara, and action in Ohio and along the Canadian border. www.41st-foot.co.uk

GREATER MANCHESTER

In *Southern Cemetery, Manchester*, a headstone marks the grave of Phillip Baybutt, a British citizen who fought on the Union side in the American Civil War. In 2002 the US Veterans Administration presented a special headstone for winners of the Congressional Medal of Honor. A special graveside service was held in September with Phillip Baybutt's granddaughter in attendance.

The American Civil War (1861–5)

A largely unknown connection between American and England involves English soldiers who fought in the American Civil War. Some of these men were British veterans of military service in the Crimea and India who migrated to the United States attracted by adventure. Others were motivated by visions of wealth – the 1849 gold rush had made America a land of dreams. Many of these men joined the Union armies, and served valiantly. At least sixty-seven Englishmen received the Congressional Medal of Honor for their service in the American Civil War.

AMERICAN CIVIL WAR RE-ENACTMENT GROUPS

In England, history re-enactment is a popular activity. Dressed as military groups did in the past, members spend time living as authentically as possible. It's not unknown to happen upon a local history group holding a Roman fete with legionnaires striding proudly around in their armor. Participants take both sides to re-enact the Battle of Hastings. Every year on 29 January, the anniversary of King Charles I's execution, re-enactors dress up as Roundheads and Cavaliers to march through London in commemoration of the king and the English Civil War. Throughout the year events are held in parks and estates in all parts of the country.

One of the most popular periods for re-enactment is the American Civil War. Groups of English history buffs don uniforms from the Union army and the armies of the Confederacy and stage re-enactments of American Civil War battles! Why? Why in the world would British people enjoy re-enacting American Civil War battles? There are many possible explanations. The American Civil War can be viewed somewhat romantically, especially if you know the war largely from books and movies like *Gone With the Wind*. Horsemanship is very popular in England, so riding around in blue or gray uniforms holding mock battles can provide an exciting weekend's entertainment. Also, the American Civil War is removed from Britain; it is an American war that the British did not fight in, except for the very rare individual. It is easier to take up the uniform of one side or the other and treat the American Civil War as a fantasy if your family or community had no real involvement with the actual conflict.

There is a theory that the American Civil War largely reflected a cultural conflict between the American northerners, who were more industrial and largely descended from the Anglo-Saxon English, and the southerners, who were more agrarian and predominantly Scotch-Irish Celts. Maybe it was one last manifestation of divisions that were seen during the English Civil War – the stern, hard-working Puritans of New England pitted against the agrarian southerners who saw themselves as a more aristocratic and paternalistic society.

Perhaps the English who participate in American Civil War re-enactments are still carrying on this cultural battle. Are they really the Celtic re-incarnations of frustrated southerners who would like to turn back the tide of industrial development, pollution, work-day stresses, and return to a simpler time when a man (or woman) jumped on a horse and fought for what he believed in?

AMERICAN CIVIL WAR GROUPS IN THE UK

Southern Skirmish Association
PO Box 485, Swindon, Wiltshire SN2 8BZ www. soskan.co.uk

Formed in July 1968, SOSKAN (Southern Skirmish Association) is the oldest American Civil War re-enactment society outside the United States. Over the years the association has performed in many venues around Britain, the Continent, and the USA. Members are trained to handle the weapons and equipment of the period using the correct drill and instruction manuals. They take part in military camp life and act out scenarios when the public can visit the camp.

The American Civil War Society
ACWS Ltd, PO Box 52, Brighouse, West Yorkshire, HD6 1HF www.acws.co.uk

The American Civil War Society (ACWS) was formed in 1975. It has close connections with American Civil War re-enactors in the USA and across Europe. Many members are experts in the history of the period and give talks at schools, colleges, and to other organizations.

The Confederation and Union Re-enactment Society
www.homestead.com/curs1/society.html

Members of this re-enactment society come largely from the west of Britain: West Wales, South Wales, Surrey, Derbyshire, the West Midlands, and Hampshire.

Armies of the Potomac and Northern Virginia Historical Society
PO BOX 1863, Northampton NN48ZQ www.apnv.co.uk

The Armies of the Potomac and Northern Virginia Historical Society or APNV was formed in June 1999 by eight people, many of whom have over thirty years of re-enacting experience. In less than a year the APNV grew to nearly 200 members with new members joining each week. The APNV consists of strong artillery, Union army of both regular blue troops and Sharpshooters, two cavalry units and a Confederate army and medical corps.

The SCALAWAG Mess
Company B, 9th Kentucky Volunteer Infantry
Contact: Chris O'Brien, 4 Maycock Grove, Northwood, Middlesex HA6 3PU
www.members.lycos.co.uk/COB9KY/scalawag.htm

The Scalawags attempt to recreate the dress, drill, camp life, and attitudes of the soldier and citizen of 1863. Not strictly "re-enactors," they try to go a bit further than just "dressing up" by researching photographs, diaries, manuscripts, newspapers, and Quartermaster returns of the period. With advice from groups in the US and visits to museums and battlefields, the Scalawags have put together a highly accurate impression of that period.

LONDON A small stained-glass window in the nave of *Westminster Abbey* was erected by Mrs. Louis Bennett of West Virginia in memory of all members of the Royal Flying Corps 1914–18 who died, including her son Louis, Jr., who was killed in France.

In the *Royal Air Force Chapel* at *Westminster Abbey*, a furled American flag can be seen in the stained-glass window as a memorial to the American pilots who flew with the RAF during the **Battle of Britain**. The only American killed during this battle was **Pilot Officer William Fiske**.

In the crypt of *St. Paul's Cathedral* there is a plaque to William Fiske.

WEST SUSSEX Pilot "Billy" Fiske is buried at *Boxgrove Priory* near *Chichester*. His parents' ashes are near his grave.

LONDON A memorial plaque in the Painted Hall of the *Royal Naval Hospital* in *Greenwich* commemorates Americans who joined the Royal Navy to fight in World War II.

SUFFOLK *Martlesham Heath Control Tower Museum* near *Ipswich* is on the site where three RAF "Eagle" squadrons of American volunteer pilots were based in 1941.

The Eagle Squadron Memorial in *Grosvenor Square, London*

World War I

More than one million American soliders fought in France during World War I. More than 75,000 of these young men died (approximately 58,480 in battle). Many wounded Americans were brought back to England for medical care and subsequently died. 486 of these fallen soldiers were buried in the special American military section of **Brookwood Cemetery** in **Woking**, which was one of the main cemeteries for British casualites in World War I. Special trains from London carried the caskets and mourners to Woking for the funeral ceremonies. 🍃

World War II

During World War II, US military forces came to England to set up bases in preparation for the invasion of Europe. The remains of some of these installations, along with memorials to their involvement in the war, can still be seen, especially in East Anglia and near **Plymouth**. The **American Military Cemetery** is located near Cambridge. At **Bletchley Park**, Americans participated in the top-secret efforts to break the German military codes. 🍃

The Battle of Britain

The Battle of Britain from July to October 1940 was the first major air attack on Britain during World War II. The US was not officially at war at this time, but there were Americans who wanted to do what they could to help in the effort to defend Britain. Some young Americans were able to join the Royal Air Force (RAF) and bravely flew in the skies above England. 🍃

William M.L. Fiske III was a young American who came to Cambridge in 1928. He led the US bobsled team to victory in the Winter Olympics, and married Rose, Countess of Warwick, in Maidenhead in 1938. The first American to join the RAF in World War II, William Fiske died on 16 August 1940 during the Battle of Britain after his damaged plane crashed on landing at the RAF base at Tangmere. 🍃

1st Eagle Squadron was formed in September 1940, mostly of American citizens who volunteered to join the RAF. The Eagle Squadron Memorial in **Grosvenor Square** in **London** is a tapering shaft of white Portland stone. On the top, with wings spread ready to fly, stands a bronze statue of an American bald eagle. The inscription reads: "They came not as warriors in search of conflict, but rather as crusaders in the cause of liberty. They became brothers in arms to their British colleagues..." 🍃

Winston Churchill

Named "The Greatest Briton of All Time" in 2002 in a nationwide poll, Winston Churchill's father was the younger son of the Duke of Marlborough and his mother was an American, **Jennie Jerome** of Brooklyn, New York, who met and charmed young Lord Randolph Churchill. They were married in Paris on 15 April 1874 when she was twenty years old. Jennie's son Winston Churchill was born at **Blenheim Palace** on 30 November 1874.

Educated at Harrow and the Royal Military Academy Sandhurst, Winston became an officer in the 4th Hussars in 1894. By 1895 he was on leave from the military and writing as a journalist for the *London Daily Graphic*. After reporting on military action in Cuba and the Sudan, in 1899 Churchill was sent to cover the war in South Africa for the *Morning Post*. His first-hand account of being captured and imprisoned by the Boers, and then making an exciting escape from the prisoner-of-war camp, gave him a taste of celebrity in Britain.

Winston Churchill returned home and was elected to Parliament in 1900. After switching from the Conservative to the Liberal Party, Churchill began to move up in government circles. By 1910 he was Home Secretary and in 1911 was appointed First Lord of the Admiralty, but the defeat of the British and French at the Battle of Gallipoli in 1915 led to his resignation. Churchill did return to government service, but it seemed he would never regain a major office. In 1924 he rejoined the Conservative Party and was appointed Chancellor of the Exchequer, but resigned in 1929 after his decision to return Britain to the gold standard led to widespread unemployment and a general strike in 1926.

Churchill left office in 1929 believing his political career to be over. He turned to writing again to support his family. His magazine and newspaper articles were a way for him to voice his concerns about the growing strength of Nazi Germany. He also wrote a biography of his famous ancestor Marlborough and started on *A History of the English Speaking Peoples*.

For a number of years Winston Churchill's warnings about the growing threat of the German military build-up were felt to be a nuisance by many in the government, but when war broke out in September 1939, Churchill returned to the office he had lost in 1915 – First Lord of the Admiralty. In May 1940, Winston Churchill became prime minister of Great Britain. During the Second World War, he inspired the nation with his stubborn determination and brilliant oratory. Churchill developed a personal relationship with American president **Franklin Roosevelt**, keeping him

OXFORDSHIRE Winston Churchill was born at *Blenheim Palace* in *Woodstock* on 30 November 1874. Today a suite of rooms at Blenheim house a display about his life.

SOMERSET On 26 July 1897 the twenty-three-year-old Winston Churchill made his first political speech at *Claverton Manor* now the *American Museum in Britain*, near *Bath*.

LONDON On 12 September 1908 Winston Churchill married Miss Clementine Hozier at *St. Margaret's Church, Westminster*.

Winston Churchill and Franklin Roosevelt were both members of *Gray's Inn*, one of the Inns of Court. Winston Churchill served as First Lord of the Admiralty from 1911 to 1915 and returned to the office in 1939. His official residence was at the *Old Admiralty Building, Whitehall*.

During the war years, Churchill's official residence as prime minister of Britain was *10 Downing Street*.

KENT *Chartwell* was Winston Churchill's home from 1924 until the end of his life. The house contains many signed photographs and letters from American statesmen, generals, and other leaders with whom Churchill was in contact, such as **General Eisenhower** and **Franklin Roosevelt**.

LANCASHIRE Family trees of the Washington and Churchill families are on view at *St. Oswald's Church* in *Warton*. They show that **George Washington** and **Winston Churchill** were both related to an ancestor who came from Warton.

LONDON The Churchill Memorial exhibit in the *Cabinet War Rooms* includes Winston's 1953 Nobel Prize for Literature. A special closet in the Cabinet War Rooms held the "hot-line" for secret communications between Churchill and Roosevelt during World War II. Much of the equipment for the transatlantic "hot-line" for secret telephone calls between Churchill and **Roosevelt** was installed in the basement of *Selfridges* department store on *Oxford Street*.

On 9 April 1963 **President John F. Kennedy** conferred honorary American citizenship on Winston Churchill.

HAMPSHIRE During the time when *Southwick House* was being used as a secret military HQ, the *Golden Lion* pub in *Southwick* became an unofficial officers' mess. One of the pub's claims is that among many others they served **General Eisenhower**, General Montgomery, and Prince Philip. There is a plaque near the entrance of the pub giving some details of its wartime history.

closely informed about the situation in Europe. When the US finally entered the war thousands of American servicemen were stationed in Britain in preparation for the invasion of Europe on D-Day.

Amazingly, at the end of the war, Winston Churchill was forced out of office when the Conservative Party lost the 1945 election. After the years of suffering and deprivation, the British public seemed to feel little thanks for what Churchill had done. They wanted a government that would focus on their social needs The Conservative Party was returned to government in 1951, and Churchill served as Prime Minister again for four years. 1953 was a special year for him – he was awarded the Nobel Prize for Literature, and he was knighted by the Queen. Churchill resigned from office in 1955 but he retained his seat in Parliament until 1964.

Winston Churchill's funeral in 1965 was one of the great state ceremonies of the century. After his coffin lay in state at Westminster Hall, the casket was placed on a gun carriage and was pulled by a Royal Navy gun crew through the streets of London. The sites passed included **St. Margaret's Church,** where he had married; the **Houses of Parliament**, **No. 10 Downing Street**, where he had lived as prime minister; the **Admiralty**, where he had served as First Lord in two wars; **Fleet Street**, where he had published so many articles; and finally **St. Paul's Cathedral**, where a state funeral service was held, the first for a commoner since 1914. After the funeral, the casket was placed on a barge which carried it to Waterloo Station. As the barge passed along the river, London's dockers lowered their cranes silently to the great man. A train from Waterloo took him to his final resting place at his family's church in **Bladon** near Blenheim where he was born. 🍃

Southwick House

Southwick House, Hampshire, was used as the secret headquarters for the Allied Expeditionary Force during World War II, and it was here that the Allied invasion of Europe, known as "Operation Overlord," was planned. At Southwick, **General Eisenhower**, as Supreme Allied Commander, made the decision to proceed with the invasion of Europe on 6 June 1944. A map in the drawing room shows the plans for the invasion. Eisenhower lived in a trailer or "circus" wagon at Advance Command Post at Portsmouth near Southwick House during the D-Day invasion. After the war, the house was purchased by the Royal Navy and used as part of the Royal Navy Maritime Warfare Training School. 🍃

WINSTON CHURCHILL SITES IN ENGLAND

SURREY During the summer of 1915, when Winston Churchill was First Lord of the Admiralty, he and his brother Jack rented **Hoe Farm** in **Hascombe, Surrey**, as a weekend retreat for their families. After the disastrous Allied defeat in the Dardanelles, Winston was forced from office. As he spent time at the farm, he watched his sister-in-law painting and decided to give it a try. Taking it up as a distraction from his political setback, Churchill became one of the world's most famous amateur painters.

At **Godalming Museum** an exhibit tells the story of Churchill's stay at Hoe Farm. Reproductions of two of his Hoe Farm paintings hang at the museum.

LONDON A bronze statue of the defiant wartime prime minister stands in **Parliament Square** facing Parliament. Created by Ivor Roberts-Jones, it was unveiled by Lady Churchill in the presence of the Queen on 1 November 1973.

A memorial commemorating the 130th anniversary of Winston Churchill's birth was unveiled at **St. Paul's Cathedral** in 2004.

In the mosaics portrait on the large staircase at the main entrance of the **National Gallery**, **Trafalgar Square**, Churchill is shown confronting the Devil in the Defiance roundel.

The **Church of St. Mary Aldermanbury** (corner of Love Lane and Aldermanbury Square) was bombed in 1940. After the war, the stones were sold to the US and rebuilt in Fulton, Missouri, as a memorial to Winston Churchill's famous "iron curtain" speech. There is a memorial garden at the site now.

Churchill died on 24 January 1965 at his home at **28 Hyde Park Gate, Kensington Gore**.

More than 320,000 people paid tribute while Churchill's body was lying in state at **Westminster Hall**.

OXFORDSHIRE As he requested, Winston Churchill's burial place was at **St. Martin's Church** in **Bladon** near **Woodstock**.

CAMBRIDGE Churchill College, which focuses on science and technology, was founded in 1960 as a memorial to Winston Churchill. Many of the most important of Churchill's papers are housed in the Churchill Archives Centre, including letters, writings (which earned him a Nobel Prize), and wartime speeches. They can be viewed by appointment only.

BUCKINGHAMSHIRE In the "A" Block of **Bletchley Park** an extensive exhibition of Winston Churchill memorabilia features a display case with items from his American mother, **Jennie Jerome**.

Winston Churchill in England The University of Dallas's summer study program offers high school students an opportunity to earn three college credits while studying the career of the great English prime minister and the ideal of leadership it exemplified.
www.congressionalgoldmedal.com/WinstonChurchill

BUCKINGHAMSHIRE A case in the "A" Block museum at *Bletchley Park* has information about the D-Day invasion and material about **General Eisenhower**, whose famous "OK, Let's Go" started the Allied invasion of Europe.

A large American flag hangs on the wall in the billiards room at *Bletchley Park*. The sign says, "This flag was given to the Bletchley Park Trust in its early days and is reputed to have been carried by American forces landing in the famous Omaha Beach during the D-Day invasion of Europe on 6 June 1944."

In the entrance hall, there is a photo of Sir Edward Travis, commander of Bletchley Park, with a certificate stating: "This Medal for Merit awarded by President Truman to Sir Edward Travis, the first non-American to be given this honour, on 12 June 1946 by Harry S. Truman, the then President of the United States and Commander in Chief."

SEE The film *Enigma* starring Kate Winslet.

READ *Station X, The Codebreakers of Bletchley Park* by Michael Smith. London: Channel 4 Books, 1998.

Bletchley Park

One of the most closely guarded secrets in Britain during World War II was the existence of a vast organization of technicians, engineers, crossword puzzle addicts, chess champions, mathematicians, and code-breakers working at Bletchley Park in Buckinghamshire. They were all working on decoding the messages that the German military were sending using the Enigma coding machines. The information that Bletchley Park provided was vital in the British and Allied effort during the war.

A small group of Polish mathematicians had broken the original Enigma code in 1932, but when the Germans made the machine more complex, the Poles did not have the financial resources to work on the new problems. In 1939 they turned their findings over to the British, who assembled a secret group at their Government Code and Cypher School. The huge calculating machine developed at Bletchley to aid in decoding the messages was called "Colossus." Some of the most complex machinery in Britain was developed at Bletchley Park, including the world's first programmable computer.

The first direct involvement of Americans in the work at Bletchley Park was in early 1941 when four Americans were briefed on aspects of the operation. Months of somewhat hesitant meetings across the Atlantic followed, and by the end of 1942, seven US military officers were working at Bletchley Park – two from the navy's Op-20-G section and five from the army's Special Branch and Signal Intelligence Service.

The British were reluctant to allow Americans to work directly on the Enigma code-breaking, but in 1943 a small group of American military officers were selected to come to work at Bletchley Park. This group of extremely capable men included Lewis Powell, who became a member of the US Supreme Court, and Alfred Friendly, who became managing editor of the *Washington Post*. The code-breakers in the group came from the US Army Special Branch and were under the command of Captain William Bundy. This was the beginning of a life-long career that led to top-level government service for Bundy, who eventually became assistant secretary of state. He was the older brother of McGeorge Bundy, who was national security advisor to Presidents **John F. Kennedy** and Lyndon B. Johnson.

At the end of the war, the computer equipment and all records and papers at Bletchley Park were destroyed. Everyone who worked at Bletchley was required to sign the Official Secrets Act, and the secret was kept for many decades. In 1991 plans were made to demolish the site and build a housing complex. However, following efforts by the Bletchley Park Trust, the British government decided to restore it and turn it into a museum. Most of Bletchley Park is restored and there are plans to completely restore it.

Exercise Tiger at Slapton Sands

Bletchley Park was not the only long-kept secret of World War II. The fate of 749 American servicemen who died at Slapton Sands in Devon on 28 April 1944 was not widely known for many years. They were part of Exercise Tiger – a training exercise held 22–30 April 1944 in preparation for the D-Day landings in Normandy. Slapton Sands was chosen as the site of operations because it resembled the beach in France where the landings would take place. Residents of local villages and farms were relocated so live naval and artillery fire could be used to make the rehearsals as real as possible.

Just after midnight on 28 April, a flotilla of eight tank landing ships, carrying hundreds of American servicemen, neared the Devon coast. Unknown to them, they were being followed by nine German torpedo boats. The Germans fired torpedoes and hit three of the landing ships. In the fire and confusion, 749 servicemen died –198 sailors and 551 soldiers.

Generals **Dwight D. Eisenhower** and Omar N. Bradley watched the exercise, and quickly ordered the strictest secrecy about the disaster – even the doctors and nurses who treated the survivors were ordered not to discuss what had happened. The commanders were concerned that word of the landing maneuvers might give clues about the impending invasion to the Germans and would also demoralize the troops who would soon be sent on the real invasion. However, this was not planned as a cover-up. In July 1944 General Eisenhower's Supreme Headquarters issued a press release about the tragedy, and the American army newspaper *The Stars and Stripes* also mentioned it. Nevertheless, many of the people who had been involved – both American servicemen and local English residents – felt that they had been ordered to keep the incident secret and they never spoke of it.

In 1954 US Army officials unveiled a monument honoring the people of the local area who left their homes and farms to provide a practice area for the invasion, but the monument did not mention the hundreds of servicemen who had died that night in April 1944. This may have been due to the American policy that only the American Battle Monuments Commission is allowed to erect monuments to the American dead killed in wars.

A private group eventually erected a memorial at the site of the Exercise Tiger disaster. A local Devon man, Ken Small, felt there should be a memorial to the fallen American servicemen. He paid to recover a Sherman tank from the

DEVON A memorial to the troops lost in Exercise Tiger has been erected at *Slapton Sands, Torcross, Devon.*

waters of the bay, and placed a memorial plaque next to it. In 1987 a commemorative plaque was unveiled at the site. In November 1995, at the Veterans' Day Ceremony at Arlington National Cemetery, **President Bill Clinton** unveiled a plaque dedicated to the 749 sailors and soldiers killed in the Exercise Tiger tragedy. The Exercise Tiger Association in the USA was founded to honor veterans of all wars, and holds annual ceremonies in the US.

There are ongoing efforts to fund a memorial at Slapton Sands with the names of the lost servicemen. Information can be found at: www.exercisetiger.org and www.friendsofthelaurel.co.uk. 🍃

American Bases in England

American military forces began to arrive in Britain in large numbers in 1943, preparing for direct involvement in the European conflict. American troops were housed all over England. Stately homes, estates, and schools were used as officers' housing, headquarters for military planning, and many secret operations. Small airfields were used by the USAAF (United States Army Air Force); and temporary airfields were built in farmland. Today many of these old airfields have been returned to farming or converted to new uses, but visitors can often find hints of the history of the area. Special signs sometimes indicate their wartime use and some airfields have special memorials to the men or squadrons that had been stationed there. In some cases the original control towers still stand and some have been restored. A few contain exhibitions and displays about their wartime use.

The 8th Air Force was the largest striking force ever committed to battle. By 1943 the USAAF had more than 100,000 US airmen stationed in Britain, housed on about a hundred bases in the east of England. Some famous Americans served in England during the Second World War, including the movie stars Clark Gable, James Stewart, Walter Matthau, and **Joseph P. Kennedy, Jr.**, son of the former US ambassador to Britain. 🍃

Glenn Miller

Glenn Miller, the famous American bandleader, came to England in 1944 with his band to work with the BBC radio service and to perform at US military bases throughout England. The band was due to leave for Paris on Saturday 16 December to play a series of concerts for the troops. Miller decided that he would go ahead of the band, but bad weather delayed his departure. When Miller discovered that a flight was going to Paris in a small Norseman aircraft, he convinced the pilot to take him along. The small plane left from Twinwood Airfield, near **Clapham, Bedfordshire**, shortly after noon on 15 December. On 20 December, an announcement was issued that Major Alton Glenn Miller and his two companions were "missing in flight, presumed to be lost." On Christmas Eve 1944, it was confirmed that Glenn Miller had died. The Glenn Miller band continued to entertain troops in England and Europe until 28 July 1945, when they gave their last concert at Le Havre. 🍃

American Military Cemetery, Madingley

Two miles outside of Cambridge is the only American military cemetery in England to honor the people of the US who gave their lives during the Second World War. The cemetery has 3,812 graves, including memorials to **Glenn Miller** and **Joseph P. Kennedy, Jr.**, brother of **President John F. Kennedy**. On the wall running from the entrance to the chapel are inscribed the names of 5,127 Americans who gave their lives in the service of their country, but whose remains were never recovered or identified. Many of the 749 American servicemen who were killed on 28 April 1944 at **Slapton Sands** by German torpedo boats during Exercise Tiger are buried at the American Military Cemetery at Madingley. 🍃

American Military Cemetery at
Madingley, Cambridgeshire

WORLD WAR II MILITARY MUSEUMS IN ENGLAND

LONDON
Churchill Museum and Cabinet War Rooms
Churchill and his staff and cabinet worked in this secret headquarters during World War II.

Imperial War Museum The Imperial War Museum focuses on military conflicts, especially those involving Britain and the Commonwealth, from the First World War to the present day. It has several components: the Imperial War Museum London, the Imperial War Museum North (Manchester), the Cabinet War Rooms, HMS *Belfast*, and Duxford Airfield.

National Army Museum in Chelsea
The museum features a display of weapons, uniforms, and other artifacts that show the history of "The Redcoats: The British Soldier 1415–1792", including British uniforms worn during the American Revolution. There is a print showing the **Battle of Concord and Lexington**, and a model of the Battle of Yorktown, the final battle of the American Revolutionary War. The gallery has a large collection of historical paintings.

BEDFORDSHIRE
Twinwood RAF Control Tower and Glenn Miller Museum, Clapham
On 27 August 1944 Glenn Miller gave the only outdoor concert he ever did at an RAF base. He

was billeted at Bedford, three miles from Twinwood, and often used the RAF base when he flew out with his band to perform at military bases around England. On 15 December 1944 he left from Twinwood on his final flight. An annual Glenn Miller Festival of Swing, Jazz and Jive is presented at Twinwood each August. Website for information: www.twinwoodevents.com

BUCKINGHAMSHIRE
Bletchley Park – top-secret location of the code-breakers of World War II.

CAMBRIDGESHIRE
American Air Museum in Duxford
One of the finest collections of tanks, military vehicles, and naval exhibits in Great Britain, this site began as an airfield in the First World War and played a vital role in World War II, first as an RAF fighter station and later as an American fighter base. The American Air Museum houses the finest collection of historic American combat aircraft outside the USA.

DORSET
The **Tank Museum** in **Bovington** is the world's leading museum devoted to military vehicles. Four impressive machines, the M41, M48, M60 and M103 represent the US.

HAMPSHIRE
Aldershot Military Museum
The Cody Gallery focuses on the achievements of **Samuel F. Cody**, the American who was instrumental in developing airplanes in England. The gallery includes a reconstruction of his Farnborough workshop and his original flying helmet.

D-Day Museum and Overlord Embroidery in Portsmouth
The D-Day Museum features an audio-visual show and displays that reconstruct wartime scenes and story of D-Day. The Overlord Embroidery depicts the Allied invasion of Normandy. Military equipment and vehicles are also on display.

The **Mary Rose** in **Portsmouth** is the only preserved sixteenth-century warship in the world. Visitors get a good idea of what ships were like at that time by touring the *Mary Rose*, King Henry VIII's warship, which sank in 1545. Richard Grenville's father died in the disaster.

Museum of Army Flying in Middle Wallop
Home in 1944–5 to the 9th USAAF, the museum houses one of the country's finest collections of military kites, gliders, aeroplanes, and helicopters. The collection includes a replica of **Cody**'s man-lifting kite. Cody was an American who built and flew the first airplane in Britain in 1908.

Winchester's Military Museums Visitor Centre
This collection of museums from six military units provides an insight into the history of British military service. The group comprises the King's Royal Hussars, the Royal Hampshire Regiment, the Light Infantry, the Gurkhas, the Adjutant General's Corps, and the Royal Green Jackets.

Royal Green Jackets Museum in Winchester
The Royal Green Jackets Regiment was formed in 1966 when several regiments were united,

including the 43rd and 52nd Light Infantry which saw long service in North America during the Revolution. The regiments fought in Massachusetts in the Battles of Lexington and Bunker Hill, suffering heavy casualties. They were more successful in a series of actions around New York in which the Americans were regularly defeated. In 1778 the units returned to England. After the French gave more support to the colonials, the 43rd was sent to Virginia to reinforce **General Cornwallis**. They were present at the British surrender at Yorktown in 1781 that brought the war to an end. The museum collection includes American flags seized during the war.

NORFOLK
City of Norwich Aviation Museum
At the City of Norwich Aviation Museum visitors can look into the cockpits of several aircraft. Displays tell the story of the US 8th Army Air Force in the area during World War II.

NORTHAMPTONSHIRE
Harrington Carpetbagger Aviation Museum
Harrington Airfield was a highly classified World War II base, built in 1944 by the US 8th Air Force Special Operations Group. It was home to the 801st Bomb Group (later changed to the 492nd). The secret role of this unit was to support resistance groups in France, Holland, and Scandinavia. On secret missions "Carpetbaggers" – secret agents with equipment – were dropped into the hostile countries. The 8th Army left Harrington in 1945. All military activity has now ended at Harrington. A museum has been opened in the old Operations Building. Exhibits, photographs, and film describe the secret missions that left from this site.

SUFFOLK
Halesworth Airfield Museum
During World War II, the airfield at Halesworth was mainly used as an American base for the 56th Fighter Group and the 489th Bomb Group. Towards the end of the war the base took on a rescue and training function before closing in February 1946.

Martlesham Heath Control Tower Museum near Ipswich
In 1916 an aerodrome was built at Martlesham. In 1924 the station became the Aeroplane and Armament Experimental Establishment In 1941 three RAF "Eagle" squadrons were based at Martlesham, manned by American volunteer pilots. 1943 saw the arrival of the USAAF's 356th Fighter Group; this group left Martlesham in August 1945. In March 1979 the last aircraft flew from Martlesham Heath. The site has been rebuilt as British Telecom's research and development center. There are displays on aviation history from 1916 to 1979 in the control tower.

Norfolk and Suffolk Aviation Museum, Flixton
The Norfolk and Suffolk Aviation Museum includes the Royal Observer Corps Museum, the 446th (H) Bomb Group Museum, the RAF Bomber Command Museum, and the Air Sea Rescue and Coastal Command Museum. The museum has material about World War II and US bases in Norfolk and Suffolk. One display focuses on Project Anvil, the top-secret project with the goal of destroying the German V3 Supergun site at Mimoyecques, France. The most famous person involved in Project Anvil was probably **Joseph P. Kennedy, Jr**., who died on 12 August 1944 when his airplane exploded over New Delight Wood, Blythborough, Suffolk. The elder brother of John F. Kennedy, he was buried at the American Military Cemetery at Madingley.

Parham Airfield Museum

The Parham Airfield Museum houses the 390th Bomb Group Memorial Air Museum and the Museum of the British Resistance Organization. The Airfield Museum exhibits include a unique collection of recovered World War II aircraft engines, parts of Allied and German aircraft, uniforms, photographs, documents, combat records, paintings, and memorabilia, all housed in an original wartime control tower. There is an additional museum dedicated to the British Resistance Organization and a World War II memorial.

Rougham Control Tower Museum

Rougham Airfield was home to the USAAF 322nd and 94th Bomb Groups during World War II. This airfield is one of the few wartime bases where the control tower still exists. The museum illustrates the history of the airfield with artifacts from the USAAF 94th Bomb Group.

Wattisham Airfield Station Museum near *Ipswich*

In 1942 the airfield was handed over to the USAAF, and for the next two years it served as a central supply depot and maintenance depot. In May 1944 the 479th Fighter Group arrived, and Wattisham became home to three squadrons of fighter planes. In January 1946 the airfield was handed back to the RAF. The museum opened in November 1991, and is housed in the original station chapel built by the USAAF in 1943. There is a plaque in the HQ building. The collection includes over 300 photos and other memorabilia.

WORLD WAR II MEMORIALS WITH AMERICAN CONNECTIONS

LONDON
Royal Air Force Chapel, Westminster Abbey

Battle of Britain Memorial Window – Among the symbols in the window, the American flag appears in tribute to several American pilots who flew with the RAF during the Battle of Britain. The roll of honor contains the names of 1,497 pilots and aircrew killed or mortally wounded during the Battle of Britain. The names include those of 47 Canadians, 47 New Zealanders, 35 Poles, 24 Australians, 20 Czechoslovaks, 17 South Africans, six Belgians, and one American, along with those from the United Kingdom and Colonies.

American Memorial Chapel, St. Paul's Cathedral

The chapel was created by the British people as a tribute "To the American dead of the Second World War from the People of Britain." On 4 July 1951 **General Eisenhower** presented a roll of honor to the dean of St. Paul's in the presence of HM Queen Elizabeth II. The roll of honor rests in a case on a marble pedestal with the inscription, "This tablet was unveiled by Her Majesty Queen Elizabeth II on 21 November 1958 in the presence of Richard M. Nixon Vice President of the United States of America."

The decoration of the chapel is filled with symbolism including the insignia of the American states and the US Army, Air Force and Navy. In the center window are an American eagle and the Stars and Stripes. Carved into the end panel of the altar end of the south side stalls is a small medallion with the portrait of President Eisenhower. On the north stalls there is a portrait of HM Queen Elizabeth II. Carvings on the stalls depict American birds, fruit, and flowers. Hidden behind the trailing leaves on the right-hand panel is a rocket, symbolizing America's achievement in space exploration.

St. Clement Danes, Strand

In 1958 St. Clement Danes was dedicated as the Central Church of the Royal Air Force. The Book of Remembrance lists the names of over 125,000 service-men and -women who lost their lives in World War II. A roll of honor also commemorates over 19,000 airmen from the United States of America who died on active service during the war.

Grosvenor Chapel, South Audley Street

Many men and women of the American armed services were headquartered in the area around Grosvenor Square and the American Embassy. They attended services here, as did General Eisenhower. At the end of the war a Thanksgiving Service was held and is commemorated with a plaque in the west wall. The American Friends of Grosvenor Chapel was set up in 1998 to further links and ties between the chapel and its American friends, who support its ongoing work.

31 St. James's Square

A plaque states that in 1942 General Eisenhower planned and launched "Operation Torch" for the liberation of North Africa from Norfolk House. In 1945 the building was again used by Eisenhower for planning "Operation Overlord" – the liberation of northwest Europe.

20 Grosvenor Square

A plaque notes that in this building was the headquarters of **General Dwight D. Eisenhower**, Supreme Commander of the Allied Expeditionary Force, January–March 1944.

Goodge Street Underground station

Deep underground tunnels at Goodge Street were equipped as **General Eisenhower**'s headquarters. Military leaders had easy access from the sation to the bunker, which was linked to the **Cabinet War Rooms** by pneumatic dispatch tube. Much of the planning for the D-Day invasion was done here. After the war the space was used as an army transit camp until a serious (but non-fatal) fire in the mid-1950s. The front of the building now bears the name "Eisenhower Centre" in large black letters. It currently is used to store film and video archives.

OTHER WORLD WAR II MEMORIALS WITH AMERICAN CONNECTIONS

BRISTOL

The **Floating Harbour** was Britain's most important port during World War II. General Douglas MacArthur, in charge of American forces in Britain, established his headquarters in **Clifton College** in Bristol. On the 4th of July each year the college raises the Stars and Stripes in recognition of its connection with the US.

BERKSHIRE

Littlecote House in **Hungerford** During preparations for the D-Day invasion, Littlecote House was requisitioned for military use by the US Army 506th Parachute Infantry Regiment, and served as headquarters for the 1st Battalion. Easy Company, the 50th Parachute Infantry, were part of the 101st Airborne Division, known as the "Screaming Eagles." The men of the 506th were among the first to go into action on D-Day.

In January 1944 battalions of the US Army 501st Parachute Regiment were encamped around the Berkshire village of Lambourn. The 2nd Battalion camped on the grounds of the old Craven mansion. During the D-Day invasion, the 501st parachuted into Normandy, where they fought for the next six weeks. During July all three battalions returned to **Hamstead Marshall** where they waited for reinforcements to replace the many soldiers lost during the invasion. On 17 September 1944 the regiment left Berkshire for the last time and was shipped to Holland. In July 1945 the regiment was deactivated and the men returned to the US.

BEDFORDSHIRE

Podington – The airfield was turned over to the USAAF in 1942. Various squadrons used the field, including the 100th Bomb Group. In May 1944 the collision of two B17s on the runway caused a huge explosion and twenty-one airmen were killed. A memorial to the 92nd Bomb Group is on the nearby road. The local church also has a memorial. Today the main runway is used for drag racing. The control tower has been converted into a private residence.

Thurleigh – The RAF began using Thurleigh as a Bomber Command base in 1941. The US 8th Air Force operated from here for three years. After 1946 the site was known as the Royal Aeronautical Establishment, Bedford. The airfield was finally closed in 1997 and the experimental operations were moved to Boscombe Down and Farnborough.

CAMBRIDGESHIRE
Bassingbourn Control Tower Museum

Housed in the original airfield control tower, the museum has photographs and documents relating to the RAF, USAAF 91st Bomb Group, and the British Army. The airfield was the wartime home of the B17 "Memphis Belle." A memorial plaque features a diagram that shows the parking "pads" where the planes were serviced.

Glatton Airfield, Conington

Glatton Airfield was built by American Army engineers in 1943. The 457th Bomb Group used the field for its B17s and then the B29 "Superfortresses." At the end of June 1945 the base was returned to civilian use. A memorial to the 457th is in **All Saints' Church** in **Conington**. Parts of the original runway are still in use for small planes.

Kimbolton Castle Estate

The USAAF 379th Bombardment Group was stationed at Kimbolton from May 1943 to June 1945. The airfield was originally a fighter base for the RAF but was leased to the United States to use as base for their heavy bombers. For information on the history of the 379th Bomb Group, see their website at www.379thbga.org.

St. Andrew's Church, Kimbolton

At the east end of the north aisle of the church there is a monument to the USAAF 379th Bombardment Group.

RAF Molesworth

In 1942 Molesworth was used as a USAAF base for the 8th Air Force: 15th Bomb Squadron and 303rd Bomb Group. In 1945 the base was handed over to the RAF, but the US Air Force returned in 1951 and the site was used by the 303rd Tactile Missile Wing. Today it is a military storage and communications center and joint analysis center. The base is not open to the public. In June 2000 an impressive memorial to the World War II aircrews was dedicated. It is located near the main gate.

Steeple Morden

In 1943 the 355th Fighter Group was stationed at the Steeple Morton airfield. In 1946 the land was returned to agricultural use, but a large stone monument which includes a P51 propeller stands next to the road that runs by the old airfield.

Wimpole Hall and Park

During World War II, the 3,000-acre Wimpole Park estate housed an American military hospital which treated army casualties of war. After being used as a teachers training college, community school and emergency local housing unit, the facility was for a while used as a US Air Force hospital, which closed in 1960. During the war, the Wimpole Park estate was also home to the 323rd Squadron, 91st Bomb Group of the US 8th Army.

DEVON

Plymouth – During preparations preceding the D-Day invasions, the majority of American troops in the Plymouth area were from the 29th Armored Division. There were encampments in **Antony Park, Saltram Park**, and **Mount Edgecumbe Park**. Special slipways built along the coastline to allow the landing vessels to enter the English Channel were called "Chocolate Box Hards" in code talk because they looked like bars of Hershey's chocolate. Examples can still be found in the Plymouth area at Turnchapel and Saltash Passage.

At **Saltash Passage** there is a memorial to the V and VII Corps of the US Army where the British and American flags fly side by side. The D-Day Memorial marks the departure of the units on 6 June 1944 for the D-Day landings in France.

Slapton Sands – Exercise Tiger Memorial (see page 129)

ESSEX

Braintree – In the **Church of Our Lady, Queen of Peace** the stained-glass window over the high altar was donated by the 322nd, 394th, 410th, and 416th Bomb Groups and 121st Station Hospital. There is a plaque commemorating their gift.

NORFOLK

Attleborough – There is a memorial to 453rd Bomb Group outside the railway station and a roll of honor in the village hall.

The 452nd Bomb Group was based at **Deopham Green**, 5 1/2 miles southwest of Wymondham. The airfield was built in 1942–3 and occupied by the 452nd on 3 January 1944. It served as a base for B17 Flying Fortresses. The airfield was closed in 1948. There is a roadside memorial.

Hingham – A memorial to the 452nd has been place outside **St. Andrew's Church**.

Hunstanton – In the **Esplanade Gardens** there is a memorial plaque with the names of the thirty-one people who died in the east coast floods of 1953. Among the dead were sixteen Americans who had been billeted in the area. Two American servicemen were awarded the George Medal for their heroism: Reis Leming and Freeman Kilpatrick.

Old Buckenham – There is a memorial at the site of the old airfield at Old Buckenham, which was occupied by the 453rd Bomb Group from December 1943. Jimmy Stewart and Walter Matthau were stationed there during World War II. Another memorial can be seen at the Old Buckenham village hall which also has a roll of honor, a plaque, and some memorabilia.

Wymondham – During World War II the main military hospital for American servicemen was near Wymondham. After the war the Nissen huts of the hospital became the dormitories and classrooms of **Wymondham College**. Only two Nissen huts from the military hospital are still standing.

NORTHAMPTONSHIRE
Chelveston Airfield – In May 1942 the RAF turned the Chelveston airfield over to the USAAF. It was used by the 60th Troop Carrier Group, followed by the 301st Bomb Group (with B17 Flying Fortresses) which was replaced by the 305th Bomb Group, commanded by Colonel Curtis LeMay. A memorial tablet to the men of the 305th can be seen at the Church of St. John at Chelveston-cum-Caldecott.

SOMERSET
Ashton Court in **Long Ashton** near **Bristol** – During World War II, Ashton Court was used as a military transit camp, RAF headquarters and American Army command HQ.

STAFFORDSHIRE
Alrewas – The Allied Special Forces Memorial Grove at the **National Memorial Arboretum** has been planted to commemorate those men, women, and children who lost their lives while serving with or assisting the Allied Special Forces or Resistance units during World War II and many conflicts since. Units from all the Allied countries who fought for the freedom of Europe are included in the list of those remembered in the peaceful memorial grove.

SUFFOLK
In 1942 there were nineteen American military airfields in Suffolk.
Bungay – The 310th and 446th Bomb Groups were based at Bungay, near Flixton. There is a memorial plaque on the gates at **St. Mary's Church** and a roll of honor plaque in the community center. Some related material can be seen in the Norfolk and Suffolk Aviation Museum.

Bury St. Edmunds – There is a memorial to the USAAF 94th Bombardment Group in the **Appleby Rose Garden** in the grounds of **St. Edmundsbury Cathedral**. The garden is supported by proceeds from the sale of *Suffolk Summer*, a book of affectionate memories written by Technical Sargent John Appleby, who was based in Lavenham and Thorpe Abbotts in 1945. The book and a pamphlet are available at the local tourist information center. A piece of the cathedral is now part of a church in San Marino, California. Through the connection with an American forces chaplain who preached in the cathedral during the war, the borough council sent a piece of stone from the abbey ruins and two carved pieces of stone to be incorporated into a new church which was built in 1952.

Debach – This airfield was used by the 493rd Bomb Group; there is a stone memorial at the original headquarters location. The land has returned to agricultural use but the control tower, several buildings and parts of runways still exist. There are plans to turn the control tower into museum. There are a flag and plaque in St. Mary's Church, Clopton.

Flixton – The 446th Bomb Group Memorial at **St. Mary's Church** in neighboring Bungay (see above) is dedicated to the memory of the 456 airmen killed in action and to those serving at Flixton from 1943 to 1945. It was unveiled by Bill Davenport, president of the 446th Bomb Group Association in 1993 during a Group reunion.

Lavenham
Lavenham Airfield was operational during World War II between March 1944 and August 1945. It was manned by the US Army Air Force 487th Bombardment Group. The airfield has largely reverted to farmland, but some cracked concrete runways are still visible, and the control tower is still maintained.

Church of St. Peter and St. Paul – the Branch Chapel in this beautiful church features an American flag that is displayed in honor of American servicemen who were stationed in this area during World War II.

Swan Hotel – preserved behind glass in the bar of the lovely half-timbered inn, a section of the wall is covered with the signatures of American airmen who were based in the district during the Second World War. There is also a large case with military insignia from many of the US military units that served in Europe, along with photos of American military personnel.

In the **Market Place** there is a memorial plaque dedicated to the "Men of the 487th Bomb Group who sacrificed their lives in World War II that the ideals of democracy might live."

Sudbury – There is a plaque by the front door of Sudbury Town Hall to the USAAF 486th Bombardment Group.

WILTSHIRE
Blue Boar in **Aldbourne** – The Blue Boar pub has a memorial to the American 101st Airborne Division which was stationed in the area during World War II. In 2004 a wooden barracks block used by the American 101st was dismantled and shipped to a museum in Toccoa, Georgia. The cost was met by donations from American veterans whose wartime exploits were shown in Steven Spielberg's television drama series *Band of Brothers*.

OTHER WORLD WAR II MEMORIALS
IN SUFFOLK

Great Ashfield (10m ENE of Bury St Edmunds)
Honington (10m NE of Bury St Edmunds)
Horham (7m SE of Diss)
Knettishall (7m E of Thetford)
Leiston (4m E of Saxmundham)
Mendlesham (6m NE of Stowmarket)

Metfield (5m NW of Halesworth)
Rattlesden (5m W of Stowmarket)
Raydon, Suffolk (3m SE of Hadleigh)

PRESENT-DAY US MILITARY BASES

There are currently two US Air Force bases in Suffolk, at **Mildenhall** and **Lakenheath**. However, these bases were not used by US forces during World War II.

RAF Mildenhall, Suffolk – Opened in October 1934, the air base first hosted American airmen in 1950. Driving tours of the US Air Force base and tours of static displays for groups of fifteen to thirty are available. Please phone for more details or to book a tour.
RAF Mildenhall Base Tours
Base Tour Organizer, Public Affairs Office
100th Air Refueling Wing
RAF Mildenhall, Suffolk IP28 8NF
Telephone: 01638 542654

RAF Lakenheath, Suffolk – home of the 48th Tactical Fighter Wing which arrived in 1960.

CHAPTER 5
POLITICAL CONNECTIONS AND
ROYAL HONORS

Politics and politicians have traveled both ways across the Atlantic since the first English colonies were established in America. Many American presidents have been able to trace their families directly back to the ancestors who left England in the seventeenth century. The first president to come to England while in office was Woodrow Wilson, who visited King George V and Prime Minister Lloyd George in 1918. Since then other presidents have crossed the Atlantic on diplomatic and personal trips. Some lived in London before they were elected president of the United States.

Political movements have also moved across the Atlantic. On 29 July 1833 slavery was abolished throughout the British Empire with the Emancipation Act. Americans who supported the ending of slavery in the United States attended the World Anti-Slavery Movement conference in London in 1840. The blatant inequality between men and women which was enforced at this conference had important repercussions in America. The women's rights movement in the US had its beginnings in the group of American women who attended the London conference. 🍃

AMERICAN PRESIDENTS IN ENGLAND
George Washington (1732–99) first president of the United States of America: 1789–97 George Washington's family name originally was "Wessyngton" (or Wessington). One of the first important members of the family was William Fitz-Patrick, alias de Wessyngton. He married the sister of the King of Scotland and settled in the town of Wessyngton (later spelled Washington) in northeast England before 1180. The Washington family coat of arms came from the coat of arms adopted by William de Wessyngton – three red five-pointed stars and two red stripes on a white background. These stars and stripes can be found in various sites around England linked to the Washington family, and on the flag of the United States.

LONDON **George Washington**'s statue stands on the soil of Virginia in front of the *National Gallery*.

TYNE AND WEAR *Washington Old Hall* near *Sunderland* incorporates the twelfth-century home of George Washington's ancestors. An exhibition celebrates the connection with George Washington. President Carter visited the hall in 1977.

COUNTY DURHAM In *Durham Cathedral*, a plaque has been placed in memory of John Wessyngton who served as prior for twenty-nine years in the fifteenth century. He was one of the earliest known ancestors of George Washington.

YORKSHIRE An ancient stained-glass window at *Selby Abbey* features John Wessington's coat of arms with the stars and stripes. It was restored in 2006 with donations from American friends.

Sulgrave Manor, Northamptonshire

George Washington was called the "Father of his Country." He was naturally held in the highest regard in his native land, but he was also widely respected in England. Upon receiving word of Washington's death in late January 1800, the admiral of the British fleet at Torbay ordered the flag to be flown at half mast in his memory. The gesture was followed by the entire British fleet. The whole of England went into mourning, according to the Sons of the American Revolution. 🌿

PLACES LINKED WITH GEORGE WASHINGTON

NORTHAMPTONSHIRE Sulgrave Manor, in **Sulgrave**, near **Banbury**, was completed by Lawrence Washington in about 1560. When a subsequent Lawrence Washington was accused of being a "malignant Royalist" during the English Civil War, the family was forced to leave Sulgrave Manor in 1643. They moved to London and had a very difficult time, becoming impoverished. John Washington was nineteen when his father died in poverty in 1652. John got married and sailed for Virginia in 1656. Unfortunately his wife died and in 1658 he married again, this time to Anne Pope. The wedding present from his father-in-law, Lieutenant Colonel Nathaniel Pope, was a 700-acre estate at Mattox Creek where their eldest son Lawrence was born in 1659. This Lawrence Washington was the great-grandfather of George Washington, who was born on 22 February 1731. Sulgrave Manor is now an important historial museum with special exhibitions and events throughout the year.

CUMBRIA Mildred Warner Gale, the grandmother of George Washington, came from **Whitehaven**. She was buried in the grounds of **St. Nicholas's Church** on 30 January 1700/1 along with her baby daughter and a servant. Unfortunately, a fire destroyed the church in 1971 and only the tower remains, but the lovely garden around the church has become a community centerpiece. The exact location of Mildred Warner Gale's grave in the church burial ground is no longer identified. When George Washington wanted paving stones for the terrace of Mount Vernon, his Virginia home, he ordered them from Whitehaven. They were ordered before the American Revolution and delivered in 1786.

CAMBRIDGE The Reverend Godfrey Washington, fellow of **Peterhouse College** and minister at **Little St. Mary's Church** in the early eighteenth century, was the great-uncle of George Washington. A memorial displays the "stars and stripes" of the Washington family coat of arms and the family crest which is an eagle.

LANCASHIRE The tower of **St. Oswald's Church** in **Warton** is thought to have been built by Robert Washington, who died in 1483. The Washington family coat of arms was engraved on the stone tower, but was moved inside the church in 1955. Eighteen members of the Washington family were baptized at St. Oswald's between 1584 and 1718. Some Washington family members are buried in the churchyard, including Thomas Washington who served as vicar from 1799 to 1823. A memorial to Elizabeth and Thomas Washington is located in the east end of the church. The family trees of the Washington and Churchill families that are on view show that George Washington and **Winston Churchill** were both related to Robert Kitson (or Kytson) of Warton, the father of Margaret Kytson who married John Washington.

The **George Washington Pub** in **Warton** features a portrait of the American president on the pub sign. Inside there are many interesting mementoes of the first president of the United States.

SUFFOLK Hengrave Hall in **Bury St. Edmunds** was built in 1534 by Sir Thomas Kytson whose sister Margaret married John Washington, ancestor of George Washington. Kytson was a member of the Company of Merchant Adventurers and traded extensively in Flanders, working with his nephew, Thomas Washington. A window in Hengrave Hall shows the arms of the Washington family including the stripes. Interestingly, in 1611, when Penelope Darcy married John Gage of Firle Place, Hengrave Hall came into the Gage family. 160 years later **General Thomas Gage** would command the British forces in America during the Revolutionary War, and George Washington would lead the Americans.

NORTHAMPTONSHIRE St. Mary's Church in **Great Brington** is the parish church of the Spencer family and holds nineteen generations of Spencer tombs. The tower was built in 1200 and the nave and north and south aisles were added by 1300. There is a memorial to Lawrence Washington who died in 1616. He was an ancestor of George Washington. The memorial features the Washington family coat of arms.

LONDON Church records at **St. Dunstan in the West** show the baptism of two children of Lawrence Washington: a daughter, Anne, in 1621 and a son, Lawrence, in 1622. Another son, also called Lawrence, was buried here in 1617. The name Lawrence was obviously important to the family; it was used in many generations. George Washington's half-brother was also named Lawrence.

KENT Lawrence Washington, George Washington's great-great-great uncle, lived in Knightrider Street in **Maidstone** in the late sixteenth century. When he died in 1619 he was buried in **All Saints' Church**. His memorial near the south door shows the Washington family coat of arms. Mary Scott Argall, the mother of **Samuel Argall**, colonial governor of Virginia, is also buried at All Saints' Church. Lawrence Washington was her second husband. Set into niches on the first floor of **89—90 Bank Street** in **Maidstone** are statues of four important local men. From left to right the figures are Lord Avebury (who introduced Bank Holidays in 1872), Lawrence Washington, William Caxton (who published the first book printed in English) and Courtney, Archbishop of Canterbury (who built All Saints' Church).

ESSEX George Washington's great-great-grandfather, also named Lawrence Washington, was born at Sulgrave Manor in 1602 and was educated at **Brasenose College, Oxford**. He was rector of **All Saints' Church** at **Purleigh** from 1632 until the Puritans removed him from office in 1643 for being a "malignant Royalist" and "oft drunk" – a charge that was refuted. After being turned out of his church because he supported the king in the Civil War, he fled to London. To honor his memory, American citizens contributed money to restore the flint church tower. This same Lawrence Washington died in poverty in 1652. The church register at **St. Peter's Church** in **Maldon** reads "Burials 1652. Mr. Lawrence Washington, 21 Jany," but the exact location of his tomb is unknown. His son John left London to sail to America in 1656. The "Washington Window" at **All Saints' Church** was presented by the citizens of Malden, Massachusetts, in 1928 and dedicated to the memory of Lawrence Washington. The window shows among other things the signing of the Declaration of Independence.

SOMERSET The *American Museum in Britain* at *Claverton Manor* near *Bath* has a replica of the garden at George Washington's home at Mount Vernon, Virginia. Mount Vernon was named in honor of Admiral Edward Vernon by George's eldest half-brother Lawrence who served on Vernon's flagship in 1741 during naval campaigns against the Spanish in the West Indies. There is a monument to Admiral Vernon in *Westminster Abbey*.

WORCESTERSHIRE According to the church guide at *St. John the Baptist's Church* in *Wickhamford*, two of Archbishop Edwin Sandys's grandsons married Washington sisters, who shared a common ancestor, John Washington, with President George Washington. There is also a monument to Penelope Sandys who died in 1697. Her first husband was Colonel Henry Washington, an ancestor of George Washington. The memorial features the Washington family coat of arms. There are two other extraordinary monuments in the parish church. One commemorates Samuel Sandys and his wife Mercy Culpeper. He died in 1623. The second is to his son Edwin Sandys who died three weeks later. Samuel Sandy was the brother of *Sir Edwin Sandys*, treasurer of the London Company. *Wickhamford Manor* is a beautiful sixteenth-century manor house. Its lakes and circular dovecote were mentioned in the 1086 Domesday Book. Penelope Washington lived and died here. The manor offers bed-and-breakfast accommodation, including a room with a four-poster bed. During the summer Shakespearean plays are performed in the grounds.

KENT Lawrence Washington, the elder brother of the future president, married Anne Fairfax in 1738 in Virginia. She was the daughter of Sir William Fairfax, cousin of Sir Thomas Fairfax, proprietor of five million acres of the Northern Neck of Virginia. Sir Thomas was born at *Leeds Castle* in 1693.

SUFFOLK In *Ipswich* a plaque on *Christ Church* in Tacket Street commemorates the Reverend William Gordon, who went to the Americas, worked for General George Washington, and wrote the first account of the American Revolution in 1788.

LONDON *George Yeardley*, a governor of the Jamestown Colony, was baptized at *Southwark Cathedral*. He and Temperance Flowerdew may have been married there. Their son Argall Yeardley was an ancestor of George Washington.

On display in the *Bank of England Museum* is a "dividend warrant" signed by both George and Martha Washington. The warrant authorized payment from a holding of bank stock which Martha Washington and her two children from her first marriage inherited jointly from John Custis, the father of her first husband. The warrant was signed on 16 November 1759, and, according to the museum display, is the earliest document giving evidence of the marriage of George and Martha which had taken place on 6 January 1759. A larger-than-life portrait of Washington in his formal Masonic attire in on display at the *Freemasons' Hall*.

The *National Portrait Gallery* has several portraits of George Washington, including two famous images by Gilbert Stuart. A portrait of Washington is on display in the British prime minister's residence at *10 Downing Street*.

A bust of George Washington has been placed in the crypt of *St. Paul's Cathedral*. The base of the marble plinth says "The Gift of the Sulgrave Institution 1931."

John Adams (1735-1826), second president: 1797-1801

John Adams was born in Braintree, Massachusetts, in 1735, a great-grandson of Henry Adams, from Braintree in Essex, who sailed to America on the *Lyon* with the **Braintree Company** in 1632. Another Adams ancestor, Edmund Quincy, sailed to Massachusetts with the **Winthrop Fleet** in 1630. At the end of the American Revolution John Adams helped negotiate the peace treaty with Britain. He became first official minister from the government of the United States to the Court of St. James, serving from May 1785 to March 1788. He was elected vice-president under Washington and was re-elected in 1792. In 1797 he was elected the second president of the United States. 🌿

LONDON Jane Randolph, Thomas Jefferson's mother, was baptised at *St. Paul's Church, Shadwell*, on 20 February 1720. A plaque commemorates this link with the US.

Thomas Jefferson (1743-1826), third president: 1801-9

Jane Randolph Jefferson was born in 1720 in Shadwell, just east of the Tower of London. Her father, Isham Randolph, was Virginia's colonial agent in London who married Jane Rogers at **Whitechapel** on 25 July 1717. They lived at **Shakespeare's Walk, Shadwell**, where their first child, Jane, was born. In 1735, when Jane Randolph was fifteen, the family moved back to Virginia. They settled on Isham's plantation which they named "Shadwell" as a reminder of England. Soon after their arrival, Jane Randolph was introduced to Peter Jefferson, whom she married in 1739. Their third child, Thomas, was born in 1743.

In March–April 1786 Thomas Jefferson visited **John Adams** in London. They toured the English countryside and visited **Painshill Park** and **Chiswick House**. Perhaps he also visited **Penshurst**, the ancestral home of **Algernon Sidney**, whose political writings greatly influenced Jefferson's own political thought. During his visit to London, Thomas Jefferson was presented at court and snubbed by **King George III**. Perhaps this increased Jefferson's cool attitude towards the British. Jefferson left London and traveled to Paris, to become the first ambassador from the US to France. 🌿

LONDON Lord Burlington's beautiful villa at *Chiswick* just west of London may have influenced Jefferson's designs for Monticello. *Chiswick House* features a central dome with an octagonal roof.

THOMAS JEFFERSON

WEST MIDLANDS While Jefferson was a student in Virginia at the ***College of William and Mary***, his mathematics teacher was ***William Small***, a member of the ***Lunar Society*** which met in **Birmingham** at Matthew Bolton's home, now called ***Soho House***. Jefferson kept in touch with his former teacher until Small's death in 1775. His last letter to Small mentions three dozen bottles of Madeira wine he was sending across the Atlantic. This gift of Madeira was not the only time wine was to find a place in thestory of Thomas Jefferson. In December 1985 the first wine auction held by Christie's auction house included a bottle of 1787 Lafitte that had apparently been found in a bricked-up cellar in Paris and is believed to have belonged to Jefferson.

LONDON In 1797 John Quincy Adams married Louisa Catherine Johnson, daughter of the U.S. consul at London. Their wedding was at *All Hallows by the Tower*.

LONDON For a while Charles Francis Adams lived at *98 Portland Place*. The building was also used as the US Embassy in 1863–6.

NORFOLK The *Angel Inn* in *Swanton Morely* claims to have been the Lincoln family home in the sixteenth century.

There is a stone bust of Lincoln in the east entrance of the *Royal Exchange*.

LONDON A large statue of Abraham Lincoln stands on the west side of *Parliament Square*.

The spire at *Christ Church, Kennington Road*, was donated by Lincoln's family to acknowledge its support for abolition.

John Quincy Adams (1767–1848), sixth president: 1825–9

John Quincy Adams came to Britain in 1785 when he was fourteen. His father was the first minister from the United States to Britain. The Adams family had a presence in London that lasted for several generations. In 1815 John Quincy Adams became Envoy Extraordinary and Minister Plenipotentiary to the British court. His son, Charles Francis Adams, was US minister to Britain from 1861 to 1868. His son, Henry Brooks Adams, taught American history at Harvard and wrote many important works, one of which was awarded the Pulitzer Prize in 1919.

Martin Van Buren (1782–1862), eighth president: 1837–41

In 1831 Martin Van Buren planned to campaign for the office of president of the US, so he resigned from his position in the US cabinet, and moved to London to serve as minister to Great Britain. He lived at *7 Stratford Place, London*. In February 1832 he learned that the Senate had failed to ratify him as ambassador. He had been liked by the British, and they treated him sympathetically, realizing that his defeat was a political move by his opponents. Van Buren returned to the US. He was elected vice-president before serving as the eighth president of the United States.

Zachary Taylor (1784–50), twelfth president: 1849–50

Taylor was a descendant of Isaac and Mary Allerton who sailed on the *Mayflower*, and of Colonel Richard Lee, progenitor of the **Lee family** of Virginia.

Abraham Lincoln (1809–65), sixteenth president: 1861–5

The village of **Swanton Morley** in **Norfolk** is the historical home of many Lincoln families prior to the seventeenth century, including Edward Lincoln who had three sons that immigrated to Massachusetts. He was President Lincoln's direct ancestor. Abraham Lincoln was president during the American Civil War, which elicited varied responses in different parts of Britain. Liverpool merchants supported the Confederacy during the war, and Liverpool ships would run the blockade to bring loads of cotton to England. The mill workers of **Manchester** refused to cooperate with this. On 31 December 1862 a group of mill workers in Manchester voted to boycott all cotton from the Confederate states as a show of support for President Lincoln's emancipation of the slaves, even though this action meant that the mills would probably be closed. President Lincoln greatly appreciated this show of support from across the ocean. He sent a message of thanks, saying that he regretted the suffering that the workers of Manchester would have to face.

LINCOLN FAMILY CONNECTIONS

SUFFOLK Abraham Lincoln's oldest known ancestor, Van Ryse (1446–1521), was from **Bures**. He died in 1521 and is buried at **St. Mary's Church, Bures**, along with other Lincoln ancestors.

LINCOLNSHIRE Samuel Lincoln was baptized in **St. Andrew's Church** in **Hingham** in 1622. He sailed to America on the *John and Dorothy* and settled in Hingham, Massachusetts. A family tree in St Andrew's shows that Samuel's great-great-great-great-grandson was Abraham Lincoln. To commemorate this connection members of the Lincoln family in the US donated a bronze bust of the US president. It was unveiled on 15 October 1919 by the American ambassador.

MANCHESTER In 1920 a statue of Abraham Lincoln was erected in Manchester's **Lincoln Square**. Excerpts from Lincoln's letter to the workers of Manchester were engraved on the plinth.

LONDON Abraham Lincoln was assassinated on 14 April 1865 in the Ford Theater, Washington, D.C. by **John Wilkes Booth**, an actor who was descended from a family from **St. John's Square** in **Clerkenwell**. (*See his entry in Chapter 12*). His great-grandfather and great-grandmother were married on 15 February 1747 at St. George's Chapel, Hyde Park Corner (on the site of the present **Lanesborough Hotel**). Six of their children were baptized at **St. John the Baptist Church** in **Clerkenwell**. The grave of a relative, also John Wilkes Booth, who died in 1836, is reported to be in the garden behind the church.

Theodore Roosevelt (1858–1919), twenty-sixth president: 1901–9
Theodore Roosevelt married his second wife, Edith Kermit Carow, on 2 December 1886 at **St. George's Church, Hanover Square, London**. Teddy was staying at **Brown's Hotel**, and walked to St. George's for the wedding, which was celebrated with a reception at Brown's. 🌿

Woodrow Wilson (1856–1924), twentieth president: 1913–21
President Woodrow Wilson's mother, Jessie Janet Woodrow Wilson, was born in **Carlisle**, in 1828. From 1832 to 1835 the Woodrow family home was at Cavendish House. Woodrow Wilson visited Carlisle in 1896 on his first trip abroad. He returned in 1903, and then spent the summers of 1906 and 1908 in the area. 🌿

Herbert Hoover (1874–1964), thirty-first president: 1929–33
Herbert Hoover lived at **39 Hyde Park Gate** in **Kensington, London**, from 1901 to 1907. He then moved his family to a house on Hornton Street just off Kensington High Street. He used these homes as his European base while he traveled as a petroleum engineer. 🌿

CUMBRIA Jessie Janet Woodrow's father was minister at a church in *Carlisle*. A plaque on the church notes this connection with an American president.

LONDON *Churchill Arms, 119 Kensington Church Street*, has a portrait gallery of American presidents from George Washington to Nixon.

The exhibition at *Madame Tussauds, Marylebone Road*, includes waxwork figures of several American presidents.

LONDON A statue of Franklin Roosevelt and Winston Churchill on *New Bond Street* frequently attracts photographers.

A larger-than-life statue of FDR stands in a place of honor in *Grosvenor Square*.

Franklin D. Roosevelt (1882–1945), thirty-second president: 1933–45

Descended from a Dutch family that settled in New Amsterdam around 1650, Franklin Roosevelt was born at his family's estate in Hyde Park, New York. He married his cousin, Eleanor Roosevelt, who had spent three of the happiest years of her life in England, while attending school in **Wimbledon** in the London suburbs. In 1905 Eleanor and Franklin Roosevelt spent part of their honeymoon at **Brown's Hotel** in **London**.

FDR was US president during the Second World War, and developed an important personal relationship with the British prime minister, **Winston Churchill**. They communicated about the important military and political issues of the times, often over the highly secret "hot-line" that linked the White House in Washington and the **Cabinet War Rooms** in **London**. 🍃

FRANKLIN D. ROOSEVELT

LONDON Near the west door of **Westminster Abbey** a memorial plaque surrounded by an American eagle honors Franklin D. Roosevelt.

Churchill's secret HQ during World War II was in the **Cabinet War Rooms**. Equipment for the secret "hot-line" between London and Washington was installed at **Selfridges** department store on **Oxford Street**.

In 1899 the fifteen-year-old Eleanor Roosevelt was sent to Madame Souvestre's school at **Allenswood**, one of the large country villas that used to line Albert Road (now **Albert Drive**) in **Wimbledon** in the late nineteenth century.

LONDON A statue of Dwight D. Eisenhower stands in front of the American Embassy at *Grosvenor Square*.

Dwight David Eisenhower (1890–1969), thirty-fourth president: 1953–61

Dwight David Eisenhower was the supreme commander of Allied forces in North Africa and Italy in 1942–3, and of the Allied invasion of Europe in 1944. He had his headquarters at **20 Grosvenor Square** and directed the invasion from **31 St. James's Square**. Much of the planning for the D-Day invasion of Europe was done in the deep underground tunnels at **Goodge Street Underground station**, which were equipped as General Eisenhower's headquarters (*see Chapter 4*). He did not like living in the center of London, so he moved to **Telegraph Cottage**, a house in **Kingston-upon-Thames**, **Surrey**. A West Point graduate (1915), he resigned from the army in 1952 to stand for the presidency and was twice elected to that office. 🍃

DWIGHT DAVID EISENHOWER

LONDON A plaque on the building at **31 St. James's Square** states that General Eisenhower directed the D-Day invasion from this building.

A plaque at **20 Grosvenor Square** states that Eisenhower directed the Allied military campaign from offices in this building.

During the Second World War, Eisenhower worshipped at **Grosvenor Chapel, South Audley Street**. There was a service of thanks here at the end of the war.

SURREY Eisenhower lived at **Telegraph Cottage, Warren Road, Kingston Hill** in **Kingston-upon-Thames** from 1942 to 1944. In 1987 the house was destroyed by fire and has been rebuilt. A plaque at the corner of Kingston Hill and Warren Road notes Eisenhower's residence here.

HAMPSHIRE Southwick House was used as the secret headquarters for the Allied Expeditionary Force during World War II. It was here that the Allied invasion of Europe, known as "Operation Overlord," was planned. At Southwick, General Eisenhower, as Supreme Allied Commander, made the decision to proceed with the invasion of Europe on 6 June 1944.

John Fitzgerald Kennedy (1917–63), thirty-fifth president 1961–3

Joseph P. Kennedy was US ambassador to England from March 1938 until October 1940. He lived in the then ambassador's residence at **14 Prince's Gate**, which had been given to the US government for this use by J.P. Morgan. On two trips to Europe, in 1937 and 1939, his son John F. Kennedy stayed at American embassies, talking to newspapermen, political leaders, and diplomats, and observing international power politics at first hand. JFK also studied at the London School of Economics.

John Kennedy's elder brother, **Joseph P. Kennedy, Jr.**, on active military duty during the Second World War, was killed on 12 August 1944 when his airplane exploded over New Delight Wood, Blythborough, Suffolk. He is buried at the **American Military Cemetery** in **Madingley, Cambridgeshire**.

Kathleen Kennedy, the sister of President John F. Kennedy, is buried in the estate village of **Edensor, Derbyshire**. During the Second World War Kathleen married William, Marquess of Hartington, the eldest son of the Duke of Devonshire. Four months later he was killed in action in Belgium. Kathleen died in an airplane crash in France in 1948.

LONDON A commemorative bust of JFK stands on *Marylebone Road* near *Great Portland Street*. The bust was paid for by funds collected by the *Sunday Telegraph* in 1965.

SURREY The John F. Kennedy memorial at *Runnymede* near Windsor stands on a one-acre site that was given to the people of America in memory of the slain president.

SUFFOLK During World War II JFK's oldest brother, **Joseph P. Kennedy, Jr.**, was part of the group working on Project Anvil, a top-secret project aimed at destroying the German V3 Supergun. A display at the *Norfolk and Suffolk Aviation Museum, Flixton*, focuses on the project.

ESSEX An American flag, which had flown over the US Capitol Building, is displayed on the church wall at *All Saints' Church* in *Messing*, with other memorabilia.

LONDON 30 *Craven Street* was Aaron Burr's home for a time.

George Bush (1924–) and **George W. Bush** (1946–), forty-first president: 1989–93 and forty-third president: 2001–
Ancestors of Presidents George Bush and George W. Bush were farmers in Essex in the fourteenth century. Their lineage can be traced back to Reynold Bush who immigrated to America in the 1630s, possibly with the **Braintree Company**. The village church where the Bush family were baptized still stands, but the font has been moved to the Church of All Saints in Wakes Colne. The register, now in the Essex County Office, records John Bushe's baptism at *All Saints' Church* in *Messing* on 20 January 1594. 🍃

William J. Clinton (1946–), forty-second president: 1993–2001
Bill Clinton attended **University College, Oxford**, on a Rhodes Scholarship 1968–70. His daughter Chelsea followed in her father's steps, attending University College on a Rhodes Scholarship in 2001–3. 🍃

A VICE-PRESIDENT AND THREE AMERICAN WOMEN

Aaron Burr was born in Newark, New Jersey, in 1756. During the Revolutionary War he served on General **George Washington**'s staff, and entered politics when the war ended. He ran successfully for the US Senate against General Philip Schuyler, the father-in-law of Alexander Hamilton. This election marked the beginning of a bitter, and eventually fatal conflict, between Burr and Hamilton. Frustrated at what he saw as a malicious personal campaign against himself, Burr challenged Hamilton to a duel which was fought on 11 July 1804 at Weehawken, New Jersey. Alexander Hamilton was killed. When warrants were issued for Burr's arrest, he fled to Philadelphia, where he met with General James Wilkinson. They developed a plan to invade Mexico with a private army and set up an independent empire, but Wilkinson betrayed Burr to **President Jefferson**. Trying to escape to Spanish territory, Burr was arrested and returned for trial at Richmond, Virginia, in May 1807. He was tried for treason, but was found innocent.

Aaron Burr's political career in the United States was completely ruined. He moved to London and lived at *30 Craven Street*. He was never able to establish himself in England and began to run out of funds, so he moved to **Clerkenwell Close**, where the rents were much lower. After four years of exile, he returned to the US where he lived for twenty-four years as a social and political outcast. 🍃

Cliveden, Berkshire

Nancy Langhorne Astor achieved a political position that no other woman, British or American, had achieved before. In 1919 she became the first woman to take her seat as an MP in the **House of Commons**. Nancy Witcher Langhorne was born in Greenwood, Virginia, one of five daughters of a wealthy tobacco auctioneer. In 1897 she married Robert Gould Shaw, but was divorced in 1903.

Nancy then traveled to England, where in 1906 she married Waldorf Astor. The groom's father, **William Waldorf Astor**, an American millionaire, had moved to England, owned the *Observer* newspaper, was generous to the Conservative Party, and became an influential member of the English aristocracy. As a wedding gift, the newlyweds received **Cliveden**, an estate that William Waldorf Astor bought in 1895. In 1910 they moved to **Plymouth** to live in the political constituency that Waldorf represented in the **House of Commons**. When Waldorf's father died in 1919, he inherited the title and a seat in the **House of Lords**, and was thus unable to continue in his seat in the House of Commons. Nancy ran for his seat and was elected. From 1919 until 1921 she was the only woman to have a seat in the House of Commons. She remained in Parliament until her retirement in 1945. Nancy Astor died in 1964, at the age of eighty-five. 🍃

Wallis Warfield Simpson (1896–1986): The Duchess of Windsor

Bessie Wallis Warfield was born in Pennsylvania in 1896. In 1916 she married Earl Winfield Spencer, Jr., and was divorced from him in 1927 after years of unhappiness. Two years later she married Ernest Simpson, a businessman who was half-English, and who worked in London. After their marriage, they moved to **5 Bryanston Court, Bryanston Square, London**. In 1931 she was introduced to Edward, Prince of Wales, by Thelma Furness, his American mistress. In 1932 and early 1933, Wallis and Ernest Simpson attended social events where the prince was present, but Wallis began to spend more time with Edward, especially at his country retreat – **Fort Belvedere**, in **Sunningdale**, not far from Windsor Castle. She was divorced from Ernest Simpson in October 1936.

Edward became King of England in January 1936, when his father died. The Prince of Wales's attachment to Wallis developed into a determination to marry her. The affair brought on a constitutional crisis. Edward was forced by the government to choose between his throne and the woman he loved. He abdicated in December 1936, having never been crowned in a royal coronation. After the abdication, he was given the title Duke of Windsor.

The Duke of Windsor and Wallis Simpson were married

BERKSHIRE *Cliveden* was Lord Astor's wedding gift to Waldorf Astor and Nancy Langhorne.

LONDON Nancy Astor's London home was at *4 St. James's Square*.

The *National Portrait Gallery* has portraits of Nancy Astor.

2 Temple Place, built in 1895, was the London residence of William Waldorf Astor. The weather vane represents the *Santa Maria*, Columbus's caravel.

Lord Astor of Hever had many links with *St. Bride's Church* on *Fleet Street*, which is known as "the printers' church." He donated the organ in 1957.

DEVON Lord and Lady Astor had a home at *3 Elliot Terrace, Plymouth*.

LONDON Thelma Furness, the twin sister of Gloria Vanderbilt, was mistress of Prince of Wales. She lived at *Farm House, 22 Farm Street*, in *Mayfair*. Thelma introduced the prince to Wallis Simpson. Reportedly Wallis entertained him at the house that earlier had belonged to American movie star, Gloria Swanson.

Wallis Warfield married Ernest Simpson on 21 July 1928 at the *Chelsea Register Office* on the *Kings Road*.

BERKSHIRE Wallis Simpson was buried next to her husband in the grounds of *Frogmore* in *Windsor Great Park*.

Buckingham Palace, London

10 Downing Street

SOMERSET A member of the Continental Congress, William Bingham, served in the US Senate from 1795 to 1801. He was president pro tempore of the Senate during the Fourth Congress. Bingham withdrew from public life and moved to *Bath* in 1801. When he died in 1804, he was interred in *Bath Abbey*.

SURREY US Representative Vincent Francis Harrington of Iowa resigned from the US House of Representatives in 1942 to serve in the US Army Air Corps in World War II. He died in Rutland, England, on 29 November 1943, while on active duty and was buried in the United States Military Section of *Brookwood Cemetery* in *Woking*.

in Tours, France, on 3 June 1937. They did not set foot in England for many years. Following the duke's death in 1972, the duchess lived virtually as a recluse in their house in Paris. She was in ill health for many years before she died at the age of ninety on 24 April 1986. Her funeral took place at *St George's Chapel, Windsor Castle.* 🍃

Queen Liliuokalani of Hawaii

When Liliuokalani was still a princess, she visited England in 1887 with Queen Kapiolani and the royal Hawaiian delegation to attend the celebrations of the Golden Jubilee of Queen Victoria. She kept a diary of the visit and wrote of her first presentation to Victoria:

> "The whole city was in commotion in view of the coming great event. Rooms were assigned to us at the Alexandra, where there were many other members of the royal families of the distant world. Amongst these were Prince Komatsu of Japan; the Siamese Prince, brother of the King of Siam; the Prince of India; and the Prince of Persia. At other leading public houses were quartered the princes and princesses of the nations of Europe. Immediately after our arrival Queen Kapiolani sent messages of congratulations to Her Majesty Victoria, Queen of Great Britain and Empress of India. Arrangements were made for us to present our felicitations in person at *Buckingham Palace* on Monday at one o'clock in the afternoon." 🍃

LOCATIONS WITH OFFICIAL GOVERNMENT CONNECTIONS
10 Downing Street, London: Official Residence of the British Prime Minister

Sir George Downing was born in Dublin in 1624. His parents were Emmanuel Downing, a barrister, and Lucy Winthrop, sister of **John Winthrop**, the governor of the Massachusetts Bay Colony. The Downing family immigrated to Massachusetts in 1638 and settled in Salem. George was the second graduate of **Harvard College**'s first class of 1642. He returned to England after the Restoration and became a government servant and diplomat, eventually renouncing the principles of the New England colony. Downing zealously hunted down the regicides Barkstead, Corbet, and Okey who were hiding in Holland. Pepys said "All the world takes note of him for a most ungrateful villain." His London house near Whitehall Palace became property of the government after his death, and the street was named **Downing Street** after him. His grandson, also named George Downing, was the founder of **Downing College, Cambridge**, based on the fortune established by the Harvard College graduate. 🌿

Embassy of the United States of America: 24 Grosvenor Square, London

The Embassy of the United States was first located in **Great Cumberland Place** and later in **Portland Place** and **Grosvenor Gardens**. In 1938 it was moved to **1 Grosvenor Square**, the building which now houses the Canadian High Commission. After the end of World War II, the US government wanted to purchase the freehold of the land on the western side of Grosvenor Square for a new embassy from the ground landlord, the Grosvenor Estate. However, the estate's condition that the USA return the Grosvenor family's 12,000 acres in Florida, confiscated after the War for Independence, was, unsurprisingly, rejected. As a result, the embassy is said to be the only one in the world for which the US does not own the freehold.

Embassy of the USA, Grosvenor Square, London

The present embassy (or "chancery,") occupying the whole west side of the square, was designed by **Eero Saarinen**. It was completed in 1960. The modern design of the building has not received universal praise – it has been referred to disparagingly by some as a concrete egg carton. 🌿

LONDON Former ambassador John Motley was buried at *Kensal Green Cemetery* in 1870.

American Ambassador's Residence 1912–55:

A passenger riding along Kensington Road might be surprised to see a row of American Indians looking back from a classical townhouse at **14 Prince's Gate**. The house has had a long association with the United States. Built in 1849, five years later the house was sold to an American banker, Junius Spencer Morgan, who came to London as a partner in the firm of **George Peabody** and Company, a merchant bank in the City.

Peabody was instrumental in organizing the US participation in the Great Exhibition of 1851, held in Hyde Park just across the street from Prince's Gate. When he died in 1890, he left the house to his son, J.P. Morgan, Jr., who loaned the house to the Council of War Relief for use as a maternity home. In 1912 the building was given to the American government as a home for American ambassadors to the Court of St. James's.

US ambassadors who lived at 14 Prince's Gate include Charles Gates Dawes (1929–31), who won the Nobel Peace Prize for the Dawes Plan, which set out the plans for German reparations after the First World War; **Andrew Mellon** (1932); Robert Worth Bingham (1932–7); and Joseph Patrick Kennedy (1938–40). John Winant was ambassador from

LONDON American Indians decorate the keystones above the windows at the former American ambassador's residence at 14 *Prince's Gate*.

US ambassador John Gilbert Winant lived at 7 *Aldford Street* from 1941 to 1946. The house was loaned to him by his good friend **Sir Winston Churchill**.

LONDON After visiting *Winfield House* in 1946, Barbara Hutton decided to offer it the US government to be used as the official residence of the American ambassador. For the token price of $1, Winfield House passed into official American ownership. The beautiful house, surrounded by tranquil gardens, has served as a peaceful and secure ambassadorial residence since January 1955.

Berry Brothers Wine Shop, St. James's Street, London

Memorial plaque in the passageway to the left of *Berry Brothers.*

LONDON Today's *Texas Embassy Restaurant* is on the corner of *Cockspur Street* near *Trafalgar Square.*

1940 to 1946, but did not stay at the ambassadorial residence. Lewis Douglas took up residence in 1949, followed by Walter Gifford (1950–3). The United States left the building while Winthrop Aldrich was ambassador and, on 18 January 1955, **Winfield House** became the official American ambassador's residence. 🍃

Winfield House, Regent's Park

In the nineteenth century John Nash, architect to the Woods and Forests Department, and friend of the Prince of Wales, the future King George IV, created an elaborate plan for the development of the whole area which involved fifty-six villas and a zoo. By the time George IV became king, costs had skyrocketed and only eight villas were built. The largest, "St. Dunstan's," was built on the site where the US ambassador's residence now stands. In 1920 many of the villas, including St. Dunstan's, were abandoned and neglected. In 1936 the house was partly destroyed by fire and was later bought by Barbara Hutton, the wealthy American heiress who had inherited some $40 million from her grandfather, Frank Winfield Woolworth, founder of the Woolworth store chain. In August 1936 the Crown Estate Commission gave permission for the old white stucco Regency villa to be pulled down and a red brick Georgian-style house built in its place. Winfield House was named after Barbara Hutton's grandfather. During the war, Winfield House was used by an RAF barrage balloon unit and later as an Air Crew Reception Center and as an American Officers' Club. It suffered from neglect and near misses. 🍃

Texas Legation, St. James's Street

Many Texans think their state is so special that it should stand alone – and indeed from 1836 to 1845 it existed as an independent country called the Republic of Texas. The Republic set up an embassy in rented rooms above Berry Brothers wine merchants at **3 St. James's Street**. A plaque on the side of the building, in a covered passage leading to Pickering Court, commemorates the short-lived independence of the Lone Star State.

The plaque identifying the Texas Legation was placed there by British novelist Graham Greene, founder and first president of the Anglo-Texan Society. The society hoped to establish closer social and cultural ties between England and Texas. The Anglo-Texan Society was dissolved in the late 1970s. 🍃

BRITISH HONORS FOR US CITIZENS

Since World War II more than sixty American citizens have been granted honorary knighthoods by the United Kingdom. The recipients cannot use the chivalric title but can use the initials after their names to indicate the honor.

Paul Mellon's generous works were honored when he was granted the rank of Honorary Knight Commander of the Order of the British Empire (KBE), an award for distinguished service to the arts.

Yehudi Menuhin received an honorary knighthood in 1965, a full knighthood in 1985, and was created Baron Menuhin in 1993.

George Bush, Snr., former US president, was appointed Knight Grand Cross of the Most Honourable Order of the Bath by Queen Elizabeth.

Wesley Clark, US general and NATO Supreme Allied Commander in Europe, was made KBE in March 2000.

Tom Foley, former Speaker of the US House of Representatives, was made a Member of the Order of the British Empire (MBE) in March 1995.

Rudolph Giuliani, mayor of New York City, was honored for his service to British citizens following the terrorist attack on the World Trade Center.

John Paul Getty II, US billionaire businessman, was appointed KBE by HM Queen Elizabeth.

Bob Hope, British-born actor, comedian, and humanitarian, was appointed a Commander of the British Empire (CBE) in 1976.

Colin Powell, US military general, was appointed in 1993 as a Knight Commander of the Most Honourable Order of the Bath.

Billy Graham, Evangelist, was created KBE in December 2001.

André Previn, US composer and orchestral maestro, was appointed KBE in 1996.

Ronald Reagan, former US president, was appointed Knight Grand Cross of the Most Honourable Order of the Bath in 1989.

Norman Schwarzkopf, US military general, was appointed Knight Commander of the Most Honourable Order of the Bath (Honorary) by HM Queen Elizabeth in 1993.

Stephen Spielberg, film director, was made KBE (Civil Division) in the 2000 New Year's Honours List.

Elizabeth Rosemond Taylor was honored for services to acting and charity in the 1999 New Year's Honours.

Caspar Weinberger, former US Secretary of Defense, was appointed Knight Grand Cross of the Most Excellent Order of the British Empire by HM Queen Elizabeth.

Sam Wanamaker was created CBE in 1993 in recognition of the "remarkable contribution he has made to relations between Britain and the US and for all he has done on behalf of the Shakespeare Globe project."

Zoë Wanamaker, American-born English actress with dual US and British citizenship, was made CBE for services to drama in the New Year's Honours List of 2000.

Microsoft billionaire **Bill Gates** received an honorary knighthood in March 2005.

CHAPTER 6
POLITICAL REFORMS

LONDON The *Museum in Docklands* was built in an old West India warehouse. Among the displays are some that focus on the largely unknown history of London's involvement with the slave trade and its abolition.

BRISTOL A plaque above the entrance to one of the *Redcliffe Caves* refers to the "Middle Passage." Local myths abound about these caves. One such story is that slaves were held in the caves, but this is very unlikely.

British reformers in the nineteenth century led efforts to improve the lives of people through the abolition of slavery, the expansion of voting rights to include women, and the improvement of housing and education for the poor. Many Americans were involved in these campaigns which, in turn, had enormous impact on life in America.

In the seventeenth and eighteenth centuries, British merchants were involved in the slave trade. Manufactured goods were shipped from Britain to Africa, to be exchanged for slaves, who were packed into British ships and transported across the Atlantic under horrible conditions in what became known as the "Middle Passage." In America and the Caribbean the slaves were sold to plantation owners who paid with sugar, tobacco, rum, cotton, and tea, which were shipped to Britain. This "triangular trade" formed the basis of huge fortunes in London, Bristol, and Liverpool. In Britain the campaign to end slavery was often led by the Society of Friends – the Quakers – who were also at the forefront of efforts to improve the lives of black people and women in America. 🌿

London
Early English exploration in America began with the hope that it would be possible to exploit the natural resources of that vast land. By the eighteenth century, this hope had become reality. In the late 1700s the West Indies merchants who carried on trade with America and the Caribbean found the existing London warehouses insecure and inefficient. They needed new facilities to store the sugar, tobacco, rum, cotton, and tea that they shipped back from America. The government built the West India import dock and six huge warehouses which were opened in 1802. At the time they were the largest brick buildings in the world. 🌿

Bristol
For hundreds of years Bristol was a major trading port.

There has been speculation that ships from Bristol reached North America several years before Christopher Columbus sailed across the Atlantic. In the seventeenth century enormous fortunes were made by Bristol merchants involved in the slave trade. The elegant homes around Queen's Square and elsewhere in Bristol reflect the money that flowed into the town.

Between 1698 and 1807 approximately 2,100 slaving ships sailed from Bristol. After American independence, Bristol continued to trade with both the northern states and the southern slave states, and the first American consulate in Britain was established in Bristol in 1792. 🍃

Liverpool

The new "Transatlantic Slavery" gallery at the **Merseyside Maritime Museum** in Liverpool tells the story of the slave trade and Liverpool's part in the cruel and inhuman business. The displays cover 500 years of transatlantic slavery and its consequences, focusing on the eighteenth and nineteenth centuries.

The Maritime Museum also offers walking tours around the city center that focus on information and places associated with the slave trade. A pamphlet giving details of a self-guided "slavery trade trail" around Liverpool is available at the museum and tourist information center and online: www.liverpoolmuseums.org.uk/maritime/trail.asp 🍃

Slaves and Free Blacks in Britain

While the great majority of black slaves from Africa were transported to the Americas to work in the great cotton and sugar cane plantations, there were black slaves and also black free people in Britain at this time. Some British planters returning from America brought slaves with them. In the seventeenth and eighteenth centuries a black pageboy became a status symbol with the English upper class; they are often seen in portraits by Hogarth and others. During the American Revolution many black people in America joined the British in the fight against the colonial rebels – the British promised to emancipate blacks who stayed loyal to the Crown. When the war ended, thousands of these former slaves sailed to England, but they often found that the situation wasn't what they expected. Many clustered around the London parish of **St. Giles-in-the-Fields** which was already a notorious slum. The beggars who filled the area were given the derogatory name of "St. Giles Blackbirds." 🍃

Olaudah Equiano

Olaudah Equiano was a former slave who was born in

BRISTOL The *Ostrich Inn* has connections with the slave trade and a secret entrance to the caves. The *Georgian House Museum* demonstrates Bristol's involvement in the slave trade.

The Tourist Information Centre in Bristol offers a pamphlet with a self-guided walking tour that focuses on the history and consequences of the slave trade. An online guide is available at www.lineone.net/~stkittsnevis/bristol.htm.

MERSEYSIDE The *Maritime Museum* in *Liverpool* includes a "Transatlantic Slavery" gallery.

Nathaniel Hawthorne was US consul in Liverpool from 1853 to 1857. He was especially interested in improving the conditions of men working on American ships at sea.

St. Giles-in-the-Fields, London

LONDON When **Olaudah Equiano** was brought to London as a young boy he lived with Captain Pascal's relatives at *111 Maze Hill* in *Greenwich*.

After he purchased his freedom, Olaudah lived at *73 Riding House Street* where he wrote his autobiography. In 2000 Westminster Council placed a plaque on the house where he lived.

LONDON The Buxton Memorial Fountain in the *Victoria Tower Gardens* next to the *Houses of Parliament* commemorates the ending of slavery in Britain in 1834.

The present *Freemasons' Hall* at 60 *Great Queen Street* was built in 1927–33, so it is not the building where the Anti-Slavery Convention was held, but it is at the same location.

Nigeria in 1745. Sold to a British sea captain in a Virginia slave market, Olaudah was taken to England. He was very lucky; he learned to read and write and saw much of the world as he traveled with the sea captain. Because he was well educated, Olaudah was able to earn the £40 required to buy his freedom. Olaudah settled in England and wrote his autobiography, *The Interesting Narrative of the Life of Olaudah Equiano, or Gustavus Vassa, the African*, published in 1789. (Gustavus Vassa was the name given to him by Captain Pascal.) He was involved in many early attempts to improve the lives of black slaves. His autobiography was very popular and was an important inspiration to the growing group of opponents of slavery.

The Abolition of Slavery in Britain

In 1807, after a long campaign led by William Wilberforce, social activists, and the Society of Friends, Parliament passed a law making it illegal for any British citizen to transport slaves. The law did not end slave trading, and at times it had a terrible consequence – ship captains sometimes tried to avoid being fined by throwing their captives overboard to drown. Led by Thomas Fowell Buxton MP, Parliament finally passed the Slavery Abolition Act in 1833 giving freedom to all slaves in the British Empire.

The World Anti-Slavery Convention

After slavery was abolished in Great Britain in 1833, the efforts of abolitionists to end slavery in the USA fueled tensions between northern and southern states and contributed to the American Civil War of the 1860s. The World Anti-Slavery Convention, held in London in June 1840, had a profound effect on American politics and culture. American delegates included many Quakers who were involved in the anti-slavery movement in the United States.

When they arrived in London for the convention, American delegates were faced with a serious problem. Most of the British male delegates did not want female delegates to be allowed to participate. After much debate a vote was taken and females were excluded from the main floor. Women delegates from America traveled all the way to London expecting to be full participants in the convention, and when the actual work began, they were forced to listen to debates from behind a curtain. They considered this an insult and an injustice. The experience kindled a determination in **Elizabeth Cady Stanton** and **Lucretia Coffin Mott** to work for women's rights back in their homeland of America.

Lucretia Coffin Mott and Elizabeth Cady Stanton

The idea of equality of ability and opportunity for women was a fundamental part of Lucretia Coffin's bringing. She grew up in a Quaker community on the island of Nantucket. Lucretia became a Quaker minister at twenty-eight, and began expressing her beliefs. Many Quakers were involved in the anti-slavery movement in the US before the American Civil War and like many of her faith, Lucretia denounced slavery. She and her husband James Mott went to London as delegates to the World Anti-Slavery Convention. Henry Stanton also came to the London convention, with his bride of a few weeks, Elizabeth Cady Stanton. Elizabeth and Lucretia met for the first time at the convention, and there was an immediate bond between the two women. Both were shocked and offended by the way women were treated at the convention. When these American women returned home, they organized the first women's rights convention in the US in 1848, in Seneca Falls, New York. 🍃

Frederick Douglass

Frederick Douglass, an escaped slave who was part of the American abolitionist movement, published the first of his three autobiographies – *The Narrative of the Life of Frederick Douglass: An American Slave* – in 1845. To escape recapture, he came to England that year to lecture on the American anti-slavery movement and spoke at many meetings around Britain, including a meeting of the Anti-Slavery Society at the **Freemasons' Hall**. Douglass so impressed the people he met that they raised enough money to purchase his freedom. He returned to the US in 1847 as a free man. During the American Civil War Douglass helped organize two regiments of Massachusetts African Americans and urged other blacks to join the Union ranks. He visited England again in 1860, fleeing possible arrest after John Brown's raid. 🍃

Moncure Conway

An American abolitionist born in 1832 into a slave-owning family in Virginia, Moncure Conway was sent to London in 1863 to convince the UK that the American Civil War was a war of abolition. He stayed in England and became minister of the South Place Chapel in Finsbury. He and the congregation left the Unitarian Church and became the Ethical Society. The group were early supporters of women's suffrage. **Conway Hall** in **Red Lion Square**, just off Theobald's Road, is named in his honor. Conway played a vital role in the return of part of **Thomas Paine**'s body to be included in his monument in New Rochelle, New York. 🍃

LONDON A statue in *Victoria Tower Gardens* next to the *Houses of Parliament* honors Emmeline Pankhurst, the woman who led the fight for women's suffrage in Britain.

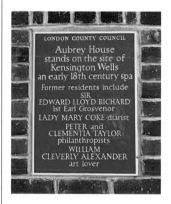

LONDON While in London in 1845, **Frederick Douglass** lived at *Aubrey House, Aubrey Street, Kensington*, with Peter Taylor, MP for Leicester, supporter of the anti-slavery movement.

MANCHESTER In 1920 a statue of President Abraham Lincoln was erected in *Manchester's Lincoln Square.* Excerpts from Lincoln's letter to the workers of Manchester were carved on the plinth.

Abraham Lincoln in *Parliament Square*

LONDON *Lancaster House* is located diagonally across from Buckingham Palace. It was built for Frederick, Duke of York, second son of **King George III** and was originally known as "York House." When the mansion was purchased by the Marquess of Stafford it was renamed "Stafford House." The marquess was elevated to the 1st Duke of Sutherland. His son, the 2nd Duke, finally completed the house, which was then known as "Sutherland House." It was regarded as the finest in London and was taxed as the most expensive private house in the city. It was renamed Lancaster House in 1912 by the new owner, Sir William Lever.

Abraham Lincoln and the Manchester Mill Workers

By the nineteenth century England had a booming textile industry. Much of the cotton for the Manchester mills came from slave plantations in the southern United States and the Caribbean. The American Civil War caused a serious problem for the Manchester mill owners – especially when Abraham Lincoln ordered a naval blockade of southern ports in an effort to cripple the economy and prevent military arms from being imported from Europe. Liverpool merchants supported the southern states of the Confederacy during the war, and Liverpool ships would run the blockade to bring loads of cotton to England. On the other hand, the mill workers of Manchester refused to cooperate with this. On 31 December 1862 a group of mill workers in Manchester voted to boycott all cotton from the Confederate states as a show of support for President Lincoln's emancipation of the slaves, even though this action meant that the mills would likely be closed. President Lincoln appreciated this show of support from across the ocean. He sent a message of thanks, saying that he regretted the suffering that the workers of Manchester would have to face. 🌿

Harriet Beecher Stowe

As the anti-slavery movement grew in the United States, one of the most celebrated events was the publication in 1852 of *Uncle Tom's Cabin* by Harriet Beecher Stowe. The story of the human cruelty of slavery was a tremendous success, selling over 300,000 copies in a year. The book was also extremely popular in Europe, especially in England where it was taken up by the abolitionists among the British elite. A number of readings and plays of *Uncle Tom's Cabin* were put on all over England. In America southerners and slave-owners tended to be very critical of the book, and Harriet Beecher Stowe was subjected to hate-mail and threats. In April 1853 she accepted invitations to tour Europe and Britain. During her tour to various cities she was greeted with tremendous enthusiasm and support.

In January 1853 the Duchess of Sutherland held an important meeting of British women to express their opposition to American slavery. The **Stafford House** Assembly of Ladies honored Harriet Beecher Stowe, presenting her with twenty-six volumes of signatures on a petition against slavery, along with a heavy gold bracelet, with links in the shape of slave shackles. A link was left blank, waiting to be engraved with the date when slavery was abolished in America. 🌿

Josiah Henson

Josiah Henson escaped from slavery in the American South in 1830 and made his way to freedom in Canada. He spent the rest of his life helping to free other slaves. He set up a technical school and work projects for former slaves in Dawn, Ontario. Josiah met **Harriet Beecher Stowe** and was reportedly the inspiration for the character of Uncle Tom in her famous anti-slavery novel *Uncle Tom's Cabin*. Henson visited England in 1849–51 and again in 1851–2 to raise money to support his Canadian projects. In May 1851 he was one of the Canadian representatives at the Great Exhibition in *Hyde Park, London*, and was reportedly the only black exhibitor. When Queen Victoria toured the exhibition she paused to look at his display of items produced at the Dawn Settlement and spoke with Henson. This led to further attention being paid to Henson by the press and influential people at a time when the effort to end slavery in America was gaining momentum. During his last trip to England, in 1877, Henson lectured and preached to large gatherings in several cities. On 5 March 1877 he and his wife were presented to Queen Victoria at *Windsor Castle*. 🌿

Elizabeth Taylor Greenfield

In May 1853 the Duchess of Sutherland held a concert at *Stafford House* to benefit the freed American slave Elizabeth Taylor Greenfield. Born in 1817 as a slave in Mississippi, Elizabeth accompanied her mistress to Philadelphia, Pennsylvania. When her mistress became a Quaker and freed her slaves, Elizabeth chose to stay with her and adopted her name. Encouraged to study music, it became evident that Elizabeth had great potential as a singer. She raised money to travel to England to study singing, but when she arrived in London for a concert tour, her supposed manager disappeared along with her money, leaving her in a very difficult position. After her concert at Stafford House, she sang at several concerts in cities around England and then on 10 May 1854 Elizabeth Taylor Greenfield sang for Queen Victoria at a performance at *Buckingham Palace*, arranged by Harriet, Duchess of Sutherland. 🌿

Booker T. Washington

Booker T. Washington was a former slave who visited England and met with influential people. He was the guest of Queen Victoria for tea at *Windsor Castle*, at a meeting that also included Susan B. Anthony. He stayed at *Skibo Castle, Dornoch*, Scotland, with **Andrew Carnegie**, and met the Duke and Duchess of Sutherland who later invited Washington and his wife to a reception at Stafford House. 🌿

BERKSHIRE *Cliveden* is one of England's finest country houses and has been a center of influence, wealth, and political power for more than 300 years. The present house was built in 1850–1 for the Duke and Duchess of Sutherland, who actively supported the anti-slavery movement.

William Waldorf Astor purchased *Cliveden* from the Duke of Westminster in 1893 and gave it to his son and **Nancy Langhorne** as a wedding gift.

SOMERSET The *American Museum in Britain* just outside *Bath* has the largest collection of American decorative arts outside the US. A portrait bust of **Josiah Henson** by W. Charles May is on exhibit at the museum, along with a portrait by Francis Walker of Henson being presented to Queen Victoria in 1877.

LONDON Josiah Henson's final trip to England took place in 1877. In March, he addressed a huge crowd at Sturgeon's Tabernacle, now known as the *Metropolitan Tabernacle*.

Windsor Castle, Berkshire

LONDON Ernestine Rose died on 4 August 1892 and was buried next to her husband William at *Highgate Cemetery*. The Roses' grave marker was restored and a dedication ceremony held at the cemetery on 4 August 2002.

Ernestine Rose

Born in Poland in 1810, Ernestine Potowski was the only child of a respected rabbi. She was well educated but was barred from full participation in religious studies because she was a woman. After her mother died, her father arranged a marriage for her, promising the inheritance she had been left by her mother. At sixteen, Ernestine already had a determination to stand up for herself. Refusing to marry a man she did not love, she appealed to a secular court for the right to keep her inheritance. After winning the case, she left home seeking freedom from the stifling bounds of religious creed and paternal oppression.

Ernestine arrived in England in 1830 and became involved in the Owenite movement, a utopian socialist movement. She married William Rose, a fellow Owenite who shared her commitments. In 1836 Ernestine traveled to New York and became involved in the effort to ensure married women's property rights. She became a life-long friend of **Elizabeth Cady Stanton** and Susan B. Anthony, leaders of the women's rights movement in America. Ernestine and William became US citizens but in 1869 they returned to England to live in retirement. She died in 1892.

Victoria Woodhull Martin

Victoria California Claflin was born in 1838 in Homer, Ohio, into a life of poverty. Her family was part of a traveling medicine show. Victoria would sing and dance in the show, and often joined her mother in telling fortunes. At fifteen, she married a brutal alcoholic. By 1868 she was married to her second husband and had moved to New York City. Through her practice of spiritualism, Victoria met the aging railroad tycoon, Cornelius Vanderbilt, whom she impressed with her ability to channel financial advice from the dead. He backed Victoria and her sister, Tennessee Celeste, in opening the first women-owned brokerage firm on Wall Street.

GLOUCESTERSHIRE In *Bredon's Norton*, Victoria Woodhull Martin's home became the headquarters for the Ladies' Automobile Club, the International Peace Society, and the Women's Aerial League of Great Britain. She also contributed £1,000 towards the purchase of *Sulgrave Manor, Northamptonshire*, George Washington's ancestral home.

Victoria attended the National Female Suffrage Convention in 1869 and became more politically oriented and outspoken about her beliefs, such as free love, women's suffrage, short skirts, spiritualism, vegetarianism, birth control, and licensed prostitution. In January 1871 she gave an address to the National Suffrage Convention but the following year Victoria's personal ambitions caused the suffrage movement to repudiate her when she tried to establish a new political party to back her own individual goals. In 1872 Victoria Claflin Woodhull became the first woman nominated to run for president of the United States, supported by her own "Equal Rights Party." As her vice-presidential running mate, she nominated **Frederick Douglass,** the former slave and renowned orator. Unfortunately, Douglass had not been approached for his consent to this nomination, and he never even acknowledged the honor.

Victoria's run for president created strong opposition, and it got nasty. When criticized for her beliefs on free love, she threatened to publish the names of men who frequented prostitutes. As the opposition became more personal, she felt much of it was being directed by Henry Ward Beecher, the brother of **Harriet Beecher Stowe**. When she named him as an adulterer in her weekly publication, she was taken to court for sending obscene material through the mail. Although the story was later proven to be true, Victoria's run for the presidential office was finished, and she was bankrupted by the case. In 1878, Victoria and Tennessee moved to England and began a new chapter in their lives.

In 1883 Victoria Woodhull married a London banker, John Biddulph Martin. She started a magazine in which she published several feminist articles. John Martin died in 1897 and Victoria moved to the family home in the village of **Bredon's Norton, Gloucestershire**. She spent the rest of her life being involved in village affairs and doing good deeds. In England, Victoria Woodhull Martin was viewed as a compassionate, courageous, and inspirational woman. She died in 1927 at the age of eighty eight. Her ashes were scattered in mid-Atlantic, between the two countries where she lived her remarkable life.

GLOUCESTERSHIRE In St. Faith's Chapel in *Tewkesbury Abbey* a memorial to Victoria Woodhull Martin notes that "she devoted herself unsparingly to all that could promote the great cause of Anglo-American friendship."

Paul Robeson

Born in Princeton, New Jersey, in 1898, Paul Robeson came from a family that had been involved in the campaign for African American civil rights. His father, a former slave and pastor of the Witherspoon Street Presbyterian Church, was also involved in working for civil rights for his people. Paul Robeson won an academic scholarship to Rutgers University, which he entered in 1915. During his four years there his academic and sports achievements were outstanding. He was elected to Phi Beta Kappa, and was valedictorian of his graduating class. In 1919 Robeson entered Columbia Law School, and in 1921 married Eslanda Cardozo Goode, the first black analytical chemist at Columbia Medical Center.

In 1920 Robeson joined a group of Afro-American students who wanted to produce plays on racial issues. He was a great success and was offered the leading role in several plays. After graduating from Columbia Law School, Robeson began a short-lived law career in New York. He was the only African American in the firm, and faced racial prejudice and abuse. Robeson decided to try the theater as a profession. Here he also faced prejudice – a journal owned

LONDON Over the years the *Royal Albert Hall* has hosted a great variety of events, including political ralllies at which Paul Robeson spoke.

by William Randolph Hearst called for a play not to be shown because it included a scene where a white actress kissed Robeson's hand. He was invited to travel to London to perform. The reactions he met there were full of praise and support. Soon Robeson was offered other roles in London, most famously a 1930 production of *Othello* at the Savoy Theatre opposite Peggy Ashcroft.

During the 1930s, Robeson made London his primary residence. He took part in labor and peace rallies, Save China assemblies, and meetings to protest British colonialism in Jamaica. On 24 June 1937, Robeson spoke at a large rally at the **Royal Albert Hall** in London in aid of those fighting against General Francisco Franco in Spain. In December 1937 he joined Labour Party leaders at a rally at the Albert Hall attacking the British government's Non-Intervention Agreement. In 1939 Paul and his wife returned to the US where he continued to be politically active.

In 1949 Robeson had a European concert tour, including the Soviet Union where his wife's brothers had emigrated. Attending the Paris Peace Conference, he stated: "It is unthinkable that American Negroes could go to war on behalf of those who have oppressed us for generations against the Soviet Union, which in one generation has raised our people to full human dignity." When he returned to the US, his concerts were cancelled. The US government confiscated his passport. In 1958 when he and Essie were allowed to leave the US, they moved back to London. Robeson returned to the US in 1963. He died in 1976. 🍃

Martin Luther King, Jr.

As a little boy, Martin Luther King saw the violence of racial hatred and the social, political, and economic oppression of African Americans. He followed his father into the Christian ministry, which was a path to leadership in the black community at that time. King's life work combined his Christian beliefs with an appeal to American ideals of freedom and justice. The effectiveness of Gandhi's non-violent campaign in India inspired King's early campaigns against racial discrimination in the US. He advocated tactics such as the bus boycott in Montgomery, Alabama, and the lunch-counter protests throughout the South. The peaceful demonstrations often resulted in violent opposition and widespread clashes where many protestors were beaten or even killed. King led a massive public march on Washington, D.C., in August 1963. The US Congress passed the Civil Rights Act on 2 July 1964. In 1967 Martin Luther King, Jr., was awarded the Nobel Peace Prize. One year later, on 4 April 1968, he was shot and killed in Memphis, Tennessee. 🍃

LONDON A statue of **Martin Luther King** is among the ten "Modern Martyrs" above the front entrance of *Westminster Abbey*.

CHAPTER 7
AMERICAN HEIRESSES

Between the end of the American Civil War and the outbreak
of the First World War, 454 American women married
European nobles. Of these, 100 married into the English
aristocracy. There were many economic and social reasons
for this movement across the ocean. For one thing, the old
aristocratic families were running out of money. The English
aristocracy was based on land and agriculture, but increasing
industrialization meant the income from these estates was
disappearing. An aristocratic estate was passed on as a
whole to the oldest son, so younger sons and daughters
usually did not inherit much. Daughters of English nobility
often did not have bountiful dowries to help a poor,
struggling peer who might have developed a taste for an
expensive lifestyle. In America, and especially in New York,
there was a great social gulf between the tightly closed "Old
Money" families and the ambitious, energetic, and intelligent
nouveaux riches who often made their money during the
period of industrial growth that accompanied and followed
the American Civil War. Their daughters were often excluded
from the social life of upper-crust New York, so they looked
elsewhere for an impressive marriage. A titled Englishman
was hard to ignore, even for the Old New York families.

1895 was the year when Anglomania peaked. Nine
American girls wed British nobles, including Maud Burke
who married Sir Bache Cunard, Mary Leiter who married the
Honorable George Curzon, and Consuelo Vanderbilt who
married the 9th Duke of Marlborough. Unfortunately, these
transatlantic marriages were not always happy. The American
brides often did not know what to expect when they arrived
at the grand family estates. Sometimes the huge family
stately homes had no electricity and very little modern
plumbing. They also faced social conventions and
expectations of behavior that were very different from those
of their home country. Their husbands were sometimes
dissolute or self-absorbed; often they did not consider wives
to be intellectually interesting or personally important. Some

LONDON Jennie Jerome's sisters also married into the British aristocracy. In June 1881 Clara Jerome married Moreton Frewen at Grace Church in New York. He was from one of the oldest landed gentry families in England. In October 1894, also at Grace Church, Leonie Jerome married Jack Leslie, son of Sir John Leslie, Baronet of Glaslough and one of the largest landowners in Ireland. After Leonie and Jack were married, they often lived with his parents at *Stratford House* on *Stratford Place*, just off *Oxford Street*.

OXFORDSHIRE A special suite of rooms at *Blenheim Palace* in *Woodstock* houses an exhibition about Jennie Jerome Churchill's son Winston.

LONDON In 1897 Jennie attended the famous ball at *Devonshire House* on 2 July 1897 dressed as the Queen of Romania.

Jennie Jerome Churchill married her second husband, George Cornwallis-West, at *St. Paul's Church, Wilton Place, Knightsbridge*, in July 1900.

BUCKINGHAMSHIRE A Churchill exhibition at *Bletchley Park* includes memorabilia connected with Jennie.

OXFORDSHIRE Jennie Jerome is buried next to her first husband in the churchyard at *Bladon* near *Woodstock*.

of these American brides were able to find a life they could enjoy, but others never did. Some marriages ended in divorce and others in years of unhappiness. What seemed a glamorous fairy tale could end up as something very different. 🍃

Jennie Jerome married Randolph Churchill, son of 7th Duke of Marlborough (m. 1874)

Jeanette ("Jennie") Jerome was born in Brooklyn, New York, on 9 January 1854. Her father, Leonard Jerome, was a prosperous financier who was involved in building a racecourse and helped found the American Jockey Club. In 1867, following a scandal involving their father and an opera singer, Jennie and her two sisters were taken to Paris by their mother.

Jennie Jerome was known for her beauty and vivacious personality. She was one of the few women in high society who had a tattoo – a snake coiled around her left wrist. In 1873 she met and charmed young Lord Randolph Churchill, second son of the 7th Duke of Marlborough. They were married in Paris on 15 April 1874 when she was twenty years old. Her American vivacity, wit, and beauty assured her of social success in London, and she became a glamorous member of English society.

As the younger son of the duke, Randolph Churchill was not in line to inherit the title or family home, Blenheim Palace. He became active in politics and was a Member of Parliament. Lord Randolph Churchill died in 1895 and Jennie was left to enjoy herself as a merry widow. In 1900 she married Captain George Cornwallis-West, an officer of the Scots Guards, who was twenty years younger than she and only sixteen days older than her son Winston. Their marriage caused much opposition among their families and members of society. The marriage ended in divorce in 1913. In 1918 Jennie married Montague Phippin Porch of the British Civil Service in Nigeria. She died on 29 June 1921. 🍃

Consuelo Yznaga married the 8th Duke of Manchester (m. 1876)

Consuelo Yznaga was born in Louisiana in 1858, daughter of Ellen Clement Yznaga, whose father had been a steamboat captain from Duchess County, New York, and Don Antonio Yznaga, the heir to sugar plantations in Cuba. After the American Civil War, she went to Paris with her mother and sisters, Emily and Natica, and was introduced to the sophisticated, extravagant lifestyle of the French Second Empire of Napoleon III and Empress Eugénie. When the family returned to America, Consuelo and her mother set off on a campaign to find a suitable husband. In 1875 they spent a summer holiday in Saratoga Springs, New York, a resort town popular among the rich. There she met George Victor Drogo Montagu, Viscount Mandeville, who was called "Kim" because of his subsidiary title of Baron Kimbolton. The heir to the Duke of Manchester was known for his racy lifestyle – he spent lavishly and loved gambling. Kim was invited to visit the Yznaga's plantation home, Ravenswood, in Louisiana. During his visit, Kim became very ill and Consuelo nursed him back to health. The couple soon became engaged.

Consuelo made a place for herself in English society, becoming the close friend of the Prince of Wales. She also became somewhat of a professional match-maker, introducing many ambitious American heiresses to English men with old noble titles and very little money. It seems she didn't have much contact with her son Kim. She was quite surprised when he married an American heiress, Helena Zimmerman. Consuelo died in London on 20 November 1909. An echo of Consuelo Yznaga's life is seen in that of her god-daughter, Consuelo Vanderbilt, whose mother Alva Smith Vanderbilt pushed her into marriage with the 9th Duke of Marlborough. 🍃

Helena Zimmerman

married the 9th Duke of Manchester (m. 1900, div. 1931)

Helena Zimmerman was the only child of Eugene Zimmerman of Cincinnati, who had made a fortune in coal, iron, railroads and petroleum – he was one of the founders of Standard Oil. On 14 November 1900 the headstrong young woman married William Angus Drogo Montagu, the twenty-three-year-old 9th Duke of Manchester, who was known as Kim, as his father had been. Neither the bride's father, a self-made millionaire, nor the groom's mother, Consuelo, the American dowager Duchess of Manchester, were happy about the marriage.

Kim turned out to be a young man who did not have a firm grasp on some of the realities of life – especially the economic realities. As a young man Kim spent time in the US and was especially impressed by the vast fortunes that some men had made, and by new technology, such as automobiles and films. Unfortunately, his aristocratic upbringing did not include any notion of hard work, organization, or a sense of responsibility. In England a duke may have been able to get away with not paying his bills for years and years, but in America, merchants and businessmen were not so forgiving. Everyone was expected to pay their bills and Kim rarely did. He also had problems in

WARWICKSHIRE In the main apartment block of *Warwick Castle* a series of rooms are furnished as they would have been around 1890. The exhibits show a "Royal Weekend Party," when royalty were entertained at the castle. Most of these rooms include life-size wax figures in period costume depicting real personalities of the period. Included among the guests are **Consuelo Vanderbilt** and **Jennie Jerome Churchill** with her second husband, George Cornwallis-West.

LONDON Consuelo Yznaga moved to *5 Grosvenor Square* in 1901. (The building was rebuilt after the Second World War.)

Consuelo Yznaga attended the *Devonshire House* ball dressed as Empress Anne of Austria.

CAMBRIDGESHIRE The seat of the dukes of Manchester is at *Kimbolton Castle*.

In the south chapel of *St. Andrew's Church* in *Kimbolton* there is a stained-glass window by American glass artist Louis Comfort Tiffany of New York. The window depicts the twin daughters of Consuelo Yznaga. In the chancel there is an unusual marble monument to Consuelo Yznaga, who died in 1909.

LONDON The elegant houses at *Carlton House Terrace* were popular with wealthy aristocrats and many American heiresses lived there:

No. 1 – bought for **Mary Leiter** of Washington, D.C., by her father when she married George Curzon in 1895.

No. 2 – **May Goelet** and Kelso (8th Duke of Roxburghe) moved here in 1923.

No. 3 – home of **Lily Hammersley** after 1895 marriage to Lord William Beresford

No. 5 – the residence of **Mary Burke** of San Francisco who married Sir Bache Cunard I in 1895

No. 7 – the residence of **Belle Wilson** and Mungo (Hon. Michael Henry) Herbert, married in 1888. She was the aunt of May Goelet, and he was the younger brother of the 13th Earl of Pembroke.

No. 18 –home of **William Waldorf Astor**

No. 20 – home of Lady Parker, American wife of Sir Gilbert Parker, MP

No. 22 – home of **Amy Phipps**, of Pittsburgh, and her husband, the Hon. Frederick Guest, MP

England – in 1928 he was brought before the bankruptcy court and in 1933 was convicted of fraud for selling jewels that belonged to his mother's estate. This time Kim was sentenced to a nine-month term in Wormwood Scrubs Prison, but in the end served only twenty-five days. By 1914 Kim and Helena were leading completely separate lives. She lived with their two sons and two daughters at Kylemore Castle in Ireland, which her father had purchased for her. Kim pursued his pipe dreams of business achievement in America and Cuba.

Helena had finally had enough of marriage to an "inveterate gambler, womanizer, liar, compulsive spender, rash schemer, and all-around fool." In February 1931 Helena served Kim with a divorce suit on the grounds of misconduct. Later that year, Kim showed up at New York's City Hall intending to marry Kathleen Dawes, an actress. Unfortunately he had forgotten to bring along a copy of his divorce papers, so the wedding had to wait until the next week. In 1937 Helena married Lord Arthur George Keith-Falconer, Earl of Kintore. They moved to Keith Hall at Inverurie in Aberdeenshire, Scotland, and Helena lived there quietly, and one hopes, happily, for thirty-four years. She died at Keith Hall in 1971 at the age of ninety-three. 🌿

Lily Hammersley
married the 8th Duke of Marlborough (m. 1888)

Lillian Hammersley was a thirty-three-year-old widow with a large inheritance when she met George Charles Spencer-Churchill, 8th Duke of Marlborough in 1887. He was called Blandford all his life because his preducal title was Marquess of Blandford. He had been married to Lady Alberta Hamilton, daughter of the Duke of Abercorn. Their marriage was unhappy and marked by Blandford's flagrant infidelities, but they had four children before finally divorcing in 1883. Their oldest son became the 9th Duke of Marlborough and married **Consuelo Vanderbilt**.

Lily and Blandford were married on 29 June 1888 in the Mayor's Office in New York City. Lily's money soon was being spent for improvements on **Blenheim Palace**, like installing central heating. Lily wasn't accepted in most aristocratic circles because of Blandford's divorce, and she lived in an uncomfortable, un-modernized stately home, but she supported Blandford, indulging his whims (such as installing a pipe organ in the Long Library at Blenheim), and funding his business schemes. Blandford also spent some of Lily's money on his long-time mistress, even setting her up in a palazzo in Venice.

The unhappy marriage came to an end in 1892, when

Blandford died of a heart attack, at the age of forty-eight. Lily left Blenheim and moved to Brighton, but she did remain on good terms with Blandford's relatives. In 1893 she gave a typewriter to the son of her sister-in-law, **Jennie Jerome Churchill**. **Winston Churchill** may have used it when he wrote as a journalist during the Boer War.

Lily's story did have a happier chapter. On 30 April 1895 she married Lord William de la Poer Beresford at *St. George's Church, Hanover Square, London*. They lived contentedly at *Deepdene*, her large comfortable house near *Dorking* in Surrey. In 1897, at the age of forty-three, Lily had a son – William Warren de la Poer. Unfortunately, this brighter interlude lasted only a few years. Lord Beresford died in 1900. Lily died at Deepdene of a heart attack in 1909. Her ashes were interred beside those of her third husband at Clonegan Church in Ireland. 🍃

Consuelo Vanderbilt
married the 9th Duke of Marlborough (m. 1895, div. 1920)

Consuelo Vanderbilt's wedding to Charles Richard John Spencer-Churchill on 6 November 1895 was the precursor of the superstar weddings of today, having the same public fascination with every detail and the same media frenzy to be the first in print with the most information. The marriage eventually made Consuelo the symbol of the unhappy rich girl when her mother forced her to marry a man whom she didn't love, a man who married her solely for her millions and who very soon disliked her. The duke was always known as "Sunny" because of his predual title of Earl of Sunderland, but his personality was far from Sunny.

On her wedding day, Consuelo was eighteen years old. Named after her mother's good friend Consuelo Yznaga, Consuelo Vanderbilt was a tall, beautiful, intelligent young woman who was brought up by an ambitious, controlling mother. Alva Smith Vanderbilt was determined to use her husband's money to place her family at the top of society's hierarchy. In New York City, the Old Money society did not acknowledge the achievements of self-made men like William K. Vanderbilt, or his grandfather, Commodore Cornelius Vanderbilt. Alva built extravagant mansions in New York and Newport, Rhode Island, gave the most outlandish parties seen in New York for a hundred years, and was determined to marry her daughter to the British man with the highest noble title available.

Sunny was a preeminent member of the English aristocracy where higher education for the heir to an aristocratic title was considered "gilding." Sunny did not show a lot of intellectual depth, whereas Consuelo was

St. George's Church,
Hanover Square, London

SURREY Lily Hammersley and her third husband lived at *Deepdene House* in *Dorking* until his death. The house was demolished in 1969, but is remembered in the name of a Dorking railway station, and many local street names. The house stood on Deepdene Avenue just south of South Drive.

LONDON In June 1894 Alva Smith Vanderbilt stayed at *Brown's Hotel* while she made her first direct attack on English society with her daughter Consuelo Vanderbilt. The following June they returned to Brown's and continued the campaign.

The Duke of Marlborough built *Sunderland House*, on the corner of Curzon Street and Shepherd's Market, in 1901 with money William K. Vanderbilt gave to his daughter Consuelo as a Christmas gift. After her separation from the duke in 1906, Consuelo moved here. The house is now called Lombard House and is owned by the ruling family of Qatar.

OXFORDSHIRE Several portraits of Consuelo are on display at *Blenheim Palace* in *Woodstock*. **John Singer Sargent**'s portrait of the duke, Consuelo, and their two sons hangs in the Red Drawing Room.

LONDON In 1897 the Duke of Marlborough rented *Spencer House* (West Front, above, by Mark Fiennes © Spencer House). Consuelo Vanderbilt Churchill's first son was born at Spencer House on 18 September 1897.

On 2 July 1897 **Consuelo Vanderbilt** and her husband attended the famous ball at *Devonshire House* on *Piccadilly* although she was uncomfortably pregnant. She was dressed as the wife of the French ambassador to the court of Catherine the Great of Russia.

OXFORDSHIRE Consuelo Vanderbilt was buried, as she requested, next to her son Ivor in the churchyard at *St. Martin's* at *Bladon* near *Blenheim Palace*.

LONDON Wimborne House at *22 Arlington Street* is now owned by the Ritz Hotel and has been renamed "William Kent House."

May Goelet and her mother rented *Spencer House* on *Green Park* for the May–July 1902 London Season.

extremely well educated, spoke several languages, and liked to read philosophy. Consuelo's dowry of $2.5million ($60m in 2005 dollars) meant that Sunny would have the huge sums of money that Blenheim Palace seemed to eat up. When Consuelo (or more probably, her mother) accepted Sunny's proposal of marriage, he sent a telegram to the Blenheim estate manager saying "HAVE THE LAKE DREDGED." He also spent huge sums of her money living a life of conspicuous consumption, buying extravagant goods for the house and clothes and jewelry for himself. He also flaunted his relationship with his long-term mistress, American Gladys Deacon.

It took eleven years of marriage before Consuelo shared her feelings with her father, who supported her in gaining her independence. Consuelo separated from Sunny in 1906, but was not actually divorced until 1920, when Sunny wanted to marry Gladys Deacon and join the Catholic Church. After the divorce, Consuelo used her wealth and position in society to make a significant contribution to social causes she personally believed in. She set up premises where the wives of imprisoned convicts could work and earn money; she equipped and ran lodging houses for poor women and working girls; she began a school to teach mothering skills to working-class women.

On 4 July 1921 Consuelo Vanderbilt married Colonel Jacques Balsan, a French man whom she had met at her first ball in Paris. They had twenty-one happy years together until Jacques died in 1956. Consuelo Vanderbilt Marlborough Balsan died at Southampton, Long Island, on 6 December 1964 at the age of eighty-seven. This unique American woman, whose story proved that riches don't guarantee happiness, used her intelligence and energy to live a fulfilling and meaningful life. 🍃

Mary Goelet
married the 8th Duke of Roxburghe (m. 1903)
Unlike many of the American heiresses that came from the families of *nouveau riche* entrepreneurs who had made their money during and after the American Civil War, Mary ("May") Goelet was from an Old Money – Old New York family. She grew up traveling in Europe. The Prince of Wales was a family friend who had been entertained on their yacht several times. The Goelet family rented a house in London for the 1897 social season, and May was one of the most sought-after young ladies that year.

On 2 July 1897 May attended the Devonshire House Ball, held in the summer of Queen Victoria's Diamond Jubilee year. She went to the costume ball dressed as Scheherazade.

Other famous American heiresses were among the many extravagantly dressed women at the famous ball. **Lily Hammersley Churchill Beresford** came up from Deepdene; **Consuelo Yznaga Manchester** attended, as did **Consuelo Vanderbilt Marlborough**, who was pregnant and unhappy. At the ball, May met one of the most handsome and eligible young aristocrats in Britain – Sir Henry John Innes-Ker, 8th Duke of Roxburghe, known as Kelso. One of the richest young men in Britain, he did not need to marry an American heiress for her money. Their courtship proceeded slowly and calmly, with time for the couple to get to know each other.

May Goelet and the Duke of Roxburghe were married on 10 November 1903 at St. Thomas's Episcopal Church in New York, with both delighted families there to celebrate the event. They had a long, happy marriage, with May enjoying her life as the mistress of **Floors Castle**. She brought new life into the centuries-old seat of the dukes of Roxburghe, and was greatly loved by the local people. Kelso died in 1932, and May died at her home at **Carlton House Terrace, London**, in 1937. They were buried next to each other at Kelso Abbey. 🍃

Lord Curzon and the American Ladies

The Kedleston estate has been owned by the Curzon family since 1297. One of the most well known of the family was George Nathaniel Curzon, Marquess Curzon of Kedleston (1859–1925). An ambitious politician who served in government as a member of the Cabinet during the First World War and as foreign secretary, Curzon is best remembered as having been viceroy of India from 1898 to 1905. He was able to fill this post largely because of the wealth brought to him through his marriage in 1895 to the wealthy American beauty, **Mary Leiter**, daughter of Chicago businessman Levi Leiter, one of the founders of the Field & Leiter department store, which became the Marshall Field's store. Mary's sister Margaret ("Daisy") also married an Englishman, the Earl of Suffolk, so she became the Countess of Suffolk. As the wife of a marquess, Mary's rank of marchioness was higher than her sister's.

Lord Curzon may have married Mary Leiter for her money, but their marriage developed into a happy one where she was devoted to her husband. Unfortunately, it was not to last long. Mary died in 1906 at the tender age of thirty-six. Her heartbroken husband built a memorial chapel at **All Saints' Church**, the ancient church in the grounds of the **Kedleston estate**. Mary Leiter and Lord Curzon had three daughters: Mary Irene (who inherited one of her father's baronies to become Baroness Ravensdale), Cynthia (first wife of Sir Oswald Mosley), and Alexandra Naldera (wife of

May Goelet attended the famous *Devonshire House* ball in 1987 dressed as Scheherazade.

SCOTLAND *Floors Castle, Kelso, Borders*, is the largest inhabited house in Scotland. The splendid entrance gates were erected in 1929 as a silver wedding gift to the 8th Duke of Roxburghe from his American wife May Goelet.

DERBYSHIRE During his time as viceroy of India, **Lord Curzon** played a leading role in the Coronation Durbar held in Delhi in January 1903, one of the greatest pageants ever staged by the British Empire. The vicereine is remembered for the fabulous "Peacock Dress" she wore during the durbar. Designed by a Parisian couturier and made by many skilled seamstresses in India, the dress was created from shining cloth of gold, semi-precious stones, gold and silver threads, and the wing cases of brilliant scarab beetles, pearls, etc., embroidered into a pattern of peacock feathers. The dress is now on display at the museum at *Kedleston Hall*, the seat of the Curzon family.

Mary and Lord Curzon are buried side by side in a beautiful tomb in *All Saints' Church* at *Kedleston*.

EAST SUSSEX A romantic story tells how Lord Curzon drove Grace Hinds into the countryside. He blindfolded her and led her to a hill overlooking *Bodiam Castle*. When he let her look at the scene, she said it was as enchanting as a fairy tale come to life. She accepted his proposal of marriage. Restoring the medieval castle became one of Lord Curzon's personal projects. When he died, the castle was bequeathed to the National Trust.

LONDON Alamric Paget and his wife Pauline Whitney moved to England in 1902 and lived at *38 Berkeley Square*.

KENT After Lady Baillie's death in 1974, *Leeds Castle* near *Maidstone* was turned over to the Leeds Castle Foundation. It is open to the public and has been the setting for several international conferences.

LONDON *Apsley House* – No. 1 London at *Hyde Park Corner* was the **Duke of Wellington's** London residence.

Edward "Fruity" Metcalfe, the best friend of King Edward VIII.

After Mary's death, it seemed Lord Curzon would never marry again. He had a long affair with Elinor Glyn, a romantic novelist who wrote love stories that sometimes seemed to reflect her relationship with Lord Curzon. She hoped to marry Curzon, but that was not to be. In 1917 he married another wealthy American woman, the former Grace Elvina Hinds, an Alabama-born widow. Lord Curzon's political career suffered a great disappointment in 1923 when he hoped to become prime minister, but was passed over in favor of Stanley Baldwin. George Curzon died in 1925; his widow Grace Elvina, Marchioness Curzon of Kedleston, died in 1958.

Olive Paget Baillie

In 1926 Lady Olive Baillie purchased **Leeds Castle**, one of the most romantic castles in England. Her father was Almeric Paget, the first and only Lord Queenborough, and her mother was an American, Pauline Whitney, another of the American heiresses who married into the British aristocracy. Pauline and Almeric Paget had married in New York on 12 November 1895, one week after Consuelo Vanderbilt married the Duke of Marlborough. Almeric worked for her father, a wealthy businessman who made a fortune as the founder of the Metropolitan Transit. The Anglo-American connection was very popular in their families: Almeric's brothers, Arthur and Sidney, married Americans; and Pauline Whitney's stepsister Adelaide Randolph married the Honorable Lionel Lambart.

Olive Paget became Lady Baillie through her marriage to Sir Adrian Baillie. She restored the romantic castle, where she centered a life of grand entertaining. Guests included relatives such as John Hay ("Jock") Whitney, who was American ambassador from 1957 to 1961, the Prince of Wales, and Grand Duke Dimitri of Russia.

The Duke of Wellington and the Baltimore Connection

An interesting American connection linked Arthur Wellesley, the Duke of Wellington, with Napoleon Bonaparte. The military leaders who faced each other on the battlefield at Waterloo were both related by marriage to an American family in Baltimore, Maryland.

In 1803 Jerome Bonaparte, Napoleon's youngest brother, was serving aboard a French ship that was forced to go into the Port of Baltimore to avoid capture by the British. Jerome met an American girl and fell in love. On Christmas Eve 1803, in Baltimore Cathedral, he married Elizabeth Patterson, the eighteen-year-old daughter of William Patterson, the second wealthiest man in Maryland. Unfortunately, Napoleon was furious. He planned to marry off his siblings in politically advantageous matches and this was not part of his plans. He had the marriage annulled by a French court and ordered Jerome to return to France. Jerome crossed the Atlantic with his pregnant wife, but ports in France refused to allow her to land. She had to go to London were her son was born in 1805. She subsequently returned to Baltimore. After Napoleon became emperor, Jerome was made an imperial prince. He married Federica Catherine, daughter of the King of Wurttemberg. From 1807 to 1813 he ruled as King of Westphalia.

Elizabeth Patterson's brother Robert married Marianne Caton of Baltimore. In 1825, after Robert's death, Marianne married Richard, Marquess Wellesley, the elder brother of Arthur, Duke of Wellesley. So, through a family in Baltimore, Maryland, the battlefield foes could have been considered (distant) brothers-in-law.

In another twist of history, Marianne Caton Patterson was the granddaughter of **Charles Carroll** of Carrollton, Maryland, the last surviving signatory of the Declaration of Independence!

Nancy Astor

When Nancy Astor of West Virginia married Waldorf Astor in 1906 she became part of an influential American family who had moved to England and become influential in British newspaper publication and politics. Nancy became the first woman to take a seat in the **House of Commons**. *(See Chapter 5 for details of her life.)*

Nancy Astor's portrait at
Cliveden, Berkshire

READ
Fortune's Daughters by Elisabeth Kehoe. London: Atlantic Books, 2004

The Buccaneers by Edith Wharton. New York: Viking Press, 1993 (first published 1938)

The Duchess of Devonshire's Ball, by Sophia Murphy. London: Sidgwick and Jackson, 1984. (It has many photos of the fantastic costumes at the famous Devonshire House Ball.)

The Glitter and the Gold, by Consuelo Vanderbilt Balsan. New York: Harper & Brothers, 1952

To Marry an English Lord, Or, How Anglomania Really Got Started by Gail MacColl and Carol McD. Wallace. New York: Workman Publishing Company, 1989

CHAPTER 8
FOUNDERS AND
PHILANTHROPISTS

LONDON Thomas Coram died in 1751 and was buried in the chapel of his Foundling Hospital.

In the 1920s the Foundling Hospital was demolished, but the many treasures that had been donated to it were saved and moved to *40 Brunswick Square*. The work with vulnerable children continued with the Thomas Coram Foundation for Children, today known as Coram Family. In 1998 the *Foundling Museum* was established and given the task of preserving and managing the collection of Thomas Coram's hospital. The museum also tells the heartbreaking story of the children who were left in the care of the hospital.

England has a long history of wealthy and powerful men becoming involved in philanthropy and creating institutions that help the needy in society. In the sixteenth and seventeenth centuries schools, hospitals, and almshouses were created by families or economic institutions. Robert Sackville, the Earl of Dorset, created **Sackville College** in **East Grinstead, West Sussex**. The Elizabethan actor Thomas Alleyn established **Dulwich College**, Sir Thomas Sutton started the **Charterhouse School** and **Sir Thomas Smythe** set up a foundation that gave money to the needy for centuries. The Merchant Venturers' companies built almshouses such as those in **Bristol** where retired seamen could live out their later years in security and comfort. Kings built colleges, orphanages, and hospitals around the country.

Americans have continued this tradition of the wealthy contributing to their communities. Whether it be starting schools or orphanages, creating institutions of learning, or donating to the arts, their generosity has enriched many lives. Many Americans see England as the home of their cultural heritage, and over the years they have enjoyed returning to visit or even live permanently in the country from which their ancestors came. Some of these Americans have made significant contributions to the social and artistic fabric of England. In a similar act of generosity, one Englishman made a lasting donation to the people of America and established one of the most important educational and research institutions in the US. 🌿

Thomas Coram (1668–1751): The Foundling Hospital

Born in **Lyme Regis, Dorset**, in 1668, Thomas Coram spent many years working as a sailor and ship maker. He moved to Massachusetts in 1694 and established a shipyard on the River Taunton. As a faithful Anglican, he must have felt an outsider in the strict Puritan culture of the Massachusetts Bay Colony, and he tried to encourage the development of an

Anglican community. In a deed dated 8 December 1703, Coram left in trust with the vestry of King's Chapel, Boston, fifty-nine acres of land that he owned "if ever hereafter the inhabitants of the town of Taunton should be more civilized than they now are, and if they should incline to have a Church of England built amongst them."

In 1705 Thomas Coram returned to England, heavily in debt and perhaps disheartened about his unsuccessful efforts to spread Anglicanism. Back in his homeland he became a successful and wealthy businessman, and was also involved in projects helping the poor. In 1732 he was named a trustee of **James Oglethorpe**'s plan to transport people from debtors' prisons in England to a new colony called Georgia.

Thomas Coram's interest in helping people turned to what was to become his lasting legacy. Horrified by the way poor and unwanted children were treated in England, he obtained a royal charter to establish a "hospital for the maintenance and education of exposed and deserted young children." The **Foundling Hospital** was completed in the mid-1740s and became the world's first incorporated charity. Coram enlisted famous and wealthy patrons to support his orphanage. William Hogarth became a governor of the hospital. He painted a portrait of his friend Thomas Coram and donated paintings to the hospital as did Gainsborough, Reynolds, and others. George Frederick Handel supported the Hospital's charitable work and christened the organ he had presented to the Foundling Hospital Chapel with a special performance of the *Messiah*. In his will Handel donated a copy of the *Messiah* to the hospital and started a musical tradition that has continued to the present day with the Coram family's Handel Concert held each February to celebrate his birthday. 🍃

James Smithson (1765–1829): The Man Behind the Smithsonian Institution

While the institution that was named for James Smithson enjoys worldwide fame, few people know anything about the man who left $508,318 to the people of the United States to establish it. It would surprise many people to discover that the Smithsonian Institution was the gift of the illegitimate son of a British duke. James Macie was born in France in 1765. His mother was Elizabeth Keate Hungerford Macie, a wealthy English widow, and his father was the 1st Duke of Northumberland, whose surname was changed from Smithson to Percy after he married the daughter of the Earl of Northumberland.

The Duke of Northumberland never acknowledged James Macie as his son. After his mother's death, James did

DORSET The *Coram Tower* in *Lyme Regis* was built to commemorate Thomas Coram who was born in the town in 1688.

LONDON *Syon Park* in *Brentford* is the London home of the Duke of Northumberland. James Smithson's portrait hangs in the dining room.

OXFORD James Macie received a Master's degree in 1786 from *Pembroke College* where he was described as the best chemist and mineralogist of his year. He became a very successful chemist, and was an active member of several organizations dedicated to advancing scientific research and using science to benefit society.

eventually take his father's original last name – Smithson. The name change had to have the approval of the king; it was opposed by the family of the duke who were afraid that Macie might claim he was entitled to inherit part of the family estate. This fear was probably not justified, because James and his half-brother inherited a considerable estate from their mother's family. Interestingly, the duke's eldest legitimate son, **Hugh Percy**, was a general in the British forces in North America during the American Revolutionary War and led the British retreat from the **Battle of Lexington and Concord**.

James Smithson died in Genoa, Italy, on 27 June 1829. In his will he left the bulk of his estate to his nephew, but stipulated that if the nephew died without children, the estate would go to "the United States of America, to found at Washington, under the name of the Smithsonian Institution, an Establishment for the increase and diffusion of knowledge..." Smithson did not explain his bequest or his motives in leaving money to the United States. Politicians in the US debated whether or not to accept the Smithson bequest. The fact that the gift was from a British citizen stirred debates among rights advocates, nationalists, federalists, and Anglophobes. Perhaps memories of British attacks during the War of 1812 were still fresh and they were suspicious of the reasons for the bequest. Eventually, in 1836, Congress authorized acceptance of the donation, and the Smithsonian Institution was established in 1846. The Smithsonian collection includes books from James Smithson's personal library.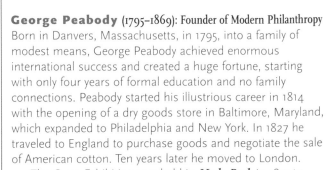

George Peabody (1795–1869): Founder of Modern Philanthropy

Born in Danvers, Massachusetts, in 1795, into a family of modest means, George Peabody achieved enormous international success and created a huge fortune, starting with only four years of formal education and no family connections. Peabody started his illustrious career in 1814 with the opening of a dry goods store in Baltimore, Maryland, which expanded to Philadelphia and New York. In 1827 he traveled to England to purchase goods and negotiate the sale of American cotton. Ten years later he moved to London.

The Great Exhibition was held in **Hyde Park** in 1851 to show off British products to new foreign markets and display manufactured goods from around the world. Invitations were sent to all nations requesting that they send exhibits. Surprisingly, there seemed to be little interest in the exhibition in the United States and Congress refused to approve funds for participation. George Peabody believed in the importance of American involvement and contributed his own money to install the American exhibits. In the end, the American

LONDON George Peabody was one of only three Americans ever to have been honored with the "Freedom of the City of London" (the others being **Dwight D. Eisenhower** and **Theodore Roosevelt**).

A statue of George Peabody can be seen behind the *Royal Exchange*. It was unveiled by the Prince of *Wales* on 23 July 1869.

At the end of his life, George Peabody lived at *80 Eaton Square*. A blue plaque marks the house.

used this as his country base for lavish entertainment.

In 1925 Selfridge leased a large London mansion on the corner of **Berkeley Square – Lansdowne House**, which had been the home of **Lord Shelburne**, British prime minister during the latter part of the American Revolution. The house had been empty for several years after the First World War. Selfridge leased it in 1925 for £5,000 a year and used it for increasingly lavish parties. He became involved with two former Hungarian cabaret singers, known as "The Dolly Sisters." Selfridge began to spend extravagantly and also developed a gambling habit. By 1931 he was almost bankrupt – he owed £150,000 in taxes. In 1940 the Board of Directors at Selfridges voted to remove him as chairman. Gordon Selfridge lived his last years in poverty. He died in a flat in Putney on 8 May 1947 when he was ninety years old. 🌿

Dennis Severs (1948–1999): A Spitalfields Experience

Born in Escondito, California, Dennis Severs moved to London after his high school graduation in 1967 and worked in a variety of jobs. In the 1960s he was running horse-drawn open carriage tours around Hyde Park. When his stable near Gloucester Road was demolished by a developer the business seemed at an end, until Queen Elizabeth II allowed him the use of a royal stable.

In 1979 Dennis Severs bought a Georgian terraced house, built in 1724, at **18 Folgate Street, Spitalfields**. Using his collection of antiques, and his study of decorative arts in period painting and prints, he developed this as a living museum. He began by sleeping in each of the house's ten rooms to judge their atmospheres. Visitors are entertained in re-created rooms with taped sound effects and atmospheric smells. Dennis Severs died in 1999. His house is now owned by the Spitalfields Trust. It is open to the public, and offers a unique "home visit" experience. 🌿

Walter Annenberg (1908–2002): Ambassador and Philanthropist

After inheriting the *Philadelphia Inquirer* and two racing publications from his father, Walter Annenberg went on to build a media empire. He had a long and distinguished career as an editor and publisher, broadcaster, diplomat, and philanthropist. In 1969 Annenberg was named ambassador to the Court of St. James's and served until 1974. Although he was not a career diplomat, he became one of the most popular American ambassadors to Britain, and the only one to be knighted. Walter Annenberg became a major art collector and made very significant donations of

DORSET Gordon Selfridge was buried next to his wife and mother in the graveyard of *St. Mary's Church, Highcliffe*. Sadly, for many years the Selfridge graves in were unattended, but today the Selfridges board of directors contribute towards the maintenance of the graves.

READ *18 Folgate Street: The Tale of a House in Spitalfields* by Dennis Severs. London: Chatto & Windus, 2001

LONDON The newly restored Reading Room at the *British Museum* is the home of the Leonore and Walter Annenberg Center which uses new technology to make information retrieval faster and easier. The Annenberg Foundation also funded the museum's multimedia object database which makes available information on objects from the museum's collections.

The *Annenberg Courtyard* at the *Royal Academy of Art, Piccadilly, London*

LONDON While Walter Annenberg was American ambassador to the Court of St. James's, he funded a complete restoration of *Winfield House*, the American ambassador's residence in Regent's Park.

Annenberg was named Honorary Knight Commander, Order of the British Empire by Queen Elizabeth II and received numerous other foreign honors including Honorary Bencher of the *Middle Temple*; Honorary Old Etonian; and Patron of the Churchill Archives Centre at *Churchill College, Cambridge*. In July 2000, Annenberg was made an Honorary Fellow of the *Royal Academy of Arts* in *London*.

LONDON When Paul Mellon died in 1999, he left $20m to endow new educational programs and preserve endangered sites in the UK. One of the most significant beneficiaries has been Nicholas Hawksmoor's beautiful London church, *St. George's Church*,

art and financial support to museums and institutions in the United States and Great Britain. He established the Annenberg Foundation to advance the public well-being through improved communication. The foundation makes grants in education, culture, the arts, and community and civic life. He also founded the Annenberg School for Communication at the University of Pennsylvania in 1958 and the Annenberg School for Communication at the University of Southern California in 1971. By the time of his death in 2002, Walter Annenberg had given more than $2 billion to schools, museums, the arts, and other civic and community groups. 🌿

Paul Mellon (1907–99): A Galloping Anglophile

Born in Pittsburgh, Pennsylvania, Paul Mellon was the son of Andrew Mellon (1855–1937), a businessman art collector and secretary of the Treasury under three American presidents. At the time Andrew Mellon was the third richest man in America, after John D. Rockefeller and Henry Ford. Paul's mother was Nora McMullen, a young woman from England who married Andrew in 1900. Paul was baptized at **St. George's Chapel, Windsor**, and spent many childhood summers in England. His parents were divorced in 1912.

After graduating from **Yale University** in 1929, Mellon studied at **Clare College, Cambridge**. He stayed in England while his father served as the American ambassador from 1932 to 1933. In 1934 he began his own collection of British arts with the purchase of George Stubbs's painting *Pumpkin with a Stable Boy*. He returned to America and began working at Mellon Bank, but within a few years decided to focus the rest of his life on philanthropy and the causes that he believed in: higher education, the arts and humanities, poetry, religion and psychiatry, and conservation and the environment.

Andrew Mellon was instrumental in the creation of the National Gallery of Art in Washington, D.C. After their father's death, Paul Mellon and his sister oversaw the development of the National Gallery. This was the beginning of a lifetime of significant contribution to art and education around the world. In addition to contributions to the National Gallery from his personal collection, Paul Mellon founded the Yale Center for British Art, refusing to have it named for him. He also was responsible for the creation of the **Paul Mellon Centre for Studies in British Art** in **London**, which supports teaching, scholarship, and publication in the field of British art and architecture.

Paul Mellon had many connections with Britain throughout his life. During World War II he served in the Office of Strategic Services in England and rose to the rank of major. Later he was able to enjoy seeing his horse Mill Reef win the English Derby in 1971. He contributed books from his personal library to the **Bodleian Library** in **Oxford** and donated millions of dollars towards saving buildings in Britain. Paul Mellon's generous works were recognized when he was granted the rank of Honorary Knight Commander of the Order of the British Empire. 🌿

Jean Paul Getty, Sr. (1892–1976): The Richest Man in the World?

The Getty fortune was founded on oil, and was originally created by George Franklin Getty, a lawyer who specialized in insurance and corporate law. His son Jean Paul Getty was born in Minneapolis, Minnesota, in 1892. In 1904 George moved from Minneapolis to Oklahoma and soon built a fortune based on his Minnehoma Oil Company. Within a few years the family moved to Los Angeles. Jean Paul studied at the University of Southern California and the University of California at Berkeley, and then traveled to England to study at **Magdalen College, Oxford**, where he graduated in 1914 with a degree in economics and political science. When Jean Paul Getty was twenty-one, his father loaned him money to invest in oil fields, and within two years he had earned $1m. The Getty Oil Company was soon incorporated, and Getty started on his path to becoming one of the richest men in the world. Interested in arts and antiques, in 1953 he founded the Getty Museum in Santa Monica, California, giving it an enormous endowment that made it one of the world's wealthiest museums. In the early 1950s J. Paul Getty moved to live in England and in 1959 he purchased **Sutton Place**, a sixteenth-century manor house on a 700-acre estate near **Guildford** in Surrey. 🌿

J. Paul Getty II (1932–2003): Playing the Game his own Way

Before graduating from the University of San Francisco, J. Paul Getty left to serve with the US Army in Korea. His relationship with his father Jean Paul wasn't always easy, but Paul Getty did work for the family's oil firm. He took over the company's operations in Italy in the 1960s. His father was said to be the richest man in the world, but in his will he left his son a bequest of just $500. However, the son did receive very generous funds from a family trust and from his grandmother. After his first wife died in Rome of a drug overdose in 1971, Paul Getty stepped down from the Getty Oil Company and moved to England. For many years J. Paul Getty II lived alone in a mansion on the banks of the River Thames in Chelsea. In 1986 he bought **Wormsley Park**, a 2,500-acre estate in Buckinghamshire. Mr. Getty became a

Bloomsbury, which was reopened in 2006 after being completely restored, largely due to Mr. Mellon's generosity.

SURREY The Tudor mansion at *Sutton Place* near *Guildford* was built around 1523 by Sir Richard Weston. It remained the Weston family home from 1523 until 1857. Since then it has been occupied by a succession of wealthy lessees or owners, such as Jean Paul Getty.

LONDON A portrait of Jean Paul Getty hangs in the *National Portrait Gallery*.

BUCKINGHAMSHIRE Introduced to the British national game by Mick Jagger, Getty developed a real love of cricket. He built a cricket ground at *Wormsley Park* and donated £2m towards construction of the Mound Stand at Lord's cricket ground. In 1986 his generosity to British charities was recognized when he was awarded an honorary knighthood. As an American citizen, he was not able to use the title "Sir," but in 1997 after twenty-five years of living in England, Getty was granted British citizenship. He decided to revoke his US citizenship and therefore was able to be called "Sir Paul."

LONDON In 2003 Sir Paul Getty donated £5m for the cleaning and restoration of the west front of *St. Paul's Cathedral*.

KENT The beautiful manor house at *Ightham Mote* is over 650 years old. It is one of the oldest houses to survive in England.

YORKSHIRE One of the largest cathedrals in Europe, *York Minster* is more than 1,000 years old.

OXFORD John Tradescant the Elder traveled widely in Europe and Russia collecting plants for the gardens he created and curiosities for his private collection, which became the basis for the *Ashmolean Museum*.

LONDON The *Museum of Garden History* is located in the church of *St.-Mary-at-Lambeth*. John Tradescant, Elder and Younger, are both buried in a tomb in the churchyard.

generous benefactor to causes that he held dear – the arts, film and cricket! J. Paul Getty II died on 17 April 2003 and was buried in the grounds of his estate. 🍃

Charles Henry Robinson: Restoring a Medieval Treasure

In 1953 **Ightham Mote** was purchased by an American, Charles Henry Robinson, who had seen the house as a young man. The ancient moated house was in a terrible condition. Initially constructed in the 1340s with a great hall, chapel, crypt, and two solars, the house was developed over 300 years until the buildings formed a quadrangle around a courtyard. A moat around the entire building provided defense. When Robinson died in 1985, he donated the property to the National Trust. A stone plaque to his memory is the only visible reminder of his part in preserving this wonderful building, which has recently been totally restored. It is a fascinating house to visit. Anna Seton, a guest in the house, heard the story about workmen who had found the skeleton of a young woman sitting on a stool in a bricked up closet in Ightham Mote. Her novel *Green Darkness* portrays life in the house in the 1400s. 🍃

The Mysterious Mrs. Howes

In the crypt at **York Minster**, the treasury houses many of the treasures given to the minster over the centuries. No gift was probably more unexpected or awe-inspiring than the 32-carat diamond donated by an American – Mrs. Howes. Mrs. Howes was a bare-back horserider and traveled around America with circuses. She and her husband bought land in various states and made a fortune when the railways were being built in the late nineteenth century. The diamond and an offer of a chalice and paten in which to set it was brought unannounced to the minster by a Miss Forepaugh one evening in 1927. She would only say that Mrs. Howes was an American friend who had recently died and she was carrying out her wishes. No one could tell of any personal connection with York or any reason why her amazing gift was made to the minster. 🍃

GARDENS

The Tradescants: Royal Gardeners and Adventurers

John Tradescant the Elder (1570–1638) and his son, **John Tradescant the Younger** (1608–1662), were gardeners to British royalty, collectors of curiosities, travelers, and importers of exotic plants. The elder Tradescant became wealthy and famous. John Tradescant the Elder started his career in the service of **Sir Robert Cecil**, the 1st Earl of Salisbury, and created the beautiful gardens at **Hatfield**

House for Cecil. As an "adventurer," he invested in the Virginia Company's settlement of a new colony to the west of Jamestown in 1617. Tradescant was appointed royal gardener to King Charles I in 1629, and his son succeeded him after his death in 1638. However, the Civil War ended royal patronage and some of the gardens they created for Charles I and Henrietta Maria were destroyed.

John Tradescant the Younger traveled to America in 1638 "to gather up all raritye of flowers, plants, shells, &c." In October 1642, just before the first pitched battle of the English Civil War, he went back to Virginia. He returned to England by January 1645, but sailed to Virginia again in 1653. This time his stay in the New World was longer. During these travels, he collected plants and brought back to England trees such as the magnolia, tulip tree, and garden plants such phlox, asters, and the Virginia creeper. He also brought curiosities, among them a leather cape reputed to have belonged to Powhatan, **Pocahontas**'s father. It is now in the collection of the ***Ashmolean Museum*** in *Oxford*. 🍃

Major Lawrence Johnson
The beautiful gardens at ***Hidcote Bartrim*** in *Gloucestershire* were created by the American Major Lawrence Johnson who began work before World War I and continued until his death in 1958. The gardens are laid out in a series of "outdoor rooms" divided by walls and hedges, and are famous for their herbaceous borders, rare shrubs, and specimen trees. The gardens are now maintained by the National Trust and are open to the public. 🍃

Bishops' Garden, Fulham Palace
Fulham Palace was the former home of the bishops of London. In its prime it was surrounded by a moat, as were many bishops' palaces. In the seventeenth century many of the missionaries sent to America by Bishop Compton had a secondary charge beyond their religious work – they sent back botanical samples that helped the bishop establish a superb collection of American shrubs and trees. The bishop grew many American plants such as the magnolia, in England for the first time. 🍃

Chelsea Physic Garden
The Chelsea Physic Garden was founded in 1673, as the Apothecaries' Garden, with the purpose of training apprentices in identifying plants. In the Garden of World Medicine, a number of plants from North America are on display, along with plants used by the Native American Indians to treat many health problems. Cotton seeds sent

READ *The John Tradescants: Gardeners to the Rose and Lily Queen* by Prudence Leith-Ross. London: Peter Owen Publishers, 1984

Earthly Joys by Phillipa Gregory, published by Harper Collins in 1998, is based on the life of John Tradescant the Elder.

Virgin Earth by Phillipa Gregory, published by Harper Collins in 1999, is a fictionalized account of the adventures of John Tradescant the Younger, including his two trips to Virginia.

GLOUCESTERSHIRE *Hidcote Manor Garden* features rare trees and shrubs, herbaceous borders and unusual plants from across the globe.

Bishop's Garden at *Fulham Palace, London*

Chelsea Physic Garden, London

A bust of *Samuel Pepys* at *Seething Lane Garden, London*

Painshill Garden, Cobham, Surrey

SOMERSET There is a replica of George Washington's Mount Vernon garden at the *American Museum* in *Bath*.

American Indian tepee at the *American Museum, Bath*

from the Chelsea Physic Garden to America started the cotton industry there. The dye used to color the British Army's red coats during the American Revolution came from the red madder plant. It is still grown at the garden. 🍃

Samuel Pepys and Seething Lane Garden

Samuel Pepys wrote one of the most famous diaries in English history. In his long career as a bureaucrat in the Naval Office, he worked closely with Admiral Penn, and Pepys mentions his young son **William Penn** in the diaries. Pepys lived for several years at the Naval Office on **Seething Lane** near the **Tower of London**. Today a quiet garden occupies the site. 🍃

Painshill Garden, Surrey

Contemporary with the famous gardens at Stourhead and Stowe, Painshill is one of Europe's finest eighteenth-century landscape gardens. It was created by the Honorable Charles Hamilton, plantsman, painter, and gifted designer, between 1738 and 1773. Hamilton imported many plants from North America, and a new display that highlights these "American Roots" has been created in Painshill's walled garden. **Thomas Jefferson** and **John Adams** both visited the Painshill garden during the 1770s and Jefferson reported that he especially liked some of the "follies" – the fanciful structures built around the garden. 🍃

The American Museum in Britain at Claverton Manor, Bath

The only museum in Europe devoted to American furniture, decorative arts, and quilts, the main collection of the American Museum at Claverton illustrates the domestic arts in America from the late seventeenth century to the end of the nineteenth century. The rooms illustrate the American cultural tradition from the English Puritans to the Spanish colonists of New Mexico. An exhibition in the museum's section on Native Americans highlights **Pocahontas**'s importance in the connection between England and America.

The museum sits on a hill overlooking the valley of the River Avon and has spacious grounds with sweeping lawns and flower gardens. Throughout the grounds are various outdoor features such as a colonial herb garden, a replica of **George Washington**'s garden at Mount Vernon, an arboretum, a Conestoga wagon and an Indian tepee.

It was at **Claverton Manor** that on 26 July 1897 the twenty-three-year-old Winston Churchill made his first political speech. The house was purchased from private owners by Dallas Pratt and John Judkyn, and the museum opened to the public on 1 July 1961. 🍃

Birkenhead Park, Liverpool

Frederick Law Olmsted, one of the best-known landscape gardeners to work in America, visited Britain in 1850. He was particularly influenced by **Birkenhead Park** in **Liverpool**, the first publicly funded park in Britain. In 1852 Olmsted won a competition for a design to develop New York City's Central Park, and Birkenhead Park is said to have particularly influenced his work in New York. 🍃

Kew Gardens

The twenty-five-year-old Joseph Banks accompanied **Captain Cook** on the voyage of the *Endeavour* which spent three years from 1768 to 1771 exploring New Zealand and Australia. Banks became one of England's most famous botanists. He was president of the Royal Society for forty-two years and was instrumental in the development of Kew Gardens. Today the Royal Botanic Gardens at Kew is a leading center of botanical research, a training ground for professional gardeners, and a popular visitor attraction. Many American trees and plants can be seen in the collection.

King George III suffered from porphyria, and had debilitating periods of illness when he seemed to be mentally unbalanced. In November 1788 he was kept at a royal cottage at Kew Gardens during his illness. 🍃

LONDON A blue plaque commemorates **Joseph Banks**'s home at *32 Soho Square*.

LONDON The Temperate House at *Kew Gardens* holds an extensive collection of temperate American plants, including fuchsias, salvias, and brugmansias.

CHAPTER 9
ACADEMIC CONNECTIONS

As a visitor walks the halls and pathways of English universities, he can listen for the echoes of students from the past. These were often the men who took part in the discovery and exploration of the New World. The ancient schools of England taught men how to think and also provided a perfect place to make connections that would last a lifetime. Many of the early investors and adventurers in the exploration of North America knew each other from their school days. In the Massachusetts Bay Colony of the 1630s many of the leaders had graduated from English universities before immigrating to the New World.

Later students contributed to the culture, politics, and artistic life of early America. The first schools in the English colonies of America were started by emigrants from London, East Anglia, and Oxford. The ties with the home country continued for many years. Among the wealthy colonial families, it was common for the sons to be sent back to England for their education. It is interesting to look at a list of the leaders of the American Revolution and see how many went to school in England.

The links continue to this day. US presidents and Supreme Court justices, scientists, writers, and poets have come to England to study. Scholarships and study programs encourage academic travel both ways across the Atlantic.

Inns of Court

The Inns of Court in London are at the center of Britain's legal system. They were originally inns – residences where students lived while they studied law. But they were more than that. Barristers came to the Inns to teach and conduct business. Wealthy families sent their sons there to be trained and to network – meeting influential and well-educated men. In the fifteenth century there were as many as fourteen Inns; today there are four, which still retain their control over admission to the legal profession.

Middle Temple, London

Middle Temple

For many centuries the Middle Temple has been an important center of legal education. It has also served as a place where men of action could network and make important personal contacts. The ancient Great Hall is decorated with the emblems of many of its former students.

In the sixteenth and seventeenth centuries the Middle Temple served as a social hub where men such as **Sir Francis Drake** and **Walter Raleigh** could meet with the rich and important. Raleigh joined his half-brother **Humphrey Gilbert** at the Middle Temple in 1575. **Richard Hakluyt**, the greatest English geographer of the sixteenth century, may have had his interest in geography sparked by his cousin, a lawyer at the Middle Temple. **Sir Edwin Sandys**, who became treasurer of the Virginia Company, was admitted to the Middle Temple in 1586 to study law. Jamestown leader **Bartholomew Gosnold** studied law at the Middle Temple, along with a friend from his years at Cambridge – **Henry Wriothesley**, the 3rd Earl of Southampton, who later became an important investor in early explorations to America, and was also a patron of William Shakespeare.

Many Americans have studied law at the Middle Temple and other Inns of Court. In the 1770s some of these law students returned to America to have great influence in the development of a new nation. A number of them were members of the Continental Congress that voted to approve the **Declaration of Independence**. A reproduction of the document hangs on the landing outside the American Law Library. Red stars mark the names of members of the Middle Temple who were signatories of the Declaration.

The ***American Law Library***, the finest and most extensive collection of American law books outside the United States, is sited in the Middle Temple grounds. After the Middle Temple was damaged by bombs during the Second World War, the Canadian and American Bar Associations contributed towards its restoration.

AMERICAN COLLEGES AND UNIVERSITIES WITH CONNECTIONS TO ENGLAND

Harvard College

Cambridge, Massachusetts – founded in 1636

John Harvard (1607–38) was baptized on 29 November 1607 at St. Saviour's Church in Southwark (now ***Southwark Cathedral***). He was educated at St. Saviour's Grammar School and then entered ***Emmanuel College, Cambridge***, receiving a BA degree in 1632 and an MA in 1636. When his mother died in 1636, she left him the Queen's Head tavern in Southwark and part of his stepfather's estate. John had

American connections with the Inns of Court in LONDON:

Gray's Inn
William Cecil
Francis Walsingham
Thomas Wriothesley
Thomas Gresham
Nathaniel Bacon
Winston Churchill
Franklin Roosevelt

Lincoln's Inn
Edward-Maria Wingfield
William Penn
President Eisenhower
Dean Acheson

Inner Temple
William Paca of Maryland – signed the Declaration of Independence

Signatories of the American Declaration of Independence who studied at the *Middle Temple*:
Edward Rutledge
Thomas Heyward
Thomas Lynch
Arthur Middleton
Thomas M. Kean

Other members of the *Middle Temple* with connections to American history:
Robert Devereux
William Penn
Richard Grenville
John Culpeper
George Percy
Sir William Berkeley
John Winthrop
Arthur Lee
W.H. Taft – former president and chief justice

American ambassadors to the Court of St. James's are granted honorary membership of the Middle Temple.

CHARTERHOUSE SCHOOL

The London Charterhouse was set up as a Carthusian monastery in 1371 but was closed in 1535 at the Dissolution of the Monasteries. It served as the home of the Duke of Norfolk and his son Thomas Howard, Earl of Suffolk. Queen Elizabeth I stayed at Charterhouse during preparations for her coronation and James I held court here in 1603 when he first came to London. In 1611 the site was purchased by Thomas Sutton who endowed a foundation that created an almshouse and school at the former monastery. The school moved to **Godalming, Surrey**, in 1872 but the ancient buildings in **London** still serve as home for eighty male pensioners.

Old Carthusians with American connections: ***John Wesley, Roger Williams, Sir Edwin Sandys***

DULWICH COLLEGE

Edward Alleyn was the best-known actor in Elizabethan England. Alleyn acted with the Admiral's Men at the Rose Theatre and, with his partner Philip Henlowe, built the Fortune Theatre. Alleyn became very rich and bought the Manor of Dulwich. He thought of building a hospital but instead built what he called "The College of God's Gift." King James I granted a letter patent in 1619.

Old Alleynians with American connections: ***Raymond Chandler*** – author

ETON COLLEGE

Founded in 1440 by King Henry VI, Eton College in **Berkshire** has educated an amazing roll-call of the best and the brightest for almost 600 years. During America's colonial period, wealthy families often sent their sons to England to be educated. Old Etonians connected with American history include:

James Oglethorpe – founder of the State of Georgia
Hugh Percy – British commander who led the retreat from the Battle of Lexington and Concord
Arthur Lee – of the Lee family of Virginia, became "America's first spy"
Thomas Lynch, Jr. – of South Carolina, signed the Declaration of Independence
Thomas Nelson – of Virginia, signed the Declaration of Independence
Charles Cornwallis – British general who lost the last battle of the American Revolution
Many members of the Astor family, including
John Jacob Astor of Hever, 1st Baron (1886–1971): proprietor, The Times
Waldorf Astor, 2nd Viscount (1879–1952): proprietor, The Observer 1911–45
Walter Annenberg, US ambassador – honorary Old Etonian

WESTMINSTER SCHOOL

In 1179 the Benedictine monks of **Westminster Abbey** in **London** began taking in students who paid fees. In the 1540s when King Henry VIII dissolved the monasteries, the school became a royal college. In 1560 Queen Elizabeth I granted the school an endowment to support "Queens Scholars." This is accepted as the date for the formal founding of the school. Old Westminsters with American connections:

Richard Hakluyt – foremost English geographer of the sixteenth and early seventeenth centuries
Charles Chauncy – second president of Harvard College 1654–72
Arthur Middleton – signed the Declaration of Independence
Charles Wesley – Methodist preacher and writer of over 6,000 hymns
Thomas Gage – commander in chief of British forces in North America in 1775
General Burgoyne – British general who surrendered to the Americans at the Battle of Saratoga
Charles Cotesworth Pinckney – member of the American Constitutional Convention
Thomas Pinckney – US minister to Great Britain in 1792
Francis Lewis of New York – signed the Declaration of Independence

already inherited part of his father's estate, so he was a wealthy young man. Deciding to immigrate to America in 1637, he sold four houses in Southwark, but kept the tavern. He spent a considerable amount on buying books, and when he sailed to Massachusetts with his wife in March or April 1637, he had an extensive library. Unfortunately he died on 14 September 1638 after a short illness. He left half of his estate and all of his library to the proposed new college in Newtown (renamed Cambridge). The school had been started by **John Bridge**, originally of Rayne Road, Braintree, who immigrated to Massachusetts with the **Braintree Company**. In his honor, the school was named Harvard College.

Other Connections with Harvard College

Benjamin Woodbridge (1622–84) was born in Wiltshire in 1622 and studied at Magdalen Hall (now *Magdalen College*), *Oxford University*. In 1639 he left England and continued his education at the newly established Harvard College. In 1642 he became the first person to receive a degree in Harvard's first graduation ceremony. By 1647 King James had been captured and the Puritans were in charge of the government in England, so Benjamin returned home and was appointed minister at *St. Nicolas's Church, Newbury*. The following year he returned to Magdalen and was awarded his MA degree. After the restoration of King Charles II, the Act of Uniformity brought the episcopal rule back into the Church of England. Nearly 2,000 Puritan preachers were forced to leave the established church. Benjamin Woodbridge was dismissed from his position at St. Nicolas's, but continued to preach privately. It is reported that he even served as a chaplain to King Charles.

George Downing (1623–84) was the second graduate of Harvard College's first class of 1642. He immigrated to New England in 1638 with his parents Lucy Winthrop (sister of **John Winthrop**) and Emmanuel Downing. He returned to England after the Restoration and zealously hunted down the regicides Barkstead, Corbet, and Okey who were hiding in Holland. Pepys said "All the world takes note of him for a most ungrateful villain." *Downing Street* in *London* was named after him because he had an estate on the site.

John Allin (died 1683/4), vicar of *St. Mary's Church, Rye, East Sussex*, graduated in the second class of students to complete their studies at Harvard College – in 1643. Each year on the second Sunday in Advent, Rye still remembers its links with Rye, New York, in prayers during morning service and in singing "The Battle Hymn of the Republic."

Henry Dunster (1609–59), born in Bury, Lancashire, graduated from *Magdalene College, Cambridge*, having

LONDON The old chapel of St. John in *Southwark Cathedral* has been rededicated as the Harvard Chapel. The East Window was a gift from Joseph H. Choate, the American ambassador from 1899 to 1905.

A plaque at *103 Borough High Street, Southwark*, states: "The Queen's Head Inn owned by the family of John Harvard, founder of Harvard University, formerly stood here."

WARWICKSHIRE John Harvard's mother was Katherine Rogers of *Stratford-upon-Avon*, daughter of Thomas Rogers, a butcher, maltster, and grazier. The Rogers lived in a substantial timber-framed house in Stratford. The house is now owned by Harvard University.

CAMBRIDGE In the New Chapel of *Emmanuel College*, designed by Sir Christopher Wren, there is a stained-glass window depicting John Harvard. The record of his entrance to the college, for a fee of one shilling, is still kept at the college.

BERKSHIRE Benjamin Woodbridge died in 1684 at Englefield Green and was buried at the *Parish Church of St. Nicolas* in *Newbury*. There is no marker for his burial place but he is listed on the church website as "dispossessed under Act of Uniformity" in 1662.

King William III at
Kensington Palace, London

WALES The Yale Chapel at *St. Tysilio's Church* in *Bryn Eglwys, Clwyd,* is built over the entrance to the family vault. It is one of the many gifts and memorials given to the church by the Yale family. *St. Giles Churchyard* in *Wrexham, North Wales,* is the site of Elihu Yale's tomb.

Yale Center for British Art
1080 Chapel Street, New Haven
Connecticut 06520
www.yale.edu/ycba/

The Yale Center for British Art houses the most comprehensive collection of English paintings, prints, drawings, rare books, and sculpture outside Great Britain. Given to Yale University by **Paul Mellon,** Class of 1929.

studied oriental languages. He immigrated to Boston, Massachusetts, in 1640 and on 27 August 27 1640 became the first president of Harvard College.

Nathaniel Eaton (1610–74), the sixth son of Rev. Richard Eaton (1565–1616), was christened 16 October 1610 at the church of **St. Giles Cripplegate, London**. He was educated at the University of Cambridge, **Trinity College**, where he was a good friend of **John Harvard**. Nathaniel's older brother, **Theophilius Eaton,** immigrated to New England in 1637 and helped found the colony at New Haven. Nathaniel immigrated to Massachusetts and became the first schoolmaster of the newly established Harvard College, but he was much more than just a school teacher – he erected Harvard's first building, established the colony's first printing press, created its first semi-public library and planted an apple orchard. After disagreeing with the ruling Puritans of the Massachusetts Bay Colony, Nathaniel moved to Virginia. He then returned to England and in 1661 he was appointed the vicar of Bishop's Castle, Shropshire. He became rector of Bideford, Devon, in 1669, but then went to Italy and studied at Padua University. Nathaniel Eaton died in 1674 in **King's Bench Prison** in **London**, where he had been jailed for a debt of £100.

THE COLLEGE OF WILLIAM AND MARY
Williamsburg, Virginia – founded in 1693

In 1693 King William III and Queen Mary II granted a charter which established in Virginia "a certain Place of universal Study, a perpetual College of Divinity, Philosophy, Languages, and other good Arts and Sciences." The Sir Christopher Wren Building at the College of William and Mary in Virginia is the oldest college building in the United States, and architecturally links the college with the monarchs who established it. Although the brick building does have similarities to William and Mary's residence at **Kensington Palace**, it was probably not designed by Wren himself.

YALE COLLEGE
New Haven, Connecticut – founded in 1701

Yale College was named to honor **Elihu Yale** (*see Chapter 2 for details of his life*), who made a donation worth £1,162 and also gave a book collection to the Collegiate School of Connecticut in Saybrook in 1718. The school subsequently moved to New Haven and was renamed Yale College.

The **Berkeley family** of Gloucestershire was very important in the early settlement of Virginia. Sir William Berkeley was named governor of Virginia in 1641. From the Irish branch of the Berkeley family, George Berkeley (1685–1753) was Dean of

Derry and Bishop of Cloyne. He donated books and land to Yale College. In 1930 Berkeley College at Yale University was named for him. Berkeley California was named for him in 1866 when one of the founders of Berkeley College recalled a poem by George Berkeley with the lines, "westward the course of empire takes its way."

PRINCETON COLLEGE
Princeton, New Jersey – founded in 1746

The town of Princeton, New Jersey, was named "Prince-Town" in honor of King William III, who as Prince of Orange was invited to come from Holland to become King of England when his wife Mary acceded to the English throne. Princeton University takes its color orange from William. One of its main halls – Nassau Hall – also takes its name from William III, who was of the "illustrious house of Nassau." Princeton University began life as the College of New Jersey in Newark. It moved to Princeton in 1756.

HAMPDEN SYDNEY COLLEGE
Hampden-Sydney, Virginia – founded in 1776

The tenth oldest college in the US, Hampden-Sydney College was named after **John Hampden** (1594–1643), a Parliamentary leader during the English Civil War, and **Algernon Sidney** (1622–83), whose book *Discourses Concerning Government* was very important to the political philosophy of early American leaders, especially **Thomas Jefferson**. Hampden and Sidney were widely held to be hero-martyrs by American colonial patriots. One of the college houses is named Penshurst after Algernon's birthplace in Kent and "Hampden House", built in 1858, is now the Alumni Headquarters and guest house.

SWARTHMORE COLLEGE
Swarthmore, Pennsylvania –founded in 1864

An excellent small private college of liberal arts and engineering, Swarthmore College was founded in 1864 by the Religious Society of Friends (Quakers). The name was taken from **Swarthmoor Hall** in **Cumbria**, the home of early Quaker supporters Judge Fell and his wife Margaret.

AMERICAN STUDY PROGRAMS IN ENGLAND
Stanford University in England

Harlaxton Manor in *Lincolnshire* was home to the Stanford University "Stanford in England" program from 1965 to 1968. When Stanford moved their program to *Cliveden* in *Berkshire*, the University of Evansville (Indiana) purchased Harlaxton Manor as the center for their British overseas study program. During college vacations, the beautiful

KENT *Penshurst Place*, Algernon Sidney's family home, is one of the best-preserved examples of fourteenth-century domestic architecture in England.

BUCKINGHAMSHIRE John Hampden's family home was *Hampden House* in *Great Hampden*. His mother was Elizabeth Cromwell Hampden, aunt of the Lord Protector Oliver Cromwell. Hampden's cousin was the regicide **Edward Whalley**. John Hampden died in 1643 after being wounded in a Civil War battle and was buried at the Church of *St. Mary Magdalene* in *Great Hampden*.

CUMBRIA *Swarthmoor Hall* in *Ulverston* was built in 1586 by George Fell. **George Fox** first came to Swarthmoor Hall in June 1652 as he traveled the countryside preaching his religious vision and building a large group of followers who called themselves "Children of the Light" or "Friends of the Truth."

LINCOLNSHIRE *Harlaxton Manor* was built in 1837 by Gregory Gregory.

BERKSHIRE From 1969 to 1983, Stanford University's UK study program was based at *Cliveden*. Stanford presently has its British Overseas Study Program at *Oxford*.

OXFORDSHIRE *Wroxton Abbey* is the English home of Fairleigh Dickinson University.

building is used for residential schools, conferences, wedding receptions, and a variety of other functions. The Stanford in England program is now based in Oxford. Information can be found at http://osp.stanford.edu/oxford.

Fairleigh Dickinson University

Wroxton Abbey near *Banbury, Oxfordshire*, became a private home after King Henry VIII dissolved the monasteries in 1536. In 1668 the estate came to the North family through marriage. The most famous resident was **Frederick, Lord North** who was British prime minister from 1770 to 1782, during the American Revolution. In 1932 ownership of the abbey was returned to Trinity College, Oxford. In 1963 Wroxton Abbey was sold to Fairleigh Dickinson College (of Madison, New Jersey) for its English literature program. The fifty-six-acre abbey gardens, which were created in 1727 and further developed from 1731 to 1751, are open to the public all year. The gardens include a serpentine lake, a cascade, and a number of follies.

For other Study in England programs
www.studyinbritain.com
www.studyabroaddirectory.com/England.cfm

UNIVERSITY OF CAMBRIDGE

The first scholars arrived in Cambridge in 1209, taking refuge from hostile townsmen in Oxford. In 1294 the Bishop of Ely founded the first college, Peterhouse. At this early period, the university was closely associated with the local churches and religious orders, such as the Benedictines, Dominicans and Franciscans. There was no separation between Church and State since education was generally seen as preparation for careers in the church as clergymen or in service for the monarch as diplomats, judges or officers of the royal household.

Three signatories of the American Declaration of Independence studied at Cambridge University during the 1770s – **Thomas Lynch** of South Carolina, **Thomas Nelson** of Virginia and **Arthur Middleton** of South Carolina.

Clare College
Paul Mellon, American philanthropist

James Watson who, with Francis Crick, discovered DNA. They received the Nobel Prize for their discoveries in 1962. In 1968 Clare College made Watson an honorary member.

Henry Louis Gates, Jr., American educator and writer

Christ's College
John Smyth, a leader of the Pilgrims in Lincolnshire; took his congregation to Holland.

Ezekiel Rogers, sailed to Massachusetts in 1638 and became a Puritan leader.

Ralph Izard, American colonial in London, signed the Thatched House Tavern petition.

Churchill College
founded in 1960 as a memorial to **Winston Churchill**

Corpus Christi College
Robert "Trouble-Church" Browne, an early Separatist leader who led his congregation to Holland

Darwin College
Dian Fossey, American researcher, earned her PhD at Darwin College. She studied gorillas in Africa and was murdered in her cabin in 1985. She wrote *Gorillas in the Mist.*

Downing College
Sir George Downing, second graduate of Harvard College. Downing Street in London was the site of his home.

Emmanuel College
Emmanuel College was founded in 1584 by *Sir Walter Mildmay*, Queen Elizabeth I's Chancellor of the Exchequer. The goal of the college was to train preaching ministers for the Church. It quickly became known as a "nursery" for Puritans. Of the first 100 college graduates who settled in the English colonies in America, one third had studied at Emmanuel College.

John Cotton, preacher from Boston, Lincolnshire, and Massachusetts Bay Colony leader

Thomas Hooker, founder of Connecticut

John Harvard, benefactor of Harvard College in Massachusetts. The New Chapel at Emmanuel College, designed by Christopher Wren, has a stained-glass window depicting John Harvard.

Herchel Smith, an Emmanuel graduate who made a fortune from patents involving the development of the contraceptive pill, established a program offering scholarships to its members for study at Harvard University.

Gonville and Caius College
Thomas Lynch, Jr., signer of the Declaration of Independence

Jesus College
Rev. John Eliot, "Pastor to the Indians" in Massachusetts

Alistair Cooke, journalist and broadcaster

King's College

King's College has had formal ties with **Berkeley College at Yale University** since 1938.

American **James Watson** worked here on the structure of DNA with Crick in the 1950s.

Magdalene College

Henry Dunster studied oriental languages at Magdelene College. He immigrated to Boston, Massachusetts, and on 27 August 1640 became the first president of Harvard College.

Newnham College

The American poet **Sylvia Plath** won a Fulbright Scholarship for study at Cambridge.

Pembroke College

Roger Williams, founder of the Colony of Rhode Island, graduated in 1627.

Peterhouse College

Rev. Godfrey Washington, fellow of Peterhouse College, and minister at Little St. Mary's, Cambridge, in the early eighteenth century, was the great-uncle of George Washington.

William Brewster, a leader of the *Mayflower* Pilgrims

Queens' College

Thomas Hooker, the founder of Connecticut, started as a student at Queens' College. When his Dixie Fellowship was confirmed, he switched to Emmanuel College.

Edmund Bohun, chief justice of South Carolina (died 1699)

Alexander Crummell was possibly the first black graduate of Cambridge. A leading figure in the movement for black rights, he was active in the US, Britain, and Liberia. He helped found the American Negro Academy.

Michael Foale, American astronaut with dual UK/US citizenship, studied at Queens' College, receiving a PhD in laboratory astrophysics in 1982.

St. Catherine's College

Nathaniel Bacon received a Master's degree from the college. He was a cousin of Frances Culpeper Berkeley, wife of Sir William Berkeley, governor of the Virginia Colony. He led "Bacon's Rebellion" in Virginia in 1676.

St. John's College

Henry Wriothesley, 3rd Earl of Southampton, backed the early exploration of America.

Sidney Sussex College

John Wheelwright, banished from Massachusetts, became the founder of New Hampshire.

Trinity College

John Cotton, Puritan preacher and leader of the Massachusetts Bay Colony

John Winthrop, leader of the Winthrop Fleet to the Massachusetts Bay Colony in 1630

Vladimir Nabokov, novelist, poet, scholar, translator, and lepidopterist. The Nabokov family became US citizens in 1945.

Nicholas James MacDonald Patrick graduated from Trinity College in 1986. He moved to America to work as an engineer for GE. He became a US citizen in 1994 and was selected for astronaut training in 1998.

Trinity Hall

Arthur Middleton, signatory of the Declaration of Independence

Cavendish Lab

J. Robert Oppenheimer, American theoretical physicist, worked for a while at Ernest Rutherford's Cavendish Lab at Cambridge.

SCHOLARSHIPS FOR STUDYING IN THE UK

The Marshall Scholarship Program
www.marshallscholarship.org

The Fulbright Program
http://exchanges.state.gov/education/fulbright

Rhodes Scholarships for study at Oxford University
www.rhodesscholar.org

Gates Scholarships for study at Cambridge University
www.gates.scholarships.cam.ac.uk

OTHER ACADEMIC CONNECTIONS

The English-Speaking Union
Dartmouth House, 37 Charles Street, London W1J 5ED
Tel: 020 7529 1550
www.esu.org
Scholarship programs for British and American students

CHAPTER 10
SCIENCE AND INDUSTRY

LONDON Members of the Royal Society who were involved in the early years of English colonization of America include **George Berkeley, George Monck, Anthony Ashley Cooper, Edward Hyde,** and **William Penn.** Those honored by election to the Royal Society have included more than 100 Americans; among them are **Benjamin Franklin, John Winthrop,** Alexander Dalles Bache (Benjamin Franklin's great-grandson), Cotton Mather (judge at the Salem witch trials), **Joseph Priestley,** William Byrd, and J.R. Oppenheimer. In the recent past, women have become eligible for election to membership. In 1989 Barbara McClintock became a member of the Royal Society; she was the first woman in her category to win an unshared Nobel Prize. Interestingly, **Elihu Yale,** was was born in Boston, Massachusetts in 1649, listed as British American, while **Benjamin Franklin,** who was also born in Boston, in 1706, is listed as a British member of society.

William Small lived in America for six years, 1758–64, teaching mathematics at the **College of William and Mary** in Virginia. One of his students was **Thomas Jefferson,** who wrote that "Dr. Small was ... to me as a father. To his

SCIENTISTS AND INVENTORS

Often the technological inventions on which we depend in our daily lives just seem to be there – light bulbs, the telephone, the Underground. The stories of how they came to be can reveal surprises. Who would expect a cowboy to have invented airplanes? Scientific and economic interests have long linked England and the United States, perhaps best exemplified by Benjamin Franklin, a colonial printer with an inquisitive mind.

The architecture that we pass every day can also reveal stories of cultural connections. Two country houses in Sussex have direct links with the US Capitol Building and the White House. Statues that at first glance seem merely decorative can tell stories of unexpected adventure or achievement.

The Royal Society

In 1660, after a lecture by Christopher Wren at Gresham College, twelve men decided to found "a College for the Promoting of Physico-Mathematical Experimentally Learning." They met weekly to conduct experiments and engage in discussions on what we would now call scientific topics. King Charles II granted the group a royal charter. From its present location on **Carlton House Terrace**, the Royal Society continues to be an independent scientific academy and funding body that assists scientists in their studies and research. 🍃

The Lunar Society

The Lunar Society counted among its members some of the most influential scientists, inventors, and natural philosophers of the late eighteenth century. From 1765 to 1813, the group met once a month in Birmingham when there was a full moon, which provided light for their travel home. They discussed their ideas, experiments, and inventions; their interests ranged from manufacturing, mining, and chemistry, to transportation, education, and medicine. They can really be considered the founding fathers of the Industrial Revolution. Initial members of the Lunar Society included:

- Matthew Boulton, one of the most inventive manufacturers of the time
- Erasmus Darwin, poet, philosopher, naturalist, and grandfather of Charles Darwin
- Thomas Day, educational reformer
- Richard Lovell Edgeworth, inventor interested in electricity and agricultural machinery
- Samuel Galton, Quaker gunmaker
- Robert Augustus Johnson, chemist
- James Keir, glass and soap manufacturer
- **Joseph Priestley**, Nonconformist preacher who discovered oxygen and the India rubber eraser (among other things)
- William Murdock, who invented gas lighting
- **William Small**, mathematics professor with interests in engineering, chemistry, and metallurgy
- Jonathan Stokes, botanist
- James Watt, inventor of the condensing and rotary engines
- Josiah Wedgwood, inventive potter, canal promoter, and Charles Darwin's other grandfather
- John Whitehurst, geologist who made clocks and scientific instruments
- William Withering, medical doctor with interests in botany, metallurgy, and chemistry.

Joseph Priestley (1733–1804)

The oldest of six children of Jonas Priestley, a weaver, and Mary Swift, a farmer's daughter, Joseph Priestley was born in Yorkshire in 1733. After his mother's death, he was sent to live with his aunt where he was exposed to discussions of theological questions and liberal political ideas. Joseph had an inquiring mind and a great ability to learn languages; he mastered Greek, Latin, French, German, Italian, Syrian, and Arabic as well as the basics of algebra and geometry before he left home to study at the Daventry Academy in Northamptonshire, one of the Dissenting academies established to provide higher education for Nonconformists who were not allowed to attend the great universities.

For several years Priestley taught chemistry in Nonconformist academies, while also preaching his unorthodox theology in small Dissenting congregations. While he was at Warrington Academy, John Forster, a

enlightened and affectionate guidance of my studies while at college, I am indebted for everything."

WEST MIDLANDS The Lunar Society met at Matthew Boulton's house. *Soho House, Birmingham*, is now a museum. Boulton's desk with globe are among the exhibits on view.

READ *The Lunar Men* by Jenny Uglow. London: Faber, 2002.

YORKSHIRE Joseph Priestley was born in *Birstall* in 1733. A family grave marker lies near the front door of *St. Peter's Church*.

NORFOLK In 1755 Priestley accepted his first preaching position with a poor Presbyterian congregation at *Needham Market* where he remained for three years.

A large statue of Joseph Priestley stands in the Market Place at *Needham Market*.

CHESHIRE In 1758 Priestley was invited to move to a Dissenting congregation in Nantwich where he opened a school for students.

In 1761 Priestley joined the teaching staff at *Warrington Academy*. A statue of Joseph Priestley stands in the foyer of the sixth-form *Priestley College* in *Warrington*.

WEST MIDLANDS Priestley's years at the Lower Meeting House (1780-91) are remembered with a memorial in the *Unitarian New Meeting House* in *Birmingham*. A statue of Joseph Priestley has been erected in the city's *Chamberlain Square*.

YORKSHIRE In 1767 Joseph Priestley accepted an invitation to preach at the *Mill Hill Chapel* in *Leeds*. During his six years there, he did basic studies of gasses that led to important later discoveries.

A statue of Joseph Priestley stands in *Leeds City Square* overlooking the chapel.

WILTSHIRE Priestley is credited with discovering oxygen on 1 August 1774 in Lord Shelburne's laboratory at *Bowood House* in *Calne*. In 2000 the American Chemical Society joined the Royal Society of Chemistry in designating Priestley's laboratory at Bowood House an International Historic Chemical Landmark.

teacher of modern languages and natural history, was invited to join **Captain Cook**'s second world voyage. Priestley had hoped to join the expedition but his Nonconformist religious beliefs were unacceptable to the clergymen on the Board of Longitude, who approved the specialists who went on the voyage. This was a great disappointment for Priestley.

Beginning in 1765 Priestley spent a month each summer in London meeting the leading men of science such as **Benjamin Franklin**, who became a life-long friend and supporter. Priestley came to endorse many of the American's political views and Franklin encouraged Priestley to write and publish *The History and Present State of Electricity*, which led to his election to the Royal Society in 1766.

Priestley became one of the best known scientists in England, but his religious beliefs continued to cause problems. He became a full-fledged Unitarian and questioned many traditional Christian teachings. Unitarianism grew among many of the scientists and thinkers of England and America. **Thomas Jefferson**, **John Adams**, and **John Quincy Adams** are among prominent Americans who had religious beliefs that followed the Unitarian tradition.

In 1773 Priestley accepted an offer from **William Petty**, Lord Shelburne, to become librarian and literary companion to the earl and tutor to his son. While he worked at **Bowood House**, Priestley expressed support for the American Revolution, while Earl Shelburne opposed the colonies' independence, so in 1780 Joseph Priestley resigned his position and returned to the ministry, moving to Birmingham where he lived for eleven years, preaching on Sundays and continuing his scientific work. He became a member of the **Lunar Society**.

In Birmingham Priestley's religious and political views met with hostility. When he voiced support for the French Revolution, he faced suspicions that his real purpose was to overthrow the Church of England and the king. The situation literally exploded in 1791. After a dinner commemorating the French overthrow of their monarch, a drunken mob gathered to show their opposition. The crowd attacked and burned the meeting house where Priestley preached. They moved on to his house. Priestley and his wife escaped with only the clothes they were wearing. The mob burned the house, destroying his manuscripts and scientific equipment. More than 100 houses and several meeting houses were destroyed in the three days and nights of destruction.

Priestley moved to London to become minister at the old **Gravel Pit Chapel** in **Hackney**. He had to live with the constant threat of possible arrest on political charges, but he wrote that "On the whole I spent my life more happily at Hackney than I had ever done before." Priestley's sons immigrated to America, and in 1794 he and his wife decided to follow them. Priestley had many friends in America. Benjamin Franklin had died in 1790, but Priestley knew **George Washington**, **John Adams**, and **Thomas Jefferson**. He joined his sons in Northumberland, Pennsylvania, a small community 150 miles west of Philadelphia. Priestley was one of the first Unitarian ministers in America, and often held services in his home. Continuing his scientific experiments, in 1799 he discovered carbon monoxide. He spent many winters in Philadelphia and continued his friendships with many of the American "Founding Fathers." Thomas Jefferson consulted him on planning classes for students at the University of Virginia. Joseph Priestley died after a brief illness in 1804. The "Father of Modern Chemistry" is buried in the Quaker cemetery in Northumberland, Pennsylvania. 🍃

Benjamin Franklin (1706–90)

One of the most famous scientists in the world during his years in London, 1757–62 and 1764–75, Benjamin Franklin's fame preceded him to London. He was elected to membership of the **Royal Society** in 1756 on the basis of his many inventions and study of electricity. During the years he spent in England, Franklin conducted many important experiments such as the "smoothing" of water with oil, and understanding the Gulf stream. He invented an "economical" clock with three wheels to ensure a perpetual twenty-four-hour cycle, a popular fireplace draught, and the glass harmonica, for which Mozart and Bach composed. He also sent seeds to America for planting, introducing new trees and vegetation to the colonies. (*See the long list of places associated with Franklin in Chapter 3.*)🍃

Samuel Morse (1791–1872)

From 1812 to 1815 the American inventor and artist Samuel Morse lived in London at **141 Cleveland Street** while studying at the **Royal Academy of Arts**. After returning to the US, he became the first president of the National Academy of Design, New York. He was also a professor at New York University from 1832. In 1837 he presented his idea for a magnetic telegraph to Congress seeking financial support. He also invented what became known as Morse code for use with the telegraph – sending messages long distances over wires. The first outdoor trial was held on a line from Baltimore, Maryland, to Washington, DC. The first official telegraph message was, "What hath God wrought." 🍃

LONDON A blue plaque marks the site of the old *Gravel Pit Chapel* at *Ram Place* in *Hackney* where Richard Price and Joseph Priestley were ministers.

A blue plaque marks the house at 113 *Lower Clapton Road, Hackney*, where Priestley lived from 1792 to 1794, before immigrating to America.

LONDON In 1775, when **Benjamin Franklin** decided that the political situation meant he had to return to America, he spent his last day in England with **Joseph Priestley**.

In 1764 Benjamin Franklin was consulted about the best way to protect the steeple at *St. Bride's Church*. He suggested installing a lightening rod with a sharp-pointed end. However, **King George III** said he thought a rounded end would be better. When Franklin's sharp ended rod was used, comments were made that "good, honest, blunt King George" had been outdone by a "sharp-witted colonist." The pointed lightening rod did protect St. Bride's steeple, along with many other buildings around the world.

KENT The *Unitarian Meeting House* in *Tenterden* has a painting of Benjamin Franklin attending service here in 1774 when he and **Joseph Priestley** were staying in Woodchurch Road. In May 1976 one of Benjamin Franklin's descendants unveiled a plaque at the meeting house to mark the bicentenary of American independence.

CUMBRIA In 1772 Franklin went to *Derwentwater* to carry out his oil-on-water experiment.

LONDON On 12 January 1882 Thomas Edison opened the world's first commercial incandescent lighting and power station at *57 Holborn Viaduct*. It supplied electricity to the Old Bailey and the General Post Office.

LONDON The Graham Bell Room at *Brown's Hotel* is named in memory of the first telephone call made in England.

Brown's Hotel has another link with American science and industry. In 1890 the International Niagara Commission met at the hotel. The commission, with representatives from the UK, France, Canada, Switzerland, and the United States met to investigate and evaluate proposals concerning the best way to use the power of the Niagara Falls. Brown's Hotel commemorates the commission in the name of the "Niagara Room."

Thomas Edison (1847–1931)

One of the world's most prolific inventors and businessmen, Thomas Edison's early business trips to England were focused on the development of the telegraph and telephone. In 1873 he demonstrated his new telegraph to the British Post Office. In August 1879 the Edison Telephone Company of London, Ltd. was incorporated and the company's first exchange opened at **11 Queen Victoria Street, London**, with ten subscribers. By the end of the following February the company had two additional exchanges serving 172 subscribers. It was one of a number of companies which, over several decades, combined and merged to finally become British Telecommunications.

Edison was also involved in generating electricity for his light bulbs. The Edison Central Station was opened at the Crystal Palace Exhibition, London, in 1882 producing electricity for 1,200 lights. Edison's first foreign kinetoscope parlor opened in London on 17 October 1894. 🍃

Alexander Graham Bell (1847–1922)

An outstanding scientist and inventor, Alexander Graham Bell was the grandson of a Scottish actor, Alexander Bell, who developed his training for the stage into a career in teaching speech and elocution publishing books titled *The Practical Elocutionist* and *Stammering and other Impediments of Speech*. The family's interest in communication problems became more personal when Alexander's son Melville married a woman who was profoundly deaf. Their son, Alexander Graham Bell, developed his own way of "talking" with his mother. He spoke in deep tones very close to her forehead, and she was able to "hear" him through vibrations from his voice.

Alexander Graham Bell was educated at Edinburgh High School and Edinburgh University. In 1867 he moved to London to study at University College. Two of his brothers died of tuberculosis, and Alexander himself also suffered from TB. Hoping that a new climate would help him recover from it, the family moved to Canada in 1870, and his health did improve. In 1871 Alexander Graham Bell moved to the US and began giving lessons in "visible speech" at the Boston School for Deaf Mutes. In 1872 he became a professor of voice physiology at Boston University and continued to study vibration, sound, electricity, and physics.

Bell hoped to develop an instrument in which sound could be transmitted over wires. On 10 March 1876, while working with Thomas Watson, an electrical craftsman, an accidental spill of battery acid on their experimental wire led to the first transmission of voice sound over a wire. Bell shouted the now famous words, "Mr. Watson, come here. I want you," and Watson heard them over the wire. In 1876 Bell patented his "electric speaking telephone." On 11 July 1877 Alexander Graham Bell married Mabel Hubbard, a young woman who was profoundly deaf. They left for a honeymoon in Europe. While in London, Bell made the first telephone call in England from a room at **Brown's Hotel, Albemarle Street, London**. 🍃

Samuel Cody (1857–1913)

Some surprising characters can turn out to be quite inventive – and Samuel Cody was quite a character! He claimed that he was born in 1851 in Birdville, Texas, and that his father was Samuel Franklin Cody, who, he said, was a Confederate officer during the American Civil War. In fact, he was born in 1857 in Iowa, and his father was Samuel Franklin Cowdery, a Confederate private. His son went to work early and found adventure in Texas as a cowboy, buffalo hunter, and gold prospector. He changed his name to Samuel Franklin Cody, perhaps trying to claim a connection to the famous cowboy, William F. Cody, "**Buffalo Bill**," who had a triumphant tour of England in 1887 with his **Wild West Show**.

Samuel Cody came to England in 1889. He set up his own cowboy stunt show, touring the country with his show "The Klondyke Nugget." He was an excellent mechanic and often experimented with new things to add to his shows. His "man-lifting kite" was more reliable than balloons in strong winds. The British Army became interested in this new technology and hired Cody as chief kite instructor to the British Army Balloon Factory at Farnborough (1902–9).

At this time, many inventors were trying to build a flying machine. In 1903 the Wright Brothers' plane made the first sustained powered flight. By 1908 Samuel Cody was working on a powered flying machine and on 16 October 1908, near **Farnborough** in **Hampshire**, he flew his British Army Aeroplane No. 1 for a quarter mile in what is recognized as the first powered sustained flight in Britain. Over the next five years, he developed several new planes. His biplane, known as Cody's Flying Cathedral, was then the world's largest plane. Flying his own planes, he won the British Empire Michelin Cup contest in 1910, and the British and international divisions of the military airplane trials in 1913.

In August 1913, during a flight, Cody's plane broke up and crashed. Cody was killed. After a funeral attended by more than 50,000 people, he was buried in the military cemetery in **Woking**. Remembered as the "Father of British Aviation," Cody's work led to the formation of the Royal Flying Corps and the Royal Naval Air Service. 🍃

HAMPSHIRE The collection at the *Museum of Army Flying* in *Middle Wallop* includes a replica of Samuel Cody's man-lifting kite.

The Cody Gallery at the *Aldershot Military Museum* focuses on the achievements of Samuel F. Cody in developing airplanes in England. He built his British Army Aeroplane No.1 in his Farnborough workshop. The gallery includes a reconstruction of his Farnborough workshop, and his original flying helmet.

In *Farnborough*, as a memorial to Cody, there is an aluminum replica of the beech tree that Cody used to tether his planes to.

LONDON A model of Cody's "war kite" hangs from the ceiling in the first room of the "Aviation" section at the *Science Museum*. Cody's bi-plane of 1912, which won the British Army's competition that year, was donated to the museum in 1913 and has been on display ever since. There is also a model of his British Army Aeroplane No. 1 of 1908.

LONDON In the "Flight" displays at the *Science Museum*, Hiram Maxim's experimental test rig of 1894, his petrol engine of 1908, and his experimental compound steam engine can all be seen. In the "Lighting" section, there is a display of one of his light bulbs with its unusual "M"-shaped filament.

LONDON A blue plaque marks the building at *57d Hatton Garden* where Hiram Maxim designed and manufactured his machine gun.

ESSEX A wood carving at *St. Mary the Virgin* in *Dedham* commemorates Neil Armstrong's landing on the moon on 20 July 1969.

LONDON The Metropolitan and District Lines of the *London Underground* network at the Gloucester Road station.

Hiram Stephens Maxim (1840–1916)

Born in Sangersville, Maine, in 1840, Hiram Maxim was one of many American inventors and entrepreneurs who came to Britain and Europe during a period of technological development in the 1870s and 1880s. Maxim possessed great mechanical skills and creativity. In 1878 he founded the United States Lighting Company, which became **Thomas Edison**'s main rival in the field of incandescent lighting. Maxim continued to develop new products including a curling iron, devices to prevent the rolling of ships, riveting machines, bombs for aircraft, an aerial torpedo gun, and a coffee substitute. In 1881 Maxim moved to London at a time when Thomas Edison was also developing business interests in Britain.

In 1883, working at a workshop in **Hatton Garden, London**, Maxim developed a design for a single-barrel gun that could fire between 300 and 500 rounds per minute. The British Army adopted the Maxim machine gun in 1889 and soon military powers around the world wanted this new deadly weapon. Hiram Maxim became extremely wealthy and famous from his invention of the machine gun. He became a naturalized British subject and was knighted in 1901. 🍃

Charles Tyson Yerkes (1837–1905)

Another American character who had an influence on life in London, Charles Yerkes was born in 1837 into a Welsh family that had moved to **William Penn**'s Quaker colony in 1682. He proved to be a very shrewd businessman, but his career had its ups and downs. He made and lost fortunes, lived an extravagant lifestyle, and was jailed for bankruptcy. Yerkes was important in the development of the Chicago city railway system. When his company was unable to meet construction deadlines in 1899, he was accused of handing out more than a million dollars in bribes and was politically and socially ostracized.

Yerkes sold his holdings in Chicago and in 1900 moved to London. He invested in the building and electrification of the **London Underground** railway system, which had been operating since 1863. He headed the syndicate that built the Metropolitan and District Lines and was involved in developing and extending the Bakerloo, Northern, and Piccadilly Lines. Within five years the London Underground system had been transformed; unfortunately, his business vision was not founded on sound financial practice – when he died in 1905 the transport system was on the verge of bankruptcy! 🍃

Isaac Merritt Singer (1811–75)

Isaac Singer was an American inventor, actor, and entrepreneur. He was also a larger-than-life character! Born in Pittstown, New York, in 1811, he was a man who definitely lived life at a very fast pace. His early career focused on acting, and he often used his business ventures to fund his career on the stage. As an entrepreneur, he tried to develop markets for many early machines, finally making an enormous fortune with the sewing machine. Many people believe that Singer invented the sewing machine – so closely is his name is linked worldwide with the device. In fact, his main contributions were to suggest improvements to the way early machines worked, and then to get in at the beginning of marketing mass-produced sewing machines for home use. Through I.M. Singer & Company and then the Singer Manufacturing Company, he became one of the richest men in the world.

Singer's personal life must have been a non-stop soap opera. After a nasty legal problem in New York when his wife discovered he had a second family, Isaac was arrested for domestic violence. Released from prison on bond, he fled to London and then to France to live with yet another woman, Isabella Eugénie Boyer (said to be the model for the Statue of Liberty!) In 1871 the Franco-Prussian War made life in France less appealing, so the family moved to England, first living in London. Singer bought an estate in **Paignton** on the **Devon** coast and spent four years remodeling the house in a grandiose way. He died in 1875, just before the work was completed. Isaac Merritt Singer was buried in the Torquay cemetery. He left twenty-two living children, and a number of wives, ex-wives, and mistresses.

Two of Singer's daughters married into European royal families. His third son, Paris Eugene Singer, took a great interest in Oldway Mansion. In 1904 he began substantial alterations – inspired by the Palace of Versailles! Especially impressive are the grand staircase of marble with balusters of bronze and marble pillars with gilding, and the Gallery, a miniature reproduction of the "Hall of Mirrors" at Versailles. A copy of a huge painting, *The Crowning of Josephine by Napoleon* by Lebrun hangs above the stairs. The orginial, painted for this house, was sold by Torbay Borough Council and now hangs in the Palace of Versailles. The grounds were laid out by a French designer and many of the features remain today.

Paris must have inherited his father's love of beautiful women – he had a love affair with the famous dancer, Isadora Duncan. In 1917 Paris moved to the United States and became an American citizen.

DEVON Paignton Council purchased *Oldways Mansion, Paignton,* in 1946. Today the building is used mainly as council offices and for civil wedding ceremonies. There are also offices for the BBC local radio station. The house and grounds have been used in several film and TV productions – once standing in for Buckingham Palace! The mansion and grounds can be visited by the public free of charge.

The Latrobe family were French Protestants who settled in Ireland at the end of the seventeenth century after the French king revoked the Treaty of Nantes and Protestants were forced to leave the country.

LONDON The great British architect Sir John Soane influenced the young Benjamin Latrobe. Drawings and models of Soane's work can be seen at his former residence which is now the *Sir John Soane's Museum.*

Hammerwood Park, East Grinstead, East Sussex

EAST SUSSEX The half-round entrance portico at Latrobe's *Ashdown House, Forest Row,* may have been a precursor of the Oval Office at the White House in Washington.

During World War I, Paris Singer funded the use of the mansion as the American Women's War Hospital. Trains with wounded soldiers would arrive at the Paignton Station from which the men would be carried by stretcher to the house. It must have seemed a bit surreal. The Singer family sold Oldway Mansion in 1918. In 1926 the estate became the Torbay Country Club. During World War II it was used by the RAF. 🍃

ARCHITECTS
Benjamin Henry Latrobe (1764–1820)
After his early education at the Moravian school at *Fulneck, West Yorkshire,* where his father was a teacher, Benjamin Latrobe went to university in Germany and traveled widely in Germany, France, Italy, and England. One place in Italy had a lasting influence on him – Paestum, near Naples, where he saw ancient Greek temples built in the Doric style that he later used in his own work.

Latrobe returned to live in England and, by 1787, he was working in the office of John Smeaton, one of the most respected engineers in England. As an apprentice to S.P. Cockerell he was exposed to some of the greatest architects of the era, including George Dance the Younger and Sir John Soane. After Latrobe married, he opened his own architectural office, working primarily on alterations to existing buildings. As his reputation grew, he was commissioned to design two houses in East Sussex – *Ashdown House* in *Forest Row* and *Hammerwood Park* near *East Grinstead*. These houses are early examples of the Greek Revival style in England. Both houses have elements that featured in his later, more famous work in America.

Times were difficult for a young architect in Britain. His wife had died and the British economy was declining so there were fewer architectural projects to work on. Latrobe was near bankruptcy. He left England and arrived in Norfolk, Virginia, in May 1796. Setting up an office in Richmond, Virginia, he became the first fully trained engineer and architect to practice and teach in America. By 1798 he was working on some of the first important public buildings of the new nation, including the US Capitol Building and the White House in Washington, D.C. He was hired to build the waterworks for the city of New Orleans. His son went to New Orleans to supervise the construction but he died of yellow fever in 1817. In 1818 Latrobe sailed to New Orleans to complete the project; he also contracted yellow fever and died in New Orleans in September 1820. His legacy can be seen in the public architecture of the US. Benjamin Latrobe was largely responsible for the classical look of the nation's capital city. 🍃

Frank Lloyd Wright (1867-1959)

One of the most famous architects America has ever produced, Frank Lloyd Wright had family connections with Britain. His mother's family, the Lloyd Jones, were Welsh. He used the Welsh world "Taliesin" (which means "shining brow") for his house in Green Spring, Wisconsin, and also for his home and architectural center in Scottsdale, Arizona. Wright was influenced by the work of nineteenth-century British designers and theorists such as John Ruskin, Owen Jones, and William Morris, and his designs show the influence of the British Arts and Crafts Movement. Frank Lloyd Wright received many honors from British institutions including the Royal Institute of British Architects (RIBA) and from the University of Wales. 🍃

LONDON The office that Frank Lloyd Wright designed for Mr. Kaufmann is on display at the *Victoria and Albert Museum* along with drawings and other small items designed by Wright.

Eero Saarinen (1910-61)

The present Embassy of the United States, which occupies the whole west side of **Grosvenor Square**, was designed by Eero Saarinen and completed in 1960. The modern design of the building has not found universal praise – some people refer to it as a concrete egg carton. Born in Finland, Saarinen's family immigrated to the US when he was thirteen and Eero became an American citizen. He graduated from the Yale School of Architecture, and created many modern structures, including the Gateway Arch in St. Louis, Dulles Airport outside Washington, D.C., the TWA Terminal at JFK Airport and the Yale Hockey Rink. 🍃

The *US Embassy, London,* by Eero Saarinen

Robert Venturi (1925-)

After working with **Eero Saarinen** and Louis I. Kahn, the American-born architect Robert Venturi set up his own architectural firm with his British-born wife, Denise Scott Brown and their third partner, John Rauch. In London Venturi's postmodern **Sainsbury Wing** of the **National Gallery** combines sleek modern stone and glass with a witty reference to the classical details of the classical National Gallery. If you look closely, you will see the window treatment of the original building fading away across the Sainsbury wing. 🍃

César Pelli (1926-)

The Argentinean-born César Pelli immigrated to America with his family in 1952. He became a naturalized US citizen in 1964. After studying architecture at the University of Tucuman in Argentina, and the University of Illinois, he worked at the firm of **Eero Saarinen** from 1954 to 1964. He founded his own firm in 1977 in New Haven, Connecticut. Cesar Pelli and Associates have been instrumental in the

The *Sainsbury Wing* of the *National Gallery, London,* by Robert Venturi

One Canada Square, London,
by César Pelli

Bush House,
Aldwych, London

development of London's new financial center at Canary Wharf. He designed **One Canada Square**, the pyramid-topped building that was completed in 1991. At fifty stories, it was the first skyscraper in England. Cesar Pelli and Associates also designed the **Citigroup Building, Docklands Station** at **Canary Wharf**, the **Lehman Brothers Building, East** and **West Winter Gardens**, and **30** and **40 Bank Street Buildings** at **Heron Quay**. 🍃

Bush House, Aldwych
Bush House is the home of BBC's Overseas Service. It was designed by American architects Helmle and Corbett, and built from 1925 to 1935. Over the portico with its giant Corinthian columns stand two statues in classical drapery. The figure on the right represents America and holds a shield decorated with an American eagle. Across the base where they stand is carved the motto "Friendship Between English Speaking Peoples." 🍃

ASTRONAUTS
Neil Armstrong (1930–)
The American astronaut Neil Armstrong is remembered in **York Minster**, where one of the new bosses on the ceiling of the south transept depicts the first astronaut to step on the moon, holding an American flag. The "Space Exploration" boss also shows an American flag. American astronaut Alan Shepherd is a descendant of Richard Warren and his wife Elizabeth, who sailed on the *Mayflower*. 🍃

Michael Foale (1957–)
After receiving a PhD in laboratory astrophysics in 1982, at **Queens' College, Cambridge**, Michael Foale joined the mission operations division at NASA. An astronaut with dual UK/US citizenship, he participated in several space shuttle missions and spent four months on the Russian space station Mir. 🍃

Nicholas James MacDonald Patrick (1964–)
Born in Yorkshire in 1964, Nicholas Patrick graduated from **Trinity College, Cambridge**, in 1986. He learned to fly as a member of the Royal Air Force's Cambridge University squadron. Patrick moved to the US to work as an engineer for GE and then earned his PhD at MIT. He became a US citizen in 1994 and was selected for astronaut training in 1998. His first space shuttle flight was the 2006 *Discovery* STS-116 mission. 🍃

CHAPTER 11
CREATIVE ARTISTS

America was starting to produce its own excellent artists in the eighteenth century. The American War for Independence presented problems for creative people along with everyone else. Would they remain loyal to Britain? Colonials were British citizens, after all. Or would they join the protestors and support the effort for independence? For the American artists who had trained in England, it was tempting to stay in the country where there was a highly developed artistic tradition and a large group of wealthy patrons. Some of these American artists did return home, but others stayed and achieved great success and fame in England.

American artists continued to travel back to England for training, exposure to the work of a larger group of artists, and sometimes to escape the social or intellectual restraints of home. Painters, sculptors, writers, and poets – many found a sense of freedom when they left home. 🍃

PAINTERS
Benjamin West (1738–1820)
One of the first American artists to win a wide reputation in Europe, Benjamin West eventually became one of the most respected and influential artists in Britain. Several young American painters, including John Singleton Copley and Charles Willson Peale, came to study with him in London, and through them West had a great influence on the development of art in the United States.

Benjamin West was born in 1738 of Quaker parents in Springfield (now Swarthmore) in the Pennsylvania Colony. In his youth, he was encouraged to draw. When he was sixteen, after his Quaker community approved art training for him, West studied in Philadelphia and New York City. Next he went to Italy for three years of study. In 1763 he traveled to England where he lived for the rest of his life.

Known in London as "the American Raphael," West became a friend of Sir Joshua Reynolds, England's leading painter. **King George III** commissioned him to do several

LONDON In 1765 Benjamin West and Elizabeth Shewell of Philadelphia were married at the church of *St. Martin in the Fields.*

Five paintings by West are on view at *Spencer House,* loaned by Her Majesty the Queen. One is a version of *The Death of General Wolfe.*

The central ceiling paintings in the lobby of the *Royal Academy of Arts, Piccadilly,* are by West. A large portrait in the Slaughter Room shows West seated in his chair of office as the second president of the Academy.

Tate Britain has fourteen paintings by West in its collection.

West was also a sculptor. His work can be seen at the *Old Royal Naval College* in *Greenwich.* He created the pediment carving of the King William Court colonnade (the SW building) as a tribute to Lord Nelson. His large painting of *The Preservation of St. Paul after Shipwreck at Malta* hangs above the altar of the *Chapel of St. Peter and St. Paul.* West's sculptures can also be seen in the vestibule.

West died on 11 March 1820. He was buried in the crypt of *St. Paul's Cathedral.*

EAST SUSSEX West's portrait of Elizabeth Gideon hangs in the drawing room of the Gage family home at *Firle Place*.

LONDON John Singleton Copley and his family lived at *28 Leicester Square* from 1776 to 1783. The family lived at *25 St. George's Street, Hanover Square*, from 1783 until his death in 1815.

Copley and his son are buried at *Highgate Cemetery (East)* in *Highgate*.

Copley's famous painting *The Death of the Earl of Chatham* can be seen at the *National Portrait Gallery*. It portrays the dramatic aftermath of the Duke of Richmond's speech in 1778 calling for a withdrawal of British troops from America.

The collection at *Tate Britain* has seven works by Copley including *The Death of Major Pierson*.

LONDON The *National Portrait Gallery* has a number of **Gilbert Stuart's** works including portraits of **George Washington, Isaac Barre, Joseph Priestley, Benjamin West,** and **John Singleton Copley**.

LONDON The portraits that **Gilbert Stuart** painted for **Hugh Percy**, 2nd Duke of Northumberland, hang in the print room at *Syon Park, Brentford*.

paintings, and in 1772 the king appointed West to be his historical painter. Later West became a charter member of the **Royal Academy of Arts** and succeeded Reynolds as its second president in 1792. 🍃

John Singleton Copley (1738–1815)

Born in Boston, Massachusetts, John Singleton Copley's stepfather was a London-trained engraver who introduced John to English portrait prints. In 1765 Copley sent his *Boy with a Squirrel* (Henry Pelham) to London to be exhibited at the Society of Artists. The painting earned praise from Sir Joshua Reynolds and **Benjamin West** and won Copley election to the prestigious society.

Copley knew and painted many of the men who became leaders in the Massachusetts colony. His portrait of the silversmith Paul Revere became a symbol of the direct, strong American character. Copley was patronized by both Tories and Loyalists in Boston. One of his most famous portraits was commissioned by **General Gage**, commander in chief of the British forces in North America. Copley also painted a famous portrait of Gage's wife, **Margaret Kemble**, dressed in an exotic turban and Turkish caftan.

As the political tensions grew in America, Copley found it harder to live in Massachusetts and remain neutral. In 1770 he wrote to Benjamin West in London, "I am desireous of avoideing every imputation of party spir[it], Political contests being neither pleasing to an artist or advantageous to the Art itself..." Encouraged by the British artistic elite, Copley sailed for England in June 1774. He became one of the most successful artists of the period, painting historical canvases and portraits of British aristocrats and royalty. 🍃

Gilbert Stuart (1755–1828)

The son of a Scottish immigrant businessman who established the first snuff mill in the colonies, Gilbert Stuart was born in Rhode Island in 1755. His artistic talent became evident when he was quite young, and in 1775 he was sent to London to study painting. He was apprenticed to **Benjamin West**, and also studied with Sir Joshua Reynolds. His fame as a painter grew substantially when, in 1782, he exhibited his *Portrait of William Grant* (also known as *The Skater*) at the **Royal Academy of Arts**. He returned to America in 1793 with the specific intention of painting President Washington's portrait. This became his best-known work.

Hugh Percy (later the 2nd Duke of Northumberland), commander of the British forces in Boston, Massachusetts during the early part of the American Revolution, commissioned three paintings by Gilbert Stuart. These portraits, which still hang at **Syon Park**, are one of the duke himself, one of his family and finally a portrait of his friend, **Joseph Brandt**, an important Mohawk Indian leader who allied himself with the British.

Mather Brown (1761–1831)

Born in Boston, Massachusetts, Mather Brown was a descendant of the Puritan judge Cotton Mather and **John Cotton**, the famous Puritan preacher who immigrated from Boston, Lincolnshire, in 1633. Mather Brown showed early promise as an artist and took lessons from the young **Gilbert Stuart**. When he was twenty he arrived in London to begin his training in the studio of another son of Massachusetts, **Benjamin West**, and in 1782 he entered the school of the *Royal Academy of Arts*. Two years later he painted two religious paintings for the chancel of the church of *St. Mary-le-Strand* in **London**. Mather Brown spent most of his career painting portraits of prominent British military leaders and wealthy aristocrats, as well as Americans in London, and later in life he returned to painting large-scale religious and historical paintings. Unfortunately, his artistic talent never brought him financial success and he died in poverty in 1831.

James Abbott McNeill Whistler (1834–1903)

Although he was born in Lowell, Massachusetts, much of Whistler's childhood was spent in distant places. His father, George Washington Whistler, a graduate of the US Military Academy at West Point, was an engineer and was employed in the building of the St. Petersburg–Moscow railroad. James spent five years of his early life in St. Petersburg, Russia, and received his first art lessons in the Imperial Academy of Fine Arts. When he was fifteen, his father died and the family returned to the US. Whistler entered West Point but dropped out in his third year. In 1855 he left the US for Europe and never returned.

In 1855 Whistler arrived in Paris, and three years later moved to London where he lived until 1892. Whistler's painting style was not widely appreciated in his early years. Also, he had a flamboyant personality and didn't always make an effort to get along with people, even his patrons. A famous episode took place in 1876 involving a room that Whistler was commissioned to decorate for one of his wealthy patrons, Frederick Leyland. Whistler unleashed his creative talents and completely redid the room, creating one of the most striking "Aesthetic" interiors ever. Unfortunately, when Mr. Leyland returned to find his room transformed, he was furious. The "Peacock Room" caused a permanent break between Whistler and one of his most important patrons.

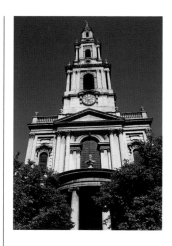

LONDON Mather Brown's paintings are on both sides of the altar at *St. Mary-le-Strand*.

LONDON *Arrangement in Grey and Black No. 1: The Artist's Mother* (1871) was painted while James Whistler lived at *96 Cheyne Walk* in Chelsea.

LONDON A statue of Whistler stands on *Chelsea Embankment* near *Battersea Bridge*, close to where he painted his *Nocturnes*.

The famous "Peacock Room" at *49 Princes Gate* is now in the Freer Gallery in Washington, D.C.

LONDON Seven portraits by Whistler are in the collection at the *National Portrait Gallery* and eleven Whistlers are in the collection at *Tate Britain*.

Whistler is buried at *St. Nicholas's Churchyard, Chiswick*.

LONDON John Singer Sargent lived and worked at *31 Tite Street* in *Chelsea* for twenty-four years.

The *National Portrait Gallery, Trafalgar Square*, has a large collection of forty-six of Sargent's portraits and drawings, as well as a portrait of the artist by Boldini. Sargent's portrait of fellow American **Henry James** was commissioned in 1913 for his seventieth birthday by a group of 269 subscribers, organized by **Edith Wharton**. In the end, Sargent waived his fee for the portrait.

Tate Britain has two Sargent paintings in its collections.

LONDON In the OBE Chapel in the crypt of *St. Paul's Cathedral* there is a memorial to John Singer Sargent. A large metal plaque tells that his sisters placed the memorial here.

SURREY John Singer Sargent is buried at *Brookwood Cemetery* in *Woking*.

MANCHESTER The *John Rylands Library* has a full, first edition of John Audubon's famous book *Birds of North America*.

In 1877 Whistler began to paint a series of pictures based on River Thames views at night. Critics were outraged by the new style of painting. John Ruskin, after seeing *Nocturne in Black and Gold: The Falling Rocket* criticized Whistler in print: "I have seen and heard much of Cockney impudence before now; but never expected to hear a coxcomb ask two hundred guineas for flinging a pot of paint in the public's face." Whistler sued Ruskin for libel and won the subsequent trial. Unfortunately the judge showed his leanings by giving Whistler an award of only a farthing in damages (the lowest possible monetary award). The legal costs of the case almost bankrupted Whistler even though he had won it. Meanwhile Whistler's reputation soared in other quarters. In 1891 *Arrangement in Grey and Black No. 1: The Artist's Mother* was acquired by the French state, and the Glasgow Corporation paid a thousand guineas for the *Portrait of Thomas Carlyle*. 🍃

John Singer Sargent (1856–1925)

Born in 1856 in Florence to expatriate American parents, John Singer Sargent received his first formal art instruction in Rome in 1868. At the 1884 Paris Salon, his portrait of the twenty-three-year-old American Virginie Gautreau scandalized the Paris establishment. The picture, which became known as *Madame X*, ruined Sargent's hopes of establishing himself as a portrait painter in Paris.

In 1886 John Singer Sargent moved to London, and in a few years became the most admired and sought-after portrait painter in Britain and the United States. By the turn of the century Sargent was recognized as the most acclaimed international society portraitist of the Edwardian era, and his clientele included many of the most affluent, aristocratic, and fashionable people of the time. Sargent felt his talent was limited by painting portraits and took every opportunity to paint a wide range of subjects. Although he was an expatriate who lived in London, Sargent also worked in America and created important mural decorations for the Boston Public Library (1890–1919), the Museum of Fine Arts, Boston and Harvard University's Widener Library. 🍃

David Hockney (born 1937)

One of the world's most influential contemporary artists, David Hockey was born and brought up near **Saltaire, Shipley, West Yorkshire**. He moved to the US in 1963 and gravitated to the sun and beach-life of California. Many of his paintings reflect the blue skies and water of California. At Saltaire (World Heritage Site – a nineteenth-century model village built by Sir Titus Salt), the internationally renowned **Salt Mill Gallery** features many of Hockney's works. 🍃

A SCULPTOR
Jacob Epstein (1880-1959)

Born in New York City to Polish parents, Jacob Epstein studied art at the Art Students League of New York, while also working in a bronze foundry. He moved to Paris in 1902 and studied with Auguste Rodin, and then moved to London in 1905. He later became a British citizen. His sculptural works, often on public buildings or in public places, were some of the earliest modern sculptures in England, and at times shocked the prim Edwardians. Often the sculptures were attacked with paint or broken and mutilated by irate mobs. Epstein was knighted in 1954. He died in 1959 and is buried at *Putney Vale Cemetery* in *London*. 🍃

LONDON Jacob Epstein lived and worked at *18 Hyde Park Gate* in *Kensington*.

WORKS BY EPSTEIN IN LONDON

Night and Day (1928–9) at ***55 Broadway***, St. James's (St. James's Park Underground station)

Madonna and Child (1950) at ***Cavendish Square***, on an arch leading to the Theology Faculty of the University of London

Pieta –War Memorial (1956) at ***Trades Union Congress House, 28 Great Russell Street***

Rima (1924), a memorial in ***Hyde Park*** to the author W.H. Hudson, with a relief sculpture that depicts a character from Hudson's novel *Green Mansions*.

At the ***National Portrait Gallery*** Epstein is the sitter in twenty-four portraits, and the artist of thirteen portraits.

Ages of Man (1907–8) Epstein's first major public piece on a building at ***429 Strand*** (now ***Zimbabwe House***), which was built for the British Medical Association, featured eighteen figures based on the work of Walt Whitman. The public was very hostile to the work, which was considered to be indecent, and the statues are now very mutilated.

Epstein memorial at ***Roper's Garden*** on ***Chelsea Embankment*** by ***Chelsea Old Church***.

Rush of Green (Pan) (1959), a group sculpture at the ***Edinburgh Gate*** entrance to ***Hyde Park***

Tate Britain has twenty-four Epsteins in its general collection.

WORKS BY EPSTEIN ELSEWHERE IN BRITAIN

Lazarus (1947–8) – ***New College Chapel, Oxford***
Christ in Majesty (1954–5) – ***Llandaff Cathedral, Cardiff, Wales***
St Michael and the Devil (1956–8) – ***Coventry Cathedral, Coventry, West Midlands***

LONDON *Rush of Green (Pan)* is a group sculpture at the *Edinburgh Gate* entrance to *Hyde Park*.

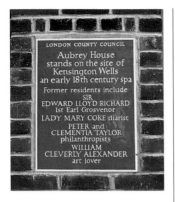

LONDON Peter and Clementia Taylor were philanthropists who lived at *Aubrey House, Aubrey Road*, in *Kensington*, in the mid-nineteenth century. They supported the anti-slavery movement, among other causes.

SURREY The idealistic group at *Ham Common* became the "British and Foreign Society for the Promotion of Humanity and the Abstinence of Animal Food," a forerunner of the Vegetarian Society. It was disbanded in 1848. "Alcott House" was subsequently used as a cholera orphanage for girls, later known as the National Orphan Home. The building was replaced in 1862, and it became a private residence, *South Lodge*. Recently it has been converted into luxury flats.

LONDON *Fleet Street* was the home of journalism when Bill Bryson worked there.

BERKSHIRE Bill Bryson tells about working at the Royal Holloway Sanatorium in *Virginia Water* in *Notes from a Small Island*. The hospital and grounds have been redeveloped into luxury housing.

WRITERS, POETS, AND JOURNALISTS
Louisa May Alcott (1832–88)
Three years before the book that made her famous, *Little Women*, was published in 1868, Louisa May Alcott came to Europe traveling as the companion of a young invalid. She spent the first ten days of June 1865 at **Aubrey House** in **Kensington**, visiting Mr. Peter Alfred Taylor, who had befriended **Frederick Douglass** in 1845 when the escaped American slave and writer visited England. Mr. Taylor took Louisa to the **Houses of Parliament** where she listened to John Stuart Mill and Benjamin Disraeli speak on the Second Reform Bill. On 10 June 1865, Louisa May Alcott rented a "pleasant little room" in Mrs. Travers's lodging house at **6 Westbourne Grove Terrace, Bayswater**.

Louisa's father Bronson Alcott had come to England in 1842 to share his educational ideas with a group at **Ham Common, Richmond**, in **Surrey**. The experimental socialistic group renamed their house "Alcott House" in his honor. Two members of the English group, Charles Lane and Henry C. Wright, traveled back to Massachusetts with Alcott and were involved with "Fruitlands," his utopian socialist experiment in farm living and nature meditation at Harvard, Massachusetts, which did not survive for long. The community at Ham Common, Richmond, was an experiment in alternative lifestyle linking educational reform with radical new ideas about gender relations, work, clothing and diet. It is likely that the term "vegetarian" was first used here. 🌿

W.H. Auden (1907–73)
Entering **Christ Church, Oxford**, in 1925, Wystan Hugh Auden first studied science but changed to English, graduating in 1928 with a third-class degree. He taught biology at several prep schools during the next seven years, but also began writing poetry and became one of the most highly regarded poets and critics of the twentieth century. He was born in England, but immigrated to the US in 1939 and became a US citizen in 1946. Auden started returning to England, and from 1956 to 1961 was professor of poetry at Oxford. 🌿

Bill Bryson (born 1951)
Born and raised in Iowa, Bill Bryson dropped out of college and decided to backpack around Europe for four months. He first traveled to England in 1973 and returned a few years later when he found a job working in a psychiatric hospital. Bryson returned to the US to complete his college degree and then moved to England where he started his career as a journalist and travel writer. Bryson became a well-loved and widely selling British author before his books were even

noticed "at home." In 1995 Bryson moved his family back to the United States where they lived in New Hampshire for a few years. While there he wrote a couple of books about America, including *A Walk in the Woods*. The family returned to England in 2003. 🍃

Raymond Chandler (1888–1959)

The author who created the classic American private eye, Raymond Chandler was born in Chicago, but was educated at **Dulwich College, London**. When his parents divorced, he moved to England with his Anglo-Irish mother. He became a British citizen in 1907 in order to be eligible for a civil service job. Chandler worked briefly as an assistant stores manager at the **Admiralty**. From 1908–1912 he worked as a journalist at the *Daily Express* on **Fleet Street** in London and at the *Western Gazette* in **Bristol** before returning to America. During World War I he fought with the Canadian Army and was briefly transferred to the Royal Air Force. In 1932 Raymond Chandler turned to writing fiction, creating the hard-boiled and cynical detective with a well-hidden soft heart, Philip Marlowe. 🍃

LONDON Raymond Chandler attended *Dulwich College* from 1900 to 1905.

The *Old Admiralty Building* on *Whitehall* was the site of the government department in charge of the navy until 1964, when it was combined with other offices to become the Ministry of Defence.

James Fenimore Cooper (1789–1851)

The American author of *The Last of the Mohicans* and many other novels, James Fenimore Cooper spent three months in England in 1828, chiefly conducting business with his British publisher. For most of that time he lived in **London** at **33 St. James's Place**. This is the way he described it in *Gleanings in Europe: England*:

> "We finally took a small house in St. James's Place, a narrow inlet that communicates with the street of the same name, and which is quite near the palace and the parks. ... The people of the house cooked for us, went to market, and attended to the rooms, while our own man and maid did the personal service. I paid a shilling extra for each fire, and as we kept three, it came to another guinea weekly." 🍃

LONDON 33 *St. James's Place* is now a modern apartment building, but you can see the character the street must have had in James Fenimore Cooper's time by the five-story Georgian townhouses across the street.

Hilda Doolittle (1886–1961)

A poet, novelist, and memoirist, Hilda Doolittle was born in Bethlehem, Pennsylvania. After her family moved to Philadelphia she met **Ezra Pound**, a student at the University of Pennsylvania. They were briefly engaged, but her family did not approve. Pound moved to London in 1908. In 1911 Hilda moved to London and lived at **6 Kensington Church Walk**, just across the small paved yard from Ezra Pound. After she married Richard Aldington in 1913 at the Kensington Register

In **LONDON**, Hilda Doolittle lived at
> *6 Kensington Church Walk*
> *5 Holland Place Chambers,*
> *Kensington*
> *44 Mecklenburgh Square,*
> *Bloomsbury*
> *16 Bullingham Mansions, Pitt Street,*
> *Kensington*

LONDON A blue plaque at *24 Russell Square* commemorates the office where **T.S. Eliot** first worked at Faber & Faber.

There is a memorial plaque at *St. Stephen's Church, Gloucester Road,* where Eliot was a churchwarden.

Eliot appears in the mosaic by Boris Anrep on the stairway inside the front entrance of the *National Gallery* on *Trafalgar Square*. His portrait, in the "Modern Virtues" on the upper landing, shows Eliot reclining and studying a paper which reads $E=mc^2$.

A blue plaque at *3 Kensington Court Gardens* marks the flat where Eliot lived and died. In the poem "Mungojerrie and Rumpelteazer" in *Old Possum's Book of Practical Cats*, on which the musical *Cats* was based, Eliot mentions many of the streets near his home in *Kensington Court Gardens* – *Victoria Grove, Cornwall Gardens, Launceston Place,* and *Kensington Square*.

A memorial to Eliot was unveiled in 1967 in *Poets' Corner, Westminster Abbey*.

SOMERSET At his request, Eliot's ashes were interred in the *Church of St. Michael and All Angels* in *East Coker*, from where his ancestors immigrated to America in the seventeenth century.

Office, they lived in a flat at **5 *Holland Place Chambers***, across the hall from Ezra Pound and his wife Dorothy Shakespear. Hilda was part of the circle of poets who called themselves "Les Imagistes," a term Pound first used in 1912 when he scribbled "H.D. Imagiste" on a manuscript that Hilda Doolittle was submitting to a poetry magazine.

H.D. (as she liked to be called) lived an unconventional life. She and Richard Aldington became estranged after he had an affair. She lived at **44 *Mecklenburg Square*** in ***Bloomsbury*** from 1917 to 1918 and from August 1919 to August 1920 at **16 *Bullingham Mansions*** in ***Kensington***. In 1933 she traveled to Vienna to undergo psychological analysis with Sigmund Freud, an experience that she wrote about in *Writing on the Wall* (later titled *Tribute to Freud*). H.D. published many poems and novels during her long career. She died in 1961 and her ashes were returned to Bethlehem, Pennsylvania. 🍃

T.S. Eliot (1888–1965)

One of the most influential poets of the twentieth century, Thomas Sterns Eliot was born in St. Louis, Missouri. He could trace his ancestry back to the earliest days of English emigration to America. His mother, Charlotte Stearns Eliot (1843–1930) was a descendant of Isaac Stearns, who came to Massachusetts with the **Winthrop Fleet**. His father's family ancestor Andrew Eliot was a cordwainer who immigrated from ***East Coker*** in ***Somerset*** in the 1660s. The Eliot family became prominent in Boston, Massachusetts, and one family member, Rev. Andrew Eliot, was elected president of **Harvard College**.

T.S. Eliot lived in England from 1911 and worked as a teacher and a bank clerk before moving into publishing. Eliot established himself as a poet with the publication of *The Love Song of J. Alfred Prufrock* in 1915. He became a very important part of the literary life of London, acquiring British citizenship in 1927. He was a friend and collaborator of **Ezra Pound**, who lived in Kensington and Holland Park from 1909 to 1920. Eliot was a member of the Bloomsbury Group, and a friend of Virginia and Leonard Wolff, E.M. Forster, and others. Some of his other most notable poems are *The Waste Land* (1932) and *Four Quartets* (1944), a section of which is named "East Coker" after the village from which his ancestors came. His most famous play is *Murder in the Cathedral* (1935). Eliot was awarded the Nobel Prize for literature in 1948. 🍃

Robert Frost (1874–1963)

Moving to England in 1912, Robert Frost hoped to establish himself as a poet and find a publisher for his poems. Initially

Frost, his wife Elinor and four children lived in Beaconsfield, Buckinghamshire. In 1913 Frost walked past a bookshop in London and read an invitation to the official opening. Joining the party he met someone who became a friend and collaborator – **Ezra Pound**, another American poet living in London. Frost often visited Pound at his home at *Kensington Church Walk.*

Frost became close friends with a young English critic and poet, Edward Thomas, whom Frost later referred to as "the only brother I ever had." During 1914 and 1915 the Frost family traveled around England. For a while they lived in Gloucestershire where Frost often took walks with Edward Thomas. Frost later said that Thomas would plan a walk to see a special sight, but then at the end of the walk he would sigh about the other possible sights they had missed by not going in a different direction. "The Road Not Taken" was published in August 1915 and became one of Frost's most famous poems. In it, Frost subtly jokes about his friend's indecision, but the poem also reflects an eternal question about the things not done in life. Edward Thomas joined the British Army and was killed in France in 1917.

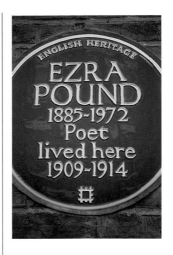

LONDON A blue plaque marks the house at 10 *Kensington Church Walk* where **Ezra Pound** lived. **Robert Frost** often visited his fellow American poet here.

> "The Road Not Taken
> Two roads diverged in a yellow wood,
> And sorry I could not travel both
> And be one traveler, long I stood
> And looked down one as far as I could
> To where it bent in the undergrowth;
> Then took the other, as just as fair
>
> Two roads diverged in a wood, and I–
> I took the one less traveled by,
> And that has made all the difference"

World War I began in July 1914, and the British market for poetry was shrinking. Frost had made a name for himself in England, and his fame had traveled back to his homeland. In February 1915 the family returned to America. 🍃

Francis Bret Harte (1836–1902)

Best remembered for his poetry and prose about pioneering life in California, Bret Harte was influenced by Dickens, and in 1870 when he heard of Dickens's death, he composed what is considered to be his poetic masterpiece, "Dickens in Camp." In 1878 Harte moved to Europe. In 1885 he settled in London, where he lived for the rest of his life. He continued to write poems, sketches, and stories that were infused with the flavor of his life in California. 🍃

LONDON Francis Bret Harte lived at 74 *Lancaster Gate*. A blue plaque marks the house.

SURREY Francis Bret Harte was buried at *St. Peter's Church, Frimley, Surrey.*

LONDON In September 1855 Nathaniel Hawthorne and his family spent some time in London and lived at *24 St. George's Street, Hanover Square*.

In 1856 the Hawthorne family visited London again and spent a month staying at a house at *4 Pond Road, Blackheath*, which Hawthorne said were "some of the happiest hours I have known since we left our American home." He met many famous people then, including Jenny Lind, Florence Nightingale, Robert Browning, and Elizabeth Barrett Browning.

At the end of 1857 the Hawthorne family returned to London before leaving for an extended trip to Europe. They stayed near the *British Museum* at *24 Great Russell Street* (now the site of the *Trades Union Congress House*).

MERSEYSIDE *The Maritime Museum, Liverpool*, has displays about the maritime history of the city. It offers walking tours around the city centre which focus on places associated with the slave trade. You will see the docks, banks, and merchants' houses.

LONDON A blue plaque marks the house at *8 Argyll Street* where **Washington Irving** lived.

LONDON Henry James lived at *32 De Vere Gardens, Kensington*, for many years.

The *National Portrait Gallery* displays the 1913 portrait of Henry James by **John Singer Sargent** that was commissioned for James's seventieth birthday by a group of 269 friends, organized by **Edith Wharton**. In the end, Sargent refused payment for the portrait.

Nathaniel Hawthorne (1804–1864)

The author of many seminal American novels, Nathaniel Hawthorne traced his family back to the first Puritans in Massachusetts. His ancestor William Hathorne sailed to America with **John Winthrop** on the *Arabella* in 1630, and settled in Dorchester, Massachusetts. (Nathaniel added the "w" to his last name.) Nathaniel's father was a sea-captain who died when his son was only four years old. His mother moved to Maine when he was fourteen, and Nathaniel attended Bowdoin College, where he was to make a lifelong friend – Franklin Pierce.

In 1846, unable to support himself and his wife with his writing, Hawthorne took a job in the Boston customs office, where he worked for three years while continuing to write. In 1850 he published his masterpiece, *The Scarlet Letter*, set in seventeenth-century Puritan New England. His college friend Franklin Pierce ran for the US presidency in 1852. Pierce appointed Hawthorne as the US consul in **Liverpool**, a lucrative position that Hawthorne held from 1853 to 1857. As consul Hawthorne was especially interested in improving the conditions of men working on American ships at sea.

While living in England, the Hawthorne family traveled extensively. Visiting London in 1855, he wandered through the city and was appalled by the squalor and drunkenness of the metropolis. After traveling in Europe, the family returned to the United States in 1860. Hawthorne wrote several books based on his travels in Europe. *The English Notebooks* and *Our Old Home* were based on the four years he lived in England.

Washington Irving (1783–1859)

In 1815 the American writer Washington Irving traveled to Liverpool as a partner in his brothers' commercial firm. When the business went into bankruptcy in 1818, Irving returned to writing for a living, but remained in Europe until 1832. Under the pen name of Geoffrey Crayon, he wrote essays and short stories collected in *The Sketch Book of Geoffrey Crayon, Gent.* (1819–20), which became his most popular work. The collection included Irving's two most famous stories: *Rip Van Winkle* and *The Legend of Sleepy Hollow*. For a short time he acted as secretary to the US legation in London. He served as US ambassador to Spain in 1842–6.

Henry James (1843–1916)

Born in New York City into a wealthy and intellectual family, Henry James published his first short story when he was twenty-one, and decided to devote himself to literature. He moved to Europe in 1875 and to London in 1886. James was host to a great many visiting Americans, particularly literary figures, including his friend the novelist **Edith Wharton**. Henry James moved to **Rye, East Sussex**, in 1898 and lived at **Lamb House** on West Street for eighteen years. In Rye, he wrote some of his best works, including *Wings of a Dove*, *The Ambassadors*, and *The Golden Bowl*.

Henry James became a naturalized British citizen on 28 July 1915. He received the Order of Merit in January 1916 and died on February 28 of that year. Henry James's funeral was held at **Chelsea Old Church**. There is a memorial to him in the church. His ashes were taken back to America by his sister-in-law and were interred in the Cambridge, Massachusetts, cemetery where his family were buried. 🌿

Rudyard Kipling (1876–1936)

The British author and poet Rudyard Kipling was born in Bombay in 1865, son of John Lockwood Kipling, an artist and teacher, and his wife Alice, one of the talented and beautiful Macdonald sisters, who married remarkable men (Sir Edward Burne-Jones, Sir Edward Poynter, Alfred Baldwin, and John Lockwood Kipling). Rudyard had a very happy early childhood in India, but when he was six years old, he and his sister were left in England to attend school; he was miserable and felt abandoned. When he was sixteen he returned to India where he started his career as a journalist writing for *The Civil and Military Gazette* and also writing short stories and poems.

In 1892 Rudyard Kipling married Caroline ("Carrie") Balestier, the sister of his American friend and literary colleague Wolcott Balestier. He and Carrie moved to live near her family in Brattleboro, Vermont, where their first two children were born. After Rudyard and Carrie's brother Beatty had a falling out, the Kipling family moved to England. He came to be regarded as the People's Laureate and the poet of the Empire. In 1907 he was awarded the Nobel Prize for Literature. Unfortunately he suffered many tragedies in his private life. His daughter Josephine died of pneumonia in 1899 and his only son John was killed in the Battle of Loos in 1915 at the age of eighteen. Rudyard Kipling died in 1936 and Carrie continued to live at **Bateman's** in **East Sussex** until her death in 1939, when she bequeathed the estate to the National Trust as a memorial to her late husband. 🌿

Henry Wadsworth Longfellow (1807–82)

Having been named a professor of modern languages at **Harvard College** in 1835, a young Henry Wadsworth Longfellow was on his way to Germany when he spent a number of days

LONDON Henry James lived at *21 Carlyle Mansions, Cheyne Walk*, from 1913 to 1916.

There is a monument to Henry James in *Poets' Corner, Westminster Abbey.*

LONDON *Chelsea Old Church* is where James's funeral was held in 1916.

EAST SUSSEX Rudyard Kipling and his wife Carrie lived in a house called *"The Elms"* in *Rottingdean* for several years. Here Rudyard wrote some of his most memorable poems and books.

EAST SUSSEX Kipling purchased *Bateman's* in *Burwash* when he was the most famous writer in the English-speaking world. Today, the house is shown as it was in his time.

LONDON A blue plaque commemorates Rudyard Kipling's home at *43 Villiers Street*.

LONDON On 20 May 1835 the twenty-eight-year-old American poet H.W. Longfellow rented rooms at *8 Princes Street, Hanover Square*, for his wife and two lady friends.

LONDON *Carlyle's House Museum* at 24 *Cheyne Row* is maintained as it was when Longfellow lived there.

In 1868 Longfellow was one of the first Americans to stay at the *Langham Hotel* on *Portland Place*. In 1870 former Confederate officer Captain James Sanderson became General Manager of the hotel which was popular with visiting Americans.

LONDON A window in *Poets' Corner* at *Westminster Abbey* commemorates James Russell Lowell.

James Russell Lowell and his wife rented a house at *37 Lowndes Street* in the spring of 1880 and stayed five years.

In 1887 the sixty-eight year-old James Russell Lowell spent the summer at *2 Radnor Place*.

KENT Robert Lowell lived at Milgate Park in Bearsted with his third wife.

LONDON Herman Melville lived at *25 Craven Street* in 1840. Benjamin Franklin and Aaron Burr lived on the same street in the 1700s.

in London purchasing books and visiting the **British Museum**. He also visited Thomas Carlyle at his home at *24 Cheyne Row, Chelsea*.

Longfellow returned to London decades later. During his two-week stay in June 1868, the sixty-one-year-old poet was given many honors, including a dinner for 300 people at the *Langham Hotel* in **London** with William Gladstone, the former prime minister, as speaker. Longfellow was the first American poet to have his bust placed in **Poets' Corner** in *Westminster Abbey*. 🍃

James Russell Lowell (1819–91)

In 1855 James Russell Lowell was elected to the Smith Professorship of Modern Languages at **Harvard College** made vacant by the retirement of **Henry Wadsworth Longfellow**. His career as a writer, critic, historian of literature, and teacher brought international recognition. After teaching for many years he entered politics and served as American minister to Spain for several years before serving as minister to England from 1880 to 1885. He was well known in England and gave a number of lectures.

After moving back to the US, James Russell Lowell returned to London in 1887 and basked in his literary reputation, dining with celebrities such as William Gladstone. He was given honorary degrees by Oxford, Cambridge, St. Andrews, and Edinburgh Universities. He also enjoyed the festivities surrounding Queen Victoria's Silver Jubilee. 🍃

Robert Lowell (1917–77)

A member of an aristocratic, intellectual Massachusetts family that included **James Russell Lowell**, the American poet Robert Lowell lived in England during the 1970s. He was a visiting fellow at **All Souls College, Oxford** (1970), visiting lecturer at the University of Essex (1970–2) and at the University of Kent (1970–5). *The Dolphin* dealt with the poet's move to England as he left one wife for another. The title poem celebrated the poet's feelings of love – the inspiration behind the poems was Lowell's third wife, the writer Caroline Blackwood. They lived for a while in Kent. 🍃

Herman Melville (1819–91)

As a young man Herman Melville first came to England as a cabin boy on a ship that sailed to Liverpool. He visited **London** briefly in 1849 when he stayed on **Craven Street**, behind Charing Cross station before leaving for New York to start work on his story "The Whale," which developed into his masterpiece *Moby Dick*. One of Melville's grandfathers participated in the **Boston Tea Party**. 🍃

William Chester Minor (1834–1920) and the *Oxford English Dictionary*

One of the strangest connections between the USA and Britain links the *Oxford English Dictionary* and the Victorian buildings of the **Broadmoor Hospital**, formerly known as the Broadmoor Asylum for the Criminally Insane, in **Crowthorne, Berkshire**. In the 1870s a huge project was begun to create a dictionary of the English language based on quotation evidence from across the centuries. In 1878 an appeal was issued for volunteers to send in contributions of words, showing how and where they had been used in English writing. One of the most productive volunteer contributors to this project was an American – William Chester Minor, a graduate of Yale University. He was a former military surgeon for the Union army, and an inmate of Broadmoor Asylum. He had been convicted of murdering a man in London, but evidence at his trial showed that he was clearly insane. On 6 April 1872 he was sent to Broadmoor to be held in permanent custody as a "certified criminal lunatic."

In some ways, Victorian care for the insane was a survival of the earlier English penal system which allowed people to provide for their own comforts while incarcerated. Because Dr. Minor was an educated man who had money to pay for his accommodations, he was allowed to furnish his rooms at Broadmoor. He built up a large personal library and often ordered books from specialist book dealers in London. It was probably through them that he learned about the appeal for volunteers to work on the project of research for the *Oxford English Dictionary*. Over the next thirty-eight years he contributed thousands upon thousands of quotations that were used in the *OED*.

In 1910 he was permitted to return to the US – to the Government Hospital for the Insane in Washington, D.C. He was diagnosed as suffering from schizophrenia. William Chester Minor died in 1920 when he eighty-five years old. He was buried in the Evergreen Cemetery in New Haven, Connecticut. 🍃

Thomas Paine (1737–1809)

The revolutionary political thinker Thomas Paine wrote *The Rights of Man* at **Angel Square** in **London**. He moved to America in 1774 with introductory letters from **Benjamin Franklin**, and wrote in support of the revolutionary cause. He also supported the French Revolution, and his *The Rights of Man* led to his trial for treason. Fleeing to France, he was again arrested, having fallen into disfavor with Robespierre, but was released because of his American citizenship. (*See also the entry for Thomas Paine in Chapter 3*). 🍃

READ *The Professor and the Madman* by Simon Winchester. New York: HarperCollins, 1998

OXFORD In November 1915 William Minor offered all his books to the Scriptorium, James Murray's headquarters for editing the *Oxford English Dictionary*. These books were later given to the *Bodleian Library*, where they are registered as having been donated "By Dr. Minor through Lady Murray."

LONDON Thomas Paine's monument in *Angel Square, Islington High Street*, is an obelisk with a bas-relief sculpture of Paine's profile.

In *Islington*, both *The Angel* pub and the *Old Red Lion* claim that Thomas Paine may have stayed with them while writing *The Rights of Man*.

LONDON Sylvia Plath's son and daughter unveiled the blue plaque at *3 Chalcot Square, Primrose Hill.* in 2000.

After her divorce from Ted Hughes, Plath and her children moved into a house at *23 Fitzroy Street* where W.B. Yeats had lived as a young boy.

YORKSHIRE Sylvia Plath is buried at *St. Thomas's Churchyard, Heptonstall,* near Ted Hughes's family.

LONDON Edgar Allan Poe lived at *172 Stoke Newington Church Street* in Hackney.

LONDON Ezra Pound lived in a small courtyard at *10 Kensington Church Walk.*

LONDON On 20 April 1914 Ezra Pound and Dorothy Shakespear were married at *St. Mary Abbot's Church, Kensington.*

LONDON On 13 January 1887 **Henry Morton Stanley** was presented with the Freedom of the City of London.

Sylvia Plath (1932–63)

Born in Boston, Massachusetts, Sylvia Plath graduated from high school in Wellesley, Massachusetts, and attended Smith College. After winning a Fulbright scholarship, Plath attended **Newnham College, Cambridge**, where she met the poet Ted Hughes. After a short, tempestuous courtship, Sylvia Plath and Ted Hughes were married on 16 June 1956 at **St. George-the-Martyr, Queen Square, Bloomsbury.** They first lived in London at **18 Rugby Street**, and later moved to a second-floor flat at **3 Chalcot Square, Primrose Hill,** where *The Bell Jar* was written. In 1962, after Ted Hughes left her, she moved to **23 Fitzroy Street** where she lived briefly before she killed herself on 11 February 1963. 🍃

Edgar Allan Poe (1809–49)

The American poet and short-story writer Edgar Allan Poe lived in England from 1815 to 1829. For three years as a boy he attended the Manor School in Hackney, east London. Among his best-known works are *The Fall of the House of Usher* and *The Murders in the Rue Morgue.* 🍃

Ezra Pound (1885–1972)

While he lived in a small house at **10 Kensington Church Walk** from 1909 to 1914, the American poet Ezra Pound knew and encouraged many other American poets including **T.S. Eliot, Robert Frost**, and **H.D. (Hilda Doolittle)**. London was awhirl with poets who were developing new types of poetry. Pound was part of a group, originally called "Les Imagistes," who wanted to break away from the late nineteenth-century Romantic poetry that stressed moralism, classical illusions, and lofty ideals, expressed with complicated or flowery language. They wanted to focus on real life and modern experience, expressed with common language, and often in free verse form. Pound was especially close to T.S. Eliot and helped to edit his important work, *The Waste Land.* World War I had a great impact on Pound and at its end he left England and moved to Paris. 🍃

Henry Morton Stanley (1841–1904)

One of the most famous scenes in the exploration of Africa took place on 10 November 1871 when the journalist Henry Morton Stanley walked up to a white man on the shores of Lake Tanganyika and said, "Doctor Livingstone, I presume." The true life history of Stanley is fairly amazing. He was born in Wales and his birth name was John Rowlands. Placed in a poor-house when he was three years old, at fifteen he sailed to New Orleans, working as a cabin-boy. He was adopted by a merchant named Mr. Stanley. During the American Civil

War, Stanley enlisted in the Confederate army, but was captured and held as a prisoner. Next he volunteered for the US Navy. When the war was over, he began his journalistic career. Hired by the *New York Herald*, Stanley reported from Abyssinia and Spain. In October 1869 the newspaper owner gave him the assignment to find Dr. Livingstone, the British explorer who had disappeared in Africa. After many adventures and hardships, Stanley did find Livingstone. His newspaper reports made him a celebrity. When he returned to England, his British citizenship was restored. In May 1890 the **Royal Geographical Society** gave Stanley and his officers a "monster reception" in the **Royal Albert Hall** and presented him with a special gold medal. Stanley was knighted by Queen Victoria in 1899. 🌿

Donald Ogden Stewart (1894–1980)
American playwright, screenwriter, and author Donald Ogden Stewart was a friend of Ernest Hemingway, F. Scott Fitzgerald, and many other leading American writers. He won an Academy Award in 1940 for his screenplay adaptation of *The Philadelphia Story* and was successful with many films, including *The Barratts of Wimpole Street* (1934), *That Certain Feeling* (1941), and *Life With Father* (1947). Blacklisted during the McCarthy era, Stewart moved to England in the 1950s. 🌿

Mark Twain (1835–1910)
The great American humorist, writer, and lecturer Mark Twain lived in London from 1896 to 1897. His great masterpieces were *The Adventures of Tom Sawyer* (1876) and *The Adventures of Huckleberry Finn* (1884). Other well-known novels include *A Tramp Abroad* (1880) and *A Connecticut Yankee in King Arthur's Court* (1889). Mark Twain (whose real name was Samuel Langhorne Clemens) returned to England in 1907 at the age of seventy-two to receive an honorary degree from Oxford University. 🌿

Edith Wharton (1862–1937)
Wharton was an American author whose books such as *The House of Mirth*, *The Age of Innocence*, and *The Buccaneers* gave a knowing insight into the social mores of the late nineteenth century. At the end of 1909 she spent a month at the **Berkeley Hotel** in **London**, enjoying her first major social whirl in England being escorted by her great friend, **Henry James**. In 1913 she organized subscriptions by a group of 269 friends to commission a portrait of Henry James from **John Singer Sargent**. In the end, Sargent waived his fee for the portrait, which now hangs in the **National Portrait Gallery**

LONDON A statue of Dr. Livingstone stands in a niche on the side of the *Royal Geographical Society*.

SURREY Stanley bought an estate, *Furzehill Place*, in *Pirbright*, where he spent his retirement. The large Victorian mansion is now a bed and breakfast.

Stanley is buried in the cemetery at the *Church of St. Michael and All Angels* in *Pirbright*. He had requested that his body be buried next to that of Dr. Livingstone in Westminster Abbey, but this was refused. On his tombstone is inscribed "Bula Matari," which was his African name.

LONDON Donald Ogden Stewart lived in *Hampstead* at *103 Frognal*.

LONDON Mark Twain lived at *23 Tedworth Square*.

LONDON A new organ was given to *St. Bride's Church* in 1957 by Lord Astor of Hever, who for many years was President of the Commonwealth Press Union. He was a descendant of William Waldorf Astor, the wealthy American who bought *Hever Castle* in 1903.

LONDON A statue of John Wilkes stands on *New Fetter Lane* just off *Fleet Street*. The champion of freedom of the press also expressed support for the rights of the American colonies in the early 1760s and 70s.

on **Trafalgar Square**. In 1913 Wharton stayed at the **Cavendish Hotel, Jermyn Street**, for ten days, during which time she visited **William Waldorf Astor** at **Cliveden**, his 300-acre country estate in **Berkshire**. 🍃

Thomas Wolfe (1900–38)

Wolfe rented the first-floor flat at **32 Wellington Square** in **Chelsea** in early August 1926. The twenty-five-year-old was working on what was to become *Look Homeward, Angel*. On 4 October 1926 he moved to **57 Gower Street** in **Bloomsbury**. At the end of the month he left for Oxford and Germany, and sailed back to New York in December. 🍃

Fleet Street

The home of British journalism for hundreds of years, Fleet Street saw many people linked with America and American history pass through its busy offices, courtyards, and pubs – **Benjamin Franklin, John Wilkes, William Cobbett, Thomas Paine**'s bones, **Raymond Chandler, William Waldorf Astor, Bill Bryson**, and many, many more. In the 1980s the newspapers finally moved away, but many reminders of the link with journalism remain. 🍃

St. Bride's Church, Fleet Street – "The Journalists' Church"

The connection between **St. Bride's Church** and journalism is exemplified by its chapel dedicated to the memory of journalists and cameramen from around the world who have gone missing or been killed in the line of duty. Prayer vigils have been held here when captured journalists are held hostage. In the Chapel of Journalists there is a plaque presented by the Overseas Press Club of America in memory of "American Journalists who have perished outside their own country." 🍃

John Wilkes

A statue of John Wilkes stands in **New Fetter Lane** just north of Fleet Street. The radical Member of Parliament supported parliamentary reform and freedom of the press during the 1760s and 1770s. In America Wilkes became a symbol of opposition to the Crown and they cheered his victories over Parliamentary repression. Wilkes Barre, Pennsylvania was partially named in his honor. (*Also see the entry for John Wilkes in Chapter 3.*) 🍃

CHAPTER 12
PERFORMING ARTISTS

The world loves a good show. American and English actors, musicians, magicians, and performers have entertained audiences on both sides of the Atlantic. During the fledgling years of the film industry in America, English comedians and actors became some of the most famous celluloid stars in Hollywood. Soon Americans transported the technology across the ocean and started making movies in England. The English stage beckoned and American actors, producers, and musicians regularly appeared in London and around the country. American theater and film writers settled in England. English actors and writers were honored in America with the highest praise given by the American film industry – the Academy Award. The cultural mix of the international entertainment world has enriched all of our lives with creativity, fantasy, music, and magic. 🍃

ACTORS, DIRECTORS, AND PRODUCERS
Birt Acres (1854–1918)
Born in Richmond, Virginia, Birt Acres's childhood was drastically changed after both of his parents were killed during the American Civil War. He was adopted by an aunt who sent him to France to study science and art. When he returned to America, Acres set out for the Wild West. He lived among the frontiersmen and Sioux Indians for several years. Around 1885 he moved to England, starting his career with a studio in Ilfracombe in Devon, where he produced portraits "by painting and photography." By 1890 he had married and moved to London. Constantly experimenting, he soon developed a way to project a series of pictures that gave the impression of movement.

In 1894 Acres experimented with celluloid film and produced a short film of the Henley Regatta. In February 1895 Acres made his first 33mm film, *Incident Outside Clovelly Cottage*, which shows his wife Annie pushing their son in front of their home. In 1895 he established his own company, Northern Photographic Works, at **45 *Salisbury Road*** in ***Barnet***.

LONDON Birt Acres worked for a short time with Robert Paul, an electrical engineer who was working on a replica of Edison's kinetoscope to project moving pictures. They produced the *Oxford and Cambridge University Boat Race*, *Rough Sea at Dover*, and *The Derby*.

The mechanism of Birt Acres's "Kineopticon" of 1895 in now displayed in the *Science Museum*.

When Acres first moved to London he worked for a company that manufactured photographic plates. He lived at the manager's house at *Clovelly Cottage, 19 Park Road, Barnet*.

Robert Paul had his electrical engineering business at *44 Hatton Garden*. Birt Acres worked here with him on the Kinetoscope.

Acres traveled and filmed public events in Germany and Britain. These became some of the first movie news reels. He was so well known that in July 1896 he was invited to an evening with seventy-five members of the royal families of Europe at Marlborough House to show his film of the Prince and Princess of Wales at the Cardiff Exhibition. This was the first ever Royal Command Film Performance. Acres gradually moved away from the technical forefront, and spent his later years giving lectures and demonstrations. Although never financially successful, Birt Acres is considered a pioneer of the film industry in Britain. 🍃

John Wilkes Booth (1838–65)

President Abraham Lincoln was assassinated on 14 April 1865 in the Ford Theater, Washington, D.C., by John Wilkes Booth, a well-known stage actor of his day. Booth was the son of Junius Brutus Booth, a famous international actor who started his career on the stage at the Covent Garden Theatre and Drury Lane Theatre in London. In 1821 he eloped to the United States with Mary Ann Holmes, abandoning his wife Adelaide and their young son. After touring many of the major cities of America and becoming a well-known theatrical star, he made two tours of England and then returned to live the rest of his life in America.

Junius Brutus was born in London and was descended from a Clerkenwell family. His father Richard Booth was an affluent silversmith who had radical political views. It was said that Richard Booth would make visitors to his Bloomsbury home pay respects to a portrait of **George Washington**. He named one of his sons **Algernon Sydney** in honor of the aristocratic political writer who was executed in 1683 for his part in a plot to restore an independent parliament under King Charles II. His father was John Booth, also a silversmith, who married Elizabeth Wilkes, a relative of the radical politician **John Wilkes**, who was born in **St. John's Square, Clerkenwell**.

John Wilkes Booth's great-grandparents were married on 15 February 1747 at St. George's Chapel, Hyde Park Corner (on the site of the present **Lanesborough Hotel**). Six of their children were baptized at **St. John the Baptist Church** in **Clerkenwell**. The grave of a relative, also named John Wilkes Booth, who died in 1836, is reported to be in the garden behind the church. 🍃

Charlie Chaplin (1889–1977)

Born into a family of music hall entertainers, Charlie Chaplin's childhood was one of extreme poverty. His father left soon after Charlie was born and his mother Hannah was

Cherie Booth Blair, wife of former Prime Minister Tony Blair, is the great-great-great granddaughter of Algernon Sydney Booth.

LONDON A statue of Chaplin dressed as the Little Tramp stands in *Leicester Square.*

unable to cope with life or care for Charlie and his older half-brother Sydney. In 1896 the children and their mother were sent to the **Lambeth Workhouse**. Next the boys were sent to the **Hanwell School of Orphans and Destitute Children**. Life at the school was very harsh, with hard work and hard discipline. Sydney left when he was eleven to go to the training ship *Exmouth*. Charlie stayed at Hanwell until January 1898. Hannah was for a time held at the **Bethlem Royal Hospital for the Insane** in **Lambeth** and was then committed to the Cane Hill Asylum.

Chaplin soon found a place on the stage. He gave his first public performance when he was five years old, having sung in place of his mother when her voice went hoarse. In December 1900 Chaplin played a comic role as a Cat in *Cinderella* at the London Hippodrome. From 1906 he was appearing as a clown in Fred Karno's Mumming Birds Company. His first appearance in the USA was in 1910 on a tour with the Karno Troupe. He returned to the US in 1912–13 and in May 1913 accepted an offer to work for the Keystone Film Company for $125 a week. Chaplin made his first film in 1914: *Making a Living*. His rise in popularity was truly meteoric. By 1920 he was earning $10,000 a week.

Charlie Chaplin lived in the USA for many years, but never became a US citizen. His personal life and political opinions drew attention during the anti-Communist witch-hunt of the late 1940s and early 50s. His four marriages, a 1944 paternity suit, and his refusal to accept US citizenship, gained him adverse publicity in America. In 1953, accused of Communist sympathies, Chaplin was denied reentry into the US and chose to settle in Switzerland. After the anti-Communist hysteria calmed a bit in the US, America's affection for Charlie Chaplin was rekindled. He retuned to Hollywood in 1972 to receive an honorary Oscar for his contributions to the motion picture industry. In 1975 he was knighted by the Queen. ❦

Walt Disney (1901–66)

After William the Conqueror defeated Harold Godwinson in 1066, many men in the victorious French army were granted property in England. One of these was a man from the town of Isignes near Bayeux in Normandy who received a manor in Lincolnshire. The family name was Anglicized from d'Isignes to Disney. During the Civil War William Disney fought with the winning Parliamentarians, but he later joined the unsuccessful attempt of the Duke of Monmouth (the illegitimate son of King Charles II) to overthrow King James II. William Disney was arrested and held in the **Tower of London** before being executed on 29 June 1685. Many

LONDON A plaque has been placed at 227 *Walworth Road* in 2005 near Charlie Chaplin's birthplace.

The Chaplin family lived in a one-room garret at 3 Pownall Terrace at 287 *Kennington Road*. A blue plaque marks the building.

A plaque marks the house at 39 *Methley Street* where Charlie Chaplin lived briefly with his mother and brother Stanley.

Today the *Imperial War Museum* is housed in the buildings of the former Bethlem Royal Hospital.

There has been public entertainment on this site since 1848 when The Eagle pub/music hall was built. This became Lusby's Music Hall where Charlie Chaplin performed before his Hollywood fame. Now it is the *Genesis Cinema, 93–95 Mile End Road*.

There is a photographic portrait of Chaplin by Peyton Straus (1920) at the *National Portrait Gallery*.

Charlie Chaplin has a memorial plaque in the "Actors' Church"– St. *Paul's Covent Garden*.

LINCOLNSHIRE *St. Peter's Church* in *Norton Disney* has a number of memorials to members of the Disney family. The oldest is from about 1300 – the figure of Joan d'Iseney who lies with her hands at prayer, a dog at her feet.

LONDON In 1970 the Judy Garland Fan Club organized for a portrait and plaque to be placed at the *London Palladium*, and in 1998 they placed a plaque and photograph at the *Dominion Theatre*.

The eccentric décor at the *Gore Hotel* in *Kensington* features bedrooms named after famous people who have stayed there. The Venus Room has a lavish gilded bed that once belonged to Judy Garland.

BUCKINGHAMSHIRE The Judy Garland Fan Club organized the creation of the award-winning "Judy Garland Rose" by the famous English rose growers Harkness. A bed of these roses at the *Garden of Remembrance, Stokes Poges*, is a memorial to Judy.

BRISTOL In 2001 a life-size statue of Cary Grant was unveiled in *Millennium Square* near the *Bristol Hippodrome* where he used to watch shows from backstage as a young boy.

branches of the family owned property in Lincolnshire, but some of them immigrated to Ireland, and it was from here that Elias Disney's father moved to Canada in 1834. Elias married and later moved to Chicago, where his son Walter Elias Disney was born in 1901.

Walt Disney visited **Norton Disney, Lincolnshire**, in 1949 and saw the remains of the manor house and **St. Peter's Church** with its many Disney memorials. 🍃

Judy Garland (1922–69)

Starting her career as a child star, Judy Garland appeared many times on stages in London. On 18 November 1957 she performed at the Palladium in a Royal Variety Show. Her first solo show at the **London Palladium** was in 1960. English fans idolized Judy; they packed the theater when she performed. She appeared at the Palladium a total of sixty-eight times. Her last performance there was on 19 January 1969. On 15 March 1969 Judy married Mickey Deans at the **Chelsea Register Office**.

Judy Garland's last movie was *I Could Go on Singing* in which she played a part that had some similarities with her own life. Many scenes were filmed on location in London and in a churchyard at **Stoke Poges, Buckinghamshire.** Judy Garland died at her home at **4 Cadogan Lane** in **Belgravia** on 22 June 1969. 🍃

Ava Gardner (1922–90)

An ornamental urn commemorates the actress Ava Gardner who lived at **34 Ennismore Gardens, London**, for seventeen years. Born in Grabtown, North Carolina, into a family of poor tobacco farmers, Gardner starred in over sixty films. She died in this flat on 25 January 1990 at the age of sixty-seven. 🍃

Cary Grant (1904–86)

The movie star we know as Cary Grant was born into a lower-middle-class family in **Horfield, Bristol**, in 1904, and was named Archibald Leach. He ran away from home at fourteen to join a group of Bob Pender's traveling comedians. In 1920 he was one of several boys selected to go to America for a production that ran on Broadway for 456 performances. When the group returned to England, Grant stayed in America and soon headed to Hollywood, where he became a leading star in light comedy movies. Handsome and charming, he appeared in such films as *Bringing Up Baby* (1938), *The Philadelphia Story* (1940), and *North by Northwest* (1959). In 1970 he received the Academy Award for general excellence. Grant starred in several movies directed by another Brit, **Alfred Hitchcock**. 🍃

Sir Alfred Hitchcock (1899–1980)

The English-born film director was born in **Leytonstone, London**, in 1899. From 1926 to 1939, when he was working on films at the **Gainsborough Studios**, Hitchcock and his wife lived on **Cromwell Road** in **Kensington**. The couple moved to the USA in 1939 with their ten-year-old daughter Patricia. Hitchcock went to Hollywood, where he became an internationally acclaimed producer of films and TV programs based on mystery and stylish suspense. He obtained US citizenship in 1955. 🍃

LONDON There is a blue plaque at *517 Leytonstone High Street* near the site where **Alfred Hitchcock** was born.

The *National Portrait Gallery* has a photographic portrait of Alfred Hitchcock by Yousuf Karsh.

LONDON LOCATIONS CONNECTED TO ALFRED HITCHCOCK

Alfred Hitchcock married Alma Reville on 2 December 1926 at **Brompton Oratory**.

Hitchcock filmed two versions of *The Man Who Knew Too Much* in the **Royal Albert Hall** in 1934 and 1956.

On Friday 13 August 1999 Patricia Hitchcock O'Connell unveiled a commemorative plaque on the house at **153 Cromwell Road, Kensington**, where the family lived from 1926 to 1939 to mark her father's 100th birthday.

In the Piazza of the new residential housing on the site of the **Gainsborough Studios** there are plans for a sculpture of Alfred Hitchcock, designed by the internationally acclaimed sculptor Anthony Donaldson.

Bob Hope (1903–2003)

Leslie Townes Hope was born on **Craigton Road** in **Eltham**, southeast London, in 1903. His family moved to Cleveland, Ohio, when he was four years old. As a young teenager, "Bob" earned pocket money by busking; his dance and comedy act was a forerunner of his long career. After working in vaudeville for a few years, he made his first film appearance in 1934. Hope went on to become a popular broadcaster with his own regular show and starred with Bing Crosby in a series of "Road" films between 1940 and 1961. His greatest fame came from entertaining the American military troops during World War II, the Korean War, and Vietnam War. In 1976 he was appointed a Commander of the British Empire by Queen Elizabeth II. Bob Hope kept his connections with his family's hometown. When the Eltham Little Theatre was in danger of closing, it was rescued by a generous donation from Bob Hope, who provided funds for the purchase of the property, which was renamed the **Bob Hope Theatre**. He often visited the theater when he was in London. 🍃

LONDON A blue plaque marks Bob Hope's childhood home at *44 Craigton Road, Eltham*.

The Eltham Little Theatre was renamed the *Bob Hope Theatre* in his honor in 1982. On Bob Hope's 100th birthday – 29 May 2003 – the theater celebrated his birthday and sent greetings and thanks to their native son.

LONDON Boris Karloff was born at *36 Forest Hill Rd, East Dulwich*. There is a plaque on the house.

A memorial plaque honors Boris Karloff at *St. Paul's Covent Garden*.

SURREY Karloff was cremated at *Guildford Crematorium* in *Surrey*. His ashes were placed in the Garden of Remembrance.

LONDON *Rules Restaurant* in *Covent Garden* was a favorite dining place for the Prince of Wales and **Lillie Langtry**. The restaurant now has their portraits in the King Edward VII Room.

LONDON Lillie Langtry lived at *21 Pont Street* from 1892 to 1897. Her house became part of the *Cadogan Hotel* where the "Lillie Langtry Room" and "Langtry's Restaurant" are reminders of Edwardian romance and scandal.

The collection of the *National Portrait Gallery* includes a number of photograph albums with Lillie's portrait, including an album that belonged to her daughter.

DORSET The house that the Prince of Wales bought for Lillie Langtry in *Bournemouth* is now the *Langtry Manor Hotel*.

JERSEY Lillie's burial place in St. Savior's Churchyard, Jersey, is marked by a lovely portrait sculpture.

Boris Karloff (1877–1969)

Born 23 November 1887 in **East Dulwich, London**, Boris Karloff began life as William Henry Pratt. He changed his name after moving to Canada in 1909 to pursue an acting career. Karloff arrived in Los Angeles in 1919 and had a long career as a character actor, often playing monsters in Hollywood films. He returned to live in England and died on 2 February 1969 at the King Edward VIII Hospital, Midhurst, Sussex. In the mid-1970s a commemorative plaque was placed in **St. Paul's Church** at **Covent Garden** in **London**, known as the "Actors' Church." On it was inscribed a few lines from Andrew Marvell's poem "Horatian Ode upon Cromwell's Return from Ireland," which refers to Charles I:

"He nothing common did or mean
Upon that memorable scene."

Lillie Langtry (1853–1929)

One of the most celebrated beauties of her era, Emilie Charlotte Le Breton was born in 1853 in Jersey, Channel Islands. An early marriage to Edward Langtry brought her to London. Soon Lillie was being invited to social soirées at which she was introduced to some of London's most famous artists. She quickly became one of the beautiful young women of the time known as "professional beauties," and many famous artists wanted to paint her portrait. Lillie became a friend of Oscar Wilde and the American painter **James Abbott McNeill Whistler**. Her portrait by Sir John Everett Millais was hung at the **Royal Academy of Arts** and was nominated for the "Painting of the Year." The press followed her everywhere and she was called the "Most Beautiful Woman in the World."

Lillie soon met the Prince of Wales, who was known for his affairs with beautiful women. She became Prince Albert's official mistress, and he purchased a house in **Bournemouth** for her. In 1881 Lillie gave birth to a daughter whose father was rumored to be Prince Louis of Battenberg. Royal affairs were tolerated at the time – as long as the social rules of behavior were followed. Lillie's affair with the Prince of Wales came to an abrupt end after she behaved recklessly at a party – she dropped a piece of ice down the prince's back!

No longer supported by royal largesse and the financial credits given to a prince's favorite, Lillie had to find a way to support herself. Going on stage was a natural step for a woman with her energy, beauty, and notoriety. When she then traveled to America, her fame and fortune grew enormously. In the 1882–3 season, she earned a huge amount of money, and proved to have a good head for business, buying a winery in California that turned out to be financially successful. Her fame in America became part of western legend when a small town judge and tavern owner in Texas claimed to have named his town Langtry in her honor. Judge Roy Bean named his saloon the "Jersey Lily" and invited her to visit the town on the Rio Grande River. Lillie did actually visit Langtry, Texas, but it was several months after Judge Roy's death. Her experiences in America were so successful and she was so fond of the country that she became a US citizen in 1887. 🌿

NOTE In Langtry, Texas, the Jersey Lilly Saloon/Courtroom is attached to the Judge Roy Bean Visitor Center

NOTE Lillie bought a vineyard in California which she owned from 1888 to 1906. Langtry Estate & Vineyard, www.langtryestate.com

Charles Laughton (1899–1962)
The character actor Charles Laughton was born on 1 July 1899 in the **Victoria Hotel, Scarborough**. After mainly Shakespearian stage performances, he turned to films, his most notable roles being the title part in *Henry VIII* (1932) for which he received an Oscar, Captain Bligh in *The Mutiny on the Bounty* (1935) and Quasimodo in *The Hunchback of Notre Dame* (1939). He became an American citizen in 1950. 🌿

YORKSHIRE A plaque on the *Victoria Hotel, Scarborough*, commemorates Charles Laughton's birth here.

LONDON Charles Laughton lived at 15 *Percy Street* from 1928 to 1931. A blue plaque marks the house.

Stan Laurel (1890–1965)
Half of the legendary Laurel and Hardy comedy duo, Stan Laurel was born in **Ulverston, Cumbria**. His father was an actor and theater manager. Stan was destined for a career on the stage, making his debut in Glasgow when he was sixteen. In 1910, as part of Fred Karno's vaudeville company that traveled to the US, Stan was Charlie Chaplin's understudy. Like Chaplin, Stan soon became part of the new film industry. In 1917 he appeared in *Nuts in May*. In 1926 he and Oliver Hardy appeared in their first film, *Forty-five Minutes from Hollywood*, and then went on to star together in many comic roles over the next twenty years. In 1960 Stan Laurel received a special Oscar "for his creative pioneering in the field of cinema comedy." 🌿

CUMBRIA The *Laurel and Hardy Museum* in *Ulverston* is the world's only museum devoted to Laurel and Hardy. Stan Laurel was born in Ulverston in 1890. He died in Santa Monica, California, on 23 February 1965, and was buried in Los Angeles, California. His grave is in the George Washington section of the Forest Lawn Cemetery.

Paul Robeson
(For information on the legendary actor and civil rights activist, see entry in Chapter 6.) 🌿

LONDON The *Theatre Museum* in *Covent Garden* has an exhibit about Paul Robeson's life.

George Bernard Shaw (1856–1950)
From 1906 until his death in 1950, the Irish-born dramatist, literary critic, socialist spokesman, and author George Bernard Shaw lived in **Ayot St. Lawrence**. As a young man of twenty-three he worked briefly for **Thomas Edison** as a telephone salesman. It was Shaw's last non-literary employment. George Bernard Shaw won the Nobel Prize for Literature in 1925. He wrote the screenplays for several movies – *Pygmalion* (1938) and *Major Barbara* (1941). His story of "Androcles and the Lion" was adapted as a movie in

HERTFORDSHIRE George Bernard Shaw's Oscar is on display at his home: *Shaw's Corner, Ayot St. Lawrence, Welwyn*.

1952. George Bernard Shaw won an Oscar in 1938 for his screenplay of the film version of his play *Pygmalion*. It is on display at his house, probably the only Oscar on display in a National Trust property. 🍂

Kevin Spacey (born 1959)

The London theatrical world was surprised in February 2003 when the Academy Award-winning actor Kevin Spacey was named artistic director at the **Old Vic Theatre** near **Waterloo Station, London**. The American actor was actually returning to the Old Vic, since his parents had brought him to London as a child and he remembers seeing Shakespeare performed on the stage there. He had also appeared on the Old Vic stage in 1998 in a production of Eugene O'Neill's *The Iceman Cometh.* 🍂

Gloria Swanson (1897–1983)

The American actress Gloria Swanson made her film debut in 1915 and became a major film star, playing opposite the leading romantic men of the day. Swanson's personal life was somewhat turbulent. It was rumored that she had a romantic relationship with Joseph Kennedy (US ambassador to the UK 1938–40 and father of **President John F. Kennedy**). She also had six husbands. She married her fourth husband, Michael Farmer, in 1931 and was soon looking for a home in London where she would have the baby she was expecting. The house she settled in gives a hint of the interesting connections of film stars and the upper-crust social circle of Americans in London. In her autobiography, Swanson writes:

> *"Lady Thelma Furness had a charming house on Farm Street, where her friend Wallis Simpson has kept the Prince of Wales company while Thelma was away in the States."*

"Farm House" is one of the most unusual residences in Mayfair – it looks like a half-timbered Tudor-style farmhouse. In the dining room a mural depicts Swanson, her films, and her foibles. In the picture there is a champagne bottle and glass, a cigarette holder, a riding whip and hat, a Harlequin, some cards and a candelabra. It's interesting to walk past this little architectural gem and think of all the glamorous ghosts that may be gliding around inside. 🍂

LONDON Thelma Furness is rumored to have introduced the Prince of Wales to Wallis Simpson at her home at 22 *Farm Street, Mayfair.*

Jessica Tandy (1909–94)

Stage and screen actress Jessica Tandy was born in London. She began her career on the London stage working with Laurence Olivier and John Gielgud. At the end of her first

LONDON A blue plaque commemorates **Jessica Tandy**'s childhood home at *58a Geldeston Road.*

marriage she moved to New York where she had a long and illustrious career. She appeared in many stage and film productions with her second husband, the Canadian actor Hume Cronyn. She is best remembered for her role in the film *Driving Miss Daisy* for which she won an Academy Award in 1989. 🍃

Elizabeth Taylor (born 1932)

Although she was born in London on 27 February 1932, Elizabeth Taylor's parents were American. They were art dealers from St. Louis, Missouri, who had moved to London to set up an art gallery. Her mother had been a stage actress but gave up her career when she married. Elizabeth lived in London for the first seven years of her life, the family moving to Los Angeles, California, in 1939. A family friend noticed the beautiful little Elizabeth and suggested that she be taken for a screen test. She was signed to a contract with Universal Studios. Elizabeth was a leading child star by the age of twelve after her performance in MGM's National Velvet. She went on to become one of the most glamorous stars of motion pictures. In 1999 Elizabeth Taylor was made a Dame of the British Empire in the New Year's Honours List. She was reported to have said proudly, "I've always been a broad, and now I'm a dame." 🍃

Sam Wanamaker (1919–93)

An American with a life-long interest in William Shakespeare was the driving force behind the rebuilding of one of England's iconic buildings. In 1934, as a fifteen-year-old student, Sam Wanamaker visited the Chicago World's Fair, where he saw a half-scale Globe Theatre and a thirty-minute Shakespeare play. Two years later Sam performed at the Great Lakes Festival in Cleveland, Ohio, which included a mock Globe. His troupe performed several condensed versions of Elizabethan plays.

Sam first visited England in 1949 to film *Give Us This Day*. While there, he went in search of William Shakespeare's original theater and discovered there was nothing left of the building. All he could find was a plaque on the wall of a brewer's bottling plant at the site believed to be where the Globe once stood. Shocking to an actor who loved the Bard!

Sam Wanamaker left America and moved to England in 1951. He became committed to creating a fitting memorial to William Shakespeare, and spent the rest of his life working to make this dream a reality. He launched a campaign to rebuild **Shakespeare's Globe Theatre**. In 1970 Wanamaker set up the Globe Playhouse Trust, and for the next twenty-three years he lobbied tirelessly to win support for his dream. He

LONDON Elizabeth Taylor's childhood home was at *8 Wildwood Road* in *Hampstead.*

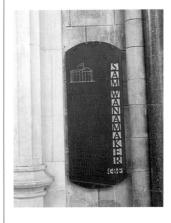

LONDON At *Southwark Cathedral* a memorial plaque to **Sam Wanamaker** has appropriately been placed next to William Shakespeare's memorial.

LONDON *Shakespeare's Globe Theatre:* reborn due to the determination of Sam Wanamaker.

The actress **Zoë Wanamaker** was born in New York in 1949 and moved to England when she was three years old. She attended the Central School of Speech and Drama but left in 1970, determined to avoid Shakespearian roles. Zoë established herself as a highly respected actress on stage, film, and TV. In December 2000 she was awarded an honorary CBE.

finally obtained permission to build on Bankside close to the site of the original Globe, and work began in 1987.

In July 1993 Sam Wanamaker was made a CBE in recognition of the "remarkable contribution he has made to relations between Britain and the US and, of course, for all he has done on behalf of the Shakespeare Globe project." Tragically, Wanamaker died on 18 December 1993, but thanks to his tireless determination, the Globe Theatre opened in 1997. On the opening night, his daughter Zoë was the first actor to speak on stage, delivering a short prologue honoring her father's work in being the main force behind the rebuilding of one of the world's most historic theaters.🌿

PERFORMERS
Buffalo Bill and the Wild West Show
On 14 April 1887 William Cody and his Wild West Show arrived in London. Three trains carried the animals and equipment to the **Earl's Court** exhibition site, and 28,000 people attended the opening show, the first at the new centre in west London.

Buffalo Bill's Wild West Show was a huge success: almost everyone in English society visited Earl's Court to see the show. Buffalo Bill even drew a smile from Queen Victoria. After she attended the show at Earl's Court, Victoria requested that he bring the show to Windsor Castle for a special performance, but Buffalo Bill said it was impossible. In November 1887 the tour moved on to Birmingham and then Manchester, where it also played to packed audiences.

Native Americans in Britain
The English interest in Native Americans did not end with Buffalo Bill's Wild West Show. Today, members of the Cherokee, Apache, and Dakota tribes often stage pow-wows at **Bush Farm Bison Centre** in **West Knoyle, Wiltshire**. The public is invited to enjoy the traditional ceremony of song and dance with Native American dancers, musicians, and costumes. The pow-wow is usually held for two days during the second week of July. The Bison Centre, created by Lord Colin Seaford, is home to other native North American animals such as buffalo, elk, red deer, turkey, chipmunks, and raccoons.

Inspired by such Native American groups as the Ironwood Singers, Porcupine Singers, and Badland Singers, a group of English singers formed the Centreland Singers, based in **Cheltenham, Gloucestershire**. They have regular practice sessions and sing at UK pow-wows. The Centreland Singers have also performed at events in Denmark and the United States. 🌿

LONDON American Sioux Indian chief, **Long Wolf**, was part of **Buffalo Bill**'s Wild West Show. He died of pneumonia in 1892 at the age of fifty-nine and was buried at the *Brompton Cemetery*. Elizabeth Knight, a Worcestershire housewife, learned of his story, traced his family and campaigned with them for the return of his body to his native land. In 1997 Long Wolf's body was moved to the Wolf Creek Community Cemetery at Pine Ridge, South Dakota.

LONDON The *British Library* has publications in Native American languages.

The *Horniman Museum* has a permanent exhibition on North American Indians.

DEVON The collection at the *Ashburton Museum* includes a number of North American Indian artifacts.

Chung Ling Soo (1861–1918)

"The Marvellous Chinese Conjurer" is one of the featured magicians in the **Magic Circle Museum** in **London**. Chung Ling Soo became widely popular in England in the early twentieth century. After his death this star of British magic was revealed to have been William Ellsworth Robinson, born in 1861 in New York. He died on stage at the Wood Green Empire on 23 March 1918 when something went wrong with his famous trick of catching bullets. The **Magic Circle Museum** has exhibitions about many world-famous magicians, including the American, Harry Houdini.

MUSICIANS

Larry Adler (1914–2001)

The world's most famous harmonica player was undoubtedly Larry Adler. Born in Baltimore, Maryland, in 1914, he left the US in 1949 after being accused of sympathizing with Communism. He lived in England for the rest of his life. Adler played at many London venues including the **Royal Albert Hall** in **London**. He was a friend of Hollywood greats such as **Charlie Chaplin** and collaborated with musicians such as George Gershwin, Ralph Vaughan Williams, and Sting.

Oscar Hammerstein (1895–1960)

In 1961 the Hammerstein Chanters were established at **Southwark Cathedral** after a donation was made by the American playwright and lyricist Oscar Hammerstein. A memorial plaque can be found in the Harvard Chapel.

Jimi Hendrix (1942–70)

The American guitarist and singer Jimi Hendrix came to England in 1966 at the height of his career. From 1968 to 1969 he lived in a flat on **Brook Street** in **London** in a building next door to the home of Frederick Handel (now the Handel Museum). On 18 September 1970 Jimi Hendrix was staying at the Samarkland Hotel in Lansdowne Crescent with his girlfriend. During the night he apparently choked as a result of alcohol and drugs and was unconscious when he was rushed by ambulance to St. Mary Abbots Hospital on Marloes Road (now named **Stone Hall** at **Kensington Green**). Jimi Hendrix was just twenty-seven when he died.

Blanche Roosevelt Macchetta (1853–98)

Born in Sandusky, Ohio, Blanche Roosevelt became the first American woman to sing opera at the Covent Garden Opera House. The daughter of Senator Tucker of Wisconsin, she traveled to Europe with her mother to study opera and singing in Paris and Milan. Using her stage name of Mme.

LONDON *Golders Green Crematorium* is the final resting place of **Larry Adler**.

LONDON A plaque at *Southwark Cathedral* commemorates Oscar Hammerstein's donation in 1961 establishing the Hammerstein Chanters.

LONDON Jimi Hendrix lived at *23 Brook Street* next door to Fredrick Handel's home.

St. Mary Abbot's Hospital was built in 1849 as the Kensington Workhouse. Now known as Stone Hall, it is the center of *Kensington Green*, an expensive residential complex.

LONDON Blanche Roosevelt Macchetta died in London in 1898 and was buried at *Brompton Cemetery*.

*Royal Opera House,
Convent Garden, London*

SURREY **Lord Menuhin** died on 12 March 1999. He was buried in *Stoke d'Abernon, Cobham,* in he grounds of the *Yehudi Menuhin School of Music* under a tree he had planted two years earlier.

Rosevilla, she made her operatic debut at the Royal Italian Opera Company in Covent Garden (now the **Royal Opera House, Covent Garden**) in 1876 as Violetta in *La Traviata.*

Blanche married a wealthy Italian aristocrat and became Madame Macchetta. "Discovered" by Arthur Sullivan, she was hired to appear in the original D'Oyle Carte production of *H.M.S. Pinafore.* Blanche was part of the touring company that took Gilbert and Sullivan operettas to New York. After retiring from the stage in March 1880, Blanche Roosevelt Macchetta, Marchesa d'Alligri, began a career in writing. She became a special correspondent, reporting from Paris for newspapers in Chicago and London. She published a collection of her newspaper dispatches and several books. 🌿

Yehudi Menuhin (1916–99)

Showing great musical talent at a very early age, Yehudi Menuhin began to play the violin when he was just four years old. Born in New York City to Russian Jewish parents, he made his debut with the San Francisco Symphony Orchestra at the age of seven. After studying in Europe, he had a successful world tour from 1934 to 1936.

During World War II he performed in hundreds of concerts for Allied soldiers, and in April 1945 he went with Benjamin Britten to perform for the inmates of the Bergen-Belsen concentration camp after its liberation. In 1962 he established the **Yehudi Menuhin School** in **Stoke d'Abernon, Cobham, Surrey**, and also established the music program at the Nueva School in Hillsborough, California. As a show of appreciation for his work, he was granted an honorary knighthood in 1965. In 1985 he became a British citizen and his honorary knighthood was upgraded to a full one. In 1993 he was created a life peer as Baron Menuhin. 🌿

André Previn (born 1929)

One of the world's leading conductors, André Previn has held chief artistic posts with many of the world's great orchestras. Born in Berlin, he began studying at the Berlin Conservatory of Music when he was six years old. His family immigrated to the United States in 1938 and he became a US citizen in 1943. In 1968 he moved to London where he spent eleven years as the principal conductor of the London Symphony Orchestra and as principal conductor of the Royal Philharmonic Orchestra. In 1996 Mr. Previn was awarded an honorary knighthood (KBE) by Queen Elizabeth II. 🌿

Paul Simon (born 1941)

The American singer-songwriter Paul Simon spent a lot of time in England during 1964 and 1965 after the release of his first album with Art Garfunkel, *Wednesday Morning 3am*, which flopped in the US. In England, his music was played on the radio and TV and he recorded an album called *The Paul Simon Songbook* in May 1965 at Levy's Studio in Bond Street, London. On the album cover was a photo of Kathleen Mary ("Kathy") Chitty, Paul's girlfriend in England. Looking back from the great success that Paul achieved, it is hard to picture the two of them at that time – Paul playing for the sidewalk crowds and Kathy collecting the money just before the police arrived. It should encourage people to stop and listen to buskers in the Underground!

Traveling around England, playing one-night stands at folk-clubs, Paul got to know English rock 'n' roll music, and the English folk tradition. A plaque at the train station in **Widnes, Cheshire**, now reminds people of the night in 1964 when Paul Simon sat in a lonely railway station waiting for a train and started writing a song that became a musical classic – *Homeward Bound*.

Paul returned to the US in 1965 after *The Sounds of Silence* began rising in the charts. He rejoined his childhood friend and music partner, Art Garfunkel, to form one of the most celebrated duos in popular music. His time in England is reflected is several of his songs. *Kathy's Song* is about the English girl who was so important during that time. *America*, written in 1968, reflects a cross-country holiday he and Kathy took in the US in 1965. Paul and Kathy broke up and he did not hear from her for over twenty-five years. She wrote to him in 1991 when he was touring England, and they got together for a private reunion. 🍃

LONDON For a while **Paul Simon** lived in a flat on Brompton Road in Knightsbridge. He was introduced to the London folk scene at the famous *Troubadour Club* on *Old Brompton Road* where Bob Dylan, Joni Mitchell and Jimi Hendrix all played in the 1960s.

CHESHIRE A plaque at the train station in *Widnes* memorializes Paul Simon's song *Homeward Bound*.

Leopold Stokowski (1882–1977)

Born in London in 1882 to a Polish cabinetmaker father and an Irish mother, Leopold Stokowski studied at the Royal College of Music in London, sang in the choir at St. Marylebone Church and was an assistant organist at the **Middle Temple**. In 1900 he formed the choir of St. Mary's Church, Charing Cross Road, and in 1902 was appointed organist and choir director of **St. James's Church, Piccadilly**. He also attended **Queen's College, Oxford**, where he earned a Bachelor of Music degree in 1903. Leopold Stokowski moved to America in 1905, becoming organist and choirmaster at St. Bartholomew's Church, New York City (1905–8). Deciding to start a career in orchestral conducting, he studied in Paris and then was appointed conductor of the Cincinnati Symphony. As conductor of the Philadelphia Orchestra (1912–36) he became one of the leading conductors in America. In 1940 he organized the All-American Youth Orchestra. Stokowski was musical supervisor of Walt

HAMPSHIRE Leopold Stokowski died in 1977 at *Nether Wallop*.

THE ROYAL ALBERT HALL, LONDON

The Royal Albert Hall on **Kensington Gore** has been the setting for many historic concerts given by American musicians:

Leonard Bernstein appeared at the Albert Hall several times, the first time in 1947. In 1970 he was a guest conductor of the London Symphony Orchestra, and in 1988 he organized and conducted a *Songfest* for his eightieth birthday.

Bob Dylan performed in the Hall on the last stop of his 1966 world tour.

In the late 1960s **Janis Joplin** and **Jimi Hendrix** had solo concerts, and **Ike and Tina Turner** appeared with the Rolling Stones. **Frank Zappa** and the Mothers of Invention had a concert there in June 1969.

In 1983 the **Everly Brothers** staged two reunion concerts at which they hugged and made up after ten years of not speaking to each other. **Fats Domino** played in the Hall in 1986. **B.B. King**, "The King of the Blues," **Stevie Wonder**, **Tina Turner**, and **James Brown** have all appeared there.

Paul Simon appeared with Ladysmith Black Mombazo in 1987.

James Taylor played in the Albert Hall in 1988.

Frank Sinatra appeared in the Albert Hall for two nights in 1975 during a world tour. He sang at the Hall several times over the next fifteen years, and in 1989 he performed with **Judy Garland** and **Sammy Davis, Jr.**, in what was called "The Ultimate Event". Judy Garland died soon after.

The Hall has been used for many other types of events:

In 1970, Evangelist **Billy Graham** took part in a program celebrating the 350th anniversary of the Pilgrim Fathers' voyage to the New World.

Alfred Hitchcock used the interior of the Royal Albert Hall twice in two versions of *The Man Who Knew Too Much*, in 1934 and 1956.

In 2002 **Henry Kissinger** spoke to the Institute of Directors, while outside hundreds of protestors demonstrated against globalization and US foreign policies.

Muhammad Ali fought an exhibition match in the Hall in 1971.

The Hall is often used for tennis. In 1978 Virginia Wade and Sue Barker beat **Chris Evert** and **Pam Shriver**. When John McEnroe played in the Hall, he said it was "the most beautiful setting for indoor tennis in the world."

Information courtesy of the Royal Albert Hall

Disney's film *Fantasia* (1940) in which he also made an appearance. In 1962 he founded the American Symphony Orchestra, New York City, a forum for young performers, and served as music director of the orchestra until he was eighty years old. After spending his professional life in America, Leopold Stokowski returned to England in 1972.

Mrs. Fanny Ronalds (1839–1916)

An American singer who was for many years the mistress of the composer Sir Arthur Sullivan, Mary Francis Carter was born in Boston in 1839. She moved to New York City where she met and married Mr. Ronalds, a socialite. In New York she became a close friend of the Jerome family. When **Jennie Jerome** and her two sisters were taken to Paris by their mother in 1867, Mrs. Ronalds traveled with them. After the fall of Napoleon III, she moved to London where she became well known for her musical entertainments. She often held Sunday afternoon musical "At Homes" in her little house in Cadogan Square, which became a gathering place for musicians including Sir Arthur Sullivan, the composing partner of the Gilbert and Sullivan musicals. She became a popular hostess and was a close friend of the Prince and Princess of Wales.

Mrs. Ronalds attended the 1897 **Devonshire House** Ball in an amazing costume – she was dressed as the Spirit of Music. Her dress was embroidered with musical notes and her headdress was a diamond-covered lyre that could be lit up by electricity from a tiny battery hidden in her hair. 🍃

A NOTORIOUS CRIMINAL
Hawley Harvey Crippen (1862–1910)

One of England's most infamous criminals in the early twentieth century was an American. The hunt for Dr. Crippen was an enormous media event followed by newspaper readers across England. Hawley Harvey Crippen was born in Coldwater, Michigan, in 1862. In 1897 he moved to England as a salesman for patented medicines. In 1910 he was convicted of murdering his wife. Crippen fled to Canada with his mistress Ethel LeNeve, but was apprehended after the captain of the ship telegraphed Scotland Yard of his suspicions about two passengers. His trial at the **Central Criminal Court** (better known as the **Old Bailey**) lasted five days. After being convicted, he was hanged at Pentonville Prison on 23 November 1910. 🍃

SPORTS

The Lawn Tennis Championships have taken place at Wimbledon since 1877. Nearly half a million people attend

Mike Leigh's excellent 1999 film *Topsy-Turvy* portrays the relationship between Arthur Sullivan and **Mrs. Ronalds.**

The *Devonshire House* Ball was one of the most fabulous balls held in the nineteenth century. (*See Chapter 7 for a description of the many American heiresses who attended.*) The house was demolished in 1926, and only the beatuful gates remain – at Green Park.

LONDON Gilbert and Sullivan operettas are still performed at the *Savoy Theatre* on the *Strand.*

Old Bailey, London

LONDON The police and neighbors were afraid that **Crippen's** house at 39 Hilldrop Crescent would attract crowds. Hoping to discourage morbid sightseers, they eventually changed the numbers of the houses on the street. The house was destroyed by German bombs during World War II.

The waxwork museum *Madame Tussauds* on *Marylebone Road* features a likeness of the infamous Dr. H.H. Crippen.

*All England Lawn
Tennis Club, Wimbledon, London*

British Baseball-Softball
www.baseballsoftballuk.com

British Basketball League
www.bbl.org.uk

British American Football League
www.gridironuk.co.uk

each year, enjoying the atmosphere that mixes festival and sport. Americans have been listed among the champions since 1905. The **Wimbledon Lawn Tennis Museum** at the All England Club Lawn Tennis Club features displays, memorabilia, and artwork connected with the game, and the tennis timeline includes many American achievements. The championship trophies, displayed prominently in large glass cases in the museum, have the names of American champions engraved along with all the other legendary tennis champions who have won the major Men's and Women's titles at Wimbledon. 🍃

THEME PARKS

The American Adventure Theme Park
Ilkeston, Derbyshire DE7 5SX
Telephone 01773 531521
www.americanadventure.co.uk

Spirit of the West – American Theme Park
Retallack Park – Winnard's Perch
Near St. Columb, Cornwall TR9 6DE
Telephone 01637 881160
sheriffjb@wildwestthemepark.co.uk

GAZETTEER

LONDON

1. OFFICIAL BUILDINGS
Government, Diplomatic and Royal Buildings, and Grand Houses
2. HEALTH, EDUCATION, AND WELFARE
Livery Guilds, Inns of Court, Schools, Orphanages, Hospitals,
Workhouses, and Prisons
3. SOCIALIZING, SHOPPING, AND TRADE
Pubs, Clubs, Taverns and Restaurants, Stores, Hotels, Commerce,
Wharfs, Docks, and a Ship
4. FUN AND GAMES
Theaters, Opera Houses, Museums, Sports, and an Exhibition Center
5. CHURCHES and CEMETERIES
6. THE GREAT OUTDOORS
Sculpture, Statues, and Monuments, Parks and Gardens
7. WHERE THEY LIVED AND WORKED
The Streets of London and Beyond

The extensive urban area that we call "London" is made up of numerous villages and
neighborhoods that developed as individual communities and were later absorbed into
metropolitan London. These names, such as Westminster, Kensington, and Islington, have been
used in the Gazetteer. This Gazetteer has also been extended to include locations within the M25
motorway that circles London. Several counties have been included, such as Middlesex and parts
of Surrey, Berkshire, and Essex. Windsor and Eton, which are just outside the M25, are also
included. This was to allow visitors to London to easily locate places within a short trip outside
of the official London municipal boundaries.

The postal codes given are to help in locating the sites on an internet or GPS mapping system.
They are not necessarily the mailing codes for businesses or museums which may use an off-site
mailing location. Some historical sites are now private property and other locations may be
closed to the public. All information is correct at the time of going to press, but should be
confirmed before a visit is planned.

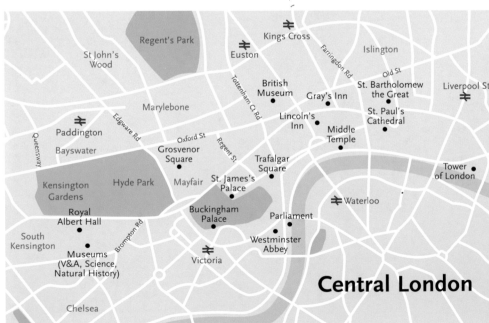

OFFICIAL BUILDINGS
Government, Diplomatic and Royal Buildings, and Grand Houses

Important events that directly affected the course of American history have taken place in the royal palaces and government buildings of London, and official visitors from America have been welcomed here.

Apsley House
Hyde Park Corner, Mayfair W1J 7NT
Tel. 020 7499 5676
www.english-heritage.org.uk
  Arthur Wellesley,
    Duke of Wellington
  Edward Pakenham
  Stephen Sayre

Banqueting House
Whitehall, Westminster SW1A 2ER
Information line: 0870 751 5178
www.hrp.org.uk
  Pocahontas
  John Rolfe
  The regicides Edward Whalley
    and William Goffe

Buckingham Palace
The Mall SW1A 1AA
Information line: 020 7766 7300
www.royal.gov.uk/output/page555.asp
  Queen Victoria
  Queen Elizabeth II
  Queen Liliuokalani of Hawaii
  Harriet, Duchess of Sutherland
  Elizabeth Taylor Greenfield
  Americans who have received
    official honors

Cabinet War Rooms
Clive Steps, King Charles Street
Westminster SW1A 2AQ
www.iwm.org.uk/cabinet
  Winston Churchill
  President Roosevelt

Chelsea Register Office
Old Town Hall, King's Road
Chelsea SW3 5EE
  Bessie Wallis Warfield
  Judy Garland

Chiswick House
Burlington Lane, Chiswick W4 2RP
Tel. 020 8995 0508
www.english-heritage.org.uk
  Thomas Jefferson

College of Arms
Queen Victoria Street, City of London
EC4V 4BT
Tel. 020 7248 2762

www.college-of-arms.gov.uk
  William Strickland
  Walter Raleigh

Devonshire House
78 Piccadilly, Mayfair W1J 8AQ
  John Berkeley
  Devonshire House Ball
  Consuelo Vanderbilt
  May Goelet

Downing Street, 10
Whitehall, Westminster SW1A 2AA
  Sir George Downing
  John Winthrop
  George Washington

**Foreign and
Commonwealth Office**
King Charles Street
Westminster SW1A 2AH
www.fco.gov.uk
  Statue of Charles Cornwallis
  Various symbols of America; the
    "Stars and Stripes" can be
    found inside and outside the
    building.

Greenwich Visitors' Centre
2 Cutty Sark Gardens
Greenwich SE10 9LW
  Sir Walter Raleigh

Hampton Court Palace
East Molesey, Surrey KT8 9AU
Tel. 0870 752 7777
www.hrp.org.uk/hampton
  King Charles I
  Edward Whalley

Houses of Parliament (see Palace of Westminster)

House of Commons/House of Lords (see Palace of Westminster)

Holland House
Holland Park, Kensington W8 7QU
  William Penn

Kensington Palace
Kensington Gardens
Kensington W8 4PX

Information line: 0870 751 5170
www.royal.gov.uk/output/page563.asp
and
www.hrp.org.uk/webcode/content.asp?
ID=35
  James Oglethorpe
  Chief Tomochichi
  King William III
  College of William and Mary in
    Williamsburg, Virginia

Lancaster House (previously called
"Stafford House")
Green Park SW1A 1BB
  Harriet, Duchess of Sutherland
  Harriet Beecher Stowe
  Elizabeth Taylor Greenfield
  Mrs. Mary E. Webb
  Booker T. Washington

Lansdowne House
9 Fitzmaurice Place, Mayfair W1J 5JD
Tel. 020 7629 7200
www.lansdowneclub.com
  Lord Shelburne
  Treaty of Paris (1783)
  Benjamin Franklin
  Joseph Priestley
  William Waldorf Astor
  Gordon Selfridge

Mansion House
(Official residence of the Lord Mayor
of London)
Victoria Street
City of London EC4N 8BH
www.cityoflondon.gov.uk
  Thomas "Customer" Symthe
  Captain John Martin at
    Jamestown
  Sir Richard Saltonstall,
    a long-time supporter of
    Captain John Smith
  John Wilkes

Old Treasury Building
70 Whitehall, Westminster SW1A 2AU
  Benjamin Franklin
  "The Cock Pit"

Palace of Westminster
Parliament Square
Westminster SW1A 0AA

Tel. 020 7219 3000
www.parliament.uk/works/palace.cfm#
pahistor
  A copy of the death warrant of
    King Charles I signed by the
    regicides Edward Whalley and
    Thomas Goffe
  John Hampden – statue in
    Central Lobby of House of
    Commons
  John Wilkes
  Isaac Barré
  "The Thatched House
    Tavern Petition"

**In the Tudor Room of the House of Lords,
the dark carved wood frieze shows:**
  Sir Walter Raleigh putting down
    his cloak for Queen Elizabeth I to
    walk across
  Queen Elizabeth I knighting
    Sir Francis Drake
  Sebastian Cabot before Henry VIII

**In the House of Lords Corridor, a large
mural shows :**
  "The Embarkation of the Pilgrims
    for New England"; Pilgrims are
    boarding the *Mayflower* ship.

**In the Strangers' Gallery, a large
mural shows:**
  "Queen Elizabeth the Fairie Queen
    with her knights and merchant
    venturers commissions Sir Walter
    Raleigh to sail for America to
    discover a new country. 1584."

Prince's Gate, 14
Kensington Road
Knightsbridge SW7 1PU
  Junius Spencer Morgan
  George Peabody
  American ambassador's
    residence 1912–55
  Charles Gates Dawes
  Andrew Mellon
  Robert Worth Bingham
  Joseph Patrick Kennedy
  John Winant

Old Admiralty Building
Whitehall, Westminster SW1A 2PA
  Winston Churchill
  Raymond Chandler

Richmond Palace
Old Palace Yard, Richmond
Surrey TW9 1PB
The old palace gatehouse, with Henry

VII's coat of arms, and parts of the
wardrobe are all that is left of the
Tudor palace. Visitors can walk
through the gatehouse and down to
the river, but the buildings that remain
are private residences.
  Thomas Dale

Royal Geographical Society
1 Kensington Gore
Kensington SW7 2AR
Tel. 020 7591 3000
www.rgs.org
  Henry Morton Stanley
  Maps of the exploration of North
    America and maps of the early
    North American colonies
  Military maps of the American
    Revolutionary War

Royal Hospital Chelsea
Royal Hospital Road
Chelsea SW3 4SR
Tel. 020 7881 5204
www.chelsea-pensioners.co.uk
  War of 1812

Royal Society
6–9 Carlton House Terrace
St. James's SW1Y 5AG
Tel. 020 7451 2500
www.royalsoc.ac.uk
  George Berkeley
  George Monck
  Anthony Ashley Cooper, Lord
    Shaftesbury
  Edward Hyde, Earl of Clarendon
  William Penn
  John Winthrop
  Alexander Dalles Bache
    (Benjamin Franklin's great
    grandson)
  Cotton Mather (judge at the
    Salem witch trials)
  Joseph Priestley
  William Byrd
  J.R. Oppenheimer
  Elihu Yale
  Benjamin Franklin – a portrait by
    Joseph Wright of Derby

Royal Society for the Arts
8 John Adam Street
Charing Cross WC2N 6EZ
Tel. 020 7930 5115
www.rsa.org.uk
  Benjamin Franklin Medal
  Benjamin Franklin Room

George Washington Carver
  became a fellow of the society
  in 1916.
Walter Annenberg

St. James's Palace
St. James's Street and
Pall Mall SW1A 1BS
www.royal.gov.uk/output/page562.asp
  King George III
  Peter Schuyler
  Five Mohawk Indian chiefs
  Queen Anne

Spencer House
27 St. James's Place
St. James's SW1A 1NR
Tel. 020 7499 8620
www.spencerhouse.co.uk
  Consuelo Vanderbilt
  May Goelet
  Benjamin West

Stafford House *(see Lancaster
House)*

Sunderland House *(now "Lombard
House")*
38 Curzon Street, Mayfair W1J 7US
  Consuelo Vanderbilt

Syon Park
Brentford, Middlesex TW8 8JF
Tel. 020 8560 0881
www.syonpark.co.uk
  George Percy at Jamestown
    Colony
  Hugh Percy at Battle of
    Lexington and Concord
  James Smithson – the
    Smithsonian Institution
  Portrait of Algernon Sidney
  Portrait of George Washington by
    Gilbert Stuart
  Portrait of Chief Joseph Brandt
    by Gilbert Stuart
  Portrait of Teyoninhokarawen,
    known as Major John Norton

Temple Place
2 Temple Place
Victoria Embankment WC2R 3BD
Tel. 020 7836 3715
www.twotempleplace.co.uk
  William Waldorf Astor

Texas Legation
3 St. James's Street
St. James's SW1A 1EG
above Berry Brothers Wine Merchants
    Texas independence

Tower of London
Tower Hill EC3N 4AB
Information line:
0113 220 1999
Tel. 020 7480 6358
www.hrp.org.uk
www.tower-of-london.com/prisoners
    Bishop Edwin Sandys
    Sir Walter Raleigh
    Thomas Wyatt
    William Disney
    John, Lord Berkeley
    William Penn
    Sir Henry Vane the Younger
    Algernon Sidney
    Robert Devereux
    Sir Thomas Smythe
    Henry Wriothesley
    Henry Laurens
    Stephen Sayre
    John Horne Tooke

Windsor, Berkshire
Windsor Castle
SL4 1NJ
Tel. 01753 831118
www.windsor.gov.uk
    Edward-Maria Wingfield
    American guests
    Josiah Henson
    Booker T. Washington and
        Susan B. Anthony

St. George's Chapel
Windsor Castle SL4 1NJ
Tel. 01753 848888
www.stgeorges-windsor.org
    Paul Mellon

Frogmore Mausoleum
Windsor Great Park SL4 2JG
www.thamesweb.co.uk/windsor/frogm
ore/frogmore.html
    Wallis Warfield Simpson,
        Duchess of Windsor

Windsor Great Park
    statue of King George III

Cranbourne Lodge
Drift Road, Winkfield
Windsor Great Park SL4 4RP
Only the Tower remains – it is visible
from northwest of the A332 between
Windsor and Bracknell.
    George Carteret

US Embassy in London
24 Grosvenor Square
Mayfair W1K 2BY
Tel. 020 7499 9000
www.usembassy.org.uk
    John Adams
    James Monroe
    John Quincy Adams
    Martin Van Buren
    Charles Francis Adams
    Eero Saarinen

Winfield House
Outer Circle, Regent's Park NW1 4RT
American ambassador's residence
    Barbara Hutton
    Frank Winfield Woolworth
    Cary Grant

HEALTH, EDUCATION, AND WELFARE
Livery Guilds, Inns of Court, Schools, Orphanages, Hospitals, Workhouses, and Prisons

**Bethlem Royal Hospital for the
Insane**
The building now houses the Imperial
War Museum (*see below*).
Lambeth Road, Lambeth SE1 6HZ
    Charlie Chaplin

Bridewell Hospital
New Bridge Street
off Fleet Street EC4V 6AN
    A plaque marks the location of
    the hospital established by King
    Edward VI in 1553.
    More family children on the
    Mayflower

Charterhouse
Sutton's Hospital at Charterhouse
Square, Clerkenwell EC1M 6BQ
Tel. 020 7253 9503

Charterhouse School
Godalming, Surrey GU7 2DX
www.charterhouse.org.uk/Other/charte
rhouse_history.asp
    Sir Edwin Sandys

    Roger Williams
    John Wesley

Chigwell School
High Road, Chigwell, Essex IG7 6QF
Tel. 020 8501 5700
www.chigwell-school.org
    William Penn

Clink Prison Museum
1 Clink Street, Southwark SE1 9DG
Tel. 020 7378 1558
www.clink.co.uk
    Robert "Troublechurch" Browne
    Ancient Church of Southwark
    Archbishop William Laud

Clothworkers' Company
Worshipful Company of Clothworkers
Dunster Court, Mincing Lane
City of London EC3R 7AH
www.clothworkers.co.uk
    John Winthrop

Conway Hall
25 Red Lion Square

Holborn WC1R 4RL
Tel. 020 7242 8032
www.conwayhall.org.uk and
www.ethicalsoc.org.uk
    Moncure Conway
    Anti-slavery movement
    Thomas Paine

Cordwainers' Company
Worshipful Company of Cordwainers
Clothworkers' Hall, Dunster Court
Mincing Lane
City of London EC3R 7AH
www.cordwainers.org
    Captain John Smith
    T.S. Eliot

Drapers' Company
Drapers' Hall, Throgmorton Avenue
City of London EC2N 2DQ
Tel. 020 7588 5001
www.thedrapers.co.uk
    George Monck, Duke of
        Albemarle

Dulwich College
College Road, Dulwich SE21 7LD
Tel. 020 8299 9263
www.dulwich.org.uk
  Raymond Chandler

Eton College
Eton, Berkshire SL4 6DW
Tel. 01753 671000
www.etoncollege.com
*Tours of the college grounds and
buildings are available on request*
  Humphrey Gilbert
  Hugh Percy
  John Horne Tooke
  James Oglethorpe
  Arthur Lee
  Thomas Lynch, signatory of the
    American Declaration of
    Independence
  Thomas Nelson, signatory of the
    American Declaration of
    Independence
  Charles Cornwallis, 1st Marquess
  John Jacob Astor of Hever,
    1st Baron
  Waldorf Astor, 2nd Viscount

Foundling Hospital
40 Brunswick Square
St. Pancras WC1N 1AZ
Tel. 020 7841 3600
www.foundlingmuseum.org.uk
  Thomas Coram

Framework Knitters' Company
(no London address)
www.frameworkknitters.co.uk
  Arthur Lee
  Stephen Sayre

  FREEDOM OF THE CITY OF LONDON
  George Peabody
  General Dwight Eisenhower
  Theodore Roosevelt
  Henry Morton Stanley – granted
    after his British citizenship was
    reinstated

Furnival's Inn
No longer a functioning Inn of Court,
it was on the site where the Prudential
Building stands today.
High Holborn, Holborn WC1V 6DA
  Edward-Maria Wingfield

Gray's Inn
Gray's Inn Square, Holborn

WC1R 5AH
  William Cecil (later Lord Burleigh)
  Francis Walsingham
  Thomas Wriothesley, 4th Earl of
    Southampton
  Sir Thomas Gresham
  Sir Winston Churchill
  Franklin Roosevelt
  Nathaniel Bacon

**Hanwell School for Orphans and
Destitute Children** (now Hanwell
Community Centre)
Westcott Crescent, Hanwell W7 1PD
Tel. 020 8578 2586
www.hanwellcommunitycentre.com
  Charlie Chaplin

Inner Temple
The Temple
Victoria Embankment, EC4Y 7HL
www.innertemple.org.uk
  Sir Richard Grenville, admitted in
    1559
  William Paca of Maryland,
    signatory of the Declaration of
    Independence

Ironmongers' Hall
Shaftesbury Place, Barbican EC2Y 8AA
www.ironhall.co.uk
  Thomas Weston

**King's Bench Prison and St.
George's Fields**
Southwark SE1 6BT
In the sixteenth century the prison was
located on Borough High Street in
Southwark. In 1755–8 it was moved to
a new location in St. George's Fields,
the southwest corner of Blackman
Street, on the road to the Obelisk, St
George's Circus. Blackman Street was
in the location of the present-day
Newington Causeway, across the street
from SE1 6BT. Today the Imperial War
Museum, surrounded by the Geraldine
Mary Harmsworth Park, is on land that
previously was part of "St. George's
Fields"
  John Wilkes
  John Horne Tooke
  Nathaniel Eaton

Lanesborough Hotel
Hyde Park Corner, SW1X 7TA
Tel. 020 7259 5599
www.starwoodhotels.com

*Site of St. George's Chapel in the
eighteenth century*
  John Wilkes Booth

Lambeth Workhouse
Renfrew Road, Lambeth SE11 4TH
  Charlie Chaplin

Lincoln's Inn
Lincoln's Inn Fields
Holborn WC2A 3TL
  Edward-Maria Wingfield
  William Penn
  Arthur Lee
  President Eisenhower
  Dean Acheson

Marshalsea Prison, Southwark
All that remains of the notorious
prison is a bit of wall containing the
entrance arch and a plaque.
St. George's Church, Borough High
Street, Southwark SE1 1JA
www.hiddenlondon.com/marshalsea.
htm
  Francis Barrington

Middle Temple
Middle Temple Lane, Victoria
Embankment EC4Y 9AT
www.middletemple.org.uk
  Sir Francis Drake
  Walter Raleigh
  Humphrey Gilbert
  Richard Hakluyt
  Sir Edwin Sandys
  Bartholomew Gosnold
  Henry Wriothesley, 3rd Earl of
    Southampton
  Robert Devereux, Earl of Essex
  William Penn
  Richard Grenville
  John Culpeper, later of Feckenham
  George Percy
  Sir William Berkeley
  John Winthrop
  Arthur Lee
*Signatories of the American Declaration
of Independence:*
  Edward Rutledge
  Thomas Heyward, Jr,
  Thomas Lynch, Jr.
  Arthur Middleton
  Thomas M. Kean
  American Law Library

Newgate Prison
Demolished in 1902, the Central

Criminal Court (Old Bailey) was built on the site.
William Penn
William Cobbett

Old Bailey
Central Criminal Court
Newgate Street and Old Bailey
City of London EC4M 7EH
Tel. 020 7248 3277
www.hmcourts-service.gov.uk
William Penn
Dr. H. H. Crippen

Paul Mellon Centre for Studies in British Art
16 Bedford Square
Bloomsbury WC1B 3JA

Tel. 020 7580 0311
www.paul-mellon-centre.ac.uk
Paul Mellon

Princess Grace Hospital
42–52 Nottingham Place
Marylebone W1U 5NY
www.theprincessgracehospital.com
Grace Kelly

Manor School
172 Stoke Newington Church Street,
Stoke Newington N16 0JL
Edgar Allan Poe

Mill Hill School
The Ridgeway, Mill Hill Village
NW7 1QS

Tel. 020 8959 1221
www.millhill.org.uk
Benjamin Franklin

Westminster School
Little Dean's Yard, Westminster
SW1P 3PF
Tel. 020 7963 1000
www.westminster.org.uk
Richard Hakluyt
Charles Chauncy
Arthur Middleton
Charles Wesley
Thomas Gage
General Burgoyne
Charles Cotesworth Pinckney
Thomas Pinckney
Francis Lewis of New York

SOCIALIZING, SHOPPING, AND TRADE

Pubs, Clubs, Taverns and Restaurants, Stores, Hotels, Commerce, Wharfs, Docks, and a Ship

The Angel
3–5 Islington High Street
Islington N1 9LQ
Tel. 020 7837 2218
Thomas Paine

Billingsgate Market
Old Billingsgate Market
1 Old Billingsgate Walk
City of London EC3R 6DX
Tel. 020 7626 4280
www.oldbillingsgate.info/history.htm
Thomas "Customer" Smythe

Butler's Wharf
Shad Thames by Tower Bridge SE1 2YE
Thomas "Customer" Smythe

Brooks's Club
60 St. James's Street, St. James's
SW1A 1LN
John Wilkes
Isaac Barré
General Burgoyne
General Cornwallis

Brown's Hotel
Albemarle Street, Piccadilly W1S 4BP
Tel. 020 7493 6020
www.brownshotel.com
Edward Hyde, Earl of Clarendon
Alexander Graham Bell
Niagara Commission – June 1890
Theodore Roosevelt
Consuelo Vanderbilt
Franklin and Eleanor Roosevelt

Bush House (Home of BBC
World Service)
Aldwych, Strand WC2B 4PA
American architects Hemle and
Corbett

**Cadogan Hotel – Langtry's
Restaurant**
75 Sloane Street
Knightsbridge SW1X 9SG
Tel. 0207 235 7141
www.cadogan.com
Lillie Langtry

Canary Wharf
Columbus Screen at Columbus Courtyard
E14 4DA
by Wendy Ramshaw
One Canada Square E14 5AB
25 Canada Square (Citigroup Building)
E14 5LB
25 Bank Street E14 5LE
Docklands Light Railway Station Canada
Square
30 and 40 Bank Street
Heron Quay E14 5DS
East and West Winter Gardens
Heron Quay E14 5AB
all designed by Cesar Pelli and
Associates

Cavendish Hotel
Jermyn Street, St. James's SW1Y 6JF
www.devereonline.co.uk
Edith Wharton

Claridge's Hotel
Brook Street, Mayfair W1K 4HR
Tel. 020 7108 8830
www.claridgeshotellondon.com
Jennie Jerome

Chelsea Arts Club
143 Old Church Street
Chelsea SW3 6EB
www.chelseaartsclub.com
James Abbot McNeill Whistler

Christie's Auction House
8 King Street, St. James's
London SW1Y 6QT
Tel. 020 7839 9060
www.christies.com
Thomas Jefferson

Churchill Arms
Kensington Church Street
Kensington W8 7LN
Tel. 020 7727 4242
Portrait gallery of American
presidents

Devereux Hotel and Restaurant
Devereux Court, Fleet Street WC2R 3JJ
Tel. 020 7583 4562
Robert Devereux, Earl of Essex

Middle Temple
Treasury Office, Middle Temple Lane
London EC4Y 9AT
Tel. 020 7427 4800
www.middletemple.org.uk

Sir Thomas Smythe
Henry Wriothesley
Edward-Maria Wingfield
Edwin Sandys
Ferdinando Gorges

Dorchester Hotel
Park Lane, Mayfair W1K 1QA
Tel. 020 7629 8888
www.dorchesterhotel.com
General Dwight Eisenhower

Duke of Albemarle Pub
6 Stafford Street, Mayfair W1S 4RS
Tel. 020 7355 0321
George Monck, 1st Duke of
Albemarle

Earl's Court Exhibition Centre
Warwick Road, Earl's Court SW5 9TA
Tel. 020 7385 1200
www.eco.co.uk
Buffalo Bill and the
Wild West Show
Chief Long Wolf

East India Arms
67 Fenchurch Street, City of London
EC3M 4BR
Tel. 020 7265 5121
East India Company

East India Club
16 St. James's Square, St. James's
SW1Y 4LH
Tel. 020 7930 1000
www.eastindiaclub.com

East India Company
East India House
109–17 Middlesex Street,
Broadgate E1 7JF

Freemasons' Hall
60 Great Queen Street
Holborn WC2B 5AZ
Tel. 020 7831 9811
www.grandlodge-england.org
George Washington
Chief Joseph Brandt
Benjamin Franklin
Theodore Roosevelt
The World Anti-Slavery
Convention of 1840
Elizabeth Cady Stanton
Lucretia Mott
Ernestine Rose

George and Vulture
3 Castle Court, City of London
EC3V 9DL
Tel. 020 7626 9710
Hell-Fire Club
John Wilkes
Benjamin Franklin

Golden Hinde
Horseshoe Wharf, 6A Clink Street
Southwark SE1 9FE
Tel. 020 7403 0123
www.goldenhinde.co.uk
Sir Francis Drake

Gore Hotel
190 Queen's Gate
Kensington SW7 5EX
Tel. 020 7584 6601
www.gorehotel.co.uk
Judy Garland

Hamilton House Hotel
14 West Grove, Greenwich SE10 8QT
Tel. 020 8694 9899
www.hamiltonhousehotel.co.uk
Boston Tea Party

La Belle Sauvage (demolished
in 1873)
Ludgate Hill, City of London
EC4 M7LQ
Pocahontas
Thomas Wyatt

Langhams Hotel
1c Portland Place, Regent Street
W1B 1JA
Tel. 020 7636 1000
www.langhamhotels.com
Henry Wadsworth Longfellow

Lloyd's of London
Leadenhall Street, City of London
EC3M 7DX
Sir William Craven
East India Company

Mayflower Pub
17 Rotherhithe Street
Rotherhithe SE16 4NF
Tel. 020 7237 4088
Mayflower
Christopher Jones

Pakenham Arms
1 Pakenham Street, St. Pancras
WC1X 0LA

Tel. 020 7837 6933
Duke of Wellington
Battle of New Orleans
Andrew Jackson

The Pennsylvanian
115–17 High Street, Rickmansworth
Hertfordshire WD3 1AN
Tel. 01923 720348
William Penn

Old Red Lion (theater)
418 St John Street, City of London
EC1V 4NJ
Tel. 020 7837 7816
www.oldredliontheatre.co.uk
Thomas Paine

Rules of Covent Garden
Rules Restaurant, 35 Maiden Lane
Covent Garden WC2E 7LB
Tel. 020 7836 5314
www.rules.co.uk
Lillie Langtry
King Edward VII Room

St. Katherine's Dock
St. Katherine's-by-the-Tower E1W 1AT
Henry Hudson

Selfridges
400 Oxford Street, W1C 1JS
Tel. 08708 377 377
www.selfridges.com
Harry Gordon Selfridge
Cabinet War Rooms

Texas Embassy Restaurant
1 Cockspur Street, Trafalgar Square
SW1Y 5DL
Tel. 020 7925 0077
www.texasembassy.com
Texas Legation
Cunard Line – *Titanic*

Thatched House Tavern
(demolished in 1843)
69 St. James's Street, St. James's
SW1A 1PH
The Carlton Club is now located on
this site.
Boston Tea Party
Benjamin Franklin
Stephen Sayre
William Lee
Arthur Lee
Henry Laurens

Troubadour
263–7 Old Brompton Road
Earl's Court SW5 9JA
Tel. 020 7370 1434
www.troubadour.co.uk
    Paul Simon
    Jimi Hendrix
    Bob Dylan

Whitechapel Foundry
32–34 Whitechapel Road
Whitechapel E1 1DY
Tel. 020 7247 2599
www.whitechapelbellfoundry.co.uk
    The Liberty Bell

Windsor Castle Pub
114 Campden Hill Road
Kensington W8 7AR
Tel. 020 7243 9551
www.windsor-castle-pub.co.uk
    Thomas Paine

FUN AND GAMES
Theaters, Museums, Sports, and an Exhibition Center

Bank of England Museum
Threadneedle Street, City of London
EC2R 8AH
Tel. 020 7601 5545 (recorded message)
Tel. 020 7601 5491
www.bankofengland.co.uk
    George and Martha Washington
    Samuel Chase

Benjamin Franklin House Museum
36 Craven Street, Charing Cross
WC2N 5NG
Tel. 0207 839 2006
www.benjaminfranklinhouse.org
    Benjamin Franklin

Bob Hope Theatre
Wythfield Road, Eltham SE9 5TG
Box Office: 020 8850 3702
www.bobhopetheatre.co.uk
    Bob Hope

British Library
96 Euston Road, St. Pancras NW1 2DB
Tel. 020 7412 7000
www.bl.uk
The Early Printed Collections include an extensive collection of books published in America before 1776; the collection of American books printed after 1776 is one of the largest outside of the US; the King George III Topographical Collection is perhaps the finest geographical collection in the world for eighteenth-century America; and the Ansel Adams Collection focuses on American fine press material. The Library also keeps some publications in native North American languages.

British Museum
Great Russell Street, Bloomsbury
WC1B 3DG
Tel. 020 7580 1788

www.thebritishmuseum.ac.uk
    Thomas Wriothesley, 4th Earl of
        Southampton
    John White of the Roanoke
        expedition
    The Annenberg Center at the
        British Museum Reading Room
    JP Morgan Chase Gallery of
        North America showing Native
        American jewelry of the
        southwest USA

Coliseum Theatre
English National Opera, London
Coliseum, St. Martin's Lane
Trafalgar Square WC2N 4ES
www.eno.org
Many of the greatest Broadway shows opened in London at the Coliseum, such as *Annie Get Your Gun* (1947), *Kiss Me Kate* (1951), *Guys and Dolls* (1953), *Can Can* (1955), *The Pajama Game* (1955), and *Damn Yankees* (1957). In 1974 the Coliseum was renamed the English National Opera.

Clink Prison Museum
1 Clink Street, Southwark SE1 9DG
Tel. 020 7378 1558
www.clink.co.uk
    Robert "Troublechurch" Browne
    Ancient Church of Southwark
    Archbishop William Laud

Courtauld Institute of Art
Somerset House, Strand WC2R 1LA
Tel. 020 7848 2526
www.courtauld.ac.uk
    American artists

Dennis Severs' House
18 Folgate Street, Spitalfields E1 6BX
Tel. 020 7247 4013
www.dennissevershouse.co.uk
    Dennis Severs

Dominion Theatre
Tottenham Court Road and New
Oxford Street W1T 7AQ
www.dominiontheatre.co.uk
    Judy Garland

Foundling Museum
40 Brunswick Square
Bloomsbury WC1N 1AZ
Tel. 020 7841 3600
www.foundlingmuseum.org.uk
    Thomas Coram

Gainsborough Studios
1 Poole Street, London N1 5EB
    Alfred Hitchcock

Genesis Cinema
Mile End Genesis Cinema
93–95 Mile End Road, Stepney E1 4UJ
Tel. 020 7780 2000
    Charlie Chaplin

Globe Theatre
Shakespeare's Globe, 21 New Globe
Walk, Bankside, Southwark SE1 9DT
Tel. 020 7902 1400
www.shakespeares-globe.org
    Pocahontas
    Robert Devereux, Earl of Essex
    Sam Wanamaker

Guildhall Art Gallery and Roman London's Amphitheatre
Guildhall Yard EC2P 2EJ
Tel. 020 7332 3700
www.cityoflondon.gov.uk
    John Singleton Copley

Horniman Museum and Gardens
100 London Road, Forest Hill
SE23 3PQ
Tel. 020 8699 1872
www.horniman.ac.uk
    North American Indians

Imperial War Museum London
Lambeth Road, Lambeth SE1 6HZ
Tel. 020 7416 5320
www.iwm.org.uk
The Imperial War Museum has artifacts, paintings, posters, drawings and sculpture, sound and cinema records that focus on all aspects of twentieth- and twenty-first century conflict involving Britain and the Commonwealth. It is also a major national art gallery, a national records archive, and a research center. The museum is housed in the buildings that were originally the Bethlem Royal Hospital for the Insane (*see above*).

London Palladium
Argyll Street, Oxford Circus W1F 7TF
Box Office: 020 7656 1800
www.london-palladium.co.uk
After the Second World War many American stars made their London debuts at the Palladium.
    Bob Hope
    Judy Garland

Magic Circle Museum
10 Stephenson Way, Euston NW1 2HD
Tel. 020 7388 6480
www.themagiccircle.co.uk
    Chung Ling Soo
    Harry Houdini

Madame Tussauds
Marylebone Road, Marylebone NW1 5LR
Tel. 020 7935 6861
www.madame-tussauds.co.uk
    Presidents of the USA
    Dr. H.H. Crippen

Museum in Docklands
No. 1 Warehouse, West India Quay
Hertsmere Road, Poplar E14 4AL
Tel. 0870 444 3857
Recorded Information line:
0870 444 3856
www.museumindocklands.org.uk/English/
    East India Company, Muscovy Company
    1588 – Queen Elizabeth's "Legal Quays"
    Thomas "Customer" Smythe
    Pocahontas
    Slave trade
    William Wilberforce – 1807 slave transport outlawed

Museum of London
150 London Wall, London EC2Y 5HN
Tel. 0870 444 3852
www.museumoflondon.org.uk
    John Wesley and history of early Methodism

National Army Museum
Royal Hospital Road
Chelsea, SW3 4HT
Tel. 020 7730 0717
www.national-army-museum.ac.uk
    American Revolution
    Battle of Yorktown
    General Cornwallis
    Battle of Lexington and Concord

National Gallery
St. Martin's Place, Trafalgar Square
WC2N 5DN
Tel. 020 7747 2885
www.nationalgallery.org.uk
    T.S. Eliot
    Winston Churchill
    J. Paul Getty, Jr.
    John Trumbull
    Sir Joshua Reynolds's portrait of Banaster Tarleton
    Sir Joshua Reynolds's portrait of Robert Orme
    Andrew Jackson

Sainsbury Wing at the National Gallery
    Robert Venturi

National Maritime Museum
Park Row, Greenwich SE10 9NF
Tel. 020 8858 4422
Recorded information line:
020 8312 6565
www.nmm.ac.uk
    Captain James Cook
    Mather Brown

Natural History Museum
Cromwell Road, South Kensington
SW7 5BD
Tel. 020 7938 9123
www.nhm.ac.uk
    Andrew Carnegie

National Portrait Gallery
St. Martin's Place, Trafalgar Square
WC2H 0HE
Tel. 020 7306 0055
www.npg.org.uk
The collection contains a large number of portraits both by American artists and of American sitters.

Old Vic Theatre
The Cut, Waterloo SE1 8NB
Box Office: 020 7928 7616
www.oldvictheatre.com
    Kevin Spacey

Royal Academy of Arts
Burlington House, Piccadilly W1J 0BD
Tel. 020 7300 8000
www.royalacademy.org.uk
    Benjamin West
    John Singleton Copley
    Annenberg Courtyard
    American artists

Royal Albert Hall
Kensington Gore, Kensington
SW7 2AP
Tel. 020 7589 8212
www.royalalberthall.com
    Henry Morton Stanley
    Paul Robeson
    Albert Hitchcock
    John McEnroe
    Billy Graham
    Henry Kissinger
    Frank Sinatra
    Judy Garland
    Mohammad Ali
    Paul Simon
    Tina Turner
    Stevie Wonder

Royal Opera House
Bow Street, Covent Garden
WC2E 9DD
Tel. 020 7304 4000
www.royalopera.org
    Blanche Roosevelt Macchetta

Savoy Theatre
Savoy Court, Strand WC2R 0ET
Box Office: 0870 164 8787
www.savoytheatre.co.uk
    Blanche Roosevelt Macchetta
    Paul Robeson

Science Museum
Exhibition Road, South Kensington
SW7 2DD
Tel. 020 7942 4455/4454
www.nmsi.ac.uk
    Hiram Stephens Maxim
    Thomas Edison

Samuel Cody
Birt Acres

Sir John Soane Museum
13 Lincoln's Inn Field
Holborn WC2A 3BP
Tel. 020 7405 2107
www.soane.org
Benjamin Latrobe

Tate Britain
Millbank, Pimlico SW1P 4RG
Tel. 020 7887 8000
www.tate.org.uk/britain
John Singleton Copley – *Death of Major Pierson*
Benjamin West
James Abbott McNeill Whistler

John Singer Sargent

Tate Modern
Bankside, Southwark SE1 9TG
Tel. 020 7887 8000
www.tate.org.uk/modern
American artists

Theatre Museum
1e Tavistock Street, Covent Garden
WC2E 7PR
Tel. 020 7943 4700
www.theatremuseum.org
Paul Robeson

Victoria and Albert Museum
Cromwell Road, South Kensington
SW7 2RL

Tel. 020 7942 2000
www.vam.ac.uk
Frank Lloyd Wright Gallery
Norfolk Room – King George III

Vinopolis
1 Bank End, Southwark SE1 9BU
Tel. 0870 241 4040
www.vinopolis.co.uk
Thomas Jefferson

Wimbledon Lawn Tennis Museum
All England Lawn Tennis and Croquet
Club, Church Road
Wimbledon SW19 5AG
Tel. 0208 944 1066
www.wimbledon.org
Lawn Tennis Museum

CHURCHES and CEMETERIES

Connections with American history can be found in many London churches. Stained-glass windows, statues and memorial plaques tell stories of adventure, bravery, and deceit.

All Hallows by the Tower
Byward Street, Tower Hill EC3R 5BJ
Tel. 020 7481 2928
www.allhallowsbythetower.org.uk
William Penn
John Quincy Adams

Brompton Cemetery
Fulham Road, West Brompton
SW10 9UG
Tel. 020 7352 1201
www.brompton.org
American Sioux Indian chief Long Wolf
Blanche Roosevelt d'Alligri

Brompton Oratory
The London Oratory, Brompton Road,
South Kensington SW7 2RP
Tel. 020 7808 0900
www.bromptonoratory.com
Alfred Hitchcock

Bunhill Fields (*Dissenters' burial ground*)
38 City Road, St. Luke's EC1Y 1AU
Tel. 020 8472 3584
www.cityoflondon.gov.uk/Corporation/living_environment/open_spaces/bunhill.htm
Susannah Wesley, mother of John and Charles Wesley
George Fox, founder of the Religious Society of Friends

Chapel of St. Peter and St. Paul
Old Royal Naval College, Park Row
Greenwich SE10 9JF
Tel. 020 8269 4747
www.greenwichfoundation.org.uk/newpage3.htm and
www.oldroyalnavalcollege.org
Benjamin West

Chelsea Old Church
Old Church Street, Chelsea SW3 5LT
Henry James

Christ Church Kennington
Christ Church and Upton Chapel
1a Kennington Road
Lambeth SE1 7QP
Tel. 020 7633 2090
www.inclusivechurch.vineyardchurch.org
Abraham Lincoln
Anti-slavery movement

Chiswick Cemetery (St. Nicholas's Churchyard)
Chiswick Mall, Chiswick W4 2PJ
James Abbott McNeill Whistler

East Finchley Cemetery
East End Road, East Finchley N2 0RZ
www.westminster.gov.uk/communityandliving/burials/eastfinchley.cfm
Leopold Stokowski

Fetter Lane Congregation and Moravian Burial Ground
Fetter Lane Moravian Church
Moravian Close, 381 King's Road
Chelsea SW10 0LP
Tel. 020 7352 2624
Benjamin Latrobe

Gravel Pit Chapel
Ram Place at Morning Lane
Hackney E9 6LT
Joseph Priestley

Golders Green Crematorium
62 Hoop Lane, Golders Green
NW11 7NL
Lily Hammersley
Larry Adler
T.S. Eliot

Grosvenor Chapel
South Audley Street, Mayfair W1K 2PA
Tel. 020 7499 1684
www.grosvenorchapel.org.uk
John Wilkes
General Eisenhower
Thanksgiving Service at the end of World War II
American Friends of Grosvenor Chapel
An annual Thanksgiving service is celebrated in November.
A commemorative service is held on the Sunday nearest the 4th of July.

Highgate Cemetery
Swains Lane, Dartmouth Park,
Highgate N6 6PJ
Tel. 020 8340 1834
www.highgate-cemetery.org
    John Singleton Copley and his
        son John Jr.
    Ernestine Rose

Kensal Green Cemetery
Harrow Road, Kensal Green W10 4RA
Tel. 020 8969 0152
www.kensalgreen.co.uk
    John Motley

Methodist Central Hall
Storey's Gate, Westminster
SW1H 9NH
Tel. 020 7222 8010
www.methodist-central-hall.org.uk
    John Wesley
    Billy Graham
    United Nations

Metropolitan Tabernacle
(Spurgeon's Tabernacle)
Metropolitan Tabernacle, Elephant
and Castle SE1 6SD
www.metropolitantabernacle.org
    Josiah Henson

Putney Vale Cemetery
Stag Lane, Putney Vale SW15 3DZ
Tel. 020 8788 2113
    Jacob Epstein

St. Barnabas's Church
23 Addison Road, Kensington
W14 8LH
www.stbk.org.uk
    T.S. Eliot

St. Bartholomew the Great
Little Britain, Smithfield EC1A 7HP
Tel. 020 7606 5171
www.greatstbarts.com
    Benjamin Franklin
    Sir Walter Mildmay
    John Wesley
    American Friends of St.
        Bartholomew the Great

St. Botolph's Parish Church
Aldersgate Street EC1A 4EU
    John and Charles Wesley
    Late eighteenth-century Wesley
        window inside church
    Plaque on railings of churchyard

St. Bride's Fleet Street
Fleet Street EC4Y 8AU
Tel. 020 7427 0133
www.stbrides.com
    Virginia Dare
    Eleanor White
    Ananias Dare, John White
    Sir Walter Raleigh
    Pilgrim Fathers
    Bridewell Hospital
    Edward Winslow
    Benjamin Franklin
    Lord Astor of Hever, descendant
        of William Waldorf Astor
    Journalists' Memorial

St. Clement Danes
Strand WC2R 1DH
Tel. 020 7242 8282
www.st-clement-danes.co.uk
Central church for the Royal Air Force
    A roll of honor for 19,000 US
        airmen

St. Dunstan-in-the-West
186a Fleet Street EC4A 2HR
Tel. 020 7405 1929
www.stdunstaninthewest.org
    George Washington
    Thomas, Lord De La Warr
    George Calvert, 1st first
        Lord Baltimore

St. Ethelburga-the-Virgin
St Ethelburga's Centre for
Reconciliation and Peace
78 Bishopsgate, City of London
EC2N 4AG
Tel. 020 7496 1610
www.stethelburgas.org
    Henry Hudson

St. George's Bloomsbury
Bloomsbury Way, Bloomsbury
WC1A 2HS
Tel. 020 7405 3044
www.stgeorgesbloomsbury.org.uk
    Paul Mellon
    East India Company

St. George's Hanover Square
Mayfair W1S 1FX
Tel. 020 7629 0874
www.stgeorgeshanoversquare.org
    Theodore Roosevelt
    Lily Price Hammersley
    Spencer-Churchill

St. George the Martyr
Queen Square, Bloomsbury
WC1N 3AH
Tel. 020 7404 4407
www.sgtm.org
    Sylvia Plath

St. George the Martyr Southwark
Borough High Street, Southwark
SE1 1JA
    King's Bench Prison
    John Wilkes
    John Horne Tooke

St. Giles's Cripplegate
Wood Street, Barbican EC2Y 8BJ
www.stgilescripplegate.org.uk
    Rev. Dr. Samuel Annesley, vicar
        1658–62, grandfather of
        John Wesley

St. Giles-in-the-Fields
60 St. Giles High Street
Charing Cross WC2H 8LG
Tel. 020 7240 2532
www.stgilesonline.org
    Cecilius Calvert, 2nd Lord
        Baltimore
    John and Charles Wesley

St. Helen's Bishopsgate
Great St. Helen's, City of London
EC3A 6AT
www.st-helens.org.uk
    John Crosby
    Andrew Judd
    Thomas Gresham

St. James's Clerkenwell
Clerkenwell Close, Clerkenwell
EC1R 0EA
Tel. 020 7251 1190
www.jc-church.org
    Ferdinando Gorges

St. James's Piccadilly
197 Piccadilly W1J 1LL
Tel. 020 7734 4511
www.st-james-piccadilly.org
    Benjamin Franklin
    Leopold Stokowski

St. John the Baptist *(no longer exists)*
St. John's Square, Clerkenwell
EC1M 4EA
A parish church until united with St.
James's Clerkenwell in 1869, St. John's

was a remnant of the priory of St. John, which is now the headquarters of the Hospital of St. John of Jerusalem. The order's museum is housed in the medieval gatehouse of the priory.

John Wilkes – born in
St. John's Square
John Wilkes Booth

Museum of the Order of St. John
St. John's Gate, St. John's Lane
Clerkenwell EC1M 4DA
Tel. 020 7324 4070
www.orderofstjohn.org

St. Lawrence, Old Jewry
Gresham Street, City of London
EC2V 5AA
Tel. 020 7600 9478
www.cityoflondonchurches.com/stlawrence
Reverend John Davenport

St. Luke's Church
161 Old Street, City of London
EC1V 9NG
www.lso.co.uk
John Wesley

St. Margaret's Church, Barking
The Broadway, Barking, Essex IG11 8AS
Tel. 020 8594 2932
www.saintmargarets.org.uk
Captain James Cook

St. Margaret's, Westminster
St. Margaret Street, Westminster
SW1P 3JX
Tel. 020 7654 4847
www.westminster-abbey.org/stmargarets/
Sir Walter Raleigh was executed on the Palace Green on 29 October 1618. He was buried in the chancel. The west window, above the entrance, commemorates the famous explorer. The window, funded with subscriptions from the USA, shows the US coat of arms and a verse by James Russell Lowell. There is another memorial to Walter Raleigh next to the east door.
Barnardus La Grange, "an American loyalist" who died in 1797, has a monument in the church.
There is a memorial to **Sir Peter Parker** who died in a skirmish on the American coast during the War of

1812.
James Rumsey (1743–92), whom the State of Virginia honors as the inventor of the steamboat, is buried in the churchyard and memorialized with a plaque.
There is a memorial to **Sir James Wright**, the last royal governor of Georgia.
Phillips Brooks, Bishop of Massachusetts, d. 1893, who wrote the hymn "O Little Town of Bethlehem," has a memorial in the south aisle of St Margaret's Church. In 1875 **George W. Childs** of Philadelphia gave money for the John Milton window in St. Margaret's, which includes lines by John Greenleaf Whittier.
Viscount Sherbrooke's late nineteenth-century bust in the east porch of St. Margaret's is by the American sculptor Moses Ezekiel.
On 12 September 1908 **Winston Churchill** married Miss Clementine Hozier at St. Margaret's.
The escort carrier HMS *Speaker* was commissioned in the USA in 1943 and served in the Far East. A small plate and badge are affixed to the west inner doorway of the church.
John and Eleanor Elliott of New York City set up the Chapel of Christ the Intercessor in St. Margaret's Church in 1981.

St. Martin-in-the-Fields
Trafalgar Square WC2N 4JJ
Tel. 020 7839 8362
www.stmartin-in-the-fields.org
Georgius Thorp
Benjamin West

St. Mary Abbots Church
Kensington Church Street
Kensington W8 4LA
www.stmaryabbotschurch.org
Ezra Pound and Dorothy Shakespear

St. Mary Aldermanbury
Love Lane and Aldermanbury Square northwest of the Guildhall
City of London EC2V 7SB
http://london.lovesguide.com/mary_aldermanbury.htm
Winston Churchill

John Stoughton

St. Mary's Battersea
Battersea Church Road
Battersea SW11 3NA
Tel. 020 7228 9648
www.stmarysbattersea.org.uk
Benedict Arnold

St. Mary's Rotherhithe
St. Marychurch Street
Rotherhithe SE16 4JE
www.stmaryrotherhithe.org
Captain Christopher Jones

St. Mary-at-Lambeth (*see also Museum of Garden History*)
Lambeth Palace Road
Lambeth SE1 7LB
Tel. 020 7401 8865
www.museumgardenhistory.org
John Tradescant the Elder
John Tradescant the Younger
Hatfield House
Ashmolean Museum in Oxford

St. Mary-le-Bow
Cheapside, City of London EC2V 6AU
Tel. 020 7248 5139
www.stmarylebow.co.uk
Captain John Smith

St. Mary-le-Strand
Strand WC2R 1ES
Tel. 020 7405 1929
www.stmarylestrand.org
Mather Brown

St. Mary the Virgin, Twickenham
Church Street, Twickenham
Middlesex TW1 3NJ
Tel. 020 8744 2693
www.st-mary-twick.freeserve.co.uk
William Berkeley
John Berkeley

St. Marylebone Parish Church
Marylebone Road NW1 5LT
Tel. 020 7935 7315
www.stmarylebone.org.uk
Charles Wesley
Benjamin West
Leopold Stokowski

St. Matthias's Church
Poplar High Street, Poplar E14 0AE
East India Company

St. Paul's Cathedral

City of London EC4M 8AD
Tel. 020 7236 4128
www.stpauls.co.uk
Queen Anne statue
John Wesley
George Washington
Charles Cornwallis, 1st Marquess
Edward Michael Pakenham –
Battle of New Orleans
Benjamin West
John Singer Sargent
American Memorial Chapel
Pilot Officer William M.L. Fiske III
Winston Churchill
J. Paul Getty Foundation

St. Paul's Covent Garden

Bedford Street, Covent Garden
WC2E 9ED
Tel. 020 7836 5221
www.actorschurch.org
Boris Karloff (William Henry Pratt)
Charlie Chaplin

St. Paul's Shadwell

302 The Highway, Shadwell E1W 3DH
Tel. 020 7680 2772
www.stpaulsshadwell.org
"Sea Captains' Church"
Jane Randolph Jefferson
James Cook, the eldest son of
Captain James Cook

St. Paul's Knightsbridge

32 Wilton Place, Knightsbridge
SW1X 8SH
Tel. 020 7201 9999
www.stpaulsknightsbridge.org
Jennie Jerome Churchill

St. Sepulchre-without-Newgate

Holborn Viaduct, London EC1A 9DE
Tel. 020 7248 1660
www.st-sepulchre.org.uk
Captain John Smith
The Jamestown Kneeler Collection
Roger Williams

St. Stephen's Church

Gloucester Road, Kensington SW7 4RL
Tel. 020 370 3418
T.S. Eliot

Savoy Chapel

The Queen's Chapel of the Savoy
Savoy Hill, Strand WC2R 0DA
Tel. 020 7379 8088

www.duchyoflancaster.org.uk/output/p
age42.asp
Richard Hakluyt

Southwark Cathedral

London Bridge, Southwark SE1 9DA
Tel. 020 7367 6700
www.southwark.anglican.org/cathedral
/index.htm
John Harvard
Joseph H. Choate
Oscar Hammerstein
Sam Wanamaker
George Yeardley
Mohegan chieftain Sachem
Mahomet Weyonomon

Unitarian Church headquarters

1–6 Essex Street, Strand WC2R 3HY
Joseph Priestley

Wesley's Chapel, House, and Museum of Methodism

49 City Road, St. Luke's EC1Y 1AU
Tel. 020 7253 2262
www.wesleyschapel.org.uk
Charles Wesley
John Wesley
James Oglethorpe
Dissenters' burial ground

Westminster Abbey

Broad Sanctuary, Westminster
SW1P 3PA
Tel. 020 7654 4900
www.westminster-abbey.org
Modern Martyrs Statues – above west
entrance
Martin Luther King
Poets' Corner
Henry James
T.S. Eliot
Henry W. Longfellow
Royal Air Force Chapel
Battle of Britain Memorial Window
Navigators' Memorial
Sir Francis Drake
Captain James Cook
Other memorials linked to Americans
George Peabody
Lord Baden-Powell
Stained-glass window – south side of
the nave
George W. Childs of Philadelphia
presented the stained-glass window
to the English poets George
Herbert and William
Cowper in 1875 and also gave

money for the John Milton window
in St. Margaret's.
Military Connections
Richard Hakluyt (1553–16) is buried in
the south transept (no marker).
Admiral Edward Vernon: George
Washington's eldest half-brother
Lawrence served on Vernon's
flagship in 1741 during naval
campaigns against the Spanish in
the West Indies. There is a
monument to Admiral Vernon in
the abbey.
John Thorndike from New England
died in 1668 on a visit to his
brother in England. Both are buried
under an unmarked stone in the
east cloister.
Colonel Roger Townshend was killed on
an expedition to Ticonderoga, New
York State, in 1759. He is buried at
Albany. His monument in the nave
includes two figures of Native
Americans from the region.
George, 3rd Viscount Howe (1725–8)
was killed on an expedition to
Ticonderoga in New York State. His
monument in the northwest tower
chapel in the nave was erected by
the Province of Massachusetts.
General John Burgoyne surrendered to
the Americans at Saratoga. He is
buried in the north cloister under a
simple stone. He was baptized at
St. Margaret's Westminster and
educated at Westminster School.
William Pitt, Earl of Chatham (d. 1778):
his life-size wax effigy in the abbey's
museum was modeled by an
American, Patience Wright. His
grave and large monument are in
the north transept.
Major John Andre, spymaster who
recruited Benedict Arnold
General Staats-Long Morris of New
York served in the army in Scotland
and married into the British
aristocracy. He died in 1800 and
was buried in the nave with his wife
(grave not marked).
Royal Flying Corps 1914–18: a small
stained-glass window in the nave of
the abbey was erected by Mrs.
Louis Bennett of West Virginia in
memory of all members of this
corps who died, including her son
Louis Jr., who was killed in France.
Congressional Medal of Honor: awarded

to the British Unknown Warrior on 17 October 1921. It hangs on a pillar near the grave in the nave and was presented by General Pershing.

Church-related memorials

John and Charles Wesley – memorial tablet to the brothers who founded the Methodist Church

Trinity Church, New York: a bronze plaque in the south aisle of the Lady Chapel was presented by this church in memory of Queen Anne and William III, who granted land for the first Anglican church in New York.

Charles McIlvaine, Bishop of Ohio, died while in Florence. A brass plaque in St. Faith's Chapel records the resting of his coffin here in 1873 on its way to the USA.

Rodman Wanamaker of New York presented a jeweled processional cross to the abbey in 1922 which is still used at most services today.

Joseph L. Chester: an American genealogist who edited the "Westminster Abbey Registers" in 1876. There is a memorial tablet to him in the south choir aisle, and he is buried at Nunhead Cemetery in London.

Political figures

Sir James Wright, the last royal governor of Georgia (d. 1785), is buried in the north transept. (The inscription on his grave is now very faint.)

James Gerard, US ambassador in Berlin, gave the stained-glass window which commemorates British prisoners of war 1914–18 in the north choir aisle. The US coat of arms is included in the design.

James Russell Lowell, poet and US minister in London 1880–5, died in 1891. A tablet and stained-glass window to his memory can be seen in the vestibule of the chapter house.

Walter Hines Page (1855–1918), US ambassador in London 1913–18, has a memorial tablet in the vestibule of the chapter house.

Franklin D. Roosevelt, US president, has a memorial tablet in the nave erected 1948. The plaque is surrounded by American eagles.

Other connections

United States citizens and charitable foundations gave money to the abbey's restoration appeals. Small

stained-glass windows in the Lady Chapel and plaques in the chapel vestibule commemorate their gifts.

William Wragg of South Carolina was drowned in 1777 on his way to England. His memorial is in the south choir aisle.

Memorial services have taken place in the abbey for several eminent Americans including President Ulysses S. Grant in 1885, J. Pierpont Morgan in 1913, and President Harding in 1923. A commemoration for President Kennedy was held in 1963. President Cleveland's daughter married at the abbey in 1918. Between 1942 and 1944 **Thanksgiving Day** services were held for the US forces, and the United States bicentennial was celebrated at a service here in 1976.

James Oglethorpe married Lady Elizabeth Wright on 15 September 1744, in the King Henry VII Chapel. Much of the above information was obtained from:
http://www.westminster-abbey.org/

THE GREAT OUTDOORS
Sculpture, Statues and Monuments, Parks and Gardens

Admiralty Arch
The Mall SW1A 2WH
    Captain James Cook – statue

Albert Memorial
Kensington Gore, Kensington SW7 2AP
    American Indians – in group of carvings on northwest corner

Aldersgate Street
Nettleton Court, St. Paul's EC2Y 5HN
    John Wesley – "Methodist Flame" memorial

Angel Square
Islington High Street, Islington N1 8XB
    Thomas Paine monument

Belgrave Square
south corner, opposite SW1X 8QA
    Christopher Columbus – statue

Berkeley Square
Mayfair W1J 6AA
    John, Lord Berkeley

Blackheath, Greenwich SE3
    Palatine immigrants
    Queen Anne
    Mohawk Indians
    Peter Schuyler

Cavendish Square
Theology Faculty of the University of London W1G 0PQ
    Sir Jacob Epstein sculpture – *Madonna and Child*

55 Broadway
St. James's Park Underground Station, Westminster SW1H 0QW
    Sir Jacob Epstein sculpture – *Night and Day*

Chelsea Embankment
just west of Battersea Bridge SW3
    James Abbott McNeill Whistler – statue

Chelsea Physic Garden
66 Royal Hospital Road, Chelsea SW3 4HS
Tel. 020 7352 5646
www.chelseaphysicgarden.co.uk
    American connections

Cockspur Street
Trafalgar Square SW1Y 5DL
    King George III – statue

Columbus Courtyard
Canary Wharf E14 4DA
    Wendy Ramshaw's "Columbus Screen"

East India Dock
Virginia Quay, Blackwall E14 2DE

First Settlers Memorial

Edinburgh Gate entrance to
Hyde Park
Knightsbridge SW1X 7LT
    Sir Jacob Epstein, sculpture – *Rush of Green*

Fulham Palace and Museum
Bishops Avenue, Fulham SW6 6EA
Tel. 020 7736 3233
www.lbhf.gov.uk/index3.htm
www.touruk.co.uk/london_houses/fulh
ampalace_house1.htm
    American trees and plants

Greenwich Quay
Just across Deptford Creek from
Greenwich, SE8 3ET
    Tsar Peter the Great of Russia – statue

Grosvenor Square
Mayfair, across from W1K 6US
    Diplomatic Gates
    Eagle Squadron Memorial
    September 11 Memorial
    Statue of President Franklin D. Roosevelt

Hyde Park
W2 2UH
    Sir Jacob Epstein sculptures – *Rima* and *Pan*
    South Carriage Drive
    Great Exhibition of 1851 – the Exhibition Hall was located on the site that is now the Hyde Park Tennis Centre.
    Josiah Henson
    George Peabody

Kew Gardens
Royal Botanic Gardens, Kew Road
Kew, Surrey TW9 3AB
Tel. 020 8332 5655
www.rbgkew.org.uk
    King George III
    Joseph Banks

Leicester Square
in garden opposite WC2H 7NA
    Charlie Chaplin – statue

Marylebone Road
near corner of Great Portland Street
Marylebone W1B 1SH
    Bust of President John F. Kennedy

Museum of Garden History
Lambeth Palace Road
Lambeth SE1 7LB
Tel. 020 7401 8865
www.museumgardenhistory.org
    Tomb of John Tradescant the Elder and John Tradescant the Younger
    Stained-glass west window presented in 1904 by American churchmen and -women in memory of Archbishop Moore

National Gallery
Trafalgar Square WC2N 5DN
    George Washington – statue
    King James II – statue

New Bond Street
Mayfair W1S 2YA
    Franklin Roosevelt – statue
    Winston Churchill – statue

New Fetter Lane
off Fleet Street EC4A 1ES
    John Wilkes – statue

Parliament Square
Westminster SW1A 0AA
    Abraham Lincoln – statue
    Winston Churchilll – statue

Roper's Garden
Old Church Street, Chelsea
Embankment SW3 5DJ
    Sir Jacob Epstein memorial sculpture

Royal Botanic Gardens Kew *(see Kew Gardens)*

Royal Exchange
Cornhill and Treadneedle Streets, City
of London EC3V 3LT
    Thomas Gresham
    Henry Hudson
    Abraham Lincoln – bust
    George Peabody – statue

Seething Lane Garden
corner of Seething Lane and Pepys
Street, Tower Hill EC3R 7NB
    Admiral Penn
    William Penn
    Samuel Pepys – bust on plinth

Somerset House
Strand WC2R 1LA
    King George III – statue

Trades Union Congress House
28 Great Russell Street, Bloomsbury
WC1B 3LQ
    Sir Jacob Epstein sculpture – *Pieta*

Trinity Gardens
Trinity Square, Tower Hill EC3N 4AA
    Algernon Sidney – plaque
    Sir Henry Vane – plaque
    William Russell – plaque
    Robert Devereux – plaque
    Archbishop William Laud – plaque

Victoria Tower Gardens
near the Houses of Parliament
Westminster SW1A 0AA
    Buxton Memorial Fountain – monument to the ending of slavery
    Statue of Emmeline Pankhurst – women's suffrage in Britain

Zimbabwe House
429 Strand WC2R 0QE
    Jacob Epstein's sculpture *Ages of Man* – Epstein's first major public commission featured eighteen figures based on the work of Walt Whitman

WHERE THEY LIVED AND WORKED

Albemarle Street
Piccadilly W1S 4BP
> George Monck, 1st Duke of
> Albemarle, one of the eight lord
> proprietors of the Province of
> Carolina

Aldford Street, 7
Mayfair W1K 2AQ
> John Winant, ambassador 1941–6 –
> blue plaque

Allenswood
Albert Drive, Wimbledon SW19 6JX
> Eleanor Roosevelt – attended
> Mademoiselle Souvestre's school
> at Allenswood

Angel Square
Islington High Street, Islington
EC1V 1NY
> Site of the Angel Inn
> Thomas Paine

Argyll Street, 8 (off Oxford Street)
W1F 7TF
> "Washington Irving lived here.
> 1783–1859"

Arlington Street, 22
St. James's SW1A 1RD
"Wimborne House" is now called the
"William Kent House."
> May Goelet

Aubrey House
Aubrey Road, Kensington W8 7JJ
> Mr. P.A. Taylor, Member of
> Parliament for Leicester
> Frederick Douglass
> Louisa May Alcott in 1865

Basing House
Watersmeet, Three Rivers Museum
20 High Street, Rickmansworth
Hertfordshire WD3 1ER
Tel. 01923 775882
www.threerivers.gov.uk
> William Penn

Berkeley Square, 38
Mayfair, W1J 5AE
> Almaric Paget and Pauline
> Whitney Paget
> Olive Paget, Lady Baillie

Bloomsbury
WC1A 2NS
> Henry Wriothesley, 3rd Earl of
> Southampton
> Thomas Wriothesley, 4th Earl of
> Southampton
> Rachel Wriothesley
> William Russell
> Algernon Sidney
> Wriothesley Russell, 2nd Duke of
> Bedford

Borough High Street, 103
Southwark SE1 1NL
> John Harvard

Branch Hill
2 The Chestnuts, Camden NW3 7LS
> Paul Robeson

Brook Street, 23
Mayfair W1K 4HB
> Jimi Hendrix

Bruton Place
Piccadilly, Mayfair W1J 6QR
> Berkeley family – lords of the
> manor of Bruton in Somerset

Bullingham Mansions
16 Pitt Street, Kensington W8 4JH
> Hilda Doolittle

Bryanston Court, 5
near Marble Arch W1H
> Wallis Warfield Simpson

Cadogan Lane, 4
Belgravia SW1X 9EB
> Judy Garland

Carnaby Street
off Regent Street W1F 9PS
> Lord Craven – one of the lord
> proprietors of Carolina

Carlton House Terrace
St. James's SW1Y 5AH
No. 1 – Bought for Mary Leiter of
Washington, D.C., by her father when
she married Hon. George Curzon in
1895.
No. 2 – May Goelet and Kelso (8th
Duke of Roxburghe) moved here in
1923.
No. 3 – Residence of Mary Hammersley

after 1895 marriage to Lord Beresford
No. 5 – Once the residence of Mary
Burke of San Francisco who married
Sir Bache Cunard I in 1895
No. 7 – The residence of Belle Wilson
and Mungo (Hon. Michael Henry)
Herbert, who married in 1888. (She
was the aunt of May Goelet, and he
was the younger brother of the 13th
Earl of Pembroke)
No. 18 – Belonged to William Waldorf
Astor
No. 20 – Residence of Lady Parker,
American wife of Sir Gilbert Parker,
M.P.
No. 22 – Once belonged to Amy
Phipps, of Pittsburgh, and her
husband, Hon. Frederick Guest, M.P.

Chalcot Square, 3
Primrose Hill NW1 8YA
> Sylvia Plath – blue plaque

Chester House, 3
Westside Common
Wimbledon SW19 4TN
> John Horne Tooke
> Thomas Paine

Cheyne Row, 24
Chelsea SW3 5HL (Carlyle's House)
> Henry Wadsworth Longfellow

Cheyne Walk, 21
Carlyle Mansions, Chelsea SW3 5RA
> Henry James

Cheyne Walk, 96
Chelsea SW3 5LR
> James Abbott McNeill Whistler

City Road, 49
St. Luke's EC1Y 1AU
> "Wesley's House" – a blue plaque
> John Wesley

Clarges Street (off Piccadilly)
Mayfair W1J 7EN
> George Monck, later Duke of
> Albemarle, a lord proprietor of
> Carolina

Clerkenwell Close
Clerkenwell EC1R 0AT
> Aaron Burr

Cleveland Street, 141
Fitzrovia W1T 6QG
  Samuel Morse

Commercial Road, 135–53
Whitechapel E1 1PX
  George Peabody/Peabody Estates

Craigton Road, 44
Eltham SE9 1QG
  Bob Hope

Craven Street, 25
Charing Cross WC2N 5NT
  Herman Melville

Craven Street, 30
Charing Cross WC2N 5NF
  Aaron Burr

Craven Street, 36
Charing Cross WC2N 5NG
  Benjamin Franklin

Cromwell Road, 153
Earl's Court SW5 0TQ
  Alfred Hitchcock

Crosby Hall
Chelsea Embankment SW3 5AZ
Now a private home
  Sir Walter Raleigh
  East India Company

Czar Street
Deptford, SE8 3JL
  William Penn

De Vere Gardens, 34
Kensington W8 5AQ
  Henry James

Eaton Square, 80
Belgravia SW1W 9AP
  George Peabody

Eisenhower Centre
Goodge Street Underground Station
Chenies Street WC1E 7EU
  Dwight Eisenhower

Ennismore Gardens, 34
Knightsbridge SW7 1HZ
  Ava Gardner

Farm House
22 Farm Street, Mayfair W1J 5RQ
  Gloria Swanson

Thelma Furness
Wallis Warfield Simpson

Fitzroy Street, 23
Fitzrovia W1T 4BA
  Sylvia Plath

Fleet Street
City of London EC4A 2DQ
  Traditional home of journalism

Forest Hill Road, 36
East Dulwich SE22 0RR
  Boris Karloff

Frognal, 103
Hampstead NW3 6XR
  Donald Ogden Stewart

Geldeston Road, 58a
Hackney E5 8SB
  Jessica Tandy

Gloucester Place, 62
Marylebone W1U 8HW
  Benedict Arnold

Gower Street, 57
Bloomsbury WC1E 6AA
  Thomas Wolfe

Great Cumberland Place, 35
Marble Arch W1H 7DS
  Jennie Jerome Churchill

Great Russell Street, 28
Bloomsbury WC1B 3LQ
Now the site of Trades Union
Congress House
  Nathaniel Hawthorne

Grosvenor Square, 5
Mayfair W1K 4AF
  Consuelo Yznaga

Grosvenor Square, 9
Mayfair W1K 5AE
  John Adams
  John Quincy Adams
  Thomas Jefferson

Grosvenor Square, 20
Mayfair W1K 6US
  General Dwight Eisenhower

Ham Common
South Lodge, Richmond
Surrey TW10 7JL

Bronson Alcott

Hatton Garden, 44
Holborn EC1N 8ER
  Birt Acres

Hatton Garden, 57d
Holborn EC1N 8HP
  Hiram Stephens Maxim

Hertford Street, 10
Mayfair W1J 7RL
  General Burgoyne

The Highway, 340
Shadwell E1W 3ES
  Captain James Cook

Holborn Viaduct, 57
Holborn EC1A 2FD
  Thomas Edison

Holland Place Chambers, 5
Kensington Church Street
Kensington W8 4LS
  T.S. Eliot
  Hilda Doolittle

Hyde Park Gate, 18
Kensington SW7 5DH
  Jacob Epstein – blue plaque

Hyde Park Gate, 28
Kensington SW7 5DJ
  Winston Churchill – blue plaque

Hyde Park Gate, 39
Kensington SW7 5DS
  Herbert Hoover

Kennington Road, 287
Lambeth SE11 6BY
  Charlie Chaplin

Kensington Church Walk, 10
Kensington W8 4NB
  Ezra Pound
  Robert Frost
  T.S. Eliot
  Hilda Doolittle

Kensington Court Gardens, 3
Kensington, W8 5QE
  T.S. Eliot

Kensington Green
Stone Hall, Marloes Road
Kensington W8 5UU

Stone Hall was formerly the home of
St. Mary Abbots Hospital.
    Jimi Hendrix

Islington High Street, 1
Angel Square, Islington N1 9TR
    Site of the Angel Inn
    Thomas Paine

Lancaster Gate, 74
Bayswater W2 3NH
    Francis Bret Harte

Leicester Square, 28
WC2H 7LE
    John Singleton Copley

Leytonstone High Street, 517
Leytonstone E11
    Alfred Hitchcock

Little Britain, 12
Barbican EC2Y 5HN
(John Bray's House)
John Bray's House was where Charles
Wesley was converted on 21 May 1738.
Both John and Charles Wesley lodged
here 1738–9 and wrote and published
Hymns and Sacred Poems. There is a
blue plaque on the later building.

Lower Clapton Road, 113
Hackney E5 0NP
    Joseph Priestley

Lowndes Street, 37
Belgravia SW1X 9HX
    James Russell Lowell

Maze Hill Street, 111
Greenwich SE10 8XQ
    Olaudah Equiano

Mecklenburgh Square, 44
Bloomsbury WC1N 2AD
    Hilda Doolittle

Methley Street, 39
Kennington SE11 4AL
    Charlie Chaplin

Mile End Road, 89
Stepney E1 4UJ
    Captain James Cook

Muscovy Street
Trinity Square, Tower Hill EC3N 4AA
    Sebastian Cabot

Muscovy Company

Park Road, 19
Clovelly Cottage, Barnet EN5 5RY
    Birt Acres

Percy Street, 15
off Tottenham Court Road, W1T 1EE
    Charles Laughton

Pond Road, 4
Blackheath, SE3 9JL
    Nathaniel Hawthorne

Portland Place, 41
Marylebone W1B 1BN
    Thomas Gage

Portland Place, 52
Marylebone W1B 1NH
    Edith Wharton
    William Waldorf Astor

Portland Place, 86
Marylebone W1B 1NU
    Charles Francis Adams

Portland Place, 98
Marylebone W1B 1ET
    Charles Francis Adams
    American Chancery

Princes Street, 8
Hanover Square, Mayfair W1S 1HJ
    Henry Wadsworth Longfellow

Prince's Gate, 49
Kensington SW7 2PG
    J.A.M. Whistler
    The Peacock Room

Queen Victoria Street, 11
City of London EC4N 4UJ
    Thomas Edison
    George Bernard Shaw

Radnor Place, 2
Bayswater W2 2TE
    James Russell Lowell

Ravenscourt Park
Hammersmith W6 0TJ
    Alexander Graham Bell

Riding House Street, 73
W1W 7EJ
    Olaudah Equiano – blue plaque

Rosslyn Hill
Hampstead, NW3 5UJ (Vane House)
    Henry Vane

Rugby Street 18
Holborn WC1N 3QZ
    Sylvia Plath

Russell Square, 24
Bloomsbury WC1B 5EA
    T.S. Eliot

Salisbury Road, 45
Barnet EN5 4JL
    Birt Acres

Samuel Annesley's House
Spital Yard, Spitalfields E1 6DY
    Susanna Wesley
    John and Charles Wesley

Soho Square, 32
Soho W1D 3AP
    Joseph Banks

St. George's Street, 24
Hanover Square, Mayfair W1S 1FX
    Nathaniel Hawthorne

St. George's Street, 25
Hanover Square, Mayfair W1S 1FX
    John Singleton Copley

St. James's Place, 33
St. James's SW1A 1NR
    James Fenimore Cooper

St. James's Square, 4
St. James's SW1Y 4JU
    Nancy Langhorne Astor –
    blue plaque

St. James's Square, 31
St. James's SW1Y 4JR
    King George III
    Dwight D. Eisenhower

St. John's Square, 10
Clerkenwell EC1M 4NL
    John Wilkes
    John Wilkes Booth

Shaftesbury Avenue
Piccadilly W1D 7EF
    Anthony Ashley Cooper, 1st Earl
    of Shaftesbury

"Shakespeare's Walk"
Shadwell, Whitechapel E1
This street no longer exists.
  Thomas Jefferson
  Jane Randolph Jefferson

Stratford Place, 7
Near Oxford Street, W1C 1ST
  Martin Van Buren

Stratton Street
Piccadilly W1J 8LN
  Berkeley family

**Sugar Quay – on the
River Thames**
Tower Hill EC3R 6DU
*Located between the Customs House
and the Tower of London*
  Boston Tea Party

Tedworth Square, 23
Chelsea SW3 4DR
  Mark Twain

Telegraph Cottage
Warren Road, Kingston-upon-Thames
Surrey KT2 7HU
  Dwight D. Eisenhower

Throgmorton Street
City of London EC2R 8AH
  Elizabeth Throckmorton
  Sir Walter Raleigh

Tite Street, 31
Chelsea SW3 4JP
  John Singer Sargent

Upper Street, 98
Islington N1 0NP
  Sir Walter Raleigh

Villiers Street, 43
Charing Cross WC2N 6NE
  Rudyard Kipling

Walworth Road, 227
London SE17 1RL
  Charlie Chaplin

Wellington Square, 32
Chelsea SW3 4NR
  Thomas Wolfe

West Street, 24
near Cambridge Circus WC2H 9NE
  John Wesley – blue plaque

Westbourne Grove Terrace, 6
Bayswater W2 5SD
  Louisa May Alcott

Wheatley Street
Marylebone W1G 8PS
Charles Wesley lived and died in Great
Chesterfield Street (now Wheatley
Street), where the site is marked by a
plaque on the King's Head public
house.

Wildwood Road 8
Hampstead, NW11 6TB
  Elizabeth Taylor

The Underground System
  Charles Tyson Yerkes
  Goodge Street – Eisenhower
  St. James's Park station – Jacob

Towns and Villages with American Connections

The postal codes given are to help in locating the sites on an internet or GPS mapping system. They are not necessarily the mailing codes for the sites which may use an off-site postal location. Some historical sites are now private property and other locations may be closed to the public. All information is correct at the time of going to press, but should be confirmed before a visit is planned.

England

SCOTLAND

YORKSHIRE
& NORTH

York

Manchester   Sheffield
Liverpool

Lincoln

Nottingham

MIDLANDS   Norwich

Birmingham   EAST

Cambridge   Ipswich

WALES

Gloucester   Oxford   Chelmsford

Bristol   London   Gravesend
Guildford
Bath   Maidstone   Canterbury

HOME COUNTIES
& SOUTH/SOUTHEAST

SOUTHWEST   Lewes

Southampton
Portsmouth

Plymouth

Towns and Villages with American Connections

EAST

Clapham	Bedfordshire
Haynes Church End	Bedfordshire
Henlow	Bedfordshire
Podington	Bedfordshire
Thurleigh	Bedfordshire
Woburn	Bedfordshire
Arrington	Cambridgeshire
Bassingbourn	Cambridgeshire
Cambridge	Cambridgeshire
Conington	Cambridgeshire
Duxford	Cambridgeshire
Ely	Cambridgeshire
Huntingdon	Cambridgeshire
Kimbolton	Cambridgeshire
Madingley	Cambridgeshire
Molesworth	Cambridgeshire
Steeple Morden	Cambridgeshire
Wimpole Hall	Cambridgeshire
Billericay	Essex
Bocking	Essex
Boreham	Essex
Bradwell-on-Sea	Essex
Braintree	Essex
Chelmsford	Essex
Chigwell	Essex
Coggeshall	Essex
Copford Green	Essex
Cranham	Essex
Dedham	Essex
Great Burstead	Essex
Great Stambridge	Essex
Harwich	Essex
Hatfield Broad Oak	Essex
High Laver	Essex
Little Baddow	Essex
Maldon	Essex
Messing	Essex
Nazeing	Essex
Purleigh	Essex
Attleborough	Norfolk
Deopham Green	Norfolk
Heacham	Norfolk
Hethersett	Norfolk
Hingham	Norfolk
Hunstanton	Norfolk
King's Lynn	Norfolk
Norwich	Norfolk
Old Buckenham	Norfolk
Redenhall	Norfolk
Swanton Morely	Norfolk
Thetford	Norfolk
West Raynham	Norfolk
Wymondham	Norfolk
Bungay	Suffolk

Bures	Suffolk
Bury St. Edmunds	Suffolk
Clopton	Suffolk
Culford	Suffolk
Debach	Suffolk
Flixton	Suffolk
Great Ashfield	Suffolk
Groton	Suffolk
Halesworth	Suffolk
Haverhill	Suffolk
Honington	Suffolk
Horham	Suffolk
Ipswich	Suffolk
Knettishall	Suffolk
Lakenheath	Suffolk
Lavenham	Suffolk
Leiston	Suffolk
Letheringham	Suffolk
Little Glemham	Suffolk
Martlesham Heath	Suffolk
Mendelsham	Suffolk
Metfield	Suffolk
Mildenhall	Suffolk
Needham Market	Suffolk
Orford	Suffolk
Otley	Suffolk
Parham	Suffolk
Rattlesden	Suffolk
Raydon	Suffolk
Rougham	Suffolk
Shelley	Suffolk
Stowmarket	Suffolk
Sudbury	Suffolk
Walpole	Suffolk
Wattisham	Suffolk
Wetheringsett	Suffolk
Wingfield	Suffolk

HOME COUNTIES & SOUTH/SOUTHEAST

Crowthorne	Berkshire
Eton	Berkshire
Hamstead Marshall	Berkshire
Hungerford	Berkshire
Lambourn	Berkshire
Newbury	Berkshire
Sunninghill near Ascot	Berkshire
Virginia Water	Berkshire
Bletchley	Buckinghamshire
Chalfont St. Giles	Buckinghamshire
Chenies	Buckinghamshire
Cliveden	Buckinghamshire
Great Hampden	Buckinghamshire
Jordans, Beaconsfield	Buckinghamshire
Medmenham	Buckinghamshire
Penn	Buckinghamshire
Stoke Poges	Buckinghamshire
Waddesdon	Buckinghamshire
West Wycombe	Buckinghamshire
Wormsley Park	Buckinghamshire

Bexhill-on-Sea	East Sussex
Bodiam	East Sussex
Brighton	East Sussex
Burwash	East Sussex
Firle	East Sussex
Forest Row	East Sussex
Lewes	East Sussex
Old Heathfield	East Sussex
Rottingdean	East Sussex
Rye	East Sussex
Upper Dicker	East Sussex
Aldershot	Hampshire
Beaulieu	Hampshire
Botley	Hampshire
Farnborough	Hampshire
Middle Wallop	Hampshire
Mottisfont	Hampshire
Portsmouth	Hampshire
Sherborne St. John	Hampshire
Southampton	Hampshire
Southwick	Hampshire
Winchester	Hampshire
Ayot St. Lawrence	Hertfordshire
Hatfield	Hertfordshire
Nuthampstead	Hertfordshire
Welwyn Garden City	Hertfordshire
Widford	Hertfordshire
Allington	Kent
Ashford	Kent
Aylesford	Kent
Boxley	Kent
Canterbury	Kent
Chartwell	Kent
Deal	Kent
East Sutton	Kent
Edenbridge	Kent
Goudhurst	Kent
Hadlow	Kent
Hollingbourne	Kent
Ightham Mote	Kent
Leeds Castle	Kent
Maidstone	Kent
Northbourne	Kent
Pembury	Kent
Penshurst	Kent
Plaxtol	Kent
Reculver	Kent
Rochester	Kent
Sevenoaks	Kent
Shipbourne	Kent
Sissinghurst	Kent
Sutton-at-Hone	Kent
Tenterden	Kent
Gravesend	Kent
Bladon	Oxfordshire
Oxford	Oxfordshire
Sulgrave Manor	Oxfordshire
Woodstock	Oxfordshire

Wroxton	Oxfordshire
Cobham	Surrey
Dorking	Surrey
Epsom	Surrey
Esher	Surrey
Farnham	Surrey
Frimley	Surrey
Godalming	Surrey
Guildford	Surrey
Hascombe	Surrey
Ockley	Surrey
Pirbright	Surrey
Runnymede	Surrey
Stoke d'Abernon	Surrey
Woking	Surrey
Worplesdon	Surrey
Ardingly	West Sussex
Boxgrove Priory	West Sussex
Easebourne	West Sussex
East Grinstead	West Sussex
Goodwood	West Sussex
Steyning	West Sussex
Aldbourne	Wiltshire
Calne	Wiltshire
Corsham	Wiltshire
Salisbury	Wiltshire
West Knoyle	Wiltshire

MIDLANDS

Chatsworth	Derbyshire
Edensor	Derbyshire
Kedleston	Derbyshire
Ilkeston	Derbyshire
Leintwardine	Herefordshire
Marefield	Leicestershire
Market Bosworth	Leicestershire
Stoke Dry	Leicestershire
Tickencote	Leicestershire
Tilton on the Hill	Leicestershire
Alford	Lincolnshire
Bilsby	Lincolnshire
Boston	Lincolnshire
Gainsborough	Lincolnshire
Grimsthorpe	Lincolnshire
Harlaxton	Lincolnshire
Lincoln	Lincolnshire
Little Casterton	Lincolnshire
Norton Disney	Lincolnshire
Sempringham	Lincolnshire
Willoughby	Lincolnshire
Chelveston	Northamptonshire
Ecton	Northamptonshire
Grafton Underwood	Northamptonshire
Great Brington	Northamptonshire
Harrington	Northamptonshire
Kettering	Northamptonshire
Babworth	Nottinghamshire
Newark	Nottinghamshire
Scrooby	Nottinghamshire

Sturton-le-Steeple	Nottinghamshire
Workshop	Nottinghamshire
Acton Burnell	Shropshire
Alveley	Shropshire
Shipton	Shropshire
Alrewas	Staffordshire
Coughton	Warwickshire
Fenny Drayton	Warwickshire
Stratford-Upon-Avon	Warwickshire
Warwick	Warwickshire
Birmingham	West Midlands
Coventry	West Midlands
Droitwich	Worcestershire
Ombersley	Worcestershire
Wickhamford	Worcestershire
Worcester	Worcestershire

SOUTHWEST

Kilkhampton	Cornwall
St. Columb	Cornwall
Ashburton	Devon
Bideford	Devon
Buckland Monachorum	Devon
Chagford	Devon
Compton	Devon
Dartmouth	Devon
East Budleigh	Devon
Greenway	Devon
Hemyock	Devon
Paignton	Devon
Plymouth	Devon
Princetown	Devon
Slapton	Devon
Bournemouth	Dorset
Bovington	Dorset
Christchurch	Dorset
Dorchester	Dorset
Highcliffe	Dorset
Lyme Regis	Dorset
Portland, Island of	Dorset
Sherborne	Dorset
Berkeley	Gloucestershire
Bourton-on-Water	Gloucestershire
Bredon's Norton	Gloucestershire
Cheltenham	Gloucestershire
Down Hatherly	Gloucestershire
Gloucester	Gloucestershire
Hidcote Bartrim	Gloucestershire
Tewkesbury	Gloucestershire
Tortworth	Gloucestershire
Bath	Somerset
Bristol	Somerset
Bruton	Somerset
East Coker	Somerset
Hunstrete	Somerset
Long Ashton	Somerset
Wellington	Somerset
Wells	Somerset
Wraxhall, near Bristol	Somerset

YORKSHIRE & NORTH

Widnes	Cheshire
Durham	Co. Durham
Ireshopeburn	Co. Durham
Killhope	Co. Durham
Newbiggin-In-Teesdale	Co. Durham
Staindrop, Raby Castle	Co. Durham
Kendal	Cumbria
Keswick	Cumbria
Ulverston	Cumbria
Whitehaven	Cumbria
Accrington	Lancashire
Pendle Hill	Lancashire
Warrington	Lancashire
Warton	Lancashire
Manchester	Manchester
Liverpool	Merseyside
Alnwick	Northumberland
Carlisle	Northumberland
Monkwearmouth	Tyne and Wear
Sunderland	Tyne and Wear
Washington	Tyne and Wear
York	Yorkshire
Boynton	Yorkshire ERiding
Immingham	Yorkshire ERiding
Beverley	Yorkshire, East
Little Weighton	Yorkshire, East
Flamborough Head	Yorkshire, East
Stockton on Tees	Yorkshire, North
Filey	Yorkshire, North
Great Ayton	Yorkshire, North
Hemingbrough	Yorkshire, North
Kiplin	Yorkshire, North
Marske	Yorkshire, North
Marton	Yorkshire, North
Middlesbrough	Yorkshire, North
Scarborough	Yorkshire, North
Selby	Yorkshire, North
Staithes	Yorkshire, North
Whitby	Yorkshire, North
Austerfield	Yorkshire, South
Epworth	Yorkshire, South
Sheffield	Yorkshire, South
Birstall, Leeds	Yorkshire, West
Fulneck	Yorkshire, West
Leeds	Yorkshire, West
Parlington	Yorkshire, West
Saltaire, Bradford	Yorkshire, West
Heptonstall	Yorkshire, West

SCOTLAND

Arbigland, Dumfries	Scotland
Dornach, Sutherland	Scotland
Dunfermline	Scotland
Kelso, Borders	Scotland

WALES

Bryn Eglwys, Clwyd	Wales
Wrexham	Wales

GAZETTEER

Accrington, Lancashire
Haworth Art Gallery, Haworth Park
Manchester Road, Accrington
Lancashire BB5 2JS
Tel. 01254 233 782
Haworth Art Gallery has a prized
collection of Tiffany glass, a gift from
Joseph Briggs who was born and
raised in Accrington. He immigrated to
New York to work for Louis Comfort
Tiffany in 1890 at the age of seventeen
and remained with him for the rest of
his life.

Acton Burnell, Shropshire
St. Mary's Church by Acton Burnell
Castle, Acton Burnell
Shropshire SY5 7PE
    Colonel Richard E. Lee

Aldbourne, Wiltshire
Blue Boar, 20 The Green, Aldbourne
Wiltshire SN8 2EN
Tel. 01672 540237
    Memorial to the American 101st
    Airborne Division
    Barrack block moved to a museum
    in Toccoa, Georgia

Aldershot, Hampshire
Aldershot Military Museum
Queens Avenue, Aldershot
Hampshire GU11 2LG
Tel. 01252 314598
www.hants.gov.uk/museum/aldershot
    Samuel F. Cody

Alford, Lincolnshire
    Anne Marbury Hutchinson

Alford Manor House, West Street
Alford, Lincolnshire LN13 9HT
Tel. 01507 463073
www.alford.info/manorhouse.htm
The thatched manor house is now a
folk museum with an exhibit on early
American settlers from Lincolnshire.

Windmill Hotel, Market Place
Alford LN13 9EB
Tel. 01507 463377
www.alfordwindmillhotel.com
    Thomas Paine

Allington, Kent
Allington Castle, Castle Road, Allington
near Maidstone, Kent ME16 0NB
Tel. 01622 691 666

Email: sec@allingtoncastle.org
www.touruk.co.uk/castles/castle_alling
ton.htm
In the 1950s the castle was purchased
by the Carmelite religious order which
later moved to The Friars in nearby
Aylesford. Allington Castle is now a
private home but it can be glimpsed
from the to path of the Medway River.
    Thomas Wyatt
    Francis Wyatt

Alnwick, Northumberland
Alnwick Castle, Alnwick
Northumberland NE66 1NQ
Tel. 01665 510777
Information line: 01665 511 100
www.alnwickcastle.com
    George Percy
    Hugh Percy
    James Smithson

Alveley, Shropshire
Coton Hall, Hollow Ash Lane
Alveley, Shropshire WV15 6ES
northwest of Stourbridge off the A442
    Colonel Richard E. Lee

Ayot St. Lawrence, Hertfordshire
Shaw's Corner, Ayot St. Lawrence
nr Welwyn, Hertfordshire AL6 9BX
Tel. 01438 820307
www.nationaltrust.org.uk
    George Bernard Shaw

Alrewas, Staffordshire
National Memorial Arboretum
Croxall Road, Alrewas
Staffordshire DE13 7AR
www.nationalmemorialarboretum.org.uk
    Allied Special Forces Memorial
    Grove

Arbigland, Dumfries, Scotland
John Paul Jones Cottage Museum
Arbigland, Kirkbean, Dumfries
Scotland DG2 8BQ
Tel. 01387 880613
www.jpj.demon.co.uk
    John Paul Jones

Ardingly, West Sussex
Wakehurst Place
Royal Botanic Gardens
Ardingly, West Sussex RH17 6TN
Tel. 01444 894000
www.rbgkew.org.uk
    Thomas Culpeper

    Catherine Culpeper Fairfax

St. Peter's Church
Street Lane, Ardingly
West Sussex RH17 6UR
www.ardinglychurch.co.uk
    Culpeper family

Arrington, Cambridgeshire
Wimpole Hall and Park
Arrington near Royston
Cambridgeshire SG8 0BW
Tel. 01223 207 257
www.nationaltrust.org.uk and
www.wimpole.info
    US military hospital on estate
    during World War II
    Memorial plaque to 323rd
    Squadron, 91st Bomb Group,
    US 8th Army
    Control Tower Museum at
    Bassingbourn

Ashburton, Devon
Ashburton Museum, The Bull Ring
Ashburton, Devon TQ13 7AB
Tel. 01364 652648
www.ashburton.org/museum
Ashburton Museum houses a unique
collection of North American Indian
artifacts.

Ashford, Kent
Church of St. Mary the Virgin
The Churchyard, Ashford
Kent TN23 1QG
    Thomas "Customer" Smythe

Attleborough, Norfolk
Train station, Station Road
Attleborough, Norfolk NR17 2AS
    453rd Bomb Group memorial
    Jimmy Stewart and Walter Matthau

Austerfield, South Yorkshire
St. Helena's Church
High Street, Austerfield
South Yorkshire DN10 6QS
Tel. 01302 710298
    William Bradford

Bradford's Cottage, Austerfield
South Yorkshire

Austerfield Field Centre, Old Primary
School, Austerfield
South Yorkshire DN10 6RG
www.austerfieldfsc82.freeserve.co.uk

William Bradford
William Butten
Mayflower

Aylesford, Kent
Aylesford Priory, Aylesford
Kent ME20 7BX
Tel. 01622 717272
www.carmelite.org/aylesford/index.htm
Thomas Wyatt the Younger
Francis Wyatt

Babworth, Nottinghamshire
All Saints' Church
The church is kept locked, but details
of keyholders are given in the porch.
Contact: All Saints' Church, The
Incumbent, Babworth Rectory,
Babworth, Retford, Nottinghamshire
DN22 8EP
Tel. 01777 703253
Richard Clyfton
William Brewster
Mayflower

Bassingbourn, Cambridgeshire
Bassingbourn Control Tower Museum
Bassingbourn near Royston
Cambridgeshire SG8 5LX
Tel. 01763 243500
www.bassingbourntowermuseum.co.uk
Memphis Belle

Bath, Somerset
American Museum in Britain
Claverton Manor, Bath
Somerset BA2 7BD
Tel. 01225 460503
www.americanmuseum.org
Mount Vernon
Pocahontas
Josiah Henson
George Washington
Winston Churchill

Bath Abbey, Bath BA1 1LT
Tel. 01225 422462
www.bathabbey.org
William Bingham

Beaulieu, Hampshire
Beaulieu Palace House, Beaulieu
Brockenhurst, Hampshire SO42 7ZN
Tel. 01590 612345
www.beaulieu.co.uk
The National Motor Museum
collection at Beaulieu includes
American cars such as a Cord, a 1901

Columbia Electric Car, a 1914 Model T,
and the first Cadillac to be brought to
Britain.
Thomas Wriothesley, 1st Earl of
Southampton

Berkeley, Gloucestershire
Berkeley Castle, Berkeley
Gloucestershire GL13 9BQ
Tel. 01453 810332
www.berkeley-castle.com
John, Lord Berkeley
Francis Drake

Beverley, East Yorkshire
Beverley Minster, Beverley
East Yorkshire HU17 0DP
Tel. 01482 868540
www.beverleyminster.co.uk
George Percy
Hugh Percy
James Smithson

Bexhill-on-Sea, East Sussex
De La Warr Pavilion, Marina, Bexhill
East Sussex TN40 1DP
www.dlwp.com
Thomas West, 3rd Baron de la Warr

Bideford, Devon
St. Mary's Church, Church Walk
Bideford, Devon EX39 2BT
www.bidefordstmarys.co.uk
Richard Grenville
American Indian baptized as
"Rawleigh"

Hoops Hotel, Horns Cross
west of Bideford, Devon EX39 5DL
Francis Drake
Walter Raleigh
Richard Grenville

Billericay, Essex
Chantry House, 8–10 High Street
Billericay, Essex CM12 9BQ
Mayflower
Christopher Martin

Bilsby, Lincolnshire
Holy Trinity Church, Sutton Road
Bilsby near Alford
Lincolnshire LN13 9PY
John Wheelwright

Birmingham, West Midlands
Chamberlain Square, Birmingham
West Midlands B3 3HQ

Statue of Joseph Priestley

Soho House, Soho Avenue, Handsworth
Birmingham, West Midlands B18 5LB
Tel. 0121 554 9122
www.bmag.org.uk/soho_house/
Lunar Society
Benjamin Franklin
Joseph Priestley
Thomas Jefferson

Unitarian New Meeting House, 31 Ryland
Street, Five Ways, Birmingham
West Midlands B16 8BL
Tel. 0121 455 8818
www.birminghamnewmeeting.org.uk
Joseph Priestley

Birstall, West Yorkshire
Church of St. Peter, Kirkgate, Birstall
West Yorkshire WF17 9PB
off Bradford Road (A652)
www.stpetersbirstall.co.uk
Joseph Priestley

Market Place, Birstall
West Yorkshire WF17 9EN
Statue of Joseph Priestley

Bladon, Oxfordshire
St. Martin's Church, Bladon, Woodstock
Oxfordshire OX20 1RS
Winston Churchill
Jennie Jerome Churchill
Cornwallis-West
Consuelo Vanderbilt,
Duchess of Marlborough

Bletchley, Buckinghamshire
Bletchley Park, Wilton Avenue, Bletchley
Milton Keynes, Buckinghamshire
MK3 6EB
Tel. 01908 640404
www.bletchleypark.org.uk
Secret code-breakers of World War II
D-Day flag
Winston Churchill and
Jennie Jerome
General Eisenhower

Bocking, Essex
Parish Church of St. Mary the Virgin
Church Street, Bocking, Braintree
Essex CM7 5JY
www.stmarys-bocking.co.uk
Thomas Hooker

Lyons Hall, Lyons Hall Road, Bocking
Essex CH7 9SH
    Thomas Hooker
    Braintree Company

Bodiam, East Sussex
Bodiam Castle, Bodiam near
Robertsbridge, East Sussex TN32 5UA
Tel. 01580 830436
www.nationaltrust.org.uk
    George Nathaniel Curzon
    Grace Hinds

Boreham, Essex
St. Andrew's Parish Church and
Old Rectory, Church Rd, Boreham near
Chelmsford, Essex CM3 3EP
    Benjamin Rush

Boston, Lincolnshire
St. Botolph's Church, Wormgate, Boston
Lincolnshire PE21 6NP
Tel. 01295 362864
www.parish-of-boston.org.uk
    John Cotton
    Plaque to the five Boston men who
      became governors of
      Massachusetts

Guildhall Museum, South Street, Boston
Lincolnshire PE21 6HT
Tel. 01205 356656
www.bostonuk.com/visitors/att_guildh
all.htm
    Pilgrim Fathers

Fydell House, South Square, Boston
Lincolnshire PE21 6HU
Tel. 01205 351520
www.bostonuk.com/visitors/att_fydell
    American Room

Pilgrim Fathers' Memorial, River Witham
(Scotia Creek), Fishtoft near Boston
Lincolnshire PE21 0SH
past Scalp Road
www.bostonuk.com/history/sites_pilgri
mfathers.htm
    Pilgrims

Botley, Hampshire
Market Square, Botley near
Southampton, Hampshire SO30 2EJ
    William Cobbett

Bournemouth, Dorset
Langtry Manor Hotel, Derby Road
Bournemouth, Dorset BH1 3QB

Tel. 01202 553887
www.langtrymanor.co.uk
The house that the Prince of Wales
bought for his mistress Lillie Langtry is
now a hotel.

Bourton-on-the-Water
Gloucestershire
Cotswold Motor Museum and Toy Collection
Old Mill, Bourton-on-the-Water
Gloucestershire GL54 2BY
Tel. 01451 821255
www.cotswold-motor-museum.com

Bovington, Dorset
Tank Museum, Bovington
Dorset BH20 6JG
Tel. 01929 405096
www.tankmuseum.co.uk

Boxgrove, West Sussex
Boxgrove Priory, Church Lane
Boxgrove near Chichester
West Sussex PO18 0ED
www.english-heritage.org.uk
    Pilot Officer William M.L. Fiske III
    Battle of Britain

Boxley, Kent
Church of St. Mary and All Saints
The Street, Boxley, Kent ME14 3DX
Tel. 01622 758606
www.boxleychurch.ik.com
    Haute Wyatt
    Edwin Sandys
    George Sandys

Boxley Abbey, Boarley Lane, Boxley
Kent ME14 3BT
The ragstone barn, built in 1280, is the
only remaining part of Boxley Manor. It
can be seen from the road that leads
from Sandling to Penenden Heath.
(Private residence)
    Francis Wyatt
    Edwin Sandys

Boynton, East Yorkshire
St. Andrew's Church, Main Street
Boynton, East Yorkshire YO16 4XQ
    William Strickland

Boynton Hall, Boynton near Bridlington
East Yorkshire YO16 4XJ
www.statelyholidayhomes.co.uk
The dairy at Boynton Hall has been
converted into a modern holiday home
with many of the original features

preserved.
    Strickland family

Bradwell-on-Sea, Essex
Parish Church of St. Thomas
High Street, Bradwell-on-Sea
Essex CM0 7QL
    Dr. John Sherman

Braintree, Essex
Braintree District Museum, Manor Street
Braintree, Essex CM7 3YG
Tel. 01376 325266
www.enjoybraintreedistrict.co.uk/
museum/
    Braintree Company
    John Bridge
    Harvard College

Braintree Town Hall, Market Place
Braintree, Essex CM7 3YG
Tel. 01376 557776
    "Sailing of the Braintree Company
      in the *Lyon*, 1632"
    Braintree "Company of
      Twenty-Four"

Church of Our Lady, Queen of Peace
The Avenue, Braintree CM7 3HY
    Memorial window – 322nd, 394th,
      410th, and 416th Bomb Groups
    121st Station Hospital

Bredon's Norton, Gloucestershire
GL20 7HA
    Victoria California Claflin Martin
    Thomas Copley

Brighton, East Sussex
Franklin Tavern, 158 Lewes Road
Brighton, East Sussex BN2 3LF
    Benjamin Franklin

Bruton, Somerset
St. Mary's Parish Church, Bruton
Somerset BA10 0EB
    Maurice Berkeley
    George, William, and John Berkeley
    Virginia
    New Jersey

Bryn Eglwys, Clwyd, Wales
St. Tysilio's Church, Bryn Eglwys, Clwyd,
A5 west from LLangollen (LL20 8PW),
then northeast on the A5104 in
Denbighshire
www.colegygroes.co.uk/bryneglw.htm
    Elihu Yale

Bristol

Christopher Columbus visited Bristol.

George Clymer of Pennsylvania signed the Declaration of Independence. His father immigrated to America from Bristol.

American Consulate
37 Queen Square, Bristol BS1 4QS
Triangle slave trade

Bristol's Floating Harbour BS1 6JN

British Empire and Commonwealth Museum
Clock Tower Yard, Temple Meads
Bristol BS1 6QH
Tel. 0117 925 4980
www.empiremuseum.co.uk
Exploration of the New World
Trade with America
Slave trade and anti-slavery movement

Cabot Tower on Brandon Hill
Charlotte Street, Bristol BS1 5PX
John Cabot

City Museum & Art Gallery
Queen's Road, Bristol BS8 1RL
Tel. 0117 922 3571
www.bristol-city.gov.uk
John Cabot

Church of St. Mary Redcliffe
Redcliffe Way, Bristol BS1 6NL
www.stmaryredcliffe.co.uk

Richard Ameryck
American Chapel
John Cabot – whale bone
Matthew
Giles Penn
Admiral William Penn – burial marker and memorial with armor

Church of St. Stephen
St. Stephen's Avenue, Bristol BS1 1YL
Tel. 0117 927 7977
Martin Pring

Clifton College
College Road, Bristol BS8 3JH
www.cliftoncollegeuk.com
General Douglas McArthur
The college flies the American flag on the 4th of July.

Georgian House Museum
7 Great George Street
Bristol BS1 5RR
Triangle slave trade

Great Western Dockyard
Bristol BS1 6TY
Tel. 0117 9225737
www.matthew.co.uk
Replica of John Cabot's ship, the *Matthew*

15 Hughenden Road
Horfield, Bristol BS7 8SF
Cary Grant

Merchant Venturers Almshouses
King Street, Bristol BS1 4DZ

Millennium Square
Bristol BS1 5DB
Statue of William Penn
Statue of Cary Grant

The New Room
Methodist Chapel
36 The Horsefair, Bristol, BS1 3JE
Tel. 0117 9264740
http://newroombristol.org.uk
Both the New Room and Charles Wesley's house are open to the public, Charles's house by appointment.
John Wesley
Charles Wesley

Ostrich Inn
Lower Guinea Street, Redcliffe
Bristol BS1 6TJ
Tel. 0117 927 3774

Redcliffe Caves
Bristol BS1 6TJ
Triangle slave trade

Tourist Information Centre
The Annexe, Wildscreen Walk
Harbourside, Bristol BS1 5DB
Tel. 0117 926 0767
http://visitbristol.co.uk/site/home
Online walking tour:
http://Website.lineone.net/~stkittsnevis/bristol.htm
Triangle slave trade

Venturers' House
King Street, Bristol BS1 4DZ

Buckland Monachorum, Devon
Buckland Abbey, Yelverton, Devon
PL20 6EY
Tel. 01822 853607
www.nationaltrust.org.uk
Buckland Abbey is now a maritime and
folk museum.
 Richard Grenville
 Mary Rose – Plymouth
 Walter Raleigh
 Lost Colony of Roanoke
 Francis Drake

Bungay, Suffolk
St. Mary's Church, Church Lane
Bungay, Suffolk NR35 1NX
www.2ndair.org.uk/Bases/bungay.htm
For "Bungay Bucakaroos":
www.aviationmuseum.net/446bg.htm
 310th and 446th Bomb Groups
 Parts of airfield and buildings –
 private property

Bures, Suffolk
St. Mary's Church, Church Square
Bures, Suffolk CO8 5AB
www.suffolkchurches.co.uk/bures.htm
 Abraham Lincoln

Burwash, East Sussex
Batemans, Burwash, Etchingham
East Sussex TN19 7DS
Tel. 01435 882302
www.nationaltrust.org.uk
 Rudyard Kipling

Bury St. Edmunds, Suffolk
Cathedral of St. Edmundsbury
Angel Hill, Bury St. Edmunds
Suffolk IP33 1LS
Tel. 01284 754933
www.stedscathedral.co.uk
 Cathedral treasury
 Bartholomew Gosnold
 Appleby Rose Gardens

Tourist Information Centre, 6 Angel Hill
Bury St. Edmunds IP33 1UZ
Tel. 01284 764667
www.stedmundsbury.gov.uk/sebc/visit

Hengrave Hall, Bury Road, Hengrave
Bury St. Edmunds, Suffolk IP28 6LZ
Tel. 01284 701561
www.hengravehallcentre.org.uk
Hengrave Hall is now a retreat center
for people of all denominations and
nationalities.

 George Washington
 Gage family

Calne, Wiltshire
Bowood House, Derry Hill, Calne
Wiltshire SN11 0LZ
Tel. 01249 812102
www.bowood-house.co.uk
 Joseph Priestley
 American Chemical Society
 International Historic Chemical
 Landmark
 Priestley's Pool

Canterbury, Kent
 James Chilton

Canterbury Environment Centre
St. Alphege Lane *(off Palace Street)*
Canterbury, Kent CT1 2EB
Tel. 01227 457 009
www.canterburycentre.org.uk
The centre now occupies the Church
of St. Alphege.
 Robert Cushman
 Mayflower
 Thomas Cushman
 Mary Allerton

Carlisle, Cumbria
Lowther Street Congregational Church
Carlisle, Cumbria CA3 8DA
 President Woodrow Wilson

Chagford, Devon
Endecott House, Chagford, Devon
*(on the Town Square next door to the
Three Crowns Hotel)* TQ13 8AJ
 John Endecott, a Pilgrim Father

**Chalfont St. Giles,
Buckinghamshire**
Captain Cook Memorial *(in field off Vache
Lane)*, Chalfont St. Giles
Buckinghamshire HP8 4XX
The Vache is private property, but there
is public access to the monument
from Vache Lane.
 Captain Cook

Chartwell, Kent
Chartwell, Mapleton Road, Chartwell
near Westerham, Kent TN16 1PS
Tel. 01732 868381
Infoline: 01732 866368
www.nationaltrust.org.uk
 Winston Churchill

Chatsworth, Derbyshire
Chatsworth, Bakewell
Derbyshire DE45 1PP
Tel. 01246 565300
www.chatsworth-house.co.uk
 Kathleen Kennedy
 President John F. Kennedy

Chelmsford, Essex
Chelmsford Cathedral, New Street
Chelmsford, Essex CM1 1TY
Tel. 01245 294480
www.cathedral.chelmsford.anglican.org
 Thomas Hooker
 Archbishop William Laud
 George Washington
 Thomas Mildmay

Guy Harlings, New Street, Cathedral
Close, Chelmsford, Essex CM1 1TY
 Mildmay family

Cheltenham, Gloucestershire
The Centreland Singers
Tel. 01242 237948
www.centreland.org.uk
 Native American music
 UK pow-wows

Chelveston, Northamptonshire
Chelveston Airfield, Station 105, south of
Kimbolton Road, Chelveston
Northamptonshire NN9 6AN
www.mighty8thaf.preller.us/php/1Loc.p
hp?Base=Chelveston
 8th USAAF – 60th Troop
 Carrier Group
 8th USAAF – 301st Bombardment
 Group
 8th USAAF – 305th Bombardment
 Group, commanded by
 Colonel Curtis LeMay

Church of St. John the Baptist, Caldecott
Road, Chelveston, Northamptonshire
NN9 6AT
On the tower wall is a war memorial to
the 305th USAAF Bomb Group, who
were based at RAF Chelveston during
World War II. The 305th Bomb Group
helped fund the restoration of the
church tower.

Chenies, Buckinghamshire
Chenies Manor House, Village Green
Chenies, Buckinghamshire WD3 6ER
Tel. 01494 762888

CAMBRIDGE

Cambridge Visitor Information Centre
The Old Library, Wheeler Street
Cambridge CB2 3QB
Tel. 0871 2268006
www.visitcambridge.org

Church of St. Mary the Less (also known as "Little St. Mary's Church")
at the corner of Trumpington Street and Little St. Mary Lane
Cambridge CB2 1RR
Tel. 01223 366202
www.ely.anglican.org/parishes/camlsm
   Rev. Godfrey Washington
   The "Stars and Stripes"

Church of St. Andrew the Great
St. Andrew's Street
Cambridge CB2 3AX
Tel. 01223 518218
www.stag.org
   Captain Cook

UNIVERSITY OF CAMBRIDGE
Website for information about the colleges: www.cam.ac.uk

Christ's College, St Andrew's Street
Cambridge CB2 3BU
Tel. 01223 334900
www.christs.cam.ac.uk
   John Smyth
   Ezekiel Rogers
   Ralph Izard

Churchill College, Storey's Way
Cambridge CB3 0DS
Tel. 01223 336000
www.chu.cam.ac.uk
   Winston Churchill

Clare College, Trinity Lane
Cambridge CB2 1TL
Tel. 01223 333200
www.clare.cam.ac.uk
   Paul Mellon
   James Watson
   Henry Louis Gates, Jr.

Corpus Christi College, Trumpington Street, Cambridge CB2 1RH
Tel. 01223 338000
www.corpus.cam.ac.uk
   Robert "Trouble-Church" Browne

Darwin College, Silver Street
Cambridge CB3 9EU
Tel. 01223 335660

www.dar.cam.ac.uk
   Dian Fossey

Downing College, Downing Street
Cambridge CB2 1DQ
Tel. +44 1223 334800
http://www.dow.cam.ac.uk
   George Downing

Emmanuel College, St Andrew's Street
Cambridge CB2 3AP
Tel. 01223 334200
www.emma.cam.ac.uk
   Walter Mildmay
   College graduates who immigrated
      to American colonies
   John Cotton
   Thomas Hooker
   John Harvard
   Herchel Smith

Gonville and Caius College, Trinity Street
Cambridge CB2 1TA
Tel. 01223 332400
www.cai.cam.ac.uk
   Thomas Lynch, Jr.

Jesus College, Jesus Lane
Cambridge CB5 8BL
Tel. 01223 339339
www.jesus.cam.ac.uk
   Rev. John Eliot
   Alistair Cooke

King's College, King's Parade
Cambridge CB2 1ST
Tel. 01223 331100
www.kings.cam.ac.uk
   Berkeley College, Yale University
   James Watson

Magdalene College, Magdalene Street
Cambridge CB3 0AG
Tel. 01223 332100
www.magd.cam.ac.uk
   Henry Dunster

Newnham College, Sidgwick Avenue
Cambridge CB3 9DF
Tel. 01223 335700
www.newn.cam.ac.uk
   Sylvia Plath

Pembroke College, Trumpington Street
Cambridge CB2 1RF
Tel. 01223 338100
www.pem.cam.ac.uk
   Roger Williams

Peterhouse, Trumpington Street
Cambridge CB2 1RD
Tel. 01223 338200
www.pet.cam.ac.uk

   Rev. Godfrey Washington
   William Brewster

Queens' College, Silver Street
Cambridge CB3 9ET
Tel. 01223 335511
www.queens.cam.ac.uk
   Thomas Hooker
   Edmund Bohun
   Alexander Crummell
   Michael Foale

St. Catherine's College, Trumpington Street, Cambridge CB2 1RL
Tel. 01223 338300
www.caths.cam.ac.uk
   Nathaniel Bacon

St. John's College, St John's Street
Cambridge CB2 1TP
Tel. 01223 338600
www.joh.cam.ac.uk
   Henry Wriothesley, 3rd
      Earl of Southampton

Sidney Sussex College, Sidney Street
Cambridge CB2 3HU
Tel. 01223 338800
www.sid.cam.ac.uk
   John Wheelwright

Trinity College, Trinity Street
Cambridge CB2 1TQ
Tel. 01223 338400
www.trin.cam.ac.uk
   Jon Cotton
   John Winthrop
   Vladimir Nabokov
   Nicholas James MacDonald

Trinity Hall, Trinity Lane
Cambridge CB2 1TJ
Tel. 01223 332500
www.trinhall.cam.ac.uk
   Arthur Middleton

Cavendish Laboratory
Department of Physics
J J Thomson Avenue
Cambridge CB3 0HE
Tel. 01223 337200
www.phy.cam.ac.uk
   J. Robert Oppenheimer

www.visitbuckinghamshire.org/attracti
ons/info/housegdn/chenies/
    Henry Wriothesley
    Rachel Wriothesley
    William Russell

St. Michael's Church, Village Green
Chenies, Buckinghamshire WD3 6ER
Tel. 01494 762233
www.chenieschurch.cwc.net
    Russell family
    William Russell

Chigwell, Essex
Chigwell School, High Road, Chigwell
Essex IG7 6QF
Tel. 020 8501 5700
www.chigwell-school.org
    William Penn

Christchurch, Dorset
Hengistbury Head (near BH6 4NA)
    Gordon Selfridge

Clapham, Bedfordshire
Twinwood RAF Control Tower and **Glenn
Miller Museum**
Twinwood Road, Clapham
Bedfordshire MK41 6AD
Tel. 01234 350413
www.twinwoodevents.com
    Glenn Miller

Cliveden, Berkshire
Cliveden House, Cliveden near Taplow
Berkshire SL6 0JF
Tel. 01628 605069
Tel. 01628 668561 (hotel)
www.nationaltrust.org.uk
and www.clivedenhouse.co.uk
    Duke and Duchess of Sutherland
    William Waldorf Astor
    Nancy Langhorne (Lady Astor)
    Stanford University

Clopton, Suffolk
Debach Airfield, Grove Farm
Clopton, Suffolk IP13 6QS
www.mighty8thaf.preller.us/php/1Unit.
php?Unitkey=493
    8th USAAF, 3rd Bomb Division,
    93rd Combat Bombardment Wing
    493rd Bombardment Group,
    known as "Helton's Hellcats"

St. Mary the Virgin, Grundisburgh Road
Clopton, Suffolk IP13 6QB
A large memorial board at the west

end lists the names of over 200 men
of the USAAF 493rd Bombardment
Group killed during World War II who
were stationed at Debach/Clopton
airfield. The original flag from the base
hangs over the memorial.

Cobham, Surrey
Painshill Landscape Park, Portsmouth
Road, Cobham, Surrey KT11 1JE
Tel. 01932 868113
www.painshill.co.uk
    "American Roots"
    Thomas Jefferson
    John Adams

Coggeshall, Essex
Church of St. Peter-ad-Vincula, Church
Green, Coggeshall, Essex CO6 1UD
Tel. 01376 561234
www.st-peter-ad-vincula.org.uk
    Thomas Stoughton

Compton, Devon
Compton Castle, Compton near
Paignton, Devon TQ3 1TA
Tel. 01803 875740 (answerphone)
www.nationaltrust.org.uk
    Humphrey Gilbert
    Walter Raleigh

Conington, Cambridgeshire
Church of All Saints, Church Road,
Conington, Cambridgeshire PE7 3QA
    USAAF 457th Bombardment
    Group Memorial

Glatton Airfield (*now Peterborough
Business Airfield*), Conington
Cambridgeshire PE7 3PX
www.mighty8thaf.preller.us/php/1Unit.
php?Unitkey=457
    8th USAAF, 1st Bombardment
    Division, 94th Combat
    Bombardment Wing
    457th Bombardment
    Group Memorial

Copford Green, Essex
Copford Hall, Church Road, Copford
Green near Colchester
Essex CO6 1DG
    John Haynes
    Thomas Hooker
    Roger Williams

St. Michael and All Saints, Copford Green
near Colchester, Essex CO6 1DG

www.copfordchurch.org.uk and
www.british-history.ac.uk/
report.asp?compid=15213
    Haynes family

Corsham, Wiltshire
Corsham Court, Corsham
Wiltshire SN13 0BZ
Tel. 01249 701610
www.corsham-court.co.uk
    Thomas Smythe

Coughton, Warwickshire
Coughton Court, Coughton near Alcester
Warwickshire B49 5JA
Tel. 01789 400777/01789 762435
(Infoline)
www.coughtoncourt.co.uk and
www.nationaltrust.org.uk
    Walter Raleigh

Coventry, West Midlands
Coventry Cathedral, Hill Top, Coventry
West Midlands CV1 5AB
www.coventrycathedral.org.uk
    Jacob Epstein – *St. Michael*
    and the Devil

Cranham, Essex
Parish Church of All Saints, The Chase
Cranham, Upminster, Essex RM14 3YB
    James Oglethorpe

Cranham Hall, Cranham, Upminster
Essex RM14 3YB
    James Oglethorpe

Crowthorne, Berkshire
Broadmoor Hospital, Crowthorne
Berkshire RG45 7EG
Tel. 0800 064 3330
    William Chester Minor

Culford, Suffolk
Culford Hall, Culford near Bury St
Edmunds, Suffolk IP28 6TX
Tel. 01284 728615
www.culford.co.uk/history
Culford Hall is open annually for
heritage days, usually in September.
    Charles Cornwallis

Dartmouth, Devon
    Captain George Weymouth –
    Discovery
    Captain John Drew – *Godspeed*
    Henry Hudson
    Humphrey Gilbert

Bayard's Cove, Lower Street, Dartmouth
Devon TQ6 9AT
  Mayflower and *Speedwell*

Deal, Kent
St. Leonard's Church, Rectory Road, Deal
Kent CT14 9LU
  Silas Deane

Dedham, Essex
Church of St. Mary the Virgin, High Street
Dedham, Colchester, Essex CO7 6DE
Tel. 01206 322136
www.dedham-parishchurch.org.uk
  Roger Sherman

Deopham Green, Norfolk
Stalland Road, Deopham Green, Norfolk
NR18 9DN
  USAAF 452nd Bomb Group

Dornoch, Sutherland, Scotland
Skibo Castle, Dornoch, Sutherland
Scotland IV25 3RQ
Tel. 01862 894600
www.carnegieclub.co.uk
  Andrew Carnegie
  Booker T. Washington

Dorchester, Dorset
Holy Trinity Church, Dorchester, Dorset
DT1 1XA
Tel. 01305 251976
  Rev. John White

St. Peter's Church, High West Street
Dorchester, Dorset DT1 1XA
  Rev. John White
  Dorchester Company

Old Rectory, Colliton Street, Dorchester
Dorset DT1 1XH
  Rev. John White

Dorking, Surrey
Mullins House, West Street, Dorking
Surrey RH4 1BS
  William Mullins
  Priscilla Mullins
  Merchant Adventurers
  Mayflower

Deepdene House *(house now demolished)*
Deepdene Avenue, Dorking, Surrey
  Lily Price Hammersley
    Spencer-Churchill

Down Hatherley, Gloucestershire
St. Mary and Corpus Christi Church, Down
Hatherley Lane, Down Hatherley
Gloucestershire GL2 9QA
Tel. 01452 731483
www.downhatherleyparishchurch.co.uk
  Button Gwinnet

Droitwich, Worcestershire
St. Peter's Church, St. Peter's Church
Lane, Droitwich, Worcestershire
WR9 7AN
Tel. 01905 794952
www.st-peter-de-witton.fsnet.co.uk
  Edward Winslow

Dunfermline, Scotland
Andrew Carnegie Birthplace Museum
Moodie Street, Dunfermline, Fife
Scotland KY12 7PL
Tel. 01383 723638
www.carnegiebirthplace.com
  Andrew Carnegie

Durham, County Durham
Durham Cathedral, Palace Green
Durham, County Durham DH1 3RN
Tel. 0191 386 4266
www.durhamcathedral.co.uk
  John Wessyngton
  George Washington

Duxford, Cambridgeshire
**American Air Museum, Imperial War
Museum Duxford**, Cambridgeshire
CB2 4QR
Tel. 01223 835000
www.iwm.org.uk/duxford
The museum houses the largest
collection of historic American combat
aircraft outside the USA.

Easebourne, West Sussex
Cowdray Castle, Easebourne near
Midhurst, West Sussex GU29 OAQ
Tel. 01730 812423
www.cowdray.co.uk
In 1793 Cowdray Castle was destroyed
by fire and is now a romantic ruin. It is
possible to visit the ruins and the
small museum contained in the upper
story.
  Henry Wriothesley, 3rd
    Earl of Southampton

East Budleigh, Devon
All Saints' Church, High Street
East Budleigh, Devon EX9 7ED

  Walter Raleigh
  Roger Conant

Hayes Barton Cottage, Hayes Lane
East Budleigh, Devon EX9 7BS
  Walter Raleigh

East Coker, Somerset
Church of St. Michael and All Angels
East Coker near Yeovil
Somerset BA22 9JG
  T.S. Eliot

East Grinstead, West Sussex
Hammerwood Park, East Grinstead
West Sussex RH19 3QE
Tel. 01342 850594
www.hammerwood.mistral.co.uk/ and
www.touruk.co.uk/houses/housewsuss
_hammer.htm
  Benjamin Henry Latrobe

Sackville College, Church Lane off High
Street, East Grinstead
West Sussex RH19 3AZ
Tel. 01342 321 930
www.sackville-college.co.uk
  Robert Sackville, Earl of Dorset
  Sackville-West family

East Sutton, Kent
Church of St. Peter and St. Paul, Church
Lane off Workhouse Lane, East Sutton
Kent ME17 3DH
  Samuel Argall
  Mary Scott
  George Washington

Ecton, Northamptonshire
Franklin's smithy behind Three
Horseshoes Inn, High Street, Ecton
Northamptonshire NN6 0QA
  Benjamin Franklin

St. Mary Madgalene Church, West Street
Ecton, Northamptonshire NN6 0QE
Tel. 01604 416326
  Benjamin Franklin

Edenbridge, Kent
Hever Castle, Edenbridge
Kent TN8 7NG
Tel. 01732 865224
www.hever-castle.co.uk
  William Waldorf Astor
  John Jacob V

Edensor, Derbyshire
St. Peter's Church, Edensor
Derbyshire DE45 1PH
   Kathleen Kennedy

Ely, Cambridgeshire
Ely Cathedral, High Street, Ely
Cambridgeshire CB7 4DL
Tel. 01353 667735
www.cathedral.ely.anglican.org
   John Eliot

Epsom, Surrey
RAC Woodcote Park Golf Club
Wilmerhatch Lane, Epsom
Surrey KT18 7EW
Tel. 01372 276311
www.royalautomobileclub.co.uk
   Charles, 3rd Lord Baltimore
   Frederick Calvert,
     6th Lord Baltimore
   Henry Harford
   Royal Automobile Club

Epworth, South Yorkshire
Old Rectory, 1 Rectory Street, Epworth
South Yorkshire DN9 1HX
Tel. 01427 872268
www.oldrectory63.freeserve.co.uk
   Samuel Wesley
   John and Charles Wesley

St. Andrew's Church, Market Square
Epworth, South Yorkshire DN9 1EU
Tel. 01427 872471
www.churchmousewebsite.co.uk/
StAndrew
   Samuel Wesley
   John and Charles Wesley

Wesley Memorial Church, High Street
Epworth, South Yorkshire DN9 1EP
www.wesley-memorial.co.uk

Epworth's market cross
   John Wesley

Esher, Surrey
St. George's Church, Esher
Surrey KT10 9QY
St. George's Esher is behind the Bear
Hotel. It is no longer in regular use,
but is open for visiting every Saturday
April to September 10.30am –
12.30pm. At other times, check with
the parish office at Christ Church, just
across the road at The Green.
   Thomas Hooker – "Hooker pulpit"

Wayneflete Tower, Wayneflete Tower
Avenue, Esher Place Estate, Esher
Surrey KT10 8QG
www.waynefletetower.com
Wayneflete Tower is a private
residence, but can be seen from
Pelham Walk.
   Thomas Hooker

Eton, Berkshire
Eton College, Eton near Windsor
Berkshire SL4 6DW
Tel. 01753 671000
www.etoncollege.com
   Hugh Percy
   Arthur Lee
   Thomas Lynch, Jr.
   Thomas Nelson
   Charles Cornwallis
   Many members of the Astor family,
     including John Jacob Astor of
     Hever, 1st Baron (1886–1971:
     proprietor, *The Times* newspaper)
     and Waldorf Astor, 2nd Viscount
     (1879–1952: proprietor, *The*
     Observer newspaper 1911–45)

Farnborough, Hampshire
   Samuel Cody
   British Army balloon factory

Cody Building of the Defence Evaluation and
Research Agency (DERA), Ively Road
Farnborough, Hampshire GU14 0LX
   Samuel Cody

Farnham, Surrey
William Cobbett (pub), Bridge Square
Farnham, Surrey GU9 7PS
Tel. 01252 726281
   William Cobbett

St. Andrew's Church, Upper Church Lane,
Farnham, Surrey GU9 7PW
Tel. 01252 715412
William Cobbett's tomb stands just
outside the door.

Museum of Farnham, Willmer House
38 West Street, Farnham
Surrey GU9 7DX
Tel. 01252 715094
www.waverley.gov.uk/museumoffarnham
   William Cobbett

Fenny Drayton, Warwickshire
St Michael and All Angels
Church Lane, Fenny Drayton

Warwickshire CV13 6BA
   George Fox

Filey, North Yorkshire
Filey Museum, 8–10 Queen Street, Filey
North Yorkshire YO14 9HB
Tel. 01723 515 013
www.discoveryorkshirecoast.com
   Filey's maritime heritage

Filey Bay, near Scarborough
North Yorkshire YO14 9LA
   John Paul Jones
   Bonhomme Richard

Firle, East Sussex
Firle Place, Firle near Lewes
East Sussex BN8 6LP
Tel. 01273 858307
www.firleplace.co.uk
   General Thomas Gage
   Margaret Kemble Gage
   Benjamin West's portrait of
     Elizabeth Gideon
   Address giving the Freedom of the
     City of New York to General Gage
   Order from the Provisional
     Congress of Massachusetts
     rescinding honors given to
     General Gage
   "Plan of the City of New York,"
     drawn by Captain John Montresor
     in 1775
   Nathan Hale

Flamborough Head
near Bridlington, East Yorkshire
YO15 1AR
   John Paul Jones

Flixton, Suffolk
Norfolk and Suffolk Aviation Museum
The Street, Flixton near Bungay
Suffolk NR35 1NZ
Tel. 01986 896644
www.aviationmuseum.net
   World War II and US bases in
     Norfolk and Suffolk
   Project Anvil
   Joseph P. Kennedy, Jr.

St. Mary's Church, Church Road
Flixton, Suffolk NR35 1NX
   Wooden gates donated by 446th
     Bomb Group

Forest Row, East Sussex
Ashdown House, Forest Row

East Sussex RH18 5JY
Tel. 01342 822574
www.ashdownhouse.co.uk
Ashdown House has been used as a
school since 1843.
   Benjamin Henry Latrobe

Frimley, Surrey
St Peter's Church, Frimley Green Road
Frimley near Camberley
Surrey GU16 8JT
Tel. 01276 23309
www.frimleyparish.org.uk
   Francis Bret Hart

Fulneck, West Yorkshire
Fulneck School, Fulneck near Pudsey
West Yorkshire LS28 8DS
Tel. 0113 257 0235
www.fulneckschool.co.uk
   Benjamin Henry Latrobe

Gainsborough, Lincolnshire
Gainsborough Old Hall, Parnell Street
Gainsborough, Lincolnshire DN21 2NB
Tel. 01427 612669
www.gainsboroughholdhall.co.uk
   John Smyth
   William Bradford
   William Brewster

John Robinson Memorial Church
Church Street, Gainsborough
Lincolnshire DN21 2JR
   John Robinson

Gloucester, Gloucestershire
Gloucester Cathedral, St. Mary's Square
Gloucester, Gloucestershire GL1 2LR
Tel. 01452 528095
www.gloucestercathedral.org.uk
   John Stafford Smith
   "Star-Spangled Banner"
   War of 1812
   General William Lyman

Godalming, Surrey
Westbrook Manor (now named The
Meath), Westbrook Road
Godalming, Surrey GU7 2QH
The Oglethorpe family home has been
called The Meath since 1892 when it
was purchased by the Countess of
Meath. It is a residential facility for
women and men with neurological
disorders.
   Theophilus Oglethorpe
   James Oglethorpe

Colony of Georgia

Godalming Museum, 109a High Street
Godalming, Surrey GU7 1AQ
Tel. 01483 426510
www.godalming-museum.org.uk
   James Oglethorpe
   Winston Churchill

Church of St. Peter and St. Paul
Church Street, Godalming
Surrey GU7 1EP
Tel. 01483 414135
www.godalming.org.uk/twochurches.html
   Westbrook Chapel
   James Oglethorpe

Goodwood, West Sussex
Goodwood House and Racecourse
Goodwood near Chichester, West
Sussex PO18 0PX
Tel. 01243 755000
www.goodwood.co.uk
   Charles Lennox,
      3rd Duke of Richmond

Goudhurst, Kent
St. Mary the Virgin Church, Church Road
Goudhurst, Kent TN17 1BH
   Bedgebury Chapel
   Culpeper family
   John Culpeper (1430–80)
   Thomas Culpeper,
      2nd Baron, of Virginia

Bedgebury Manor, Goudhurst
Kent TN17 2SH
   Walter Culpeper of Goudhurst
   Agnes Roper, widow of
   John Bedgebury

**Grafton Underwood,
Northamptonshire**
Airfield north of Geddington Road
Grafton Underwood
Northamptonshire NN14 3B
www.384thbombgroup.com/pages/gu.
html
   8th USAAF, 384th
      Bombardment Group
   Memorial on Geddington
   Road, with the inscription:
   THE FIRST AND LAST BOMBS
   DROPPED BY THE 8th AIR FORCE
   WERE FROM AIRPLANES FLYING
   FROM GRAFTON UNDERWOOD

Church of St. James the Apostle, Brigstock
Road, Grafton Underwood
Northamptonshire NN14 3AA
Ask the postmaster for the key to the
church to see a stained-glass window
that commemorates the men of the
USAAF based at Grafton Underwood
during the Second World War.

Gravesend, Kent
   Henry Hudson

St. George's Church, Church Street
Gravesend, Kent DA11 0DJ
Tel. 01474 534965
www.stgeorgesgravesend.org.uk
   Pocahontas

Great Ashfield, Suffolk
Great Ashfield airfield, to the west of
Elmswell Road, Great Ashfield
Suffolk IP31 3HL (private property)
The village sign shows an airplane
flying over the parish church.
   8th USAAF, 3rd Air Division,
      385th Bombardment Group

All Saints' Church, Elmswell Road
Great Ashfield, Suffolk IP31 3HF
http://8thcontrails.com/ipw-
web/gallery/album50?page=1
   A stained-glass window as a
   memorial to the 385th
   Bomb Group
   Memorial in the churchyard

Great Ayton, North Yorkshire
All Saints' Church, Low Green, Great
Ayton, North Yorkshire TS9 6NN
Tel. 01642 722173
   Captain James Cook

Aireyholme Farm, Great Ayton
North Yorkshire near TS9 6HP
Aireyholme Farm is a working farm
and there is no public access.

Captain Cook Schoolroom Museum
47 High Street, Great Ayton
North Yorkshire TS9 6NH
Tel. 01642 723358
www.captaincookschoolroommuseum.
co.uk

Site of Captain Cook's father's cottage
on Bridge Street, Great Ayton
North Yorkshire TS9 6NP

Captain Cook Monument – Easby Moor, Great Ayton, North Yorkshire TS9 6HJ

James Cook Sculpture, High Green Great Ayton, North Yorkshire TS9 6BJ

Great Brington, Northamptonshire
St. Mary the Virgin Church, Great Brington Northamptonshire NN7 4JB
Tel. 01604 770402
    Spencer family
    Laurence Washington
    George Washington

Great Burstead, Essex
St. Mary Magdalene Church, Church Street Great Burstead near Billericay
Essex CM11 2TR
    Christopher Martin
    Speedwell
    Mayflower

Great Hampden, Buckinghamshire
Hampden House, Great Hampden Buckinghamshire HP16 9RD
    John Hampden
    Francis Barrington
    Oliver Cromwell
    Edward Whalley
    Hampden Sydney College

Church of St. Mary Magdalene, next to Hampden House
There is an impressive monument to John Hampden, who was buried here after his death following a Civil War battle.

Great Stambridge, Essex
Church of St. Mary and All Saints
Stambridge Road, Great Stambridge near Rochford, Essex SS4 2AP
    John Winthrop

Greenway, Devon
Greenway, Greenway Road, Galmpton near Brixham, Devon TQ5 0ES
Tel. 01803 842382
www.nationaltrust.org.uk
In the twentieth century Greenway was the home of the mystery writer Agatha Christie. The gardens are now owned by the National Trust, and are open to the public.
    Humphrey Gilbert
    Walter Raleigh

Agatha Christie

Grimsthorpe, Lincolnshire
Grimsthorpe Castle, Grimsthorpe near Bourne, Lincolnshire PE10 0LY
Tel. 01778 591205
www.grimsthorpe.co.uk
    Peregrine Bertie, Lord Willoughby
    Captain John Smith

Groton, Suffolk
The town of Groton, Connecticut, is located on the River Thames in New London County. Groton was settled by Europeans when John Winthrop, Jr., came from Massachusetts Bay in 1646. It was named in honor of the Winthrop estate in England.

St. Bartholomew's Church, Church Street Groton, Suffolk CO10 5ED
    John Winthrop

Guildford, Surrey
Sutton Place, between the A3 and Blanchards Hill, Jacobs Wells Guildford, Surrey GU4 7QN
Tel. 01483 504455
Open by appointment only
    J. Paul Getty

Guildford Crematorium, New Pond Road Godalming near Guildford Surrey GU7 3DB
Tel. 01483 444711
    Boris Karloff

Halesworth, Suffolk
Halesworth Airfield Museum, Sparrowhawk Road, Halesworth, Suffolk IP19 8NJ
www.halesworthairfieldmuseum.org.uk
    56th Fighter Group and the
    489th Bomb Group

Hadlow, Kent
St. Mary's Church, Church Street Hadlow, Kent TN11 0DB
    Henry Vane

Hamstead Marshall, Berkshire
Hamstead Marhsall Park, Park Lane Hamstead Marshall Berkshire RG20 0JG
Today the elaborate gate piers at three entrances to the house are all that remain. The gateposts near the parish church are the easiest to see.
    William, 1st Earl of Craven

US Army 501st Parachute Regiment

St. Mary's Church, Park Lane, Hamstead Marshall, Berkshire RG20 0JG
    William Craven, 2nd Earl of Craven

Harlaxton, Lincolnshire
Harlaxton Manor, Harlaxton near Grantham, Lincolnshire NG32 1AG
Tel. 01476 403000
E-mail: webmaster@ueharlax.ac.uk
    Stanford University
    University of Evansville (Indiana)

Harrington, Northamptonshire
Carpetbagger Aviation Museum, Sunnyvale Farm, off Lamport Road, Harrington Northamptonshire NN6 9PF
Tel. 01604 686608
www.harringtonmuseum.org.uk
    World War II base for operations to support resistance groups

Harwich, Essex
Harwich has been a shipping center for a thousand years. The famous Elizabethan seafarers John Hawkins, Martin Frobisher, and Francis Drake sailed from Harwich on various expeditions.

House of Christopher Jones, 21 King's Head Street, just off the Quay Harwich, Essex CO12 3EE
    Christopher Jones, captain and part-owner of the *Mayflower*

St. Nicholas's Church, Church Street, Harwich, Essex CO12 3DS
There has been a church on this site since 1177. The church was a resting place for Crusaders on their way to the Holy Land. Many early voyages of exploration sailed from Harwich, and the captains would have attended services at St. Nicholas's.
    Captain Christopher Jones

Hascombe, Surrey
Hoe Farm, Hascombe, Surrey GU8 4JQ
    Winston Churchill

Hatfield, Hertfordshire
Hatfield House, North Road, Hatfield Hertfordshire AL9 5NQ
Tel. 01707 287010
www.hatfield-house.co.uk
    William Cecil

Robert Cecil
1609 Jamestown Charter –
    King James I
George Calvert
John Tradescant the Elder
John Tradescant the Younger
Powhatan

Hatfield Broad Oak, Essex
Barrington Hall, Dunmow Road, Hatfield
Broad Oak near Bishop's Stortford
Essex CM22 7LE
www.cplaromas.com
The hall is now the administrative
headquarters and creative center for
CPL Aromas Ltd.
    Francis Barrington
    Oliver Cromwell
    Ezekiel Rogers
    Roger Williams

Haverhill, Suffolk
John Ward
Samuel Ward
Nathaniel Ward
"Body of Liberties," the first code of
laws established in New England
Haverhill, Massachusetts

St. Mary's Church, Market Hill
Haverhill, Suffolk CB9 8AX
John Ward

Haynes Church End
Bedfordshire
Haynes Park, Haynes Church End
Bedfordshire MK45 3BL
www.haynesvillageuk.co.uk/8.html
Today Haynes Park is the home of an
esoteric religious group from India.
    George Carteret

Heacham, Norfolk
Pocahontas's portrait is on the
Heacham town sign

Church of St. Mary the Virgin, Heacham
Norfolk PE31 7HJ
    Rolfe family coat of arms
    Memorial to Pocahontas

Hemingbrough, North Yorkshire
St. Mary's Church, Hemingbrough, Selby
North Yorkshire YO8 6QE
    John Wessyngton
    George Washington

Hemyock, Devon
Hemyock Castle, Cornhill Road
Hemyock, Cullompton
Devon EX15 3RJ
www.hemyockcastle.co.uk
    John Popham
    Walter Raleigh
    Native Indians from America
    Captain George Weymouth

Henlow, Bedfordshire
St. Mary the Virgin Church, Church Road
Henlow, Bedfordshire SG16 6AN
www.henlowchurch.org.uk
    Tilley Family
    Mayflower
    John Howland

Heptonstall, Yorkshire
St. Thomas's Churchyard, Church Street
Heptonstall, West Yorkshire HX7 7PL
    Sylvia Plath

Hethersett, Norfolk
St. Remigius's Church, Norwich Road
Hethersett, Norfolk NR9 3AR
    Temperance Flowerdew

Hidcote Bartrim, Gloucestershire
Hidcote Manor Garden, Hidcote Bartrim
near Chipping Campden,
Gloucestershire GL55 6LR
Tel. 01386 438333
www.nationaltrust.org.uk
    Major Lawrence Johnson

High Laver, Essex
All Saints' Church, High Laver near
Harlow, Essex CM5 0DU
Contact: Lavers Rectory, Magdalen
Laver, Ongar, Essex CM5 0ES
Tel. 01279 426774
    Roger Williams

Highcliffe, Dorset
Highcliffe Castle, Rothesay Drive
Highcliffe near Christchurch
Dorset BH23 4LE
Tel. 01425 278807
www.highcliffecastle.co.uk
    John Stuart, 3rd Earl of Bute
    Gordon Selfridge

St. Mary's Church, Hinton Wood Avenue
Highcliffe near Christchurch
Dorset BH23 5AA
    Gordon Selfridge

Hingham, Norfolk
The Hingham town sign in the market
place shows parishioners of the early
seventeenth century leaving for the
New World. A similar sign stands in
Hingham, Massachusetts, where many
of those travelers settled. The two
towns maintain a close connection.

St. Andrew's Church, Attleborough Road
Hingham, Norfolk NR9 4HP
www.hingham.churchnorfolk.com
    Samuel Lincoln
    Abraham Lincoln
    Memorial to the 452nd
    Bomb Group

Hollingbourne, Kent
All Saints' Church, Hollingbourne
Kent ME17 1UJ
    John Culpeper of Fekenham
    John, Lord Culpeper,
    Baron of Thoresway
    Grant of the Northern
    Neck of Virginia
    Frances Culpeper Berkeley

Honington, Suffolk
RAF Honington, Green Lane, Honington
near Bury St Edmunds
Suffolk IP31 1EE
8th USAAF, 364th Fighter Group
    and Air Depot
    8th USAAF memorial on today's
    operational RAF base

Horham, Suffolk
St. Mary's Church, The Street, Horham
Suffolk IP21 5DY
A memorial to the 95th Bomb Group
is on the B1117 opposite the church.

Horsham Airfield, visible to the east of
Horham Road, opposite IP21 5DQ
www.95thbg-horham.com
Some wartime buildings remain and
there is a small museum on the
former airfield.
    8th USAAF, 95th Bomb Group and
    334th Bomb Squadron

Hungerford, Berkshire
Littlecote House Hotel, Littlecote
Hungerford, Berkshire RG17 0SU
Tel. 01488 682509
www.warnerholidays.com/hotels/
littlecotehouse
Littlecote is now a country house

hotel. The gardens and ground-floor rooms are open to day visitors.

John Popham
Captain George Weymouth
Indians brought to England in 1605 by Captain Weymouth
US Army 506th Parachute Infantry Regiment
101st Airborne Division, "Screaming Eagles"

Hunstanton, Norfolk
Esplanade Gardens, Beach Terrace Road Hunstanton, Norfolk PE36 5BQ
A memorial plaque has the names of victims of the floods of 1953. Sixteen Americans were among the dead. Two American servicemen were awarded the George Medal for their heroism.

Hunstrete, Somerset
Hunstrete House Hotel, Hunstrete near Bristol, Somerset BS39 4NS
Tel. 01761 490490
www.hunstretehouse.co.uk
Hunstrete House is now a luxury country house hotel.
John Popham
Popham Colony

Huntingdon, Cambridgeshire
Hinchingbrooke School
Brampton Road, Huntingdon Cambridgeshire PE29 3BN
Tel. 01480 375700
www.hinchingbrookeschool.org.uk
Hinchingbrooke House is now a school, but is open to the public on Sunday afternoons during the summer months.
Edward Whalley
Frances Cromwell, a sister of Oliver Cromwell's father
William Goffe
Regicides

Ightham Mote, Kent
Ightham Mote, Ivy Hatch near Sevenoaks, Kent TN15 0NT
Tel. 01732 810378
Infoline: 01732 811145
www.nationaltrust.org.uk
Charles Henry Robinson
Anna Seton, *Green Darkness*

Ilkeston, Derbyshire
American Adventure Theme Park, Ilkeston Derbyshire DE7 5SX

Tel. 01773 531521
www.americanadventure.co.uk

Immingham, Yorkshire
Pilgrims Monument, opposite St. Andrew's Church, Immingham near Grimsby, Humberside Yorkshire DN40 2EU

Ireshopeburn, County Durham
Weardale Museum, High House Chapel Ireshopeburn near Stanhope County Durham DL13 1HD
Tel. 01388 537417
www.weardalemuseum.co.uk
John and Charles Wesley

Ipswich, Suffolk
Ipswich Tourist Information Centre
St. Stephen's Church, St Stephen's Lane, Ipswich, Suffolk IP1 1DP
Tel. 01473 258070
E-mail: tourist@ipswich.gov.uk

Christ Church, Tacket Street, Ipswich Suffolk IP4 1AU
Rev. William Gordon
George Washington

Ipswich Museum and Gallery, High Street Ipswich, Suffolk IP1 3QH
www.ipswich.gov.uk/Services/Museum
The museum has an exhibit about Puritan migration to New England.

Jordans, Buckinghamshire
Old Jordans Hotel and Conference Centre
Jordans near Beaconsfield Buckinghamshire HP9 2SW
Tel. 01494 879700
www.oldjordans.org.uk
William Penn
Mayflower Barn

Quaker Burial Ground, Jordans near Beaconsfield Buckinghamshire HP9 2SN
William Penn

Kedleston, Derbyshire
Kedleston estate, Kedleston Derbyshire DE22 5JH
Tel. 01332 842191
www.nationaltrust.org.uk
George Nathaniel Curzon
Mary Leiter
Grace Alvina Hinds

Kelso, Borders, Scotland
Floors Castle, Roxburghe Estates Office Kelso, Borders, Scotland TD5 7SF
Tel. 01573 223333
www.roxburghe.bordernet.co.uk
May Goelet

Kendal, Cumbria
Friends Meeting House, Stramongate Kendal, Cumbria LA9 4BH
Tel. 01539 722975
www.quaker-tapestry.co.uk
George Fox
William Penn

Keswick, Derwentwater
Cumbria CA12 5DJ
Benjamin Franklin

Kettering, Northamptonshire
Boughton House, Kettering Northamptonshire NN14 1BJ
Tel. 01536 515731
www.boughtonhouse.org.uk
Elizabeth Wriothesley
Ralph Montagu

Kilkhampton, Cornwall
Stowe Barton Farm, Kilkhampton near Bude, Cornwall EX23 9JW
www.nationaltrust.org.uk
Richard Grenville
Walter Raleigh

St. James's Church, Kilkhampton near Bude, Cornwall EX23 9QQ
Richard Grenville

Killhope, County Durham
North of England Lead Mining Museum
Killhope near Cowshill, Upper Weardale, County Durham DL13 1AR
Tel. 01388 537505
www.northpennines.com/killhope1.htm
and www.durham.gov.uk/killhope
Killhope Lead Mining Museum features an exhibition entitled "A Bidding to a Funeral," based on letters from miners at Killhope to their relatives in America. These were brought to Killhope in the late 1980s by an American woman who was doing genealogical research.

Kimbolton, Cambridgeshire
Kimbolton Castle, Kimbolton Cambridgeshire PE28 0EA
Tel. 01480 860505

www.kimbolton.cambs.sch.uk
Although the castle now belongs to
Kimbolton School, visitors can still see
the impressive range of State Rooms.
Kimbolton Castle is open to groups by
arrangement throughout the year.
Edward-Maria Wingfield
John Popham
Consuelo Yznaga
Helena Zimmerman

St. Andrew's Church, St. Andrew's Lane
Kimbolton, Cambridgeshire PE28 0HN
www.standrew-kimbolton.org.uk
Tiffany window
Consuelo Yznaga
USAAF 379th Bombardment
Group memorial
Stonely Priory, Kimbolton
Edward-Maria Wingfield –
"First President and Founder of
Jamestown, Virginia"

King's Lynn, Norfolk
Town House Museum, 46 Queen Street,
King's Lynn, Norfolk PE30 5DQ
Tel. 01553 773450
www.museums.norfolk.gov.uk
Pilgrims

Kiplin, North Yorkshire
Kiplin Hall, Bolton Road, Kiplin near
Scorton, North Yorkshire DL10 6AT
Tel. 01748 818178
www.kiplinhall.co.uk
Visitors are welcomed for tours, or to
spend the night.
George Calvert

Knettishall, Suffolk
Knettishall Airfield, The Street, Coney
Weston near Knettishall
Suffolk IP31 1HG
www.controltowers.co.uk/H-
K/Knettishall.htm
Memorial to 8th USAAF, 388th
Bomb Group

All Saints' Church, south of the A1066,
Knettishall, Suffolk IP22 2TJ
Remains of the airfield are visible
south of the church on private land.
The church is now a private home.

Lakenheath, Suffolk
RAF Lakenheath, Suffolk IP27 9DS
The airfield is now the home base for

the 48th Tactical Fighter Wing.
USAAF base in World War II

Lambourn, Berkshire
Ashdown Park, Lambourn near
Hungerford, Berkshire RG17 8RE
Tel. 01793 762209
www.nationaltrust.org.uk
William, 1st Earl of Craven
King Charles II
US 501st Parachute Regiment

Lavenham, Suffolk
John Winthrop

Church of St. Peter and St. Paul
Church Street, Lavenham
Suffolk CO10-9SA
www.suffolkchurches.co.uk/Lavenham
In the Branch Chapel an American flag
honors American servicemen stationed
in this area during World War II.

Swan Hotel, High Street, Lavenham
Suffolk CO10 9QA
Tel. 01787 247477
www.theswanatlavenham.co.uk
The hotel has mementoes from
American airmen who were based in
the district during World War I.

Market Place, Lavenham
Suffolk CO10 9QZ
Memorial plaque "Men of the
487th Bomb Group"

Lavenham Airfield and Control Tower
Old Bury Road, Alpheton
Lavenham, Suffolk CO10 9LR
www.lavenham.co.uk/airfield/
Most of the site is now private property.
Before visiting, contact by e-mail
jspawsey@hotmail.com or phone 01284
828226.
USAAF 487th Bombardment Group

Leeds, West Yorkshire
Mill Hill Chapel, City Square, Leeds
West Yorkshire LS1 5EB
Tel. 0113 243 3845
www.millhillchapel.org.uk
A statue of Joseph Priestley stands on
the City Square overlooking the chapel.

Leintwardine, Herefordshire
Church of St. Mary Magdalene,
Church Street, Leintwardine
Herefordshire SY7 0LD

Tel. 01547 540235
www.wigmore-
abbey.org.uk/leintwardine.htm
and www.banastretarleton.org
Banastre Tarleton

Leiston, Suffolk
Parts of **Leiston Airfield** runway are
visible from Cakes & Ale Holiday Park,
Abbey Lane, Leiston, Suffolk IP16 4TE
(private property)
www.friendsofleistonairfield.co.uk
8th USAAF, 357th Fighter Group
US astronaut Chuck Yeager
flew out of Leiston

Memorial to USAAF 357th on Harrow
Road, Leiston, Suffolk IP16 4TF

Letheringham, Suffolk
Church of St. Mary, Letheringham near
Whickam Market, Suffolk IP13 7QY
www.syllysuffolk.co.uk/htm/letheringham
Thomas Wingfield
Wingfield family

Lewes, East Sussex
Bull House, Sussex Archaeological Society
92 High Street, Lewes
East Sussex BN7 1XH
Tel. 01273 486260
www.sussexpast.co.uk
Tom Paine Project festivals run from 4
to 14 July – American Independence to
Bastille Day.
Thomas Paine

White Hart Hotel, 55 High Street
Lewes, East Sussex BN7 1XE
Tel. 01273 476694
www.whitehartlewes.co.uk
Headstrong Club
Thomas Paine

Royal Oak, 3 Station Road, Lewes
East Sussex BN7 2DA
Tel. 01273 474803
Headstrong Club

St. Michael's Church, High Street
Lewes, East Sussex BN7 2LX
Thomas Paine married Elizabeth
Ollive, 26 March 1771

Lincoln, Lincolnshire
Lincoln Cathedral, Minster Yard, Lincoln
Lincolnshire LN2 1PX
www.lincolncathedral.com

Captain John Smith
Arbella, lead ship of the
Winthrop Fleet

Little Baddow, Essex
Cuckoos Farmhouse and School
Church Road, Little Baddow
Essex CM3 4BN
The interior can be viewed by prior
arrangement.
Thomas Hooker
John Eliot

Meeting House and Manse
Church End, Little Baddow
Essex CM3 4BE
Thomas Hooker's birthday is
commemorated in July.

Parish Church of St. Mary the Virgin Church
Road, Little Baddow
Essex CM3 4BE
Thomas Hooker
John Eliot
Henry Mildmay

Great Graces, Graces Lane
Little Baddow, Essex CM3 4AY
Henry Baddow
Walter Mildmay

Little Casterton, Lincolnshire
Rutland Open Air Theatre, Tolethorpe Hall,
Little Casterton near Stamford
Lincolnshire PE9 4BH
Tel. 01780 754381
www.rutnet.co.uk/customers/stamford
shakespearecompany/
Tolethorpe Hall was purchased by the
Stamford Shakespeare Company in
1977 and is now a venue for theatrical
productions.
Robert "Trouble-Church" Browne
Winthrop Fleet
Battle of Lexington and Concord
Solomon Brown of Lexington
John Brown of Lexington

Little Glemham, Suffolk
Glemham Hall, Little Glemham
Suffolk IP13 0BT *just off the A12 north of
Wickham Market*
Tel. 01728 746219
www.glemhamhall.co.uk
Glemham Hall is the setting for a
variety of entertainments from country
fairs to opera.
Catherine Yale

Little Weighton, East Yorkshire
St. Peter's Church, Old Village Road Little
Weighton near Kingston upon Hull,
East Yorkshire HU20 3UU
www.littleweighton.com
Ezekiel Rogers window
Archbishop William Laud
Rowley, Massachusetts

Rowley Manor Hotel, Little Weighton near
Kingston upon Hull
East Yorkshire HU20 3XR
Tel. 01482 848248
www.rowleymanor.com
Ezekiel Rogers

Liverpool, Merseyside
Robert Morris of Pennsylvania
signatory of the Declaration of
Independence
Nathaniel Hawthorne

Merseyside Maritime Museum, Albert
Dock, Liverpool, Merseyside L3 4AQ
Tel. 0151 478 4499
www.liverpoolmuseums.org.uk/maritime
Online historic walking tour:
www.liverpoolmuseums.org.uk/mariti
me/trail/trail.asp
The museum includes a Transatlantic
Slavery Gallery and an exhibition on
emigration. Self-guided walking tours
around the city center follow a Slavery
Trade Trail.

Tourist Information Centre, Queen Square
Building, Roe Street, Liverpool
Merseyside L1 1RG
Tel. 09066 806886
www.visitliverpool.com

Birkenhead Park, Park Road North
Birkenhead, Merseyside CH41 4HD
Tel. 0151 652 5197
www.visitliverpool.com/site/product-
p44211
The design of New York City's Central
Park was based on Birkenhead Park in
Liverpool.
Frederick Law Olmsted

Sefton Park Palm House, Sefton Park
Mossley Hill Drive, Liverpool
Merseyside L17 1AP
Tel. 0151 726 9304
www.visitliverpool.com/conferences/ve
nue-portfolio/sefton-park-palm-house-
p18040

Christopher Columbus

Water Street, Liverpool, Merseyside
L3 1AB
Site of the US Consulate
Nathaniel Hawthorne

Water Street, Liverpool, Merseyside
Banastre Tarleton – a plaque marks
his house

Long Ashton, Somerset
Ashton Court Estate, Long Ashton
near Bristol, Somerset BS41 9JN
Tel. 0117 963 3438
www.bristol-city.gov.uk/acm
Ferdinando Gorges
Military transit camp,
RAF headquarters and
American Army Command HQ

All Saints' Church, Church Lane
Long Ashton, Somerset BS41 9LU
Tel. 01275 393 109
Sir Ferdinando Gorges
Hugh Smythe

Ashton Phillips Estate, Lower Court
Yanley Lane, Long Ashton
Somerset BS41 9LW
Ferdinando Gorges
Richard Ameryck

Lyme Regis, Dorset
Coram Tower, Pound Road
Lyme Regis, Dorset DT7 3HX
Thomas Coram

Madingley, Cambridgeshire
American Military Cemetery, Coton Road
Madingley CB3 7PH
www.usabmc.com/ca.htm
administered by: American Battle
Monuments Commission, Courthouse
Plaza II, Suite 500, 2300 Clarendon
Boulevard, Arlington, VA 22201, USA
Tel. 011-703-696-6897
Olmsted Brothers, landscape
architects
Glenn Miller
Joseph P. Kennedy, Jr.
Exercise Tiger

Maidstone, Kent
Leeds Castle, Maidstone
Kent ME17 1PL
Tel. 01622 765400
www.leeds-castle.com

Frances Culpeper
William Berkeley
Warham St. Leger and Walter
  Raleigh
Richard Smythe
Thomas Smythe
Thomas Culpeper, 2nd Baron of
  Thoresway
Catherine Culpeper
Thomas Fairfax
Lady Olive Baillie

All Saints' Church, Mill Street
Maidstone, Kent ME15 6YE
Tel. 01622 843298
www.maidstoneallsaints.freeserve.co.uk
  Lawrence Washington
  Mary Scott Argall
  Samuel Argall

89–90 Bank Street, Maidstone
Kent ME14 1SD
One of the statues in the niches on the
first floor of the timbered building is of
Lawrence Washington.

Maldon, Essex
St. Peter's Church, Market Hill
Maldon, Essex CM9 4PZ
The church is now home to the
Maeldune Heritage Centre.
Tel. 01621 851628
www.maldon.gov.uk/VisitingTheDistrict
/museums.htm
  Lawrence Washington
  George Washington

All Saints' Church, High Street, Maldon
Essex CM9 5PE
www.allsaintsmaldon.co.uk
  "Washington Window" –
  Lawrence Washington
  George Washington
  Signing of the Declaration
  of Independence

Manchester, Greater Manchester
Lincoln Square, Brazenose Street
Manchester M2 6LW
  Anti-slavery movement
  Abraham Lincoln statue

John Rylands University Library, University
of Manchester, Burlington Street
Manchester M13 9PP
Tel. 0161 275 3751
www.library.manchester.ac.uk
  John Audubon's famous book

Birds of North America

Southern Cemetery, Barlow Moor Road
Manchester M21 7GL
  Phillip Baybutt – American Civil War

Marefield, Leicestershire
Marefield Manor Farm, Marefield
Leicestershire LE7 9LE
  Thomas Hooker

Market Bosworth, Leicestershire
Dixie Grammar School, Station Road
Market Bosworth, Leicestershire
CV13 0LE
Tel. 01455 292 244
www.dixie.org.uk
  Thomas Hooker

Marske, North Yorkshire
St. Germain's Church, St. Germain's
Lane, Marske near Middlesbrough
North Yorkshire TS11 7EL
  Captain James Cook

Martlesham Heath, Suffolk
Martlesham Heath Aviation Control Tower
Museum, Parkers Place, Martlesham
Heath, Suffolk IP5 3UX
Tel. 01473 624510
www.mhas.org.uk
  "Eagle" squadrons

Marton, North Yorkshire
St. Cuthbert's Parish Church, Stokesley
Road, Marton near Middlesbrough,
North Yorkshire TS7 8JU
Tel. 01642 316201
www.communigate.co.uk/ne/stcuth
bertsmarton
  Captain James Cook

Captain Cook Birthplace Museum, Stewart
Park, Marton near Middlesbrough
North Yorkshire TS7 8AT
Tel. 01642 311211
www.captcook.ne.co.uk
  Captain Cook

Medmenham, Buckinghamshire
Medmenham Abbey, Medmenham
Buckinghamshire SL7 2HB
The abbey remains in ruins and is not
open to the public but it is visible from
the River Thames.
  "Monks of Medmenham" – "Hell-
  Fire Club"
  Francis Dashwood

John Wilkes
Benjamin Franklin

Mendelsham, Suffolk
Mendelsham Airfield, east of the A140
Mendelsham, Suffolk IP14 5NA
Remains of airfield on private property
  8th USAAF, 34th Bomb Group
  Memorial on the A140

Messing, Essex
All Saints' Church, The Street, Messing
near Colchester, Essex CO5 9TR
  George Bush and George W. Bush

Metfield, Suffolk
Metfield Airfield – remains of the airfield
can be seen southwest of Metfield on
Christmas Lane, Metfield, Suffolk
IP20 0JZ
www.suffolkcam.co.uk/metfield200420
02.htm
  8th USAAF, 353rd Fighter Group
    and 491st Bomb Group
  Memorial on B1123, Metfield
    Common, Suffolk opposite
    P20 0LP
  8th USAAF, 491st Bomb Group

Middle Wallop, Hampshire
Museum of Army Flying, Middle Wallop
near Andover, Hampshire SO20 8DY
Tel. 01264 784421
www.flying-museum.org.uk
  Samuel Cody's man-lifting kite

Middlesbrough, North Yorkshire
"Bottle of Notes," Russell Street Central
Gardens, Middlesbrough, North
Yorkshire TS1 2AE
  Captain James Cook

Mildenhall, Suffolk –
US military base

Molesworth, Cambridgeshire
RAF Molesworth, near Huntingdon
Cambridgeshire PE28 0QB
  World War II US military base –
  US 8th Air Force: 15th Bomb
    Squadron, 303rd Bomb Group,
    B17s
  Memorial at gate

Monkwearmouth, Tyne and Wear
St. Peter's Church, St. Peter's Way
Monkwearmouth, Sunderland
Tyne and Wear SR6 0DY

Tel. 0191 516 0135
www.freespace.virgin.net/stephen.harts
horne/parish.html
    The Venerable Bede
    Hylton family

Mottisfont, Hampshire
Mottisfont Abbey, Mottisfont near
Romsey, Hampshire SO51 0LP
Tel. 01794 340757
www.nationaltrust.org.uk
    William, Lord Sandys, father of
      Archbishop Edwin Sandys

Nazeing, Essex
All Saints' Church, Betts Lane, Nazeing
near Harlow, Essex EN9 2DB
Tel. 01992 893167
    John Eliot
    National Society of the
      Descendants of John and
      Elizabeth Curtiss

Needham Market, Suffolk
Christ Church, High Street, Needham
Market, Suffolk IP6 8AP
Tel. 01449 723444
    Joseph Priestley

Newark, Nottinghamshire
County Showground, Winthorpe near
Newark, Nottinghamshire NG24 2NY
www.americana-promotions.co.uk
    Annual American car show with
      live music entertainment

Newbiggin-in-Teesdale
County Durham
Methodist Chapel and **Wesley Manse**
Miry Lane, Newbiggin-in-Teesdale
County Durham DL12 0TY
Tel. 01833 640329
    John Wesley

Newbury, Berkshire
St. Nicolas's Church, West Mills Newbury,
Berkshire RG14 5HP
www.st-nicolas-newbury.org
    Benjamin Woodbridge
    Magdalen Hall, Oxford University
⸮ Harvard College

Northbourne, Kent
St. Augustine's Church, The Street
Northbourne near Deal
Kent CT14 0LG
www.eastrybenefice.co.uk/NORTHOM
E.htm

Edwin Sandys and his wife

Norton Disney, Lincolnshire
St. Peter's Church, Church Lane, Norton
Disney, Lincolnshire LN6 9JX
    Walt Disney

Norwich, Norfolk
St. Andrew's Church, St. Andrew's Street
Norwich, Norfolk NR2 4TP
http://website.lineone.net/~mcrouch/c
hurch2.html and
www.eatonparish.com/St.%20Andrews
1.htm
    John Robinson

City of Norwich Aviation Museum
Old Norwich Road, Horsham St. Faith
near Norwich, Norfolk NR10 3JF
Tel. 01603 893080
www.cnam.co.uk
Displays tell the story of the US 8th
Army Air Force in the area during
World War II.

Nuthampstead, Hertfordshire
Nuthampstead Airfield, Nuthampstead
Hertfordshire SG8 8NB
    8th USAAF – 398th Bomb Group
    Memorial "Hell From Heaven" –
      near Woodman Inn

Ockley, Surrey
St. Margaret's Church, Coles Lane, Ockley
near Dorking, Surrey RH5 5LS
Tel. 01306 711550
www.surreyplacesofworship.org.uk/edu
cation-detail.asp?ID=117
    Rev. Henry Whitfield

Ockley Rectory, Stane Street, Ockley
Surrey RH5 5SY
    John Cotton

Old Buckenham, Norfolk
Old Buckenham Airfield, Abbey Road
Old Buckenham near Attleborough
Norfolk NR17 1PU
www.touchdownaerocentre.co.uk/html
/453rd_gallery.htm
    US 453rd Bomb Group
    James Stewart
    Walter Matthau

Old Buckenham Village Hall, Abbey Road
Old Buckenham near Attleborough
Norfolk NR17 1QA
    Memorial, roll of honor, plaque,

and memorabilia

Old Heathfield, East Sussex
All Saints' Church, Church Street
Old Heathfield, East Sussex TN21 9AH
Tel. 01435 862457
    Robert Hunt

Ombersley, Worcestershire
Ombersley Court, Ombersley near
Droitwich, Worcestershire WR9 0HH
Tel. 01905 620220
www.charitiesdirect.com/charity9/cho1
9399.htm
    Edwin Sandys

St. Andrew's Church, Church Lane
Ombersley, Worcestershire WR9 0ER
Tel. 01905 620950
    Sandys mausoleum

Crown and Sandys Arms Hotel, Main
Road, Ombersley, Worcestershire
WR9 0EW
Tel. 01905 620252
www.crownandsandys.co.uk
    Samuel Sandys, sheriff of
      Worcestershire
    Archbishop Edwin Sandys

Orford, Suffolk
Castle Terrace, Orford Castle
Suffolk IP12 2ND
www.english-heritage.org.uk
    Henry Wingfield, Knight of Rhodes
    Edward-Maria Wingfield

Otley, Suffolk
Otley Hall, Otley, Suffolk IP6 9PA
Tel. 01473 890264
www.otleyhall.co.uk
    Bartholomew Gosnold
    Edward-Maria Wingfield

Paignton, Devon
Oldway Mansion, Torquay Road
Paignton, Devon TQ3 2TD
Tel. 01803 207933
www. oldwaymansion.co.uk
    Isaac M. Singer
    American Women's War Hospital

Parham, Suffolk
Parham Airfield Museum 390th Bomb
Group Memorial Air Museum &
Museum of the British Resistance
Organisation, Parham, Suffolk IP13 9AF
Tel. 01728 621373

OXFORD

Oxford Tourist Information Centre
15–16 Broad Street, Oxford OX1 3AS
Tel. 01865 726871
http://www.oxford.gov.uk/tourism/oic
.cfm

UNIVERSITY OF OXFORD
Website for information about the
colleges: www.ox.ac.uk
   Benjamin Franklin
   Edward Rutledge

All Souls College, Radcliffe Square
Oxford OX1 4AL
Tel. 01865 279379
www.all-souls.ox.ac.uk
   Robert Lowell, poet

Brasenose College, Brasenose Lane
Oxford OX1 4AJ
Tel. 01865 277823
www.bnc.ox.ac.uk
   Rev. Lawrence Washington

Christ Church, St. Aldate's
Oxford OX1 1DP
Tel. 01865 276150
www.chch.ox.ac.uk
   Richard Hakluyt
   William Penn
   William Petty, 2nd
     Earl of Shelburne
   John Wesley
   W.H. Auden

Corpus Christi College, Merton Street
Oxford OX1 4JF
Tel. 01865 276700
www.ccc.ox.ac.uk
   Edwin Sandys
   James Oglethorpe

Green College, at the Radcliffe
Observatory, Woodstock Road
Oxford OX2 6HG
Tel. 01865 274770
www.green.ox.ac.uk
   Dr. Cecil Green

Harris Manchester College, Mansfield
Road, Oxford OX1 3TD
Te. 01865 271009
www.hmc.ox.ac.uk
   Joseph Priestley

Hertford College, Cattle Street
Oxford OX1 3BW
Tel. 01865 279 400
www.hertford.ox.ac.uk
   Alain Locke
   Byron White

Lincoln College, Turl Street
Oxford OX1 3DR
Tel. 01865 279800
www.linc.ox.ac.uk
   Theodor Seuss Geisel
   John Wesley

Magdalen College, The Plain
Oxford OX1 4AU
Tel. 01865 276000
www.magd.ox.ac.uk
   Henry Vane
   John Davenport
   Benjamin Woodbridge
   Jean Paul Getty, Sr.
   Stephen Breyer
   David Souter

Merton College, Merton Street
Oxford OX1 4JD
Tel. 01865 276310
www.merton.ox.ac.uk
   T.S. Eliot
   John Davenport
   William Berkeley

New College, Holywell Street
Oxford OX1 3BN
Tel. 01865 279555
www.new.ox.ac.uk
   John White
   Jacob Epstein – *Lazarus*

Oriel College, Oriel Street
Oxford OX1 4EW
Tel. 01865 276555
www.oriel.ox.ac.uk
   Walter Raleigh

Pembroke College, Pembroke Street
Oxford OX1 1DW
Tel. 01865 276444
www.pmb.ox.ac.uk
   James Smithson
   Senator Richard Lugar
   Senator William Fulbright
   The Hon. Philip Lader, American

ambassador to the UK

Queen's College, Queen's Lane and High
Street, Oxford OX1 4AW
Tel. 01865 279120
www.queens.ox.ac.uk
   Thomas West, 3rd Lord De La Warr

St. John's College, Saint Giles
Oxford OX1 3JP
Tel. 01865 277318
www.sjc.ox.ac.uk
   Archbishop William Laud

Trinity College, Broad Street
Oxford OX1 3BH
Tel. 01865 279900
www.trinity.ox.ac.uk
   George Calvert, 1st Lord Baltimore
   Cecil Calvert, 2nd Lord Baltimore

University College, High Street
Oxford OX1 4BH
Tel. 01865 276602
www.univ.ox.ac.uk
   Bill Clinton
   Chelsea Clinton

Other American Connections at Oxford

Ashmolean Museum of Art and Archaeology
Beaumont Street, Oxford OX1 2PH
Tel. 01865 278000
www.ashmol.ox.ac.uk/ash
   John Tradescant the Elder
   Powhatan – Pocahontas's father

Bodleian Library, Broad Street
Oxford OX1 3BG
Tel. 01865 277180
www.bodley.ox.ac.uk
   William Chester Minor
   Paul Mellon

Pitt Rivers Museum, South Parks Road
Oxford OX1 3PP
Tel. 01865 270949
www.prm.ox.ac.uk/cook
   Captain James Cook

Museum of the History of Science
Broad Street, Oxford OX1 3AZ
Tel. 01865 277280
www.mhs.ox.ac.uk

www.parhamairfieldmuseum.co.uk
World War II aircraft and
memorabilia

Parlington, West Yorkshire
Parlington Hall Estate, Parlington
West Yorkshire LS25 3EG
The Triumphal Arch in celebration of
American independence is just north
of Parlington Hall.

Pembury, Kent
St. Peter's Old Church, Hastings Road
Pembury, Kent TN2 4PA
www.pemburychurch.net/
John Culpeper of Bayhall
Thomas Culpeper

Pendle Hill, Lancashire
Near Clitheroe, Lancashire BB12 9JE
George Fox
Religious Society of Friends
("Quakers")

Penn, Buckinghamshire
Crown Inn, Witheridge Lane, Penn
Buckinghamshire HP10 8NY
Tel. 01494 812640
William Penn

Penshurst, Kent
Penshurst Place and Gardens, Penshurst
Kent TN11 8DG
Tel. 01892 870307
www.penshurstplace.com
Algernon Sidney
Thomas Jefferson
William Penn

Pirbright, Surrey
Church of St. Michael and All Angels
Church Lane, Pirbright GU24 0JF

Furzehill Place, Stanley Hill,
Pirbright GU24 0DN
Henry Morton Stanley

Plaxtol, Kent
"Fairlawne", The Street
Fairlawne TN15 0PZ
Now a private house
Henry Vane the Younger

Podington, Bedfordshire
Church of St. Mary the Virgin, High Street
Podington, Bedfordshire NN29 7HS

Airfield Monument, Airfield Road,
Podington near Wellingborough
Bedfordshire NN29 7XA
US 8th Army Air Force, 92nd
Bombardment Group

Portland, Island of, Dorset
Pennsylvania Castle, Pennsylvania Road
Island of Portland, Dorset DT5 1HU
The castle was a hotel in the 1980s.
Private residence
John Penn, grandson of
William Penn

Portsmouth, Hampshire
D-Day Museum and Overlord Embroidery
Clarence Esplanade, Southsea
Portsmouth, Hampshire PO5 3NT
Tel. 023 9282 7261
www.ddaymuseum.co.uk

Mary Rose
Mary Rose Ship Hall, Main Road, HM
Naval Base, Portsmouth Hampshire
PO1 3PY. Flagship Portsmouth Trust
Building 1/7, Porter's Lodge, College
Road, HM Naval Base, Portsmouth
Hampshire PO1 3LJ
Tel. 023 9286 1533
www.maryrose.org
Richard Grenville

Princetown, Devon
American prisoners captured
during the War of 1812

Dartmoor Prison Museum, Princetown
Devon PL20 6RR
www.dartmoor-prison.co.uk

High Moorland Visitor Centre, Tavistock
Road, Princetown, Devon PL20 6QF
Tel. 01822 890414
www.dartmoor-npa.gov.uk/dnp/centres

Church of St. Michael and All Angels,
Princetown, Devon, PL20
French and American prisoners
of war

Purleigh, Essex
All Saints' Church, Church Hill, Purleigh
near Chelmsford, Essex CM3 6QH
Tel. 01621 826905
George Washington's great-great-
grandfather, Lawrence
Washington

Rattlesden, Suffolk
Rattlesden Airfield – remains visible west
of Benton Lane, Rattlesden, Suffolk
IP30 0SX *(private property)*
Memorial to the 8th USAAF, 447th
Bomb Group

Church of St. Nicholas, High Street
Rattlesden, Suffolk IP30 0RA
American flag behind prayer desk
Plaque to Richard Kimball
(1595–1675) who immigrated to
Ipswich, Massachusetts

Raydon, Suffolk
Raydon Airfield
The remains of Station 157 can be seen
at Notley Enterprise Park Unit 54
Raydon Road off Woodlands Road
Raydon, Suffolk CO7 6QD
www.controltowers.co.uk/R/Raydon.ht
m and
www.airforcememorials.co.uk/
_sgg/mlmq_1
8th USAAF, 353rd Bomb Group
Memorial just north of the
Enterprise Park

St. Mary's Church, The Street, Raydon
Suffolk IP7 5LP
The vestry doors are a memorial to the
men of the 353rd Bomb Group.

Reculver, Kent
Reculver Abbey ruins, Herne Bay
Reculver, Kent CT6 6SU
Rev. Robert Hunt
Jamestown expedition

Redenhall, Norfolk
St. Mary's Church, Redenhall near
Harleston, Norfolk IP20 9QS
Edward and Samuel Fuller
Mayflower
Barbican Stone in Plymouth

Rochester, Kent
Rochester Castle, Castle Hill, Rochester
Kent ME1 1SW
www.english-heritage.org.uk
Samuel Argall

Rottingdean, East Sussex
"The Elms," The Green, Rottingdean
near Brighton, East Sussex BN2 7HA
Kipling's home at "The Elms" is a
private residence, but Rudyard
Kipling's garden was saved from

PLYMOUTH, DEVON

Antony Park, Saltram Park PL7 1UH
and Mount Edgecumbe Park
PL10 1HZ
  D-Day preparations
  29th Armored Division
  "Chocolate Box Hards" at
    Turnchapel and Saltash
    Passage

Barbican Pier, Plymouth PL1 2LR
Mayflower Steps, Memorial
Colonnade with historic plaques
www.mayflowersteps.co.uk
Several plaques to the Pilgrims are
on the harbor front. One was
presented in 2000 by the Pilgrim
Monument and Provincetown
Museum and the town of
Provincetown, Massachusetts. The
Mayflower Memorial is on the harbor
front at the Barbican.
  The Pilgrims – 1620

3 Elliot Terrace, The Hoe
Plymouth PL1 2PL
The house is now maintained by the
City Council as a museum, heritage
site and venue for some official
receptions and open days.
  Lord and Lady Astor

Island House on the Barbican
Plymouth PL1 2LS
Tel. 01752 304849
plymouthbarbicantic@visit.org.uk
and
www.plymouthdata.info/IslandHouse
  Legend says the Pilgrims spent
    their last night in
    Plymouth here.
  The Council for the Governing
    of New England

58 Notte Street, Plymouth PL1 2AG
(*now a restaurant*)
  Captain Cook

Plymouth City Museum & Art Gallery Drake
Circus, Plymouth PL4 8AJ
Tel. 01752 304 774
www.plymouthmuseum.gov.uk

Prysten House, Finewell Street
Plymouth PL1 2AE
Tel. 01752 661414
A memorial service is held here
annually on 30 May.
  War of 1812
  Society of the Daughters of 1812

Royal Citadel – Fort on the Hoe
The Hoe, Plymouth PL1 2PA
The Royal Citadel is still in use by the
military, but guided tours are given.
  Ferdinando Gorges
  Squanto
  Statue of Francis Drake in Hoe Park

St. Budeaux's Church, Victoria Road
Higher St. Budeaux, Plymouth PL5 1RF
  Memorial to Ferdinando Gorges
  Francis Drake married Anne
    Newman at St. Budeaux's
    Church, Plymouth, on 4 July
    1569. She died in 1583 and is
    buried in the church.

Saltash Passage, Normandy Way
St. Budeaux, Plymouth PL5 1LA
  Memorial to the V and VII Corps of
    the United States Army
  D-Day memorial marks the
    departure of the units on 6 June
    1944 for the D-Day Landings in
    France.

Thanksgiving @ Plymouth
"The Lord Mayor and the People of
Plymouth, England invite all
Americans to join the Mother City of
Plymouth's Annual Thanksgiving
Festival, celebrating its unique
Mayflower & Transatlantic Heritage –
every U.S. Thanksgiving Weekend."

**Plymouth Chamber of Commerce and
Industry**, 22 Lockyer Street, Plymouth
PL1 2QW
Tel. 01752 220471
E-mail: chamber@plymouth-
chamber.co.uk

Western Pier, Sutton Harbour
Plymouth PL1 2NX
  Plaque to Humphrey Gilbert who
    sailed on 11 June 1583 on
    voyage to Newfoundland.
  Seven voyages to Virginia backed
    by Walter Raleigh left from here
    between 1584 and 1590.
  Richard Grenville left in 1585 with
    the expedition to the
    Roanoke Colony.
  On 2 June 1609 George Somers
    left from Plymouth on the *Sea
    Venture* which wrecked on
    Bermuda.
  The Seaplane NC4 Memorial
    commemorates the first
    transatlantic flight, from
    Long Island, USA, which
    landed in Plymouth Sound.

development and is open to the public.
  Rudyard Kipling

Rougham, Suffolk
Rougham Control Tower Museum
Rougham Industrial Estate
Rougham near Bury St Edmunds
Suffolk IP30 9XA
Tel. 01359 271471
www.rougham.org

Runnymede, Surrey
Magna Carta Memorial, Windsor Road
Runnymede, Surrey (near TW20 0AE)
www.nationaltrust.org.uk
To commemorate the signing of the
Magna Carta, the basic document of
the English legal system, this

memorial was built by the American
Bar Association on land leased by the
Magna Carta Trust. It was paid for by
donations from some 9,000 American
lawyers.

John F. Kennedy Memorial, Windsor Road
Runnymede, Surrey
(near SL4 2JN)
  President John F. Kennedy

USAAF 322nd and 94th
  Bomb Groups

Rye, East Sussex
St. Mary's Church, Church Square, Rye
East Sussex TN31 7HH
Tel. 01797 224935
www.rye-tourism.co.uk/pages/
parish.asp
John Allin

Lamb House, West Street, Rye
East Sussex TN31 7ES
Tel. 01372 453401
www.nationaltrust.org.uk
Henry James

St. Columb, Cornwall
Spirit of the West American Theme
Park, Retallack Park, Winnard's Perch
near St Columb, Cornwall TR9 6DE
www.chycor.co.uk/spirit-of-the-
west/index.htm

Salisbury, Wiltshire
White Hart Hotel, St. John Street
Salisbury, Wiltshire SP1 2SD
Tel. 01722 327476
www.whitehart-salisbury.com
Walter Raleigh
Henry Laurens

Saltaire, West Yorkshire
Salts Mill Gallery, Victoria Road, Saltaire
near Shipley, West Yorkshire BD17 7EF
Tel. 01274 531163
www.saltsmill.org.uk
David Hockney

Scarborough, North Yorkshire
Victoria Hotel, 78 Westborough Road
Scarborough, North Yorkshire
YO11 1TP
Charles Laughton

Scrooby, Nottinghamshire
St. Wilfred's Church, Church Lane
Scrooby Nottinghamshire DN10 6AR
The church is kept locked but
keyholders are listed in the porch.
Richard Clyfton
William Brewster

Scrooby Manor House, Manor Road
Scrooby, Nottinghamshire DN10 6AH
Scrooby Manor House is private
property; it can be visited by prior
arrangement only.
William Brewster
Richard Clyfton

Pilgrim Fathers Inn, Great North Road,
Scrooby, Nottinghamshire DN10 6AT
Tel. 01302 710446

Selby, North Yorkshire
Selby Abbey, The Crescent, Selby
North Yorkshire YO8 4PU
Tel. 01757 703123
www.selbyabbey.org.uk
John Wessyngton
George Washington

Sempringham, Lincolnshire
Church of St. Andrew, Sempringham
near Billingborough, Lincolnshire
NG34 0LP
*down a country lane off Pointon Road
(the B1177)*
www.sempringham.co.uk
Massachusetts Bay Company
John Cotton
Thomas Hooker
Roger Williams
4th Earl of Lincoln and his
sister Arabella
Arabella – flagship of the Winthrop
Fleet in 1630

Sevenoaks, Kent
Knole, Sevenoaks, Kent TN15 0RP
Tel. 01732 462100
www.nationaltrust.org.uk
Thomas West, Lord De la Warr,
first governor of Virginia

Sheffield, South Yorkshire
John Wesley

Paradise Square, Sheffield, South
Yorkshire S1 1UA

Sheffield Cathedral, Church Street
Sheffield, South Yorkshire S1 1HA
Tel. 0114 275 3434
www.sheffield-cathedral.co.uk

Victoria Hall Methodist Church
Norfolk Street, Sheffield, South
Yorkshire S1 2JB
Tel. 0114 281 2733

Carver Street Methodist Church
30 Rockingham Lane, Sheffield
South Yorkshire S1 4FW
Tel. 0114 266 1381

Shelley, Suffolk
Church of All Saints, Shelley Road

Suffolk IP7 5QX
Bartholomew Gosnold

Sherborne, Dorset
Sherborne Castle, Sherborne
Dorset DT9 5NR
Tel. 01935 813182
www.sherbornecastle.com
Walter Raleigh

Sherborne St John, Hampshire
The Vyne, Vyne Road, Sherborne
St. John near Basingstoke, Hampshire
RG24 9HL
Tel. 01794 340757
www.nationaltrust.org.uk
William Sandys

Shipbourne, Kent
St. Giles's Church, Ightham Road
Shipbourne near Sevenoaks
Kent TN11 9PF
Henry Vane the Younger

Shipton, Shropshire
Shipton Parish Church, Shipton
Shropshire TF13 6JZ
A plaque was placed in the church by
the Massachusetts Society of
Mayflower Descendants.
Elinor, Jasper, Richard, and
Mary More
Mayflower

Sissinghurst, Kent
Sissinghurst Castle, Sissinghurst
near Cranbrook, Kent TN17 2AB
Tel. 01580 710700
www.nationaltrust.org.uk
Thomas West, Lord De la Warr
Lady De la Warr
Pocahontas
Vita Sackville-West
Knole

Slapton, Devon
Slapton Sands, Slapton near Torcross
Devon (near TQ7 2QP)
www.exercisetiger.org and
www.friendsofthelaurel.co.uk
D-Day invasion of Europe
Exercise Tiger
American Military Cemetery,
Madingley

Southampton, Hampshire
Mayflower Memorial, Mayflower Park
Town Quay, West Esplanade

Southampton, Hampshire SO14 2AQ
A tower stands to commemorate the
Pilgrims sailing on the *Mayflower* and
the *Speedwell* in 1620 and a plaque on
West Gate records the event. Followers
of William Penn sailed to Pennsylvania
from Southampton.

Star Hotel, 26 High Street
Southampton
Hampshire SO14 2NA
   Benjamin Franklin

Southwick, Hampshire
Southwick House, South Road
Southwick near Fareham
Hampshire PO17 6EJ
off the B2177
www.d-day60.co.uk/
walk_southwick.htm
   Secret HQ for the Allied
     Expeditionary Force in World
     War II
   Operation Overlord
   General Eisenhower

Golden Lion Pub, High Street
Southwick, near Portsmouth
Hampshire PO17 6EB

Staindrop, County Durham
Raby Castle, Staindrop, Darlington
County Durham DL2 3AH
Tel. 01833 660202/660207
www.rabycastle.com
   Henry Vane the Younger,
     5th governor of the colony
     of Massachusetts

Staithes, North Yorkshire
Captain Cook and Staithes Heritage Centre
High Street, Staithes near Whitby
North Yorkshire TS13 5BQ
Tel. 01947 841454
www.staithes.co.uk/museum1.htm
   Captain James Cook

Steeple Morden, Cambridgeshire
Steeple Morden Airfield in fields just
south of Litlington Road, Morden
Green Cambridgeshire SG8 0LY
http://mighty8thaf.preller.us/php/1Loc.
php?Base=Steeple+Morden
   USAAF Station 122
   8th USAAF, 355th Fighter Group,
     4th Fighter Group
   Memorial on Litlington Road

Steyning, West Sussex
Wiston House, Mouse Lane, near
Steyning, West Sussex BN44 3DZ
Tel. 01903 815020
www.wiltonpark.org.uk
   Thomas Shirley and
     Anne Kempe Shirley
   Cecily Shirley and Thomas West

Stockton-on-Tees, County Durham
H.M. Bark *Endeavour*, Moat Street,
Stockton-on-Tees, County Durham
TS18 3AZ
Tel. 01642 608038
   Endeavour replica moored on
     River Tees

Stockton Parish Church, High Street
Stockton-on-Tees, County Durham
TS18 1SP
Tel. 01642 611734
www.communigate.co.uk/ne/spc

Stoke d'Abernon, Surrey
Yehudi Menuhin School of Music, Stoke
d'Abernon, Cobham, Surrey KT11 3QQ
Tel. 01932 864739
www.yehudimenuhinschool.co.uk

Stoke Dry, Leicestershire
Church of St. Andrew, Main Street
Stoke Dry near Uppingham
Leicestershire LE15 9JG
A mural of St. Christopher painted in
1280–5 shows two bowmen who seem
to be American Indians.

Stoke Poges, Buckinghamshire
Stoke Park Club, North Drive off
Park Road, Stoke Poges
Buckinghamshire SL2 4PG
Tel. 01753 717171
www.stokeparkclub.com

Stoke Park Manor House, North Drive off
Park Road, Stoke Poges
Buckinghamshire SL2 4PG
www.stoke-poges.com/village
   Thomas Penn, son of William Penn

Stoke Poges Garden of Remembrance
Church Lane, Stoke Poges
Buckinghamshire SL2 4NZ
   Judy Garland

Stowmarket, Suffolk
Church of St. Peter and St. Mary
Station Road West, Stowmarket
Suffolk IP14 1ES
www.stowmarketparishchurch.co.uk
   Bartholomew Gosnold

Stratford-upon-Avon, Warwickshire
Harvard House, High Street, Stratford-
upon-Avon, Warwickshire CV37 6AU
Tel. 01789 204507
www.stratford-upon-
avon.co.uk/soaharv.htm
   John Harvard
   Harvard University

Sturton-le-Steeple, Nottinghamshire
   Mayflower: William and
     Susanna White
   "Peregrine" White, the first English
     male born in the New World
   John Robinson and his wife
     Bridget White
   Bridget White's sister Catherine
     married John Carver, first
     governor of Plymouth Plantation.

Church of St. Peter and St. Paul
Church Street, Sturton-le-Steeple
Nottinghamshire DN22 9HQ
A picture depicting the *Mayflower*
hangs on the north wall of the nave.

"Crossways," Cross Street, Sturton-le-
Steeple, Nottinghamshire DN22 9HW
   John Robinson

Sudbury, Suffolk
   Thomas Davies
   William Dawes
   Paul Revere
   War of 1912 – Fort McHenry
     (Maryland)

Sudbury Town Hall, Sudbury, Suffolk
CO10 1TL
   US Air Force, 486th Bombardment
     Group

Sulgrave, Northamptonshire
Sulgrave Manor, Sulgrave near Banbury
Northamptonshire OX17 2SD
Tel. 01295 760205
www.stratford.co.uk/sulgrave
   Lawrence Washington
   John Washington
   George Washington

Church of St. James the Less
Church Street, Sulgrave
Northamptonshire OX17 2RP
   George Washington

Sunderland, Tyne and Wear
Hylton Castle and **St. Katherine's Chapel**
Craigavon Road, Sunderland
Tyne and Wear SR5 3PA
Tel. 0191 548 0152
www.hyltoncastle.com
   John Davenport
   New Haven, Connecticut
   William Hilton
   Fortune

Sunningdale, Berkshire
Fort Belvedere, London Road
Sunninghill near Ascot
Berkshire SL5 7SD
Fort Belvedere is now leased as a
private home by the Crown Estate.
   Edward Albert Christian George
   Andrew Patrick David,
     Prince of Wales
   Wallis Warfield Simpson

Sutton-at-Hone, Kent
St. John the Baptist Church, 51a Main
Road, Sutton-at-Hone, Kent DA4 9HQ
Tel. 01322 862253
   Thomas Smythe
   Virginia Company

Swanton Morley, Norfolk
Angel Inn, 66 Greengate Crescent
Swanton Morley, Norfolk NR20 4LX
   Edward Lincoln
   President Abraham Lincoln

Tenterden, Kent
Unitarian Meeting House, Old Meeting
House, Ashford Road, Tenterden
Kent TN30 6AB
Tel. 01233 628600
   Benjamin Franklin

Tewkesbury, Gloucestershire
Tewkesbury Abbey, Church Street
Tewkesbury, Gloucestershire GL20 5RZ
Tel. 01684 850959
www.tewkesburyabbey.org.uk
   Victoria Woodhull Martin

Thetford, Norfolk
Thomas Paine Hotel, White Hart Street
Thetford, Norfolk IP24 1AA
Tel. 01842 755631

   Thomas Paine

Ancient House Museum, 69 Barton
Street, Thetford, Norfolk IP24 1AA
Tel. 01842 752599
www.norfolk.gov.uk/tourism/museums
/thetford.htm

King's House, King Street, Thetford
Norfolk IP24 2AP
Tel. 01842 754247
www.thetfordtowncouncil.gov.uk/kings
house.htm
   Thomas Paine

Thurleigh, Bedfordshire
Thurleigh Airfield and **306th Bomb Group**
Museum, Thurleigh, Bedfordshire
MK44 2YP
www.306bg.co.uk/ and
www.controltowers.co.uk/T-
V/Thurleigh.htm
   8th USAAF, 306th Bomb Group

Tickencote, Rutland
St. Peter's Church, Tickencote
Rutland PE9 4AE

Tickencote Hall, Tickencote
Rutland PE9 4AE
   Wingfield family

Tilton-on-the-Hill, Leicestershire
St. Peter's Church, Main Street, Tilton-on-
the-Hill, Leicestershire LE7 9LB
http://croft.leicestershireparishcouncil
s.org/tiltononthehill/
   Thomas Hooker

Tortworth, Gloucestershire
St. Leonard's Church, Tortworth
Gloucestershire GL12 8HF
   Thomas Throckmorton
   Elizabeth Throckmorton Dale
   Thomas Dale
   Elizabeth Berkeley

Ulverston, Cumbria
Swarthmoor Hall, Ulverston
Cumbria LA12 0JQ
Tel. 01229 583204
E-mail: swarthmrhall@gn.apc.org
www.quaker.org.uk/contacts/educat/
swarth
   George Fox
   Religious Sciety of Friends
   ("Quakers")
   Swarthmore College in

   Swarthmore, Pennsylvania

Laurel and Hardy Museum
4c Upper Brook Street, Ulverston
Cumbria LA12 7BH
Tel. 01229 582292
www.laurel-and-hardy-museum.co.uk

Upper Dicker, East Sussex
Michelham Priory and Gardens
Upper Dicker near Hailsham
East Sussex BN27 3QS
www.sussexpast.co.uk/property/site.ph
p?site_id=15
Tel. 01273 486260
   Herbert Pelham – Harvard College

Virginia Water, Berkshire
(former) **Royal Holloway Sanatorium**
Stoude Road, Virginia Water
Berkshire GU25 4SR
   Bill Bryson, *Notes from*
    a Small Island

Waddesdon, Buckinghamshire
Waddesdon Manor, Waddesdon near
Aylesbury, Buckinghamshire HP18 OJH
Tel. 01296 653226
www.waddesdon.org.uk
   Declaration of Independence

Walpole, Suffolk
Walpole Old Chapel, Halesworth Road
Walpole near Halesworth IP19 9AZ
Tel. 01986 798308 or 01986 784412
www.walpoleoldchapel.co.uk
Walpole Old Chapel is regularly open
on Saturdays 11am–4pm from early
May to mid-September. In addition, by
prior arrangement, it is possible for
seriously interested parties or
individuals to visit at other times.
Bookings should be made by calling
01986 784412 or 01986 784571.
   Nonconformists of the
    seventeenth century

Warrington, Lancashire
Warrington Academy, Bridge Street
Warrington, Lancashire WA1 2HB
   Joseph Priestley

Priestley College, Loushers Lane
Warrington, Cheshire WA4 6RD
Tel. 01925 633591
www.priestleycollege.ac.uk
   Joseph Priestley, statue

Warton, Lancashire
Church of St. Oswald, Church Hill
Avenue, Warton near Carnforth
Lancashire LA5 9PG
www.lancashirechurches.co.uk/warton.
htm
Guided tours of St. Oswald's are
available.
    Robert Washington
    The Stars and Stripes
    George Washington
    Winston Churchill

George Washington Pub, Main Street
Warton near Carnforth, Lancashire
LA5 9PJ
Tel. 01542 732865
www.thegeorgewashington.co.uk

Warwick, Warwickshire
Warwick Castle, Castle Hill, Warwick
Warwickshire CV34 4QU
Tel. 01926 406600
www.warwick-castle.co.uk
Warwick Castle is over a thousand
years old, and is one of the best-
preserved castles in England.
    "Royal Weekend Party"
    Consuelo Vanderbilt, Duchess
    of Marlborough
    Jennie Jerome Churchill with
    her second husband, George
    Cornwallis-West

Washington, Tyne and Wear
Washington Old Hall, The Avenue
Washington, Tyne and Wear NE38 7LE
Tel. 0191 416 6879
    George Washington
    President Carter

Wattisham, Suffolk
Wattisham Airfield Museum, Wattisham
Suffolk IP7 7RA
Tel. 01449 728207/01449 726029
www.wattishamairfieldmuseum.
fsnet.co.uk
    USAAF – 479th Fighter Group

Wellington, Somerset
Church of St. John the Baptist
Rectory, High Street
Wellington, Somerset TA21 8RF
Tel. 01823 662248
    John Popham memorial

St. John Fisher Catholic Church, Mantle
Street, Wellington, Somerset TA21 8AX

www.our-parish.org
    John Popham – almshouses

Hospital of Sir John Popham, 11 Hoyles
Road, Wellington, Somerset TA21 9AH

Wells, Somerset
Crown Hotel, Market Place, Wells
Somerset BA5 2RP
Tel. 01749 673457
www.crownatwells.co.uk
    William Penn
    Thatcher Longstreth

Welwyn Garden City
Hertfordshire
Brocket Hall, Welwyn Garden City
Hertfordshire AL8 7XG
Tel. 01707 335241
www.brocket-hall.co.uk
Brocket Hall currently houses a sports
and leisure center which offers a range
of conference, meeting, sporting, golf,
private entertainment and dining
facilities. Important events such as the
G7 summits been held at Brocket Hall.
    John Brockett
    New Haven, Connecticut

West Knolye, Wiltshire
Bush Farm Bison Centre, West Knoyle
Wiltshire BA12 6AE
Tel. 01747 830263
www.bisonfarm.co.uk

West Raynham, Norfolk
Raynham Hall, West Raynham near
Fakenham, Norfolk NR21 7ER
Tel. 01328 701818
The Townshend family still live at
Raynham Hall.
    Charles Townshend

St. Mary the Virgin Church
West Raynham near Fakenham
Norfolk NR21 7ER
    Townshend memorials
    Whitechapel Foundry

West Wycombe
Buckinghamshire
West Wycombe Park, West Wycombe
Buckinghamshire HP14 3AL
Tel. 01494 513569
www.nationaltrust.org.uk
    Francis Dashwood
    Hell-Fire Club
    Benjamin Franklin

Church of St. Lawrence, West Wycombe
Hill, West Wycombe
Buckinghamshire HP14 3AH
Tel. 01494 529988
www.achurchnearyou.com/venue.php?
V=350&B=333
    Dashwood Mausoleum

West Wycombe Caves, High Wycombe
Buckinghamshire HP14 3AH
Tel. 01494 533739
www.hellfirecaves.co.uk
The caves have been restored and are
open to the public.
    Francis Dashwood
    Hell-Fire Club
    Benjamin Franklin

Wetheringsett, Suffolk
All Saints' Church, Church Street
Wetheringsett, Suffolk IP14 5PH
    Richard Hakluyt
    Francis Walsingham

Whitby, North Yorkshire
The Resolution Trust, 39a Flowergate
Whitby, North Yorkshire YO21 3BB
Tel. 01947 820522
www.maritimebritain.co.uk/HM%20Sl
oop%20Resolution.html
    Replica of Captain James Cook's
    Resolution

Captain Cook Memorial Museum
Grape Lane, Whitby, Yorkshire
YO22 4BA
Tel. 01947 601900
www.cookmuseumwhitby.co.uk
    Captain James Cook

Whitby Museum, Pannett Park, Whitby
North Yorkshire YO21 1RE
Tel. 01947 602908
www.durain.demon.co.uk
    Captain Cook exhibit
    Models of ships, *Resolution*
    and *Endeavour*

West Cliff, North Terrace, Whitby
North Yorkshire YO21 3EN
    Statue of Captain Cook

Whitehaven, Cumbria
    Benjamin Franklin
    John Paul Jones
    Tom Hurds Rock – memorial with
    cannon from Jones's ship

St. Nicholas's Church, Lowther Street
Whitehaven, Cumbria CA28 7DG
    Mildred Warner Gale, grandmother
    of George Washington

Beacon Museum, West Strand
Whitehaven, Cumbria CA28 7LY
Tel. 01946 592302
www.thebeacon-whitehaven.co.uk

Wickhamford, Worcestershire
St. John the Baptist Church, Wickhamford
Lane off Golden Lake, Wickhamford
Worcestershire WR11 7SD
    Samuel Sandys and his wife
      Mercy Culpeper
    Edwin Sandys
    Two of Archbishop Edwin Sandys's
      grandsons married
      Washington sisters
    Penelope Washington – her
      memorial features the
      Washington family coat of arms
      with the stars and stripes

Wickhamford Manor, Wickhamford near
Evesham, Worcestershire WR11 7SA
Tel. 01386 830296
E-mail: jeremy@wickhamfordmanor.
freeserve.co.uk
During the summer Shakespearean
plays are performed in the grounds of
the manor.
    Purchased by Sir Samuel Sandys
      in 1549
    Penelope Washington related to
      George Washington (her father,
      Colonel Henry Washington, was
      the nephew of Lawrence
      Washington)

Sandys Arms Pub, Pitchers Hill
Wickhamford, Worcestershire, WR11 7RT
Tel. 01386 830535
    Samuel Sandys

Widford, Hertfordshire
Church of St. John the Baptist, Ware Road
(B1004), Widford, Hertfordshire
SG12 8RL
    John Eliot – "Pastor to the Indians"
    Stained-glass window erected by
      Eliot's descendants

Widnes, Cheshire
Widnes train station, Victoria Avenue
Widnes, Cheshire WA8 7TJ
    Paul Simon

Willoughby, Lincolnshire
St. Helena's Church, Willoughby
Lincolnshire LN13 9NH
Contact: Rectory, Station Road,
Willoughby, Lincolnshire, LN13 9NA
www.willoughbylincs.f9.co.uk/contacts.
html
    John Smith
    American flag and flag of the State
      of Virginia
    John Smith window
    Virginia windows
    Anne Hutchinson

Winchester, Hampshire
Winchester Castle, Castle Avenue
Winchester, Hampshire SO23 8PJ
www.cityofwinchester.co.uk/history/
html/castle.html
    Walter Raleigh
    Main Plot

**Winchester's Military Museums Visitor
Centre**, Peninsula Barracks, Romsey
Road, Hampshire SO23 8TS
Tel. 01962 828549
www.winchestermilitarymuseums.co.uk
    Royal Green Jackets Museum
    43rd and 52nd Light Infantry
    Lexington and Bunker Hill
    Charles Cornwallis
    Battle of Yorktown

Wingfield, Suffolk
Wingfield College, Church Road
Wingfield, Suffolk IP21 5RA
The college is now the home of
Wingfield Arts & Music.
    John Wingfield

Wingfield Church, Wingfield, Suffolk
IP21 5RA
Collegiate church of Sir John de
Wingfield's Foundation.

Wingfield Castle, Wingfield, Suffolk
IP21 5RB
Today the moated castle with its Tudor
manor house is a private residence,
but its appearance remains the same
as when it was built.

Woburn, Bedfordshire
Woburn Abbey, Woburn, Bedfordshire
MK17 9WA
Tel. 01525 290666
www.woburn.co.uk
    Rachel Wriothesley, a

    granddaughter of Henry
    Wriothesley, 3rd Earl of
      Southampton
    William Russell, son of William
      Russell, 1st Duke of Bedford
    London: Southampton House (later
      Bedford House) on Bloomsbury
      Square, demolished in 1800
    Painting by Sir George Hayter – *The
      Trial of William, Lord Russell*
    Audubon's *Birds of America*

Woking, Surrey
Brookwood Cemetery, Woking
Surrey GU24 0BL
    American World War I veterans
    John Singer Sargent
    Samuel Cody
    US Representative Vincent
      Francis Harrington, of Iowa

Woodstock, Oxfordshire
Blenheim Palace, Woodstock
Oxfordshire OX20 1PX
Tel. 01993 811091
www.blenheimpalace.com
    Jennie Jerome
    Winston Churchill
    Consuelo Vanderbilt

Worcester, Worcestershire
**Cathedral Church of Christ and the Blessed
Virgin Mary**, College Green, Worcester
Worcestershire WR1 2LH
Tel. 01905 28854
www.cofe-worcester.org.uk
    Elizabeth I appointed Edwin Sandys
      to be Bishop of Worcester in 1559.
      In 1570 he was named Bishop of
      London. In 1576 he was named
      Archbishop of York.
    His son Edwin Sandys – treasurer
      of the London Company
    William Brewster

King's School, 5 College Green
Worcester, Worcestershire WR1 2LL
Tel. 01905 721700
www.ksw.org.uk
    Edward Winslow

Worksop, Nottinghamshire
Pilgrim Fathers Exhibition, County Library
Memorial Avenue, Worksop
Nottinghamshire S80 2BP
Tel. 01909 472408
www.nottsnet.co.uk/Worksop/worksop
_services.htm

The library has a permanent exhibition dedicated to the Pilgrim Fathers.

Wormsley Park, Buckinghamshire
Near Christmas Common
Buckinghamshire OX49 5HX
    J. Paul Getty II
    Mick Jagger

Worplesdon, Surrey
Cobbett Hill Road, Worplesdon near
Guildford GU3 2AA
    William Cobbett
    Thomas Paine

Wraxhall, Somerset
All Saints' Church, Bristol Road, Wraxall
Somerset BS48 1LB
Contact: Rectory, 8 School View
The Elms, Wraxall, Somerset BS48 1HG
Tel. 01275 857086
www.wraxallwithfailand.org.uk
    Gorges tomb
    Edmund Gorges
    Lady Anne Howard
    Anne Boleyn
    Catherine Howard
    Ferdinando Gorges

Birdcombe Court, Tower House Lane
Wraxall, Somerset BS48 1JR
The home of the Gorges family for

many years, it is now a private property.

Wrexham, North Wales
St. Giles's Churchyard, between St. Giles
Street and High Street, Wrexham
North Wales LL13 8LY
Tel. 01978 355808
    Elihu Yale

Wroxton, Oxfordshire
Wroxton Abbey, Wroxton near Banbury
Oxfordshire OX15 6PX
Tel. 01295 730551
http://view.fdu.edu
The fifty-six-acre abbey gardens are
open to the public all year.
    Frederick, Lord North
    Fairleigh Dickinson College of
        Madison, New Jersey

All Saints' Church, Church Street
Wroxton near Banbury, Oxfordshire
OX15 6QE
Tel. 01295 730344
www.achurchnearyou.com/
venue.php?V=484
    Memorial for Lord North by
        John Flaxman

Wymondham, Norfolk
Abbey Church of St. Mary and St. Thomas

of Canterbury, Church Street
Wymondham, Norfolk NR18 0PH
Tel. 01953 607062
www.wymondhamabbey.nildram.co.uk
    Rev. Richard Bucke
    Main military hospital for American
        452nd Bomb Group

York, North Yorkshire
York Minster, Minster Yard, York
North Yorkshire YO1 7JB
Tel. 01904 557216
www.yorkminster.org
    Neil Armstrong
    In the crypt – 32-carat diamond
        donated by an American,
        Mrs. Howes
    Archbishop Edwin Sandys

Fairfax House, Castlegate, York
North Yorkshire YO1 9RN
Tel. 01904 655543
www.fairfaxhouse.co.uk
    Fairfax family in Virginia

Merchant Adventurers' Hall, The Hall
Fossgate, York, North Yorkshire
YO1 9XD
Tel. 01904 654 818
www.theyorkcompany.co.uk
    Merchant Adventurers
    Sebastian Cabot

INDEX

ACKNOWLEDGMENTS

Many people have contributed to the completion of this labor of love. In my research I found the staff at local tourist information centers and guides at museums and historic sites around England to be overwhelmingly helpful and friendly. Many local historians, church secretaries, and librarians helped me uncover or confirm information. They were extremely informative and prompt – usually answering my queries within a day or two! Their interest in my project was very encouraging. I also greatly appreciated the encouragement and support of many friends who listened to my stories, read many versions of the manuscript, offered helpful suggestions, went along on trips and often pointed out "connections" I had not yet discovered. Special thanks go to Susie, Jayne, June, Stephanie, Peggy, Sherian, and Camille.

I could never have organized my files and notebooks into a coherent book without the expert guidance of the team organized by Dan Giles and Sarah McLaughlin at Giles Publishing. Eleanor Lines helped me develop a structure that could work. Sarah Kane did a heroic job editing the text and checking MANY details. Linda Wade made sure the pages looked great. They all earned my sincere appreciation and thanks.

My family have listened to years of enthusiastic stories, viewed thousands of photos, traveled many miles helping me search for hard to find treasures – thank you. But my most special thanks go to my husband who has joined me on many more adventures than we ever anticipated. I hope there will be many more.

PHOTO CREDITS

We would like to thank all those who gave their generous permission to reproduce the listed images. Every effort has been made to secure all permissions and the publishers apologize for any inadvertent errors or omissions. If notified, the publisher will endeavor to correct these at the earliest opportunity.

ABMC: p. 131; courtesy AELTC: p. 240; courtesy Alford Manor: p. 63; courtesy All Saint's Church, Old Heathfield: p. 32 (top); Alnwick Castle: p. 39; produced courtesy of The American Museum in Britain (Bath, UK): pp. 161 (top), 178 (second from bottom); Berkeley Castle (DJP): p. 46 (top); Berkeley Castle (EJH): p. 84; Birmingham Museums & Art Gallery: p. 199; photograph by Jarrold Publishing reproduced by kind permission of His Grace the Duke of Marlborough, Blenheim Palace Image Library: p. 125; image courtesy of Bletchley Park Trust, www.bletchleypark.org.uk: p. 128; by permission of Boston Borough Council: p. 55; courtesy St. Botolph's Church, Boston: p. 64; courtesy Bowood House: pp. 116, 200; © Cliveden House, Buckinghamshire, UK/National Trust Photographic Library/John Hammond/The Bridgeman Art Library. Nationality/copyright status: American/out of copyright: p. 173; Bristol Film Office, Bristol County Council: p. 22 (top); British Museum: p. 179; Chelmsford Cathedral: p. 50; © Rosie Atkins, Chelsea Physic Garden. www.chelseaphysicgarden.co.uk: p. 183 (bottom); Courtesy Clink Museum: p. 52; © Benjamin Ealovega: pp. 1, 3 (all), 5 (all), 6 (all), 7, 8, 9, 10 (top left; top, second from left; top right; bottom left), 13, 14, 20, 24 (top), 31 (all), 34, 57, 71, 72, 78, 81, 89 (top left; top, second from right), 91, 93 (top), 95, 97, 110 (top), 112 (top), 119 (top left), 124, 141 (top left; top, second from left), 145 (top), 146, 148 (top), 156 (all top), 157 (bottom), 158 (bottom), 159 (top), 160 (top), 164 (top), 165 (top left; top, second from left; top right), 169, 174 (top left; top, second from left; top right), 178, 180 (top), 183 (middle), 184 (top), 186 (top, second from left; top, second from right), 189, 198 (top left; top, second from right), 202, 204 (bottom), 207 (middle; bottom), 209 (top, second from left; top, second from right; top right), 211 (top), 212, 217, 221, 223, 224 (all), 225 (top, second from left; top right), 233 (bottom), 237, 239, 241 (top, second from left; top, second from right; top right; bottom), 268 (all); cover (all); © English Heritage Photo Library: pp. 35, 53, 145 (bottom), 172 (bottom); courtesy of the Firle Estate Trustees: pp. 102, 103; © Howard Goldbaum: p. 192 (bottom); The Trustees of the Goodwood Collection: p 94 (top); courtesy of Hammerwood Park: p. 206 (top); Harlaxton College: p. 192 (top); Historic Dockyards: p. 16; © Historic Royal Palaces: pp. 44, 96, 112; by kind permission of the Masters of the Bench of the Honourable Society of the Middle Temple: p. 186 (top left), 186 (bottom left); courtesy Kimbolton School: p. 167; courtesy Kiplin Hall: p. 75; © Ricky Leaver: p. 152 (bottom); © Leeds Castle Foundation: p. 172 (top); Lincoln Cathedral Library: p. 66; Roger Mears: pp. 25, 94 (bottom); © MGH: p. 182 (bottom); © Museum in Docklands: p. 156 (middle left); courtesy of the Council of the National Army Museum, London: p. 100; © The National Gallery, London: p. 115; National Portrait Gallery, London: p. 92; © NTPL/Matthew Antrobus: p. 171; © NTPL/John Blake: p. 83; © NTPL/N. Boyd: p. 40; © NTPL/Andrew Butler: pp. 93 (bottom), 182 (top); © NTPL/Derek Croucher: p. 150; © NTPL/Nick Meers: p. 183 (top); © NTPL/Rupert Truman: p. 219 (bottom); courtesy of Otley Hall: p. 17; © Oxford Picture Library/Chris Andrews: p. 182 (middle); © Painshill Park, Fred Holmes: p. 184 (second from top); © Viscount De L'Isle/Penshurst Place: p. 191; RGB Kew: pp. 47, 185; The Royal Collection © 2007, Her Majesty Queen Elizabeth II.: p. 90; The Royal Collection © 2007, Her Majesty Queen Elizabeth II.Photograph John Freeman: p. 161 (bottom); The Royal Collection © 2007, Her Majesty Queen Elizabeth II. Photograph Andrew Holt: p. 152 (top); by kind permission of the Governor of the Royal Hospital Chelsea: p. 119 (middle right); Science Museum/Science & Society Picture Library: p. 198 (top right); courtesy of Skibo Castle: p. 177; Mark Fiennes © Spencer House: p. 170; Sulgrave Manor: p. 142; Courtesy of Syon House: pp. 104, 109 (bottom), 119 (top, second from right), 175, 210; by permission of the Vicar and Churchwardens of Tewkesbury Abbey. ©Tewkesbury Abbey PCC: p. 163; © V&A Images/Victoria & Albert Museum, London: p. 207 (top); Virginia Historical Society, Richmond, Virginia: p. 98; courtesy Whitechapel Bell Foundry Ltd.: p. 89 (top, second from left)